NO BILLIONAIRE
LEFT BEHIND

NO BILLIONAIRE LEFT BEHIND

Satirical Activism in America

Angelique Haugerud

Stanford University Press
Stanford, California

Stanford University Press
Stanford, California

Printed in the United States of America on acid-free, archival-quality paper

Library of Congress Cataloging-in-Publication Data

Haugerud, Angelique - author.
   No billionaire left behind : satirical activism in America / Angelique Haugerud.
      pages cm
   Includes bibliographical references and index.
   ISBN 978-0-8047-8152-7 (cloth : alk. paper)--ISBN 978-0-8047-8153-4 (pbk. : alk. paper)
   1. Billionaires (Organization) 2. Political satire, American--History and criticism.
3. Street theater--Political aspects--United States--History--21st century. 4. Political
activists--United States--Case studies. 5. United States--Politics and government--
1989--Humor. I. Title.
   E902.H385 2013
   339.20973--dc23   2012051065

ISBN 978-0-8047-8631-7 (electronic)

Typeset by Bruce Lundquist in 10/14 Minion

Contents

List of Figures   vii

Introduction: The Comedy of Wealth?   1

1   Irony, Humor, Spectacle   23

2   "Times Are Good!" A New Gilded Age   55

3   Pre-Billionaires: Experiments in Satirical Activism, 1990s   81

4   Branded: Billionaires for Bush (and More)   109

5   Humor's Workshop, Humor's Witnesses   135

6   Media Players   163

7   After Satire?   187

Acknowledgments   207

Appendix: Research Methods   209

Notes   211

Works Cited   245

Index   267

List of Figures

I.1 Phil T. Rich (Andrew Boyd), cofounder of the Billionaires   2

I.2 Billionaires play games on Central Park's Great Lawn   2

I.3 Billionaires during festive demonstration in Central Park   3

I.4 Billionaires on tax day   6

2.1 Billionaires in Social Security demonstration   74

3.1 Boston tax code protest diverted   101

5.1 Iona Bigga Yacht (Alice Meaker), national director of field operations for Billionaires for Bush   155

NO BILLIONAIRE
LEFT BEHIND

Introduction

The Comedy of Wealth?

OURS IS THE AGE OF BILLIONAIRES. From a mere dozen in the early 1980s to more than a thousand today, their numbers have surged along with their influence. The world's most prosperous individuals earn incomes that exceed those of entire nations.[1] For the rest of us, such riches are a dream. "That's the state to live and die in! . . . R-r-rich!," proclaims Mr. Boffin in Charles Dickens's novel *Our Mutual Friend*. The philosopher Seneca, however, thought otherwise, declaring two thousand years ago: "A great fortune is a great slavery." If he was right, who will free the billionaires?

"Leave No Billionaire Behind!" The placard caught my eye as I scanned the crowd assembled on Central Park's Great Lawn. That Sunday morning in the park, women carrying parasols and clad in elegant gowns, tiaras, and satin gloves, and men in tuxedoes and top hats or *Great Gatsby*-like lawn-tennis whites, mingled against the backdrop of New York's skyline and a blue summer sky. Some played croquet and badminton, while others sipped champagne from fluted glasses (Figures I.1, I.2, I.3). Famous photographers snapped their pictures, journalists interviewed them, tourists and locals ogled them.[2] Were they celebrities? Consider their names: Ivan Aston Martin, Iona Bigga Yacht, Phil T. Rich, Alan Greenspend, Robin Eublind, Meg A. Bucks, Lucinda Regulations, Tex Shelter, and Noah Countability, among others. And their signs:

"Corporations Are People Too"
"Privatize the Park: Keep off the Grass"
"Widen the Income Gap"

FIGURE I.1 Phil T. Rich (Andrew Boyd), cofounder of the Billionaires, is interviewed by the *Washington Post*'s Robert Kaiser during the fanciful Billionaire croquet and badminton demonstration in Central Park on the eve of the Republican National Convention. August 29, 2004. Photo by Lucian Perkins, courtesy of the *Washington Post* and Getty Images.

FIGURE I.2 Billionaires for Bush play games as they sit in a circle on Central Park's Great Lawn while prize-winning journalists interview and photograph them during a day of protest on the eve of the Republican National Convention. August 29, 2004. Photo by author.

"Still Loyal to Big Oil"

"Taxes Are Not for Everyone"

After their lawn games, the group staged a rally opposite the Plaza Hotel and then a Million Billionaire March down New York's Fifth Avenue.

Lurking beneath the surface of this scene is a sense—only implicit—that something is not quite right. That disquiet touches historically deep debates about wealth, inequality, and democracy—concerns that stretch beyond any single election or political party.

Questions about the compatibility of wealth and democracy, though often mere shadows in contemporary public culture, have roots that reach to the very founding of the United States as a rebellion against European aristocracy and officialdom. There was a crucial duality in this legacy, writes moderate Republican Kevin Phillips: "In contrast to stratified Europe, the more fluid society in America offered a double opportunity: both to make money and to criticize its abuse by the rich, pointing out how excess wealth and stratification undercut the democracy that had nurtured them."[3] Here is an implicit ideal of a democratic society that is at once humane and entrepreneurial, admiring of wealth yet alert to its perils.

FIGURE I.3 Billionaires for Bush during their festive demonstration in Central Park on the eve of the Republican National Convention. August 29, 2004. Photo by Lucian Perkins, courtesy of the *Washington Post* and Getty Images.

By the start of the twenty-first century, the perils were stark. It was not just liberals but also moderates and avowedly apolitical social scientists such as Larry Bartels who were troubled that wealth inequality in the United States had outpaced that of more than thirty other countries the International Monetary Fund terms "advanced economies."[4] Two statistics that startled many: in 2007, the top one percent of income earners in the United States received 23.5 percent of total national (pretax) income and controlled 40 percent of the wealth—the highest levels of inequality in the United States in nearly a century.[5] Yale economist Robert Shiller said in mid-2009 that rising economic inequality—not the financial crisis per se—is America's biggest problem.[6] In millennial America great wealth could purchase outsized political power, making possible even larger fortunes for a few. For many of the rest, livelihoods grew increasingly precarious.

Yet the widening gulf between the ultrarich and the rest was one of the most important issues seldom mentioned during the U.S. presidential campaigns of 2000, 2004, and 2008. It briefly appeared during the final weeks of the 2008 campaign, when the financial crisis dominated headlines. And for a short time during the 2000 presidential campaign, outspoken critics of plutocracy ranged across the political spectrum; they included millionaires and elite politicians such as John McCain (who later shifted to a much more conservative position), Bill Bradley, and Ralph Nader.[7] Their blunt critiques sounded alarms that were soon muted. Only in 2011, fueled in part by Occupy movements, did debates about wealth inequality become more salient in campaign discourse.

This book's protagonists—satirical activists who call themselves the Billionaires—were like canaries in a mineshaft, emitting warning signals ahead of dire trouble. Since the early 2000s, they and their successors have deployed ironic humor and street theater to nudge questions about wealth and democracy into public view.

.   .   .

Why cloak such profound concerns in irony and satire? Great humorists suggest part of an answer. "The secret source of humor is not joy but sorrow," remarked Mark Twain.[8] *Doonesbury* cartoonist Garry Trudeau has said that "bad news is good for satire."[9] And Jon Stewart, host of Comedy Central's popular "fake" news program *The Daily Show*, said he and his writers focus on the morning news that most agitates them, "the sometimes somber stories he refers to as his 'morning cup of sadness.'"[10] In short, topics likely to invite ironic humor are precisely those that frighten, embarrass, pain, or affront us. Yet by the end of the day, Jon Stewart and his staff feel better because they have transposed that "little cup of sadness" to humor. For them—and likely for millions of viewers—*The Daily Show* is a "kind of catharsis machine, a therapeutic filter for grappling with upsetting issues."[11] And for some, ironic humor is much more—a political spark, an inspiration for action.

"It's a Class War and We're Winning!"

The women in elegant gowns and men in tuxedoes who attracted media throngs to Central Park on a sparkling summer morning are political activists who for more than a decade have used satirical street theater to try to spotlight serious questions about democracy and economic fairness. With a knowing wink, they say exactly the opposite of what they mean. They share affinities with trickster humor's word play or mischievous use of homonyms, ambiguity, and double entendres.[12] This is *play as subversion*, in the spirit of the court jester or wise fool who can speak safely what others dare not utter.

These activists practice an innovative genre of what scholars term "contentious politics" or "collective action" or "social movements"—if one takes these broad categories to refer, as Charles Tilly does, to "ordinary people who make collective claims on public authorities, other holders of power, competitors, enemies, and objects of popular disapproval."[13] The Billionaires' style—described by a *New York Times* reporter as a delicate balance of "earnest intent and absurdity"[14]—both mocks and upholds the genre known as political protest (Figure 1.4).

After a debut as "Billionaires for Forbes" in 1999, they morphed into "Billionaires for Bush (or Gore)" in 2000, "Billionaires for Bush" in 2004, "Billionaires for Bailouts and Lobbyists for McCain" in 2008, "Billionaires for Wealthcare" during the 2011 health care debates, "Billionaires for Plutocracy" in 2011, and "Multi-Millionaires for Mitt" in 2012. Adaptively named, they were comic sentinels for plutocracy.

Warning flags in eras of excess are *less* likely to come from the political center than from the margins, whether from humorists or serious voices that go unheeded. Cautionary words about grave instabilities in the financial system from economists such as Nouriel Roubini[15] of New York University, for example, were ignored or downplayed by most economists, pundits, and policy makers before the 2008 economic crisis. After the crisis broke, Roubini—dubbed

FIGURE I.4 Billionaires for Bush on tax day, April 15, 2004, New York City's central post office. Photo by author.

"Dr. Doom" by pundits—attracted more attention, though his positions were by no means embraced or widely publicized by corporate news media. Indeed in July 2010, *The Daily Show with Jon Stewart* included a spoof showing economist Roubini gagged in a dark closet, as pundits in news clips glibly misrepresented the logic of policy approaches to the financial crisis.

Just as Jon Stewart addresses weighty subjects such as the financial crisis and political corruption, other satirists for centuries have taken on the most serious issues of their times, at least as long ago as Aristophanes in ancient Greece.[16] Satire's "guiding premise," classical studies scholar Ralph M. Rosen remarks, is "that something is not 'as it should be,' and it takes a satirist to set the world straight."[17] But didactic messages wrapped in ironic humor—whether today or in ancient Greece—need their own warning flags. Satire is "often far more elusive and unstable than it would ever let on."[18]

Might that claim be more true of Jon Stewart, who declares himself a comedian rather than an activist,[19] than it is of the satirical Billionaires, who aspire to be simultaneously humorists and activists? Asked by Fox News anchor Chris Wallace in June 2011 what his agenda is, Stewart replied that it is "about absurdity and it's . . . anti-corruption, anti-lack of authenticity, anti-contrivance."

The Billionaires' core aim, on the other hand, is to help keep alive in the public sphere questions about economic fairness.

Two "elephants in the room"—skyrocketing wealth inequality and the influence of big money in politics—commanded the Billionaires' attention years before the emergence of Occupy Wall Street.[20] Targeting Democrats as well as Republicans, the Billionaires' ironic humor made visible what many pundits preferred to ignore, namely that wealth inequality in the United States had accelerated to record levels and that large campaign donations and lobbying yielded lopsided benefits, such as favorable tax rates for corporations and the very wealthy, the capacity to win lucrative government contracts (crony capitalism), and deregulatory legislation that risked the environment, public health, safety, and—eventually—national economic stability itself.[21]

The U.S. Supreme Court's (5–4) Citizens United decision in 2010 unleashed extraordinary new torrents of political campaign donations from often-anonymous wealthy individuals and large corporations.[22] Public opinion polls soon showed the Citizens United decision to be unpopular with a substantial majority of citizens across the political spectrum,[23] and many—such as constitutional law scholar and philosopher Ronald Dworkin—viewed it as a devastating blow to electoral democracy.[24] By mid-2012, a half dozen states had called for the U.S. Congress to draft a constitutional amendment against Citizens United. Among the signs Occupy Wall Street protesters waved in New York in 2011 and 2012 were "Democracy Not Corporatization" and "Revoke Corporate Personhood," counterpoints to the satirical Billionaires' slogan "Corporations Are People Too!" Yet in 2012 as this book went to press, U.S. congressional restraints or public disclosure mandates for corporate political contributions still appeared unlikely, leaving this momentous issue, like so many others, difficult to address through the formal institutions of representative democracy.

The Billionaires spotlight plutocracy—the intertwined growth of political and economic inequality[25]—which had ballooned faster than many cared to notice. It took deep root once again in the United States during the 1980s and 1990s and was flourishing by 2000. Billionaire investor Warren Buffett commented, "There's class warfare, all right, but it's my class, the rich class, that's making the war, and we're winning"[26]—a rarely heard pronouncement in American public culture and precisely the sentiment captured as well in the satirical Billionaires' slogan "It's a Class War and We're Winning!"

Hailed as the "rock stars of the protest scene,"[27] the Billionaires crafted an identity as genre-benders. They cultivated popular appeal through semiotic contrasts reproduced in the media (and in official discourses and practices) and reiterated through performance: Billionaire charm versus liberal anger; that is, protesters who are elegant rather than scruffy, hip rather than traditional, polite rather than offensive, and harmless rather than dangerous. Their props include champagne glasses, cigarette holders, and huge cigars, as well as bright banners and placards that are professionally printed rather than hand-lettered. Convinced that traditional forms of protest no longer worked, these artists, intellectuals, actors, corporate professionals, policy wonks, media producers, and seasoned and novice activists created a brand of theatrical political activism that evokes Information Age novelty, along with traces of earlier repertoires. In these ironic humorists we can detect echoes of late-medieval and Renaissance carnival, rituals of status reversal, charivaris, "festivals of resistance," as well as more recent Dadaists, Brechtian tactics, Situationists, surrealists, Yippie guerrilla theater, Bread and Puppet Theater, Guerrilla Girls, Ladies Against Women, Code Pink, and Reclaim the Streets.

Ostensibly harmless, the Billionaires display a witty command of policy issues and perform dissent in a way that surprises and charms. But their intentions are serious—nothing less than a reframing of current political debates. In contemporary parlance, they are "culture jammers" who aim to destabilize dominant corporate and editorial frames. By breaking common perceptual frames, political satire "*disrupt*[s] the transmission of the dominant political brand messages so competing conversations can occur."[28] Culture jammers penetrate "the subconscious of [an ad] campaign, uncovering not an opposite meaning but the deeper truth hiding behind the layers of advertising euphemisms. . . . So . . . the now-retired Joe Camel [of cigarette advertising fame] turns into Joe Chemo, hooked up to an IV machine."[29] The Billionaires—along with Jon Stewart, Stephen Colbert, Tina Fey, and the Yes Men—toy with the soft boundaries between play and seriousness. The Billionaires believed, years before Occupy Wall Street evinced a zeitgeist shift, that their elegant attire, polished visuals, and satirical pose made their dissent more palatable than it would be if conveyed more directly and conventionally. Their intentions, however, turned out to be much less opaque than those of serious journalists writing about the ultrarich.

Dinosaur Topiary

Few Americans have ever met a billionaire and must rely instead on the pseudo-intimacies of media portrayals. Such stories are not hard to find. For instance, ten months after Hurricane Katrina reminded the public of stark poverty in America, *New York Times* reporter Sharon Waxman offered this portrait of life near the top of the wealth pyramid: "At the push of a button, a 20-foot-wide screen descended from the ceiling and three huge speakers rose from beneath the wood parquet floor. At the other end of the room, a floor-to-ceiling bookcase sank—Batcave-like—revealing a projection room hidden behind it."[30] This is what passes for "warm, cozy, informal" in Southern California's Beverly Park, wrote the journalist. Here multistory palaces, some built in "classical 18th-century French style," are set in landscapes adorned with dinosaur topiary and Provençal-style gardens. Less than ten minutes by car from Los Angeles' famed Rodeo Drive, these estates sold for as much as $30 million in mid-2006. They are so luxurious that "[w]hen Eunice Kennedy Shriver visited . . . during a reception for President Vicente Fox of Mexico, she said 'I didn't know they built houses like this anymore.'" This is "Paradise Bought," the *New York Times* reporter writes, "a testament to the power of changed perspective, providing Los Angeles's micro-club of superrich and superfamous a place to feel normal."[31]

These images of opulence evoke consumer desire and fantasy, dreams that we too might one day enjoy such riches. Through such imaginative identification, America's "celebrity culture" touches gently our ambivalence about wealth inequalities and allows us, as media and culture scholar Stephen Duncombe writes, "a peek at the other side of the growing class divide while assuring us— through our intimacy with this world—that it is not really another side at all."[32]

The *Times* reporter's narrative is at once vivid and opaque. If readers, who are left guessing about intended moral messages, spot unexpected figurative meanings in Sharon Waxman's words, it could be because we suppose she expressed *less* than what she thinks—a speech form that can be ironic.[33] Perhaps the reporter is dissociating herself from the literal or purely referential meaning of her prose, or intentionally avoiding explicit judgment in her narrative—a practice media scholars say typifies much U.S. journalism.[34]

Some might see wry amusement or even light mockery in Waxman's portrait of sumptuousness. Or her narrative could call to mind judgments about the justice or injustice of such extraordinary wealth, perhaps reducing a reader's inclination to accept such riches as natural, or even prompting some to wonder if the wealth might have been acquired illegally or at the expense of employees' livelihoods. Some readers might disagree entirely with such an interpretation, in spite of America's unusual degree of wealth inequality in the early twenty-first century.[35] Indeed it may be *un*likely that readers who are not already distressed by the vast divide between the ultrarich and the rest would take Waxman's article as fodder for social justice arguments. Instead they could experience her narrative as classic comedy, journalistic understatement that captures an incongruous or surprising situation and prompts smiles. Comedy and wealth, after all, have long been friends in American popular culture.

One might expect America's great divide between affluence and poverty—wider than it has been in a century—to yield narratives of tragedy rather than humor. And of course it has. Why then has the wealth gap as comedy often shadowed American public culture? Would the Billionaires be amused by dinosaur topiary in Beverly Park? Undoubtedly. The *Times* reporter's comic overtones and the Billionaires' pointed irony, however, suggest utterly different interpretations of contemporary inequality. Indeed political satire first draws potency from comedy, and then foils it.

The Comedy of Wealth?

Comedy reassures. Restoration of harmony and reconciliation of conflict are hallmarks of comedy as plot type, as outlined in Hayden White's classic study.[36] If narrated as archetypal comedy, California's Beverly Park in the *New York Times* article becomes a tale of the ultrawealthy as mere curiosities, and vast differences between rich and poor seem harmonizable, natural, and inevitable. The interests of elites and ordinary citizens are not at odds[37] in comedic narratives about wealth, which rest easily on an imagined "state of economic nature" that supposedly precedes government and politics, where individuals' time and energies are freely exchanged, and where "rewards . . . [are] proportionate to effort" and markets are "naturally occurring democracies . . . [that] express the popular will."[38] Market forces, in this vision, are natural, benevolent, and unstoppable.

Satire (the fictional form of irony), on the other hand, upends such tales and assumes that the pleasing resolutions of comedic narratives are inadequate.[39] Satire amuses but at the same time criticizes or attacks through techniques such as ridicule, parody, or caricature. Satire's purpose nonetheless is "positive change," writes humor theorist Charles E. Schutz.[40] Plotted as satire, an economic meltdown is not a force of nature or freak accident but rather the entirely preventable outcome of politics and policy.

To choose (consciously or not) comedy, satire, romance, or tragedy as plot structure is to make a profoundly important choice about a story's meaning.[41]

Anthropologists' own archetypal narratives, as Donald Donham demonstrates, may emphasize hope, optimism, resignation, despair, or cynicism—which are in turn rooted in sharply varied assumptions about the capacities of individuals, the malleability of institutions, the contingencies of history, and the justice or injustice of a social order.[42]

The implicit paradigms of historical explanation underlying satire and irony "frustrat[e] normal expectations about the kinds of resolutions provided by stories" cast in the other three modes.[43] What scholars such as Hayden White term the metahistorical implications of satire and irony differs sharply from comedy, tragedy, and romance.[44] Satire, White says, "represents a different kind of qualification of the hopes, possibilities, and truths of human existence.... It views these hopes, possibilities, and truths Ironically, in the atmosphere generated by the apprehension of the ultimate inadequacy of consciousness to live in the world happily or to comprehend it fully."[45] Why activists who embrace irony remain passionately committed to change—even as they implicitly acknowledge the limitations of human consciousness and of language itself in representing the world—is part of this book's story. More central, however, is the question, why do individuals who are passionately committed to the common good turn to irony at this historical moment?

The Billionaires' ironic humor is at odds with the archetypal narratives embodied in dominant neoclassical economic theory, which Donham suggests are *comedy*: "Comedy, not as joke of course but as plot, appears to be a persistent feature of neoclassical analyses, so-called Pareto optimality typically providing the healthy resolution to apparent contradiction."[46] Neoclassical economic theory is grounded in models of markets as self-regulating systems and as efficient organizers of the production and consumption of goods and services. Pareto optimality, as economist George DeMartino puts it, posits that "an outcome (economic or otherwise) is 'efficient' if no one can be made better off without making at least one other person worse off . . . [but] to say that an outcome is efficient is to say nothing at all about equity or fairness."[47]

An apparent conflict between the interests of the wealthiest one percent of the population and escalating numbers of unemployed citizens—if plotted as comedy—turns out not to be a conflict after all, but rather the outcome of putatively natural market processes, or simply phases in what some economists and others interpret as the market's Darwinian processes of self-correction. Free-market cheerleaders would argue that inequality can become temporary and put to good use by arbitrageurs and that economic justice is to be found in the market.[48] Such views—repudiated by many—enable dismissal of policy moves to counteract economic precariousness, high unemployment, poverty, and extreme wealth disparities.

Further to the right than the comedic trope of Pareto optimality was the late 2000s American Tea Party ethos: "You're on your own" or "Why should anybody else have what I do not have?" or "Why should I help pay for someone else's health care or unemployment benefits?" Such questions lend themselves not to satire—which aims at inspiring hope and laughter as well as anger—but to a language of insult. Yet conservative media personalities who embrace this stance, such as Rush Limbaugh, aim to elicit laughter from their audiences, and they and liberal pundits and satirists carry out dialogues in absentia—or sometimes in person (as when Jon Stewart and Bill O'Reilly are guests on one another's shows). All contribute to contemporary political imaginings.

Resurgent since the 1970s has been a notion of natural market processes or an imaginary "free" market that conceals the laws and institutions which actually define the rules of competition in *any* market. These rules shape outcomes such as financial crises, recessions, and wealth bubbles. Many argue that different regulations over Wall Street firms' allowable debt loads and investment practices, for example, might have prevented the 2008 financial meltdown. The Glass-Steagall Act—banking reform legislation enacted during the 1930s Great Depression—separated high-risk investment banking from commercial banking that relied on citizens' deposits. But with the support of Democrats as well as Republicans, much of Glass-Steagall was repealed in 1999, paving the way for the rapid expansion of ever larger and riskier financial institutions that were free to use depositors' money for their speculative investments.

"Occupy the SEC"—an offshoot of Occupy Wall Street that includes former Wall Street professionals who favor restoration of Glass-Steagall provisions—in February 2012 drafted a 325-page comment letter to the Securities and Exchange Commission, the Federal Deposit Insurance Corporation, and the Federal Reserve Board. Their target was financial industry lobbyists' attempts to water down reforms proposed in the new Volcker Rule legislation, whose original purpose was to curtail certain highly risky, speculative investments by large banks that benefit from the Federal Reserve discount window and other implicit government backing. Thanks to lobbyists, Occupy SEC leaders said, by mid-2012 the Volcker Rule was turning into "Volcker-lite or Volcker-full-of-holes"; "Occupy the SEC" aimed to restore the legislation to its intended purposes.[49] As this example illustrates, markets are not part of a "natural" order;

they can be full of asymmetrical incentives created by humans through political processes.

Those most likely to tell stories about the American economy—and its great wealth gap—that fit the archetype of *comedy* are precisely those whom the satirical Billionaires "unmask" through irony, caricature, and paradox (satire's typical weapons).[50] Hence their slogans are "Corporations Are People Too!" and "Widen the Income Gap!" and "Taxes Are Not for Everyone!" I have seen spectators interpret these slogans literally—testament to a dominant ideology that for several decades has celebrated great wealth, enabled many large corporations to avoid paying federal taxes, and supported far lighter tax rates for the ultrarich than for the rest. In contrast, observers who detect a joke and catch the Billionaires' ironic intent sense the implied critique of such policies. For some, such irony becomes a tool for "unmasking . . . the present."[51]

Thus *hope*, not despair, is irony's gift.[52] As Jedediah Purdy writes, irony is a way to keep alive, in the spirit of Plato's Socrates, "the highest and noblest human hopes . . . if we stopped wishing for them, we would be lesser creatures—more resigned, poorer in possibility, inclined to despair."[53]

A moral vision of a more just future, not a romanticized vision of the past, inspires progressive ironic activism. And so the satirical Billionaires' cofounder Andrew Boyd writes that for a wide range of organizations participating in the 1999 World Trade Organization protests in Seattle, "Irony was no longer an expression of our lack of confidence. . . . We were neither nostalgic nor snide. We had achieved a new attitude—sly and mischievous, yet full of hope for the future."[54] The Billionaires and their satirical compatriots such as the Yes Men are not naïve about the future or about their own capacities as agents of change, yet they wholeheartedly embrace the moral vision of a fairer economy, a more just social order, and a vibrant democracy—values in sync with those of many ordinary citizens but somehow marginalized in official discourse and political practice and in mainstream news media.

Why does it matter how America's great wealth gap is portrayed by satirical activists and by a reporter writing a lighthearted piece in the *New York Times*? Citizens constitute themselves and imagine their nation partly through media consumption.[55] Furthermore, popular culture, in Stuart Hall's view, "is one of the sites where [the] struggle for and against a culture of the powerful is engaged . . . the arena of consent and resistance . . . where hegemony arises, and where it is secured."[56] In struggles over hegemony—contradictory processes aimed at ideological domination—small perturbations can foreshadow momentous changes.[57] Because corporate news journalists in the United States often adopt story frames that embody conventional wisdom rather than question dominant understandings,[58] it is left to others—including satirists—to try to stretch the boundaries of the thinkable and speakable, to destabilize common assumptions. That is precisely the intention of the satirical Billionaires.

Taunting the Powerful

Against their powerful targets do the faux Billionaires who star in this book wield mere slingshots? Like the trickster, theirs is vulnerability humor, used especially, writes Yarwood, by those who "operate from a position of weakness relative to their target."[59] The satirical Billionaires in everyday life are ordinary citizens, and as protesters they occupy a marginal social category in the United States.

But tricksters are sly. They taunt the powerful. Indeed political satire shines a spotlight on power's fault lines and contingencies.[60] And ironic activists attract serious allies, including actual billionaires and multimillionaires and sometimes even politicians—as when comedian Jon Stewart in December 2010 helped to inspire, or shame, Congress into finally passing legislation to provide health benefits for the firefighters and others who first responded to the September 11 attacks and who subsequently developed problems such as cancer and respiratory disease.[61] Stewart criticized Republicans who had blocked the bill and broadcast networks that had neglected the issue; he added, "Though, to be fair, it's not every day that the Beatles songs come to iTunes" (a story covered by the major news networks at that time). Although such an explicit link between legislative outcome and the work of a satirist may be rare, there is no reason to assume the absence of consequential if less easily traceable influences of political humor on public figures and public opinion.[62]

Plutocracy's resurgence opened an ever more lively terrain of ideological struggle and popular cultural vibrancy, where citizens' attitudes suddenly seemed to be in great flux during the early 2000s. By 2011, as Europe saw huge demonstrations against austerity programs and as protests swept across North Africa and the Middle East, the United States itself suddenly spawned Occupy Wall Street, a movement that quickly became national and global. Months earlier that same year, states such as Wisconsin saw large public protests against state austerity programs that accompanied large new tax cuts for the wealthy and big corporations, and attempts to abolish workers' collective bargaining rights.[63] Public opinion polls showed that large majorities of U.S. citizens opposed such policies and favored progressive taxation to support vital services such as education, health care, transportation, police, and fire protection, which were being slashed in the name of fiscal responsibility.[64] Yet these widely shared preferences were routinely ignored or misleadingly dismissed as out of the mainstream or too "liberal" by public figures and dominant news organizations. That disconnect, already evident at the turn of the new millennium, created a discursive opening for the billionaires—both real and pretend—who are this book's protagonists.

To capture the spirit of those moved to speak out publicly on issues such as extreme wealth inequality or the need for campaign finance reform, it is helpful to keep in mind not just their rhetorical positions on wealth, lobbyists, taxes, and corporate accountability but also matters more ineffable: a spirit of hope, a moral sensibility. There is space in the study of social movements or political activism for those who are attracted to definitive strategies and results, verifiable connections between intentions and outcomes, as well as those interested in the poetics of politics and those who approach agency as other than "a simple projection toward the future." The latter phrase is Kathleen Stewart's; her writing on affect in everyday life invites us beyond conceptions of agency as willpower so that we watch for the ways "all agency is frustrated and unstable and attracted to the potential in things."[65] Hence the personal experiences and words of the satirical Billionaires themselves, along with those of spectators, are as important to this story as larger-scale narratives about the arc of American democracy and wealth.

Million Billionaire March

When the elegant satirists played croquet and badminton on Central Park's Great Lawn, surrounded by hordes of national and international reporters and photographers (and joined by this anthropologist), they had a number of striking personal experiences: exhilaration over all the media attention; exchanges with passersby ("Who are you? The Queen of England?" shouted a man on the sidewalk to Billionaire member Contessa Frieda Markett, who wore a blue satin ball gown and tiara); enduring high humidity and heat during their energetic rally at the Plaza Hotel and then their Million Billionaire March down Fifth Avenue; hopes of being among the handful selected for Richard Avedon's studio photo shoot that afternoon[66]; keeping an eye on the police van cruising alongside their march; being careful not to occupy too much sidewalk space so that pedestrians could pass; checking their temporary tattoos bearing phone numbers for legal aid in the event of arrest; and laughing as their Billionaire marshal, Contessa Frieda Markett, directed them repeatedly to keep to the right half of the sidewalk as they marched: "to the right, Billionaires, to the right—like the country!" With astonishment, cheers, and tears of joy, the several hundred Billionaire marchers from across the country turned a Manhattan street corner and caught sight of a vastly larger multitude—hundreds of thousands of human figures bearing colorful banners and placards, singing and chanting as they walked together—affirming an expansive sense of political possibility.

That day of political electricity, on the eve of the Republican National Convention, for the Billionaires and other protesters with whom I spoke, brought on a sense of affective solidarity or social connectedness of the kind anthropologist Victor Turner would characterize as "communitas": the moral values or sentiments of humankind-ness and solidarity that cross-cut status ranks.[67] For the Billionaires for Bush, that Sunday in August 2004 became iconic, a powerfully resonant high point in the emotional arc of their organization. How pleased they were with the huge turnout of Billionaires, media, and celebrities such as Richard Avedon and cartoonist Art Spiegelman. Spiegelman took as his Billionaire name Milty National, marched with them that day, and wittily captured the experience in a half-page color cartoon sequence in the *New Yorker*.[68] New York City officials had banned a half million protesters from Central Park that day, but the Billionaires had devised a way to express dissent in that public space nonetheless. A *New York Times* reporter wrote of their "Billionaire Croquet Party" in Central Park: "Then the invasion began—dozens of Billionaires for Bush, badminton rackets held aloft, champagne flutes overflowing, waving signs that said 'Corporations Are People Too.'"[69]

The Boston Billionaire known as Arby Trajj (Chris Hartman) arrived in New York City about 10:00 that morning, after driving by rental car from Connecticut.[70] In his late twenties at the time, he worked as a researcher and graphic design consultant for a Boston nonprofit organization. He brought with him a badminton set and two costumes for the day: what he imagined as a 1920s version of an all-white lawn-tennis outfit (white slacks and white hat) for the Central Park event, and his Arby Trajj Billionaire tuxedo, top hat, and monocle. After playing croquet and badminton on the Great Lawn, he dashed to his parked car, changed into his tuxedo, and then hailed a taxi on Fifth Avenue: "I enjoyed telling the cab driver: 'to the Plaza Hotel, please,' in my Billionaire voice and he didn't miss a beat; he didn't ask me about my costume or anything."

Hartman joined the Million Billionaire March down Fifth Avenue and commented on the camaraderie: "It felt like a pretty cohesive group. . . . Probably helping the effect was that we all had distinctive costumes and we were all to varying degrees in character, so it was fun." He felt energized by the smiles and exchanges with surprised pedestrians: "I imagine if we had just been carrying signs in a normal protest march we might not have gotten the smiles we got. For me personally, I got a lot of energy from making people laugh." While he appreciated the Billionaire approach because "it was by design meant to capture the attention and imagination of the average person with humor," he felt "burnt out with the old protest-march mode of political action" and found that participating in the satirical Billionaires' actions "was a way of lightening it up for me."

When the Billionaires reached Union Square Park, he said, many "flopped down on the ground and began talking to each other." Hartman, however, said he had been "getting such a kick out of getting reactions from passersby . . . [that I] continued hailing people as they walked by and I got a lot of people taking my photograph, laughing. Some people would come up and talk to me and I would talk to them in [his Billionaire] character." To stay hydrated, he had dropped into convenience stores along the march route to buy bottles of "very fine apple juice," and then as he stood in Union Square at the end of the march, he kept refilling a champagne glass with "apple juice, which looks exactly like champagne."

The route for that day's huge march organized by United for Peace and Justice and many other political networks had been a matter of contention and was approved only a few days previously. In response to the city's denial of a permit to protest in Central Park, the Billionaires posted a tongue-in-cheek announcement on their listserv: "Billionaire Croquet Party: 500,000 anti-Bush protesters will be barred from Central Park so we can play croquet. Part of our 'Keep off the Grass' campaign to privatize Central Park. Bring your croquet sets, badminton sets, and other upper-crust lawn games. Billionaires should not gather in groups larger than 20, as it would be awfully out of character to get arrested!"[71]

Casting the satirical Billionaires as anything but protesters, yet playfully referring to the protest permit denial and free-speech issue, Billionaire cofounder Phil T. Rich (Andrew Boyd) declaimed to a reporter interviewing him in Central Park that morning: "Not a single protester to be seen . . . [We are] unencumbered by people eager to exercise their supposedly inalienable rights—just look at how alienable they are!"

Boyd's statement to that reporter echoes our era's profound contradiction: *In a political system rooted in democratic ideals but accustomed to serving the interests of large corporations and the very rich, putting ordinary citizens first had become extraordinary.* As public policy scholar and former Clinton administration labor secretary Robert Reich wrote, "Washington and the financial sector have become so tightly intertwined that public accountability has all but vanished. . . . The extraordinary wealth of America's financial class also elicits boundless cooperation from politicians who depend on it for campaign contributions and from a fawning business press . . . as well as think tanks eager to reward their generosity."[72] And so the satirical Billionaires chant, "This Is What Plutocracy Looks Like!"—itself an echo of the 1999 anti-WTO protesters' refrain as they marched in the thousands through the streets of Seattle declaring: "This Is What Democracy Looks Like!"

Humor and Specters of Calamity

This chapter's two opening vignettes—the satirical Billionaires in Central Park, and palatial homes and dinosaur topiary in California's Beverly Park—can be spun into contrasting tales of comedy or satire. Comedy soothes, while satire and irony trouble comedy's happy plot resolutions. Political satire shines a powerful spotlight on the unthinkable or invisible. If comedy and satire hold a mirror up to society,[73] what do these playful opening scenes reveal? For some, the surface images affirm the dominant political logic of an era: a wealth gap is natural, greed is good, and markets should run "free." For others, both vignettes hint at alternative attitudes and values and raise questions: What kind of economy is fair or moral? Must the quest for profit and personal responsibility trump health, safety, and security? Should society help its less fortunate members? Has the gap between the ultrarich and the rest grown too wide? Does superconsumption by a fortunate few harm the rest? Have dreams of a better life become unattainable for too many?

Perhaps more so in the early twenty-first century than at any time since the 1920s, the ultrawealthy in the United States are potent objects of both cultural fascination and resentment. Although Occupy Wall Street in 2011 and 2012 nudged questions about economic opportunity and inequality into the limelight, as a conversational topic, wealth (or more pointedly, class) in America has long been ticklish. That is one of the reasons the Billionaires chose ironic humor as their weapon.

Public imagination in the early twenty-first century is haunted by specters of financial calamity, environmental catastrophe, predatory corporations, and Wall Street robber barons. In an imaginary world of democracy in which all points of view are thoughtfully considered, where social connection and individualism are not at war, and where the richness of human variety is embraced, political satirists might be rare. But in hard times political satire and irony flourish. Should we then count comedic satirists—though often consigned to peripheries—among the makers of history?

The effects of ironic political humor—with exceptions such as Jon Stewart's public support for the 9/11 First Responders legislation—are usually difficult to trace, and scholars of humor debate its radical or reformist potential. Yet there can be little doubt that satire can reshape political imaginations in ways dictators and other leaders have long found threatening,[74] and ordinary citizens have found inspiriting.

Political humor—so vital to political imagination and everyday meaning-making—clearly merits anthropological attention. Yet humor has been a rare focus in contemporary ethnography. Exceptions include Donna Goldstein's superb study of a shantytown in Rio de Janeiro, and Dominic Boyer and Alexei Yurchak's innovative analysis of a particular form of parodic overidentification known by the Russian slang term *stiob*, which blurs the boundaries between sincerity and ridicule.[75] Otherwise it has been scholars in communication and media studies, more often than social scientists, who have analyzed contemporary American political satire.[76] I know of no other ethnographic study of the Billionaires, and this book is one of the first social science studies of satirical political activists.[77]

This study is less about practical politics than it is about the political imagination, spirit of the times, limits of public discourse, poetics of politics, and the cultural delicacy of dramatic differences in wealth. It analyzes cultural politics during a time of profound ambivalence toward politics itself. Why might the satirical Billionaires be considered a cultural touchstone, a sensitive gauge of the fragile condition of American democracy? What are the possibilities and limitations of popular activism that relies on informal networks more than formal institutions, performance parody more than community organizing or traditional canvassing, and decentralization and consensus more than hierarchy and central control?

· · ·

Chapter 1 provides a snapshot of the satirical Billionaires' trajectory from 1999 to 2012, and explores theories of ironic humor as political instrument, ironies of ethnographic fieldwork, and recent innovations in protest as spectacle by the Yes Men, Reverend Billy, Reclaim the Streets, and Stephen Colbert, among others. (The Appendix outlines my research methods.) Soaring wealth inequality and the collapse of the American middle class is one of our era's biggest stories; Chapter 2 explores the new Gilded Age as the cultural and historical period that frames the satirical Billionaire enterprise. It includes my interview with William Gates Sr. and discusses the counterintuitive melding of political concerns of satirical Billionaires and celebrity billionaires, along with popular cultural conceptions about wealth and taxes in America, and debates about whether a global economy driven by vast quantities of finance capital deployed in obscure transactions, such as derivatives, offers any recognizable object for social movement dissent.

Chapter 3 offers a rare glimpse of the embryonic stages of social movement organization, as it explores through oral history interviews how the satirical Billionaires' political network emerged after a decade of experimentation among creative activists in Massachusetts. Framed as an analysis of political ritual and antiritual, it also considers the transformative potential of resistance in political ritual. Chapters 4 and 5, building on the perspectives of participants, spectators, and media, trace the Billionaire trajectory of the 2000s: increasingly savvy strategists polishing their own "brand," growing pains as their organizational culture shifted in stages, a sharp boost in their production values during the 2004 presidential campaign, delight in their growing numbers and media coverage, an internally divisive period and demoralization after the 2004 presidential election, strategy meetings to reassess it all in mid-2005, experimentation with new modes of action and organizational names in sync with the 2008 presidential campaign and financial crisis, 2009 health care debates, the 2010 Citizens United Supreme Court decision, and 2011 austerity programs and increasingly hard economic times as a new presidential election approached. These two chapters consider as well how Billionaires can be seduced by their own theatrics, and I include close-ups of how people on the street perceive the Billionaires—with attention to those who share their political sympathies but do not necessarily appreciate their street theater, and highlighting voices that are emblematic of today's economic fracture lines.

Chapter 6 takes up a Billionaire's claim: "we cracked the code of American media culture. . . . For a brief, shining moment we outsmarted the system." So said Merchant F. Arms—social movement historian and experienced activist Jeremy Varon. How successful were the Billionaires in defying traditional images of protest in order to reach imagined publics? What did it mean to be players *in* as well as *of* the media, neither wholly compliant nor resistant? Chapter 7 offers final thoughts on humor in social movements and the contemporary political significance of satire and sincerity. I contrast the Billionaires with Occupy Wall Street and suggest not only that the satirists of the 2000s and earlier years were harbingers who helped in small ways to set the stage for the serious protests that followed, but that more sustained subversions of the status quo require humor as well as earnestness.

1 Irony, Humor, Spectacle

AVOIDING POSES AS CONTEMPORARY REAL-LIFE BILLIONAIRES such as "Star Wars" creator George Lucas, television star Oprah Winfrey, or Microsoft cofounder Bill Gates, the satirical Billionaires adopt fictive personas such as Phil T. Rich and evoke the elegance of *The Great Gatsby*'s Roaring Twenties or an even earlier era of robber barons and heiresses. "We're doing an impersonation of an imaginary subjectivity, something that is already the stuff of fiction and a complicated set of projective identifications . . . it's like a parody of a cartoon," remarked Merchant F. Arms (Jeremy Varon).[1] It is up to spectators then to historicize the present, to perceive the implied link between the early twenty first century and earlier wealth bubbles: the Roaring Twenties on the eve of the Great Depression, or the late–nineteenth-century era that Mark Twain popularized as a Gilded Age of surface glitter and vast underlying corruption, when the very rich sparkled while many went hungry.

The sheer improbability that actual billionaires of any era would be protesters is the premise of the Billionaires' ironic humor. Yet that very assumption is undone in real life by the man-bites-dog story of what *Newsweek* termed a "billionaire backlash"[2]—the multimillionaires and billionaires such as Netflix CEO Reed Hastings, Warren Buffett, George Soros, members of the Rockefeller family (and in earlier decades Presidents Franklin D. Roosevelt and Theodore Roosevelt) who support capitalism but adopt progressive public positions on wealth and taxes that catch many by surprise.[3] Indeed Franklin Roosevelt "at his legendary 1936 Madison Square Garden rally declared that he welcomed the 'hatred' of his enemies in the realms of 'business and financial monopoly, speculation, reckless banking, class antagonism, sectionalism, war profiteer-ing.'"[4] The message of today's renegade billionaires such as Warren Buffett is unmistakable: our age of excess is so extreme that even some who have gained the most are distressed enough to publicly urge reform.

This chapter begins with the double revolt of billionaires (both real and pretend) and a dash through a decade with the satirical Billionaires as they responded with quick reflexes to national political shifts. Next, since irony is the Billionaires' core weapon, I explore theories of ironic humor as political instrument: the danger in the joke, the joke in the social structure, irony as bearer of hope, ironies of ethnographic research, and Billionaire responses to having an anthropologist study them. I conclude with comparative discussion of "spectacular dissent" by the Yes Men, Reverend Billy, Stephen Colbert, and other recent satirical innovators.

A Double Revolt of Billionaires

The story's silhouette: in the mid-1980s, a Midwestern man gave away his inher-ited fortune at the age of twenty-six.[5] One year before the turn of the millen-nium, that same gentleman organized a surprise campaign stunt that shined a national media spotlight on his new cocreation, the Billionaires for Forbes, whose tagline was "Because Inequality Is Not Growing Fast Enough." After Steve Forbes dropped out of the presidential race, successors to the tongue-in-cheek protesters turned their attention to both Republican and Democratic presiden-tial candidates and during the 2000 campaign called themselves Billionaires for Bush (or Gore). They parodied the ultrawealthy, critiqued plutocracy and the outsized role of money in both major political parties, and multiplied into a media-friendly grassroots network of fifty-five chapters nationally.

Four years later, bearing a name—Billionaires for Bush—redesigned to suit a new presidential campaign, their visibility escalated dramatically as they grew in a few months from a half dozen or so members meeting in a Manhattan apartment to one hundred chapters across the country and a handful abroad. Over ten thousand people joined their online community,[6] thanks to a polished website, media coverage, eye-catching street events, personal networking, and fund-raising parties that attracted celebrities such as Electronica artist Moby (Richard Melville Hall). With a red, white, and blue piggy bank as their logo, the Billionaires for Bush cultivated high production values—protest with pol-ish. They produced music CDs,[7] a tongue-in-cheek book,[8] T-shirts, bumper stickers, and an infomercial (among other products). Their modest funding came from sales of such products and from individual donations: "Billionaire production values on a shoestring budget."[9]

The Billionaires for Bush won a spot among fifteen finalists selected from more than 1,500 contestants in a "Bush in 30 Seconds" ad competition sponsored in November 2003 by MoveOn.org.[10] In early 2004, their media coverage spiked, thanks in part to a spectacular stunt featuring a Karl Rove look-alike. They appeared in the *New Yorker* and on CNN, ABC, MSNBC, and other television networks as well as in articles in *Newsweek*, the *New York Times*, *Washington Post*, *Wall Street Journal*, *Boston Globe*, *Los Angeles Times*, *USA Today*, *Der Spiegel*, and other newspapers and magazines in the United States and abroad. *Washington Post* associate editor Robert G. Kaiser wrote that "Billionaires for Bush, no matter what your politics, must be one of the most likable protest groups ever formed."[11]

Examples of their street actions include the Million Billionaire March during Republican and Democratic National Conventions, a ballroom-dancing flashmob[12] in New York's Grand Central Station, thanking people outside post offices as they mail their tax returns on April 15, or auctioning off Social Security on President Bush's 2005 inauguration day. Their musical troupe "The Follies" produced shows such as "Dick Cheney's Holiday Spectacular." The Billionaires dubbed the U.S. Labor Day holiday "Cheap Labor Day," and displayed banners proclaiming "No Minimum Wage! No Minimum Age!" and "Subcontinents Do It Cheaper!"

In early 2008, the Billionaires produced a widely viewed video spoof, "No, You Can't," that was covered in the *New York Times*[13] and that featured a Dick Cheney look-alike and other Republican figures undercutting Barack Obama's "Yes We Can" slogan. "No, You Can't" parodied a popular video featuring celebrities and Obama's oratory that had been produced by the musician Will.i.am of the Black Eyed Peas.[14] At the 2008 Republican National Convention in St. Paul, dressed in pinstriped suits and black fedoras, the Billionaires attracted attention from the *Wall Street Journal*[15] and other media when they posed as "Lobbyists for McCain" and carried placards declaring, "No, You Can't!" and "Don't Change Horsemen Mid-Apocalypse" and "Loyal to Big Oil."

Wall Street's 2008 meltdown inspired the satirical Billionaires for Bailouts. Clad in tuxedoes and gowns or black suits and fedoras, they too were featured in a *Washington Post* article and other media when they joined Wall Street protests and held aloft signs proclaiming, "Thanks for the $700bn Check!" and

"I'm Starving, Bail Me Out!" and "Billionaires for Bailouts *Love* Tax-Payers!"[16] They pivoted during the 2009 health care reform debates to pose as Billionaires for Wealthcare ("Let Them Eat Advil!") and staged another stealth prank that attracted national media attention: a musical satirical protest—"Public Option Annie," sung to the tune of "Tomorrow" from the Broadway musical *Annie*—which caught by complete surprise health insurance industry executives at a Washington, DC, conference. That choral stunt was featured at the top of MSNBC's *Rachel Maddow Show*, in a segment captioned "Guerrillas in Their Midst."[17] Maddow said the Billionaires' prank was a "sign of the continued spunk and energy on the left to push for a robust version of [health care] reform."

In 2010, as proposals to cut Social Security benefits resurfaced—even though the Social Security trust fund is not in crisis and is not the cause of the federal budget deficit[18]—the satirical Billionaires for Social Insecurity waved signs declaring "It's a Crisis! Because We Said So" and "Feeling Entitled to Cut Your Entitlements (Since 1936)." In mid-2010, following the U.S. Supreme Court's Citizens United decision, a spin-off group dressed as the country's Founding Fathers won media coverage of their protests in Washington, DC, against massive political campaign fund-raising by corporate lobbyists.[19] Also in 2010, Agit-Pop Communications[20] (co-led by Billionaires cofounder Andrew Boyd) and MoveOn teamed up to create RepublicCorp ("Buying Democracy One Race at a Time"), a "merger between giant corporations and the GOP," which quickly sprouted offices and street actions in several cities, produced a video that MoveOn transmitted to nearly a million people, serenaded the head of the Republican front-group American Action Network, recorded a "corporate anthem," and joined Stephen Colbert's 2010 "Keep Fear Alive" rally in Washington, DC, among other activities.[21]

Andrew Boyd and other former Billionaires established a netroots organization called The Other 98%, which describes itself on its website as "a political home for the silent majority of Americans who are tired of corporate control of Washington." Its taglines include "Because the Middle Class Is Too Big to Fail" and "Making Democracy Work for the Rest of Us."[22] The Other 98% helped to organize a large flashmob of hundreds of protesters in May 2011 to spoof the renaming of a theater for ballet and opera at Lincoln Center as the David H. Koch Theatre.[23] Another of its capers: to mark the second anniversary of the Supreme Court's Citizens United decision, the Supreme Court Building's white exterior was briefly lit one night—until police arrived—with giant dollar signs and a light projection of the words "rights are for people."[24]

In April 2011, when some corporate media outlets reported that many large U.S. corporations paid no federal taxes and that some even received tax credits, the Billionaires' cofounder Andrew Boyd teamed up with the Yes Men and US Uncut[25] to concoct a widely reported media hoax asserting that the General Electric Corporation would "donate [its] entire $3.2 billion tax refund to help offset cuts and save American jobs."[26] During the half hour or so when the public believed the hoax, GE's stock plunged and then recovered quickly once the hoax was revealed, illustrating, a US Uncut spokesman said, that GE would not voluntarily "do the right thing" and pay their tax—in spite of loopholes in the law—since that would cause their stock to fall. "GE's tax avoidance is unpatriotic, it's undemocratic, it's unfair," said Andrew Boyd.[27]

In 2012, elegantly attired satirists calling themselves Multi-Millionaires for Mitt joined Occupy Wall Street protesters marching around New York's Waldorf-Astoria Hotel, where presidential candidate Mitt Romney appeared at a $2,500-per-plate fund-raising luncheon.[28] They waved placards declaring, "Corporations Are People Too!" and chanted "We're here, we're rich, get used to it!"[29] And in 2011 and 2012, Billionaires for Tar Sands staged mock counterdemonstrations to environmentalist protests against the Keystone XL pipeline project that would transport oil from the tar sands in Alberta, Canada, to the United States.

Meanwhile, the man who had given away his inherited fortune while in his twenties—the cocreator of the satirical Billionaires—redirected his attention during the early 2000s to actual billionaires and multimillionaires. He teamed up with the father of the richest man in the world to write a book subtitled *Why America Should Tax Accumulated Fortunes*.[30] He helped to found a nonprofit, nonpartisan organization (Responsible Wealth), whose members are among the wealthiest 5 percent of Americans. These privileged citizens, who include Democrats, Republicans, and Independents, spotlight the risks posed to democracy by escalating economic inequality, and call for a living wage, fair taxes, greater corporate accountability, and broadened asset ownership for all Americans.[31] Theirs began as a modest attempt to counter the outsized influence of eighteen ultrarich families—many of whom *inherited* substantial wealth—who between 1994 and 2004 spent $500 million lobbying to abolish the tax on inherited wealth (which dates back to 1916).[32] To fight back against that wellfinanced lobbying effort by heirs and heiresses (and conservative think tanks), the nonpartisan organization Responsible Wealth recruited a couple of thousand millionaires and a few billionaires to sign their petition against repeal of the federal tax on inherited wealth.

These Janus-faced insurgencies by bona fide billionaires on the one hand, and satirists who simply pretend to be billionaires on the other, were eye-catching inversions of social hierarchy. For actual billionaires and multi-millionaires to support higher taxes for the ultrarich (including a tax on inherited wealth) symbolically elevates that populist position, while the elegant self-presentation of the parodist billionaires raises the status of "protester" above its scruffy stereotype.

Embedded in these twin revolts are subtle psychological dynamics of fear and desire, imagined status reversals entailing descent into poverty or ascent into wealth. The sharpness of today's economic divide—marked some say by an "empathy gap"[33]—nonetheless offers vivid material for reciprocal imaginings of life at the opposite end of the wealth spectrum. Sometimes these ideations are projective identifications that yield anger, fear, aggression, and blame. But they can also embody an empathic capacity to imagine the lot of the other and to engage compassionately the idea of doubleness or split identity (there but for luck or grace go any of us), without which neither insurgency would carry moral or emotional force.

The Joke in the Social Structure

The "billionaire backlash" attests to what anthropologist Mary Douglas terms the "joke in the social structure"—the deep connection between a joke and its historical-political setting. Jokes about sharp inequalities of status and power, like any humor, are potent only if they tap shared understandings of context. Without that "tacit social contract" or "social congruity" as backdrop to a joke, Critchley remarks, there is "no comic incongruity."[34] That, he says, is the phenomenology of the joke.[35]

It is easy to see American life at the millennium as a social situation that *invites* symbolic reformulation into its joke pattern, given our era's runaway wealth inequality, the growing material precariousness of the middle class and working poor, the outsized role of money and huge corporations in politics, and the consequent erosion of substantive democracy in the early twenty-first century. A few years before the real estate bubble burst, and before the implosion of mortgage-backed financial derivatives helped to precipitate a global economic crisis, I asked Lois Canright (an activist in her midforties who had a couple of decades of experience with political organizing and who was active in Billionaires for Bush), What historical circumstances do you think favor satirical street theater as a protest form? Her reply, as we sat in her tree-shaded yard on a warm August day in 2004, was prescient:

> I think it arises when the real world starts to resemble a theater of the absurd . . . when the things that have become normal under Bush are so mind-blowingly imbalanced . . . his tax policy, it's just unreal that everybody just rolled over and went along with that and what that says about our society and our tolerance for this kind of opulence in the face of starvation. . . . It's pretty stark times and so maybe these more ironic or satirical [approaches] . . . rise when Rome is getting ready to roast.[36]

For many, the "roasting" had already begun. Signs of profound crisis in U.S. society, in the years immediately preceding the financial meltdown and big bailouts of 2008, included some 56 million citizens without health insurance, 36 million living in poverty,[37] hundreds of thousands of people losing homes mortgaged at subprime rates (often through deceptive lending agreements), pension funds collapsing, schools failing, physical infrastructure crumbling, an overstretched military, corporate accounting failures and fraud, "fictitious capital,"[38] government spying on citizens, growing concentration of corporate media ownership, politicians acting as courtiers of powerful corporations that funded their campaigns, and heightened political polarization and incivility in public discourse.[39]

After the 2008 financial meltdown, satirical Billionaire Merchant F. Arms said, "our core critique was utterly and completely vindicated." To understand why requires one to look no further than autopsies of the 2008 financial meltdown, such as the 2011 *Financial Crisis Inquiry Report* or Charles H. Ferguson's award-winning 2010 documentary *Inside Job*. That carefully researched film centers on the financial wizards—"masters of the universe"—whose risk-taking was enabled in part by deregulation of the financial sector and by cozy relationships with politicians and regulators. The film's director remarked in 2010: "In the case of this crisis, *nobody* has gone to prison, despite fraud that caused trillions of dollars in losses. . . . It is . . . my hope that, whatever political opinions individual viewers may have, that after seeing this film we can all agree on the importance of restoring honesty and stability to our financial system, and of holding accountable those who destroyed it."[40] Occupy Wall Street protesters echoed that sentiment.

Even though public opinion polls by 2011 showed that a large majority of U.S. citizens favored restraints on corporate political power and tax increases for corporations and the very wealthy,[41] the obstacles to translating those preferences into legislative reforms remained formidable. This historical moment—its mounting insecurities and disproportions—offered especially fertile ground for ironic humor, which softly threatened the powerful.

The Danger in the Joke

Political leaders fear jokes. In the United States, pundits have long noted that it matters when a politician becomes the object of comedian Jay Leno's or David Letterman's jokes on late-night television.[42] Even commissars in an authoritarian regime may accept citizens' hatred but fear their laughter since it dramatizes the limits of propaganda and repression.[43] Repressive regimes almost inevitably beget irony and critical humor. Although humor's pathways can scarcely be controlled, after the revolution in Russia, Pomorska writes, officials forbade writers from "certain kinds of laughter, irony, and satire."[44] Why?

Perhaps because, as Mary Douglas argues, a joke "changes the balance of power."[45] In her view, a joke exposes inadequacies and injustices, and "release[s] the pent-up power of the imagination . . . for a joke implies that anything is possible."[46] Similarly, Bakhtin argues that laughter and the carnival spirit unfetter human consciousness and open the imagination to "new potentialities."[47] George Orwell remarks that "Each joke is a tiny revolution."[48] Political jokes, in short, can be dangerous.

Or are they? The effects of such humor are hotly debated.[49] Is it harmless catharsis, or does it build solidarity and inspire political change? Is humor, as Freud suggests, sublimated aggression that eases tensions or even diffuses impulses of violence or direct attack against the objects of the satire?[50] Political humor, Schutz suggests, "is often a reaction to the greatest concentration of power in society . . . and [functions as] safe release for aggressiveness against superior force."[51] In this view, far from being threatening, political humor actually contributes to social stability, redirecting emotions people might otherwise channel to revolution.[52] From this perspective, the king who allows court jesters and carnival demonstrates his strength and authority.

To debate the "*intrinsically* radical or conservative" nature of political humor may be less productive, however, than exploring its historically contingent effects. Why, for example, do rituals of rebellion and carnival sometimes slip from ritual to open political struggle or resistance?[53] Without romanticizing political satire's revolutionary potential, we can acknowledge its capacity for shaping popular sentiments and actions and for reshaping official discourse and practices.

Humor is a delicate instrument in politics precisely because it entails a volatile mix of playfulness and derision, delight and superiority, pleasure and triumph. Lean too heavily on the second elements in the aforementioned pairs and one may offend and alienate audiences. Lean too much on the first elements and risk ineffectualness by removing a message's bite or sting. So too carnival laughter, as analyzed by Bakhtin, is ambivalent—"gay, triumphant, and at the same time mocking, deriding."[54] The boundary between laughing *at* and laughing *with* those in power is blurred. That very ambiguity is a powerful strategic weapon of the weak—as well as of the dominant.[55]

The powerful sometimes strategically embrace satire that targets them—as when former vice presidential candidate Sarah Palin appeared on *Saturday Night Live* with her sharply satiric impersonator, Tina Fey. Such tactics do not necessarily inoculate the powerful, though they may lessen humor's sting. When ordinary citizens, in turn, enjoy political satire, we implicitly laugh at ourselves for being part of the societies satirized.

Since at least the time of Aristotle, democracy has nourished political humor. Scholars of humor observe that "one of the mainsprings of humor is the discrepancy between reality and what we desire and expect."[56] The irony of a rupture between actual governance practices and the democratic ideals of political accountability of rulers to citizens inspires the Billionaires' satire as well as that of Jon Stewart and Stephen Colbert. Indeed, as a popular cultural sign of Stewart's political potency or the erosion of other channels of accountability, or both, a 2009 political cartoon depicting the death of newspapers shows a woman asking, "Without newspapers, who would hold people in positions of power accountable?" The man walking beside her replies, "Jon Stewart."[57]

In a country whose dance with democracy and wealth seemed increasingly unsteady in the 2000s, the twin billionaire "revolts" became symbolically resonant entrants into the public sphere. That historical moment, with its mounting insecurities and disproportions, offered especially fertile ground for irony.

Irony Theorized

"A nipping jest that offers the honey of pleasantness in its mouth and a sting of rebuke in its tail." So goes a seventeenth-century definition of irony.[58] Irony is a sugar-coated truth and a nettle. Analytically, it is a slippery concept. Literary scholar Wayne Booth writes, "There is no agreement among critics about what irony is, and many would hold to the romantic claim . . . that its very spirit and value are violated by the effort to be clear about it."[59] Humor and irony are "folk-concepts, with fuzzy boundaries, if any," states Attardo.[60]

The term *irony* is applied not only to figures of speech but sometimes to historical epochs, postmodernity, modernity, existence itself, or the very position of the ethnographic researcher.[61] Irony can be a state of affairs contrary to what might be expected, "a contradictory outcome of events as if in mockery of the promise and fitness of things."[62] More narrowly, verbal irony is "a subtly humorous perception of inconsistency, in which an apparently straightforward statement or event is undermined by its context so as to give it a very different significance."[63] Cosmic irony, like verbal irony, contains "a notion of a meaning or intent beyond what we manifestly say or intend."[64] But cosmic irony or the irony of fate takes us beyond the term's strictly linguistic sense, and as Colebrook writes, it "refers to the limits of human meaning; we do not see the effects of what we do, the outcomes of our actions, or the forces that exceed our choices."[65] For many anticorporate globalization activists, the September 11 attacks conveyed the cosmic irony that the global movement for social justice they had created before September 2001 would likely be undone by a chillier post–9/11 climate for dissent and popular mobilization. Irony often spotlights discrepancies between what is promised or expected and what is delivered, but it also can call into question the very norms and ideals on which expectations are based.[66]

Many see irony as a defining feature of our era, particularly of its wars.[67] Predictions that Iraqis would greet American soldiers as liberators, that oil revenues would pay for the war, and that the fighting would be over in a few days or weeks all became fodder for ironists and satirists (as in the "Mess-o-potamia" segments on comedian Jon Stewart's *The Daily Show*). Here irony marks a tragic incongruity between outcomes and intentions. Soldiers themselves are keenly attuned to the ironies of situation that war presents—war's "mortal irony" (Fussell's term). The personal events of war—trying desperately to save a bleeding comrade, following contradictory or dangerous orders, slaughtering fellow human beings—compose a horror that memory later construes as irony, a narrative arc of hope abridged, innocence lost.

The September 11 attacks brought proclamations that "irony is dead." *Vanity Fair* editor Graydon Carter famously declared in a September 2001 interview, "It's the end of the age of irony."[68] As *New York Times* reporter David D. Kirkpatrick put it, many editors and pundits assumed that "The shock of the attacks is jolting the public out of the recently fashionable skepticism toward anything purporting to be original or earnest."[69] On the other hand, the young cultural critic Jedediah Purdy—who had published a 1999 book (*For Common Things*) denouncing the age of irony—in September 2001 suggested that now might be the time for irony because it "can also work to keep dangerous excesses of passion and self-righteousness and extreme conviction at bay."[70]

Engaged irony of that kind drew praise from others such as David Beers, who wrote in an essay in Salon.com that he hoped September 11 would usher in a "golden age of irony . . . the kind that drove Socrates' queries, the irony that lies at the heart of much great literature and great religion, the irony that pays attention to contradictions and embraces paradoxes, rather than wishing them away in an orgy of purpose and certainty."[71] Engaged irony, he argued, is far removed from the cultural stereotype of "low-grade" irony as "the nihilistic shrug of an irritatingly shallow smartass . . . a handy shorthand for moral relativism and self-absorption." If anything, he suggests, ironists care too much about the world rather than too little.

Irony offers "a valuable resource for inciting the moral and political imagination against whatever is given, assumed, or imposed," Fernandez and Huber write.[72] They counter the view of irony as an evasion or subversion of moral reasoning or even a form of inaction. In highlighting the contradiction of human foibles and aspirations, irony reveals paradoxes that may inconvenience those in power even as it nourishes democratic debate and new forms of political imagination. Irony, as James Clifford writes, performs a "double function" in offering people "a means of getting some purchase on slippery power. . . . On the one hand, it helps people contain, perform, step partly outside a situation, thus gaining some control. On the other hand, by highlighting the artificial, the tactical nature of such containments, irony recognizes historical conjunctures as uncontrollable, in process, with unpredictable outcomes."[73] Irony, in short, engages power, recognizes history's unpredictability, and offers people an approach to the ineffable or incomprehensible or terrifying.

If irony in the early 2000s needed any more fuel, many found it in the words and practices of political leaders and government officials who, with media help, circulated slick narratives belied by facts or logic—a practice Jon Stewart's satirical news colleague Stephen Colbert in 2005 famously labeled "truthiness." As linguist Ben Zimmer observed, Colbert charmed many a wordsmith, pundit, and ordinary citizen when he so effectively tapped the political zeitgeist in 2005 by resurrecting the term "truthiness" for "ersatz truth."[74] Five years later, Zimmer said, "truthiness" had demonstrated impressive staying power as a "zeitgeisty word."

But even "truthiness" appears a polite term for an approach to governing and public relations that shocked many. Ron Suskind, writing in the *New York Times Magazine* in October 2004, two weeks before the presidential election, quoted a Bush administration aide dismissing what he termed the "reality-based community"[75]: "a judicious study of discernible reality [is] . . . not the way the world really works anymore. . . . We're an empire now, and when we act, we create our own reality. . . . We're history's actors . . . and you, all of you, will be left to just study what we do." In this media and political environment, news parodies such as *The Colbert Report* and Jon Stewart's *Daily Show* found increasing "cultural traction" (Frank Rich's term), since these broadcasts were among the "few reliable spots on the dial for finding something other than the government line" during the Bush administration.[76] Stewart's and Colbert's irony had the capacity, as Fernandez and Huber put it in a different context, "to reveal the deceitfulness of a leader's proclamations or the contingency of an opposing truth, thus opening eyes to the possibility of alternatives" and perhaps shaping political action.[77]

Barack Obama's election in 2008 brought new declarations, some tongue-in-cheek, that irony was dead.[78] But Joan Didion wrote that it is dangerous for a country to be in an "irony-free zone."[79] She warned against both naïve hope and a "militant idealism" that "redefin[es] political or pragmatic questions as moral questions," making them seem too easy to answer. What drove the profound transformations of the 1960s, she argued, was not partisanship translated into consumerism—babies in cute T-shirts bearing a candidate's name—"but the kind of resistance to that decade's war that in the case of our current wars, unmotivated by a draft, we have yet to see." Furthermore, the notion that Obama's victory had turned all the world into supporters of the United States, Didion suggested, "did not seem entirely different in kind from imagining in 2003 that we would be greeted with flowers when we invaded Iraq." Such imaginings obscure hard questions of politics and pragmatics, of how change is actually accomplished—hard questions that soon became salient during the Obama administration. In short, by the end of the first decade of the 2000s, irony was in no danger of extinction.

Billionaire Irony

The Billionaires' ironic humor blunts the hard edge of the American dream—"there are only winners and losers now"[80]—replacing it with a vision of solidarity and collective obligations toward the least fortunate among us. That requires turning the moral tables on the ultrarich and questioning what some among the very wealthy believe to be their legitimate privilege. Hence the Billionaires' ironic tagline, "Because we're all in this together, sort of."[81]

As the Billionaires reach out toward others through empathic laughter, they gently counter powerful ideological forces, such as the assumption that everyone has a chance at the American dream, and that individuals themselves—more than large-scale processes or institutions—are to blame if they fail to prosper. Their assumption that parody makes dissent more palatable resonates with literary theorist Hutcheon's view of parody as "less an aggressive than a conciliatory rhetorical strategy, building upon more than attacking its other, while still retaining critical difference."[82] Yet parody, a stylistic imitation that ridicules and a familiar weapon of satire, has an "ironic critical distance"[83] that distinguishes it from comedy.

Classic comedy humanizes the ultrawealthy, implying that they are after all like the rest of us. The Billionaires' parody, on the other hand, calls attention to just how disconnected and different the megarich are from most citizens. While comedy naturalizes the status quo, a turn to parody or irony in a satirical mode assumes no general satisfaction with the way things are. Irony and satire subvert comedy's harmonious resolutions of historical conflicts and its assumption that historical movement occurs "within the confines of an achieved *system* of relationships which itself is no longer conceived to change."[84] If history is plotted as comedy, then progressive billionaires such as Rockefeller and Soros—the latter a hedge fund manager who became a philanthropist and critic of economic neoliberalism—might be dismissed as quirks rather than as harbingers of or even contributors to systemic change. Irony, however, is attuned to social and political instability. Furthermore, in times of "social breakdown," Hayden White observes, irony "tends toward an Absurdist view of the world."[85]

Here we are close indeed to the Billionaires' sensibility—or at least that of their cofounder Andrew Boyd. When I asked him about possible influences of earlier activists on his generation, he mentioned the Situationists,[86] Dadaism, and "playing with meaning itself":

> the notion of an absurd universe . . . Camus . . . which allowed us an analysis . . . [of things like] death squads in El Salvador. . . . How can you be really serious and effective about your politics because horrible injustices are being committed by your government in your name and your tax dollars? But then also this

is all a dream, in a way, this is all a charade, this is all a great wonders mystery, and so how do you bring those things together? What some of us end up doing is finding these strange and beguiling and outside-the-box and provocative and playful and somewhat prophetic—and at times utopian-ish—[modes of expression that] connect with people in a very human way . . . and not just hit them over the heads with the facts, Jack.[87]

Boyd's ironic sensibility, which encompasses "horrible injustices" and the notion of an absurd universe, retains a sense that "this is all a great wonders mystery." For him, hope and human connection are nourished through political street theater that is simultaneously playful, surprising, and provocative. Irony here is partly a tool for dealing with power structures one can't control, and with historical and ideological disorder one can neither accept nor fully fathom.

Boyd's sense of absurdity and cosmic irony accompanies an assumption that the Billionaires' use of ironic humor reduces the likelihood of alienating spectators and gets the latter to reconsider conventional political claims and their own beliefs. Although scholars debate the political effects of such humor, some might agree that the dual billionaire/Billionaire revolts open new political pathways and help to unsettle common ideological assumptions.

Irony and the Ethnographer

An anthropologist who writes about irony may as well include ironies of her ethnographic position within that frame. At first that appears easy in this case, partly because my ethnographic interlocutors are adept at making jokes that reverse the observer-observed relation. During the height of the 2004 presidential campaign, when weekly meetings of the Manhattan chapter of Billionaires for Bush grew ever larger and the number of national chapters multiplied, each meeting began with introductions of everyone present, using fictive Billionaire names or real names, or both, along with any special organizational titles, such as "Master of Special Ops" or director of the "Ministry of Love."[88] During these introductions, I gave my actual name, and eventually also my Billionaire name (Ivana Itall, as in, I want it all), since any attendee was required to have a Billionaire name by her third meeting. I also stated that I am an anthropologist at Rutgers University doing research on the Billionaires, and I thanked them for allowing me to attend their meeting. At a mid-July 2004 Manhattan chapter meeting in an airy lower East Side loft apartment, when I said I was doing anthropological research on the group, Andrew Boyd (whom I had not yet met) drew laughter from the dozens of people present when he immediately shot back, "And we're studying you!"

A few months later I attended a national gathering of the Billionaires for Bush in Washington, DC, during the week of George W. Bush's second inauguration. That two-day national "convergence" included a hundred or so Billionaires from across the country, many of whom I had not met. During the initial round of introductions, when I said, "I am an anthropologist from Rutgers University, and I am studying you," some laughed because they assumed I was joking. Later a Billionaire attendee asked me if I really was studying them and said she only decided that might be the case when she noticed I was taking notes during the meeting.

Surprises in the observer-observed relationship also emerged during interactions with Billionaires and non-Billionaire activists during the street carnival that some post office plazas become on tax day. On April 15, 2004, a pleasant spring day, the Billionaires for Bush, along with other groups such as the Sierra Club and New Democratic Majority, were performing good-humored protests in front of New York City's central post office on Eighth Avenue, opposite Pennsylvania Station. A Sierra Club member was dressed as a two-headed fish. Noelle Molé, then a Rutgers University doctoral student assisting me with street-intercept interviews, described the scene in her field notes (closely paraphrased here): The post office walkway was bounded with bright yellow police tape labeled "Caution," in anticipation of the after-work rush to mail tax returns. Young women dressed in bright yellow lemon costumes—Snapple beverage company marketers—handed out free samples of cold Lemon Sour Snapple to passersby who stood in a queue. The Westin Hotel had its own promotion, a full-size bed on the sidewalk, made up in attractive linens and bearing a sign that read, "Procrastination Finally Pays Off." Westin would give a free night in the hotel to the last tax payer to enter the post office.

Noelle Molé and I together chatted with one of the first members of Billionaires for Bush to arrive, a woman Molé described as follows in her field notes: She wore a "purple sparkly scarf" and a well-worn "brown, yellow and red sweater with fake black fur . . . a blue lacey long skirt, tattered black boots, and thick layers of foundation make-up, red blush, and dark lipstick." She appeared to be in her late fifties or early sixties, and though her appearance was less polished than that of the Billionaires who arrived subsequently, her oral performance of the Billionaire role was as vibrant and high-spirited as theirs. While talking to us, she code-switched between her own slight New York accent and the faux British accent that was her Billionaire pose. When I mentioned my profession, she said in her aristocratic Billionaire accent, "Oh, isn't that cute? You don't make a lot of money, do you?"

A "What Tax Cut?" sign then prompted Molé to dash over to chat with the person carrying it. Since he and his companions were dressed in jeans and sweaters, she assumed they were not part of the Billionaires for Bush, and she intended to ask how the two groups played off each other. She approached a tall, fiftyish man with a bushy black beard and thinning brown hair, introduced herself, and asked: "Do you mind talking to me? I'm an anthropologist from Rutgers University, and I am doing a project on political activism." She had hardly finished saying "anthropologist" when he turned towards the press and, raising his voice, pointed a finger at Molé and said, "Do you see this woman? She is an anthropologist! Liberals are an endangered species, and we are being studied by anthropologists!!" He laughed in disbelief and walked off.

These vignettes illustrate not only everyday ironies of social life (for example, procrastination can be rewarded, and tax day becomes a street carnival) but also ambivalences people experience when being studied by an anthropologist. Although the man in the last vignette opted out of an interview as he offered nearby journalists the self-mocking comment about liberals being an endangered species, the woman in the first episode seemed delighted to chat with us. But much as Boyd had done with a different kind of quip, she subtly reversed any possible power inequality in the ethnographic relationship between observer and observed by teasing me about academic salaries while speaking in her Billionaire persona. These encounters embody what theorists term "sweet" rather than "bitter" ironies.[89]

I never saw the man on the street who had dodged Noelle Molé's street-intercept interview request, but I did have further pleasant conversations with the woman in the first vignette at several of the Manhattan Billionaires' weekly meetings in 2004. And I had numerous subsequent conversations and interviews with Andrew Boyd. Boyd himself has published books and articles[90] on activism, as well as wittily ironic self-help books: *Life's Little Deconstruction Book: Self-Help for the Post-Hip* and *Daily Afflictions*.[91] In 2012, Boyd and Dave Oswald Mitchell, along with dozens of activist contributors, published *Beautiful Trouble: A Toolbox for Revolution*, which Naomi Klein describes on the back cover as "A crash course for the emerging field of carnivalesque realpolitik, both elegant and incendiary." Boyd's professional identity as a writer and activist (but not an academic, he says) points to the contradictory—and indeed welcome—circumstances of conducting ethnographic research among individuals who are themselves engaged in the production of knowledge in domains that partly intersect my own.

Finally, anthropological irony emerges from the very conditions of ethnographic field research—"the partiality of knowledge and the tendentiousness of categorical understanding."[92]

Anthropologists therefore have tussled over "realist" versus self-critical or ironic modes of ethnographic description.[93] What George Marcus terms our contemporary "predicament of irony" concerns the "indeterminacy of interpretation"; it entails recognition of an "existential doubleness, deriving from a sense of being *here* with major present transformations ongoing that are intimately tied to things happening simultaneously *elsewhere* but without certainty or authoritative representations of what the connections are."[94] That leaves an individual actor to posit connections—"the behind-the-scenes structure—to read into his or her own biography the locally felt agency and effects of knowledge of great and little events happening elsewhere."[95] Such is the personal intellectual work of individuals as they decide how to enact their own citizenship, or perhaps try novel ways to influence larger political processes.[96]

Part of my own ethnographic challenge in this work then is to capture the predicament of irony as experienced by individuals who became committed political activists and who experimented with innovative forms of dissent during this second Gilded Age. To do that, even in this era of discredited paradigms and macronarratives, I must tack back and forth between my own sense of analytical and historical connections on the one hand, and those of my ethnographic interlocutors on the other, remaining alert to points of intersection, uncertainty, and ambivalence.

"Feather in Our Cap"

A well-known "Far Side" cartoon by Gary Larson shows two anthropologists arriving by boat on an island.[97] Inside a thatched-roof house, people wearing grass skirts spot the anthropologists and scurry to hide their television, VCR, and lamp. They shout, "Anthropologists! Anthropologists!" The cartoon captures the ironies of any ethnographic situation: anthropologists may fancy themselves to be scientific observers, yet they influence the behavior of those they observe, who may in turn be keenly attuned to what the anthropologists expect to find. I heard an echo of that cartoon as I was leaving one of the Manhattan

Billionaires' planning meetings a few weeks before the 2004 election. Andrew Boyd quipped to the few people remaining, "The anthropologist is leaving; now we can go back to being our true selves."[98]

A couple of years later, in mid-2006, I asked Boyd what it was like to have an anthropologist studying the Billionaires, and he replied,[99] "Very strange; it's strange and I guess flattering, it's very surreal, what is going on here?" I asked if it felt uncomfortable, and he said, "It's not uncomfortable, it just feels weird." "Weirder than having all the journalists there?" I asked, referring to news media presence at many of the Billionaires' weekly meetings and other events. His reply:

> Yes, because that's what we're about is having the journalists there, and you're much more intimate, you're a friend, and you're staying with it. You yourself are fascinated with this, it seems, and we don't understand what's the—I mean it is interesting, but at some level, we're like what's the big deal, you know? But it was also kind of cool; it was like status—in 2004, ooh, we have our own anthropologist, we rank, you know.

I replied that I was grateful that the Billionaires had graciously accepted my presence at their planning meetings, street actions, and social events, and I understood that being observed by an anthropologist might make people a little uneasy. Boyd replied, "I don't think it did; I think we kind of enjoyed it mostly; it was kind of novel, amusing, bizarre, and you know like a feather in our cap kind of feeling . . . [it was] odd in a kind of good way. . . . I think people are charmed and they are impressed with your stick-to-it-iveness."

Probably a blend of frankness and flattery, Boyd's remarks capture contradictory feelings of my interlocutors, for whom my presence seemed at once "novel," "surreal," and a "feather in our cap." Some told me they were pleased that I, unlike many journalists with whom they talked, was interested in the organization's history and origins, including its early recruitment of members from other organizations, and its pre-2004 organizational identities, rather than just their latest events.

I let my interlocutors know that I was sympathetic to their political agenda—important information to share, since subtle losses of critical information can occur when the interviewer's own voice and political position are cut out.[100] Though I share their political sympathies, I did not myself "join" the Billionaires and dress or perform the part. That symbolic distance was reflected in musician and singer Fillmore Barrels's (musician Dave Case's) gentle teasing about my non-Billionaire attire. "A bit underdressed, aren't you?" he said during the August 2004 Million Billionaire March down Manhattan's Fifth Avenue (when I wore casual black slacks and blouse). And at Reverend Billy's May 2011 show in Manhattan, billed as a "Billionaires' Costume Ball," Fillmore Barrels joked with me: "I thought you might get blinged up for this occasion—cross over to the other side," that is, the elegantly costumed Billionaire side, where many women were wearing tiaras and evening gowns or cocktail dresses. (I was wearing a silk jacket, silk blouse, black dress slacks, and understated jewelry that would not qualify as "bling," though others complimented me on my appearance.) Fillmore Barrels's jests along with others' remarks about my note-taking highlight common contradictions of participant-observation: participating, but not as a member, and observing, but not as a complete outsider.

The line between research subjects and colleagues is blurred and perhaps always has been in unacknowledged ways. Like Andrew Boyd, many of the other activists ("expert subjects"[101]) who are the focus of this book are themselves directly engaged in knowledge production about political struggles and social justice. They speak to the media, write books and articles, compose slogans and chants, research economic policies, and analyze their public image and impact. Their voices animate this work. I write not as their advocate but as their colleague in the search for and production of new knowledge, new perspectives on contemporary political life.

What did the Billionaires hope to learn from my research? Boyd talked with me about precisely that in July 2006:

> We want to learn something about ourselves, not just . . . that the outside world can learn something or that the anthropology academy can learn something about political culture. We want to learn something about ourselves that we don't already know. We want you to crystallize, theorize, synthesize, Rashomon,[102] tie together pieces . . . if the left hand doesn't know what the right hand is doing, this is a way for the left hand to realize that . . . [for example], four really different accounts of something, like from Paul and Alice and myself and some person on the street, then that's kind of interesting.[103]

"Billionaire pollster" would be a good anthropological role, said Ivan Tital (I want it all)—classical studies scholar Ken Mayer—who headed the Billionaires' Washington, DC, chapter.[104] Message testing by an anthropologist, he explained, could provide information about how audiences perceive the Billionaires and what aspects of their performances resonated with spectators.

Studying social movements poses ethnographic challenges such as possible overidentification with the groups studied, accepting their claims at face value, or representing them as more cohesive than they actually are.[105] In new domains of paraethnography with "expert or elite subjects," Holmes and Marcus caution that it is easy for an ethnographer to lose critical perspective by slipping into advisory roles or collaborative alliances.[106] At the same time, anthropologists and historians, as Edelman observes, "may have privileged access to the lived experience of activists and non-activists, as well as a window onto the 'submerged' organizing, informal networks, protest activities, ideological differences, public claim-making, fear and repression, and internal tensions, which are almost everywhere features of social movements."[107] Such research requires critical self-reflection, attention to researcher positionality, willingness to criticize the causes and movements under study, and scrutiny of both the politics and the epistemology of knowledge production. In addition, analysis of the wider social and political fields in which social movements emerge and dissipate is crucial to understanding the internal dynamics of such mobilizations and the varied responses of targeted constituencies.[108] Analysis of this form of contentious politics is well suited to a discipline attuned to blurred boundaries between informal and formal political domains and to multiple registers of political practice.

Spectacular Dissent

The Billionaires' parody is designed to be a glittering, media-friendly spectacle.[109] Like many contemporary activists, they contrast two protest modes: an older, "traditional" form that involves marches, chants, and speeches, and an ostensibly new and playful theatrical form. "Tradition" of course is a mobile term, pertinent here not as historical actuality but as a category of contingent meanings for activists and the journalists who cover them.

Protest styles said to be counter-traditional—even spectacular—include protesters who set up a medieval catapult to lob stuffed toy animals over a barricade at the 2001 anti–Free Trade Agreement protests in Quebec; a Revolutionary Anarchist Clown Bloc, some wearing rainbow wigs and playing kazoos, singing, and tossing confetti as they ride tall bicycles with streamers; and environmentalists dressed as sea turtles marching alongside teamsters in the 1999 anti-WTO protests in Seattle.[110] Comedian Jon Stewart and Stephen Colbert's 2010 Rally to Restore Sanity and/or Fear, which drew hundreds of thousands to the National Mall in Washington, DC, could be included as well. More sober examples include the throng of respectfully silent bearers of flag-draped cardboard coffins to symbolize soldiers who had died in Iraq; these mock pallbearers joined hundreds of thousands of other protesters marching in Manhattan's August 30, 2004, anti-Bush demonstration. As a participant said to me, "The U.S. government had prohibited the media from photographing flag-draped coffins coming home, so what we were doing was showing the public in the United States and abroad the very thing that the government didn't want shown." Such displays built on a long lineage, extending back to the imperial Roman circus and earlier, and including innovators such as Abbie Hoffman, who led thousands of protesters in a mock levitation of the Pentagon in 1967.[111]

Spectacular dissent does not necessarily yield predictable meanings for participants or wider publics, and participants say that is one of its strengths. It resembles an "emergent politics" that can embrace contingency, indeterminacy, and outliers, alongside clusters of shared meanings.[112] The experience of participation itself creates bonds of affective solidarity. Alternative forms of democracy are the goal of many of these activists, who experiment with consensus-building in decentralized networks through affinity groups and spokescouncils.[113]

Media and culture scholar and activist Stephen Duncombe, a member of the Billionaires' governing board, devotes a few pages to them in his 2007 book *Dream*, where he urges progressives to organize what he and Andrew Boyd term "ethical spectacles."[114] The latter are situations of popular participation and potential transformation—a vision of progressive politics that displays dreams, appeals to the imagination, and expresses itself creatively and theatrically. Duncombe and Boyd's conceptualization draws on the earlier activists known as Situationists, French activist intellectuals who were inspired decades ago by Guy Debord. Opposed to "the society of the spectacle," the Situationists "felt a responsibility to set something else in motion to replace it," and they did this by "encourag[ing] people to *dérive*—drift through unfamiliar city streets—and they showed mass culture films after '*détourning*' the dialogue, dubbing the actor's lines to comment upon (or make nonsense of) the film being shown and the commercial culture from which it came."[115]

A society of spectacle, as Debord defined it, entailed "the autocratic reign of the market economy"[116] and was marked by accelerated technological innovation, an utterly dehistoricized present unattuned to "what is actually changing" and "always returning to the same short list of trivialities, passionately proclaimed as major discoveries."[117] Similarly, Duncombe points to a contemporary world "linked by media systems and awash in advertising images; political policies are packaged by public relations experts and celebrity gossip is considered news."[118] Progressives, Duncombe argues, must be attuned to these contemporary features of culture and politics—this society of spectacle—and design their tactics accordingly.[119]

Building on theories of Foucault, Adorno, and Horkheimer, Duncombe argues against strategies of political action modeled on "sober reason" and Enlightenment notions of self-evident reality.[120] The "ethical spectacle" he endorses is participatory, active, open-ended, and transparent. Politicians who win elections and policy battles, he argues, do so not because they recite facts but because they speak effectively to "people's fantasies and desires through a language of images and associations."[121] Spectacle is not, as so many rulers have assumed, merely a tool to distract or placate citizens. Instead it is a way to engage moral passions and to shape politics and social movements in ways that are often ignored.

The Billionaires, for Duncombe, exemplify precisely the kind of ethical spectacle that defamiliarizes the familiar and questions harmful conventional wisdoms.[122] These satirists, he writes, "use their theatrical clowning to animate the abstraction of money ruling democracy—making visible an invisible reality."[123] Spectacular dissent not only dramatizes abstractions such as environmental degradation, the corruption of democracy, or the nonrepresentativeness of global trade and financial institutions, but it makes those abstractions seem contingent rather than inevitable.

Through the "power of the surface," the Billionaires engage political economy, said Merchant F. Arms (Varon). While the Yippies "knew how to manipulate the media," the Billionaires

> brought it to a new postmodern level of reflexive awareness of the power of the surface. . . . It was all about showmanship and performativity and style and costume and posturing and that's where we live as Americans. We may deny it [but] . . . that's how we play our politics out, and to connect that . . . semiotic world to . . . issues of political economy in this new kind of dialectic I think is something terribly effective. [It's] not to take flight of reality but rather to re-engage the realest of real political economy through the realm of surface.[124]

Hence the Billionaires polished their "surfaces" and protected their brand image, by monitoring the semiotics and maintaining high production values—

professionally printed placards and banners, elegant costumes, witty street performance.

Other recent examples of spectacular or counter-traditional protest abound. They include the Guerrilla Girls, "who highlighted the art world's exclusion of female artists by holding demonstrations outside the Whitney Museum in gorilla masks,"[125] ACT UP (AIDS Coalition to Unleash Power),[126] and Critical Mass, "a massive free-form bike ride in which cyclists, through the power of their numbers—their critical mass—take over city streets . . . [and] bring attention to the second-class status of bicyclists on urban streets."[127] Critical Mass began in San Francisco in the early 1990s and spread to a couple of hundred cities in North America, well over one hundred in Europe, a couple of dozen in Asia, and others in Australia, South America, and South Africa.[128]

Reclaim the Streets (RTS), an international direct action organization that drew inspiration from the Situationists and originated in London during the early 1990s, was particularly successful in replicating itself across continents.[129] RTS stages surprise conversions of public streets into zones of music, dance, and carnivals, in order to protest corporate power and the growing privatization of public space[130]: "A tall tripod is erected in the middle of the street [in New York City] and a person clambers to the top. A mobile sound system is wheeled out, tuned to the pirate station, and turned up to top volume. Broadway erupts into a party with brightly costumed dancers, fire-breathers and one particularly energetic fellow gyrating in a bright blue bunny suit." Through such festive street parties, Reclaim the Streets intended a metaphorical opening up of political space—cultivating exuberant new forms of engagement that incorporate rave culture—as well as literally reclaiming a public street from vehicle traffic.[131]

During the summer 2010 BP oil spill, creative activists posed as the country's Founding Fathers, donned dapper American Revolution-era attire and wigs, and marched into the "foyer of a powerful downtown lobbying firm, demanding that members of Congress stop meeting behind closed doors to raise money from corporate lobbyists and instead spend their time working on laws to help the American public," reported the *Washington Post*.[132] "Just got off the phone with Ben Franklin," read the message header on a listserv posting on that action from Andrew Boyd, a cocreator of Agit-Pop Communications. His announcement: "Agit-Pop and the Campaign for Fair Elections sent Benjamin Franklin and friends to razz BP's major lobbying firm . . . the framers [of the Constitution] stood guard at the biggest fundraising hot spots in DC—and caught more than a few Congressmen taking their cues from Big Money." By mid-2012, the oil spill had not yielded regulatory or industry reforms likely to prevent another similar disaster.

The Yes Men

The culture jammers known as the Yes Men[133] (Andy Bichlbaum, Mike Bonnano, and Bob Spunkmeyer) are "identity correctors," or impersonators of WTO delegates, Chamber of Commerce officials, and other leaders and corporate executives. "We have found people and institutions doing horrible things at everyone else's expense, and have assumed their identities in order to offer correctives," say the Yes Men.[134] Their technique is to present official policies and assumptions "with far more candor than usual, making them look like the absurdities that they are."[135] The Yes Men have easily fooled experts when giving outlandish lectures while posing as WTO officials; they have pretended to be Halliburton executives talking about how to profit from catastrophes (Bhopal, Chernobyl, tsunamis, hurricanes) and Dow Chemical executives addressing the legacy of the Bhopal catastrophe after Dow bought Union Carbide—explaining that Dow can't assist Bhopalis because "they aren't shareolders."[136] On the twentieth anniversary of the Bhopal disaster, a Yes Men prank drew global media attention as "Jude Finisterra," posing as a Dow representative, "went on BBC World TV to announce that the company was finally going to compensate the victims and clean up the mess in Bhopal . . . much to the chagrin of Dow, who briefly disavowed any responsibility as per policy."[137] Here, as anthropologists Boyer and Yurchak observe, the Yes Men's prank "attract[ed] the attention of dominant media and . . . expose[d] ideological principles that usually operate invisibly."[138]

The Yes Men accomplished a similar feat when they targeted the WTO's undermining of "trade unions, environmental protections, and indigenous rights."[139] After producing a website (GATT.org) in 1999 that mimicked that of the World Trade Organization (successor to GATT, the General Agreement on Tariffs and Trade, and often confused with it), the Yes Men began to receive speaking invitations from functionaries who thought they were communicating with the WTO in Geneva. After many appearances as WTO "identity correctors," they decided to try one final bold prank in that guise in a public address (titled "Agribusiness Globalisation: Directions and Implications") at a May 2002 conference of international trade experts in Sydney, Australia. There Andy Bichlbaum, dressed in a black business suit, white shirt, and gold tie and posing as "Kinnithrung Sprat" from the WTO, said that in place of the scheduled topic he would talk about "a rather dramatic development in Geneva yesterday."[140] He then described his many years of belief in the principles of free-market economics espoused by Milton Friedman and how he later was overpowered by doubt as he gradually realized that "the problems of growing poverty and inequality were not going to simply wither away" and that there might be "fundamental mistakes in the theory of laissez-faire."[141]

Bichlbaum/Sprat announced that "the World Trade Organization in its present form will cease to exist [*gasps from the audience*]. . . . Over the next two years, we of the WTO will endeavor to launch . . . [a] new [organization that] will have as its foundation . . . the United Nations Charter of Human Rights . . . [to] insur[e] that we will have human rather than business interests as our bottom line."[142] Hearty applause followed the conclusion of Bichlbaum's/Sprat's speech; those attending not only "*believed* the WTO was indeed shutting down, they were *happy* about it. And full of helpful suggestions" about how to achieve "a global economy that benefits poor people."[143] The Yes Men then sowed wider confusion when they sent out a press release about the WTO's supposed shutdown to twenty thousand people. Here again, the Yes Men drew unusual public attention to the practices of one of the world's most powerful but little understood organizations.

When I talked with Yes Man Andy Bichlbaum in 2006 at a coffee shop near Brown University (Providence, Rhode Island), he compared the satirical Billionaires and Yes Men. The Billionaires, he said, have "found a good kind of balance between clarity and satire for purposes of influencing people, like the immediate audience."[144] But the immediate audiences of the Yes Men, he remarked, usually miss their joke and think they are sincere—an outcome that at first shocked Bichlbaum and his colleagues and then led them to execute grand ruses designed to fool observers. During the 2004 election campaign, Bichlbaum recounted, they traveled in a giant bus with photos of Bush, "an extendable oil derrick that would spew black oil every once in a while," costumes of an orange orangutan, a fog machine, and slogans intended to be ironic. Yet a lot of direct observers "didn't get it," and so the Yes Men concluded that their humor works best when translated to a secondary audience. Bichlbaum suggested that Billionaires for Bush were much more effective in using clear core messages couched in satire.

Reverend Billy and the Stop Shopping Gospel Choir

"With huge facial features, a mane of dyed blond hair and an immaculate white suit, Bill Talen looks every bit the televangelist,"[145] writes a *New York Times* reporter describing the satirical evangelist Reverend Billy, who has won an Obie Award as well as international and national media attention. Reverend Billy was to confer "sainthood" on the satirical Billionaires at a May 2011 live performance I attended at Theatre 80 in the East Village. Clad that evening in white suit and clerical collar, Reverend Billy was accompanied by his Stop Shopping Gospel Choir, who were wearing bright green robes. An advance publicity notice online read: "join us in our best top hats and pearls! We are undergoing an unprecedented shift of our society's money to a small group of billionaires. . . . The latest shake-down of the middle class involves demonizing the idea of good government itself." The announcement then shifted to irony mode: "It is time to honor the activists who demanded welfare for the wealthy back when this was a scandalous phrase—the Billionaires. Numbering at its height in the thousands, with chapters across the country, [the Billionaires are] . . . activism at its most fun and effective. The Church of Earthalujah chooses to canonize the whole group, at a Billionaires' Costume Ball . . . this Sunday night."[146]

Lately emphasizing environmental issues as well as anticommercialism and commodity culture excesses, Reverend Billy ran as the Green Party candidate for mayor of New York against Michael Bloomberg in 2009. He has supported campaigns against new Walmart stores and Disney's production offshore, and has urged Starbucks to adopt Fairtrade coffee. In addition to its "absurd theatricality" or spectacular dimensions, writes Duncombe, a Reverend Billy "service is a genuine experience of communion and shared faith around a vision of a world not centered on consumption."[147]

A large color photo of the earth as seen from space was the stage backdrop at Reverend Billy's service honoring the Billionaires. The performance opened with an African American man, seated at the left edge of the stage, dolefully singing the Depression-era song "Brother, Can You Spare a Dime?"[148] and then another song that included the line "democracy is not for sale." Much of Reverend Billy's preaching that night was nonironic, with flashes of humor, as he addressed environmental abuses and the excesses of commodity culture.

Reverend Billy invited Billionaires in the audience to offer "testimonials"— to share their "wonderful nature stories." And so in irony mode, the Billionaire known as Meg A. Bucks (wearing a tiara and elegant dress) told a story about hydraulic fracturing (natural gas drilling known as "fracking"), opening with, "When I put my ear to the earth, I hear the sound of money" because there is gas under the surface. She said she would put chemicals underground and then, "I'm gonna frack it!" When Meg A. Bucks declared that she owned a water bottling company, and affirmed the safety of fracking, individuals in the audience shouted out, "Frack you!" Thurston Howell IV (writer Kurt Opprecht), dressed in the yachtsman garb he wore in Richard Avedon's 2004 studio photograph of nine Billionaires, told a story about sailing in his "little yacht" in the Gulf of Mexico. He saw oil "bespoiling those waters and it made me cry because that oil wasn't going into any tankers . . . into any plastics, and all those fish weren't going into any markets. It was a shame, Reverend, and I have to say that it touched me." After a few more environmental testimonials, Reverend Billy declared, "Amen! It's a struggle between the billionaires and the power of the earth!"

During the "canonization" ceremony, Reverend Billy acknowledged that the Billionaires and his own organization had taken divergent paths: "The Church of Stop Shopping and the Billionaires, we were always parallel to each other, but as Larry Bogad, Ben Shepherd, and Steve Duncombe, and *some of those professors who hang out with us and take notes* would tell you, we've always been at cross purposes." I had not yet met Reverend Billy, and as I sat in the audience next to Andrew Boyd's mother and Iona Bigga Yacht, I smiled in astonishment at his reference to "professors who hang out with us and take notes." That was precisely what I was doing during that performance, and the theater was small enough that my note-taking was easily visible to anyone on stage. Later some of the Billionaires present, who were quite accustomed to my notebook, mentioned his remark with amusement.

Two different activist principles drove his group and the Billionaires, said Reverend Billy: "The frontier for us is to become more and more sincere . . . to discover a real faith, like raving agnostics or something, while the frontier for the Billionaires is to become more and more absurdly true to the billionaire culture." The joke in the social structure indeed. Even though the Reverend Billy and the Billionaires, he said, had "always been going in opposite directions, we love each other as we disappear on opposite horizons, and tonight you are our saints! We'd just like to saint the Billionaires, Amen! Hallelujah!" That pronouncement cued a rousing choir performance of "When the Saints Go Marching In."

Reverend Billy then asked Andrew Boyd to recite the Billionaires' pledge of allegiance. As Boyd read each line, he paused for the audience to repeat it: "I pledge allegiance to the CEOs of the United States of America, but not to the middle class upon whom those CEOs stand. Two nations under David Koch, divided by income and influence, with liberty and justice just for us!"[149] "Huzzah!" shouted the audience and Reverend Billy. The exclamation "huzzah!"

(hooray), which dates at least to the time of Shakespeare, is probably better known in Britain than in the United States. For the Billionaires "huzzah!" encodes an upper-class cheeriness, joy, and celebratory triumph that contribute as well to their sense of in-group solidarity.

"Now, the forty-five magic words!" said Reverend Billy. A choir soloist sang slowly and solemnly the First Amendment to the U.S. Constitution: "Congress shall make no law respecting an establishment of religion; or prohibiting the free exercise thereof; or abridging the freedom of speech, or of the press; or the right of the people peaceably to assemble, and to petition the Government for a redress of grievances." Pursuing the freedom-of-speech theme, Reverend Billy extolled "shouting in public space" and publicly demanding rights enshrined in the constitution. He added, "Blessed are you who confuse consumerism with freedom," and "Blessed are the young women working in the sweatshops and the things that you make fly like magic evening gowns to the city of lights." Several times he shouted, "Blessed are you who disturb the customers!"

Activist and playwright Jason Grote provides a firsthand account of a 1999 Reverend Billy prank in a Disney Store in Times Square, where forty activists sang, "Just whistle while you work / For fifteen cents an hour / Cheap labor, dear, has brought you here / And now you work for us!"[150] Those singing were the warm-up act, a diversion for the security guards while the main attraction, Reverend Billy, walked in the store's front door, "arms above his head, preaching to a chorus of hoots and howls."[151] Reverend Billy street theater, as Grote puts it, is the use of "spectacle against itself"—that is, spectacular forms of protest against the spectacle of Disney, a glitzy Times Square, and consumption as a psychic high enabled by invisible sweatshop labor.[152]

.   .   .

While the Yes Men and the Billionaires have been collaborators in spoofs such as the 2011 GE tax refund hoax, the relationship between the Billionaires and Reverend Billy's Church of Earthalujah has seldom been directly collaborative. Their approaches to political street theater differ, though political goals and ties of friendship link the two organizations. The Billionaires' style is more lighthearted, and their street theater is designed to avoid direct confrontation with security officials. Indeed Andrew Boyd says the Billionaires' tactics and image were intended to "mainstream dissent"—to make it more widely palatable for ordinary citizens and corporate news media. Some individuals participated simultaneously or sequentially in both organizations, singing in

Reverend Billy's choir or joining flashmobs in Disney Stores as well as participating in Billionaire street theater. Robin Eublind, for example, played "Deacon Struction" in Reverend Billy's Church of Stop Shopping as well as participating in the Billionaires and other political theater groups.

Both Reverend Billy and the Billionaires were among many activist organizations taking part in a large May 11, 2011, satirical flashmob protest at New York's Lincoln Center, an event Reverend Billy described in his Theatre 80 performance a few days later as "so special . . . in a class by itself, some sort of zeitgeist thing." The cooperation of so many different organizers struck him: "How did they all get along? How did they not chase each other's boyfriends? How did that happen? Think of all the things that have screwed up activism in the past." He celebrated the ideal of a "unified force field" in activism, overcoming common divisions.

The Lincoln Center flashmob to protest the growing political influence of the conservative Koch brothers[153] had a Seattle 1999 direct-action feel, though many participants were too young to have been part of the anti-WTO protests in Seattle, said a long-term Billionaire who joined the Lincoln Center action. Also participating were the Brave New Foundation, The Other 98%, Yes Lab (affiliated with the Yes Men), Critical Mass, Agit-Pop, and Rude Mechanical Orchestra, along with the Church of Earthalujah. Billed as "guerrilla drive-in," the event featured Reverend Billy's preaching, as well as Robert Greenwald's new documentary film about the Koch brothers, which was projected from a secret location onto one of the New York State Theater's white walls. A light projected "I'm the Tea Party's wallet" just above the official "David H. Koch Theater" lettering.[154]

Stephen Colbert's Super PAC

Jumping scale to reach an audience of millions, "fake news" comedian Stephen Colbert took on the post–Citizens United U.S. election system's financing rules and in April 2012 won a Peabody Award for his satirical segments on Super PACs (political action committees). In 2010, congressional Super PACs spent more than $60 million, "managing to get their voices heard through what Mr. Colbert has described as a 'megaphone of cash.'"[155] Colbert testified before the Federal Election Commission in 2011 and obtained approval to create his own fund-raising Super PAC, "Americans for a Better Tomorrow, Tomorrow." Like any Super PAC, the one Colbert created can "raise and spend unlimited amounts of soft money in support of candidates as long as it doesn't 'coordinate' with them."[156] By early 2012, Colbert's Super PAC had raised more than one million dollars and spent some of it on subtly satirical political ads, thereby dramatizing the serious issue of campaign finance by becoming part of the very process legalized by the U.S. Supreme Court's 2010 Citizens United decision. After Mitt Romney told a heckler at an August 2011 Iowa campaign event that "corporations are people, my friend," Colbert proposed that the Republican Party in South Carolina (where he grew up) add to its January presidential primary ballot "a nonbinding referendum question that asked the voters to decide whether 'corporations are people' or 'only people are people.'"[157]

Colbert's Super PAC segments appeared deliberately didactic, especially his dialogues with Trevor Potter, former chair of the Federal Election Commission, who had become Colbert's lawyer. In the January 12, 2012, *Colbert Report* episode, Potter informed Colbert that he could not be a political candidate while running a Super PAC, but that it would be legal for him to run for office if his PAC were run by a friend or business partner—a widely criticized legal loophole. Colbert then performed a ceremony transferring control of his amply funded PAC to his satirical news colleague and friend Jon Stewart. Red and blue balloons dropped from above as he announced he would form an "exploratory committee for president of the United States of South Carolina."[158]

The Federal Election Commission, evenly divided between Republicans and Democrats, could not agree in 2012 on how to apply earlier rules to the coordination of campaign expenditures between Super PACS and candidates—leaving presidential candidates and their supporters to do as they wished. Lawyer Fred Wertheimer, of the political watchdog organization Democracy 21, expressed concern about the lack of enforcement to the Justice Department, stating, "What is going on is just absurd."[159]

Like the Yes Men and Billionaires, Colbert dramatized policies whose content is unfamiliar to many. Indeed "Colbert is literally performing the debate" about the effects on democracy of new campaign finance law, and offering more information about the law than "even the wonkiest of news reports."[160] Colbert's Super PAC both informed viewers about the post–Citizens United carousel-for-billionaires that electoral politics had become, and also became a "real" player in the very domain it parodied.

Conclusions

"Maybe the whole system has become such a joke that only jokes will serve as a corrective," writes a *New York Times* reporter.[161] For the Billionaires, and perhaps for Colbert and the Yes Men as well, the consequence of ironic humor is not meant to be simply more humor. Political satire doesn't just mirror societal incongruities or imbalances; it also helps to define what is thinkable. What matters then is "what *other* audiences—journalists, politicians, voters, nonfans, religious leaders, citizens—*do* . . . once the comedians cum political commentators have left the stage."[162]

But here didactic satire confronts a key paradox: "an inherent ambiguity, even confusion about the identity of the satirist's intended audience."[163] Satirists, writes classical studies scholar Ralph Rosen, "can never really be successful at censuring, entertaining, and instructing—the three defining pretenses of satire—the *same* group of people."[164]

That paradox raises the question: Who did the Billionaires imagine their audience to be? Charming those who already agreed with them wasn't enough, though many Billionaires certainly took pleasure in that. But they also hoped to persuade independent, undecided, or even initially hostile voters to rethink their positions. And they hoped to shape the thinking of others whose feelings about great wealth were ambivalent, or whose knowledge about America's tectonic shifts in wealth, taxes, and campaign finance was uncertain. What do we know about how their imagined audiences perceive the new Gilded Age? What makes it a new Gilded Age?

2 "Times Are Good!"

A New Gilded Age

"WHY IS EVERYBODY SO QUIET? TIMES ARE GOOD!" said Kikki Baxx in her Texas drawl as she sauntered to a front-row seat in Manhattan's Theatre 80 in the East Village. Attired in an elegant black evening dress and cowgirl hat atop blond hair in a side-of-the-head ponytail, she was one of the satirical Billionaires who had come to hear the Reverend Billy "canonize" the Billionaires. Kikki Baxx's remark, audible throughout the theater, sparked laughter among audience members waiting for the show to begin. Times of course were *not* good—at least not for many people—in that late spring of 2011. Conditions were glorious, on the other hand, for the top one percent and for large banks, oil companies, and other corporations enjoying record profits.

American opinions about why the economy had faltered and what to do about it were deeply divided. So too were notions of economic fairness—the Billionaires' core issue. Conventional liberal-versus-conservative binaries, some said, suggested that liberals think of fairness in terms of helping the weak or the poor, even if that means higher taxes on the ultrarich, while conservatives hold fast to the idea that anyone who works deserves to keep the fruits of her labor.[1] While such characterizations mask more complex public sentiments, few could avoid noticing that an increasingly polarized political culture counterposed those who construed democracy as *more* than the freedom to become ultrarich against those who bristled at any suggestion of obligations toward the less fortunate or toward the society whose commonwealth resources help some ascend to the top of the economic pyramid and stay there.

Yet foundational dilemmas about "what . . . the economy [is] ultimately *for*"[2] remained as perplexing as ever. Seldom surfacing in public discourse were fundamental questions about how to reshape market relations so as to humanize the world economy.[3] The Billionaires and other culture jammers can play with—or even jostle—political and media edifices that obscure such questions.

Four Billionaire slogans frame this chapter's examination of such "jamming" of conventional American narratives about wealth and taxes:

Leave No Billionaire Behind!
Widen the Income Gap!
Because we're all in this together, sort of.
Heirs and Heiresses Unite! Death to the Death Tax!

The associated popular narratives downplay wealth inequality, exaggerate upward economic mobility, promote the dispensability of social safety nets, and denounce the tax on inherited wealth. Their political potency is strong enough to constitute a perfect foil for the satirical Billionaires' irony.

In at least one revealing case—the Billionaires' rebranding of the tax on inherited wealth—the satirists' reframing took root in serious public domains. This chapter explores how that happened, and why some standard narratives about our new Gilded Age prompted dissent from elite reformists such as William Gates Sr. (whom I interviewed) and Warren Buffett. Finally, why has the United States seen such a surge in the number of real billionaires, and why does the emergence of financial derivatives as a key source of wealth matter politically?

(How) Do We Know What Americans Think About Wealth?

The Billionaires' slogans are premised in part on a powerful statistical narrative about the U.S. economy on which most professional economists agree.[4] Yet at the start of the millennium, the trends documented were *un*familiar to many Americans. And even those who followed the data disagreed about the political and policy implications of the numbers. Statistics may seem dry, yet as Tim Mitchell has argued and as economic historian Karl Polanyi foreshadowed, numeric data have helped to create the very notion of the economy as a freestanding object that can be measured and reshaped.[5]

Public opinion polls, in turn, offer a flawed but still useful snapshot of what some Americans think about wealth inequality. The ostensible value of opinion surveys is that they allow "citizens to be understood as consumers with preferences politicians ignore at their peril."[6] Of course opinion polls also construct rather than simply reflect what the public thinks, whether questions are crafted by nonpartisan or disinterested polling organizations, or are deliberately designed to shape opinion (as in "push polling") or to provide responses a poll's authors consider plausible.[7] Murray Edelman suggests that it would be more productive to "recognize that attitudes are inherently ambiguous and [to] . . . base analysis on the implications of that uncertainty."[8] What then did the Billionaires assume about their audiences and about how to address them?

The Billionaires' Imagined Audiences

The Billionaires' assumptions about the American public in this second Gilded Age are embodied in clear messaging advice—on their website, in listserv messages, social media, and planning meetings. Billionaire leaders through these channels advise participants to "focus on corporate takeover of democracy" or "corporate takeover of government [because] corporations are hated more than rich people, CEO's more than corporations."[9] That theme, they believe, "resonate[s] across the political spectrum, and constitute[s] the Billionaires' strongest message. . . . Corruption is a winning issue, corporate cronyism is the best cross-cutting critique of this administration." Participants are advised to know their facts and to select a few to emphasize: "vague generalities preach to the choir; swing voters are concerned with facts," states their website. A well-educated member who also participated in other progressive street theater groups said that the Billionaires worked hard to avoid appearing to "just mak[e] fun of rich people."[10] The Billionaire approach, she said, doesn't work if it's reduced to comments about one's diamonds and mere symbols of wealth rather than focusing on the economy, world issues, and how particular policies benefit the superrich. "Obviously we have many allies who happen to have a lot of money," she continued, and "they're not the people that we're rallying against, so I think that was something we had to work . . . fairly hard on to take out of our profile . . . because that's alienating."

Don't talk about capitalism, their leaders advise, since "it makes you sound like a socialist to ordinary voters."[11] Preferred alternative terms, according to their website, are corporate cronyism or Big Money, or Big Oil, since "people do have disdain for closed insider networks and corruption among CEOs." Furthermore, since "conservatives have succeeded in linking 'government spending' with 'wasteful' and 'inefficient' in the public's mind, when talking about the negative impact of Bush's tax cuts, talk about how it will reduce funding for public initiatives, rather than how it will result in cuts to government spending." Rather than deploying irony to target "liberals," Billionaires are to keep the focus on the failure of conservatives to address middle-class concerns—thereby indirectly reframing liberalism or progressivism as a corrective to policies that harm ordinary citizens. Finally, Billionaire leaders advise members to target the ultrarich rather than the merely rich.

"Leave No Billionaire Behind!"

The Billionaire known as Ivy League Legacy (actress Melody Bates) said during a New York radio appearance in which she did not depart from irony mode, "the majority of Americans think they are pre-rich . . . which of course is a delusion that is very useful to us. . . . It means that they'll vote for tax cuts for the rich."[12] Americans have long believed that the United States is a land of upward economic mobility and that it is easier here than in Europe's affluent nations to move up from one social class to another, although statistical analyses in the early 2000s demonstrated the opposite.[13] Parental income in the early 2000s was a "better predictor of whether someone would be rich or poor in America than in Canada or much of Europe."[14] Furthermore, in contrast to the myth of the self-made multimillionaire, in the late 1990s, as Gates and Collins observed, "[a]lmost a third of the Forbes 400 were born onto the list."[15]

Although corporate profits and worker productivity increased in the late twentieth and early twenty-first centuries, in the United States, the real value of the minimum wage, real median family income, and purchasing power declined—as did union membership—while the numbers of Americans living in poverty or without health insurance grew dramatically.[16] In what Hacker terms a "great risk shift," economic risk shifted away from "broad structures of insurance, including those sponsored by the corporate sector as well as by government, onto the fragile balance sheets of American families."[17] It was they who were left behind by dizzying economic opportunity for the top one percent. As income volatility grew[18] and the livelihoods of the middle class and working poor became ever more precarious, some very wealthy individuals themselves grew increasingly concerned about inequality.

"Widen the Income Gap!"

The father of the richest man in the world told me in 2006 that it is "danger-ous, and the more important thing is that it's just not right" that today we have "a real, bright line of demarcation" between the very rich and the poor, rather than a spectrum of wealth that includes a "powerful, huge middle class."[19] In explicitly nonpartisan terms, William Gates Sr. (who is a retired Seattle attor-ney, codirector of the Gates Foundation, and father of Microsoft founder Bill Gates Jr.) termed it "totally unacceptable: the degree to which the country is becoming bifurcated between the well-to-do and the barely-getting-alongs." This is not, he argues, a call for a society in which no one can become rich, but it is a moral argument about the injustice of very sharp economic inequality in a democracy—a position linked to his *support* of a tax on inherited wealth[20] and one shared by maverick billionaires such as Warren Buffett and George Soros, as well as some pundits from both major political parties.

Although the United States around 1980 began to enter a new Gilded Age, few citizens were aware in the 1990s and early 2000s of how dramatically wealth inequality was growing, and how much easier it was becoming for an ultrarich minority to pass their wealth on to children and grandchildren who would never have to work to earn a living.[21] In 2006, for the first time ever, *Forbes Magazine*'s annual list of the wealthiest four hundred Americans consisted entirely of billion-aires.[22] By 2007, even being a billionaire was no longer sufficient to make the list.

Three statistics illustrate the profound historical shift in economic inequal-ity in the United States: First, between 1980 and 2007, the share of total national income received by the top 1 percent of earners nearly tripled, rising from 8 percent to 23 percent of the nation's total income.[23] Second, when total wealth rather than income is the metric, the rise in inequality is even sharper; during the 1980s alone, "the portion of the nation's wealth held by the top one percent nearly doubled from 22 percent to 39 percent."[24] Third, between 1979 and 2007, according to a nonpartisan Congressional Budget Office study, the "average inflation-adjusted after-tax income grew by 275 percent for the 1 percent of the population with the highest income" in the United States, while incomes of most citizens stagnated.[25] The increase was still more dramatic among the top 0.01 percent, whose share of total national income quadrupled in three decades: by 2007 they earned one out of every eight dollars.[26] The widening gap between the merely rich and the ultrarich had become even more pronounced than the divide between the top one percent and the rest.

At the opposite end of the scale, even several years before the 2008 financial meltdown (in 2005), the percentage of Americans living in "deep poverty" (living below half the official poverty line income) was at its highest level since the government began to track those statistics in 1975.[27] Again, wealth inequality was even more pronounced than income inequality, and by the early 1990s, family wealth inequality in the United States exceeded that found in all industrial societies.[28] Furthermore, a popular assumption that however large the gap between rich and poor, the impoverished in the United States are much better off than the poor in many other parts of the world is sharply contradicted by indicators such as infant mortality and life expectancy.[29]

These historic transformations are not trumpeted by mainstream news media, and they are not even statistics some Americans believe if told. For example, when I mentioned to a multimillionaire businessman I interviewed in Seattle in 2006 that economic inequality in this country was higher than it had been for nearly a century, he responded, "Are you sure?"[30]

Underestimating the magnitude of inequality may be surprisingly common, as suggested in research by Michael I. Norton (Harvard Business School) and Dan Ariely (Duke University). In addition to assuming that wealth in the United States was more equally distributed than it actually was, when asked to state their ideal distribution, 92 percent of their respondents selected one that was even more equitable.[31] Furthermore, answers to Harris Poll questions from 1965 to 2005, Bartels states, show that "perceptions of economic inequality were no more prevalent at the end of George W. Bush's first term than during Gerald Ford's administration," in spite of the sharp rise in actual inequality between those two time periods.[32]

If some Americans tolerate inequality because they are unaware of how much more unequal we have become since the 1970s, others view wealth inequality as an inevitable outcome of what they assume to be approximate equality of opportunity, or as morally justifiable, or—in terms of efficiencies—economically reasonable. Although the arc of opinion appeared to shift with deepening recession and the emergence of Occupy Wall Street in 2011, as this book went to press there remained strong tendencies—reinforced by dominant news media—to downplay or naturalize inequality and to consider seriously only a narrow range of economic policy options (excluding, for example, significant tax increases on the ultrarich or substantial Keynesian stimulus in the form of massive hiring to improve public infrastructure). Furthermore, the very subject of class makes Americans uncomfortable.

However much "love of money" has gripped the hearts of Americans since at least the time of de Tocqueville, class distinctions in the United States remain a zone of cultural puzzlement, embarrassment, ambiguity, and denial.[33] Class is a subject that this consumerist society discusses indirectly through "code and euphemism," or views as "yet another personal trait or lifestyle choice."[34] As historians Steve Fraser and Gary Gerstle observe, "[i]t is a cherished American folk belief . . . that classes do not exist or, if they do, are always going out of existence."[35] While conceptualizations and category definitions of class vary, all recognize that "societies are organized unequally in a vertical fashion, with some people at the top possessing more power, income and wealth, and privileges than people at the bottom. These advantages (or disadvantages) are rooted (at least in part) in the economic relationships between individuals and households."[36]

Contrary to popular perceptions that it was "the normal state of our society," the era of a middle-class America was actually rather short—a mere interregnum between two Gilded Ages—lasting from about 1945 to the mid-1970s.[37] Economists Claudia Goldin and Robert Margo term that period of declining economic inequality the Great Compression.[38] As the middle class flourished, the previous era's great wealth gap shrank dramatically thanks not to the invisible hand of the market but because of social forces and political action, including Roosevelt's New Deal, wage controls during World War II, unions, tax changes, and institutional norms against huge salaries for CEOs and managers. Though the wealthy could no longer afford to live in Gilded Age mansions or to maintain the necessary servants for such vast living quarters, many still had very comfortable, even luxurious, lives,[39] and the growing middle class enjoyed a material security that in the early 2000s seemed an elusive dream.

The more widely shared prosperity of that earlier era was partly enabled by tax rates deemed too high even to warrant discussion in the 2000s. The marginal income tax on the highest incomes was 70 to 90 percent in the decades immediately following World War II,[40] as compared to 36 percent on income and 15 percent on capital gains in 2010. During an earlier era of sharp economic inequality, the 1920s, "the top income tax rate was only 24 percent and . . . the inheritance tax on even the largest estates was only 20 percent . . . [which meant that] wealthy dynasties had little difficulty maintaining themselves."[41] But counter to conservatives' favorite antitax arguments, World Bank economist William Easterly and others have stated that there is no evidence that high taxes inhibit economic growth or that low taxes promote growth.[42]

To reverse post-1970s increases in economic inequality, economist Larry Summers calculated, would require "every household in the top 1 percent of the distribution, which makes $1.7 million on average . . . to write a check for $800,000. This money could then be pooled and used to send out a $10,000 check to every household in the bottom 80 percent of the distribution, those making less than $120,000."[43] Summers termed the stagnation of middle-class incomes since the 1970s as "the defining issue of our time."

America's political right turn by the early 1980s brought an end to an era when extraordinarily high executive pay "provoke[d] public scrutiny, congressional hearings, and even presidential intervention."[44] If economic and technological changes loosely associated with "globalization" are only part of the story of rising economic inequality and the decline of America's middle class, political and organizational shifts have been decisive. These include the force of conservative ideology propelled by heavy investment in conservative think tanks and political organizations, along with massive fund-raising by the Chamber of Commerce and growing reliance (with the decline of unions) by Democratic as well as Republican politicians on campaign funds from corporations and very wealthy individuals. As a result, scholars such as Hacker and Pierson argue, without strong organizational pressure to defend the economic interests of ordinary citizens, the United States shifted to the right on political issues and inequality soared.[45] The "center" of the political spectrum in the United States shifted so decidedly rightward that positions on taxes and the social safety net once held by solid Republicans in the 1970s were deemed quite liberal by the early 2000s.[46]

Economic inequality and precariousness are deeply connected to intangibles such as dignity, self-worth, and workplace morale, as well as to health. High inequality, many studies suggest, is harmful to physical and emotional health and can reduce productivity and workplace morale.[47] Longevity and health are related to class, not just because of variable access to health care but because of "class differences in working conditions, stress, diet, neighborhood, family structure," and other factors.[48] Most strikingly, a study by epidemiologists Wilkinson and Pickett argues that pronounced inequality harms the health of the rich as well as the poor, partly by raising stress and anxiety levels that have harmful biological effects, as well as contributing to higher rates of crime and violence and reducing access to good education.[49] Economic growth, they write, can no longer improve life expectancy if growth is not accompanied by diminished inequality.

Again, today we see contrasting historical narratives about the economy—one that naturalizes wealth disparities and lends itself to comedy's tidy plot resolutions by assuming that markets are self-correcting, and the other that questions Darwinian visions of wealth, rejects the notion of self-correcting markets, and so lends itself to irony and satire. Paradoxically, at a time when wealth concentration was materially more substantial than ever, many legislators in both major parties did not seem burdened by any sense of obligation to lessen the disparities. To the contrary, as Phillips observes, we have seen multiple examples of "disproportionate favoritism to the top income and wealth brackets" and a series of government bailouts of savings and loan institutions, banks, hedge funds, foreign currencies, and Wall Street.[50] In 2011 and 2012, political debate centered on conservative narratives about a debt crisis rather than alternative narratives about a revenue crisis that could be alleviated through tax increases on the very wealthy. In the new millennium, economic dislocations and sharp economic inequality, which are the result of deliberate policy shifts, left Americans "liv[ing] among the ruins of the New Deal."[51]

"Because We're All in This Together, Sort Of"

A conservative narrative about wealth in the United States in the 2000s suggested that there was substantial public support for large corporations and the government to reduce their commitments to the New Deal social contract that built the middle class and to shift even more of the burden of risk to individuals—a move away from the assumption that we are all in this together. Hence we see the Billionaire slogan "Because we're all in this together, sort of." Yet a majority of Americans do not support the withering of the social safety net that helped to build the middle class through support of living wages, retirement pensions, and health insurance.[52] As public opposition to such cutbacks grew in the early 2000s, that dissent attracted little attention from corporate news media or many elected politicians.[53] Moyers, for example, points to public support for "such broad goals as affordable medical coverage for all, decent wages for working people, safe working conditions, a secure retirement, and clean air and water, [yet] there is no government to deliver on those aspirations."[54] Instead, he says, "our elections are bought out from under us."[55] Such gaps between public sentiment and official response are catnip for satirists.

Although some polls in the early 2000s showed that fewer than one third of Americans labeled themselves liberals, the actual policies large majorities apparently favor are what is normally called liberal[56] (which suggests a large potential audience of Billionaire sympathizers). Polls suggest that "public opinion, unlike the Republican Party, hasn't shifted sharply to the right"—indeed it has instead moved somewhat to the left.[57] A question asked in 1982 and 2004 in the American National Election Studies showed a rising percentage of citizens favoring an increase in government services and spending.[58] However uncertain the meanings of public opinion polls, these certainly do not imply any widespread aversion to government services.

Instead, Jacobs and Skocpol argue, "Americans are pragmatic statists."[59] Far from wishing to condemn their fellow citizens to poverty and suffering or rejecting redistributive claims on the state, many Americans do look to the government to ensure equality of opportunity, economic fairness, and a helping hand when disaster strikes.[60] Many expected much more help from their government for victims of Hurricane Katrina. These public sentiments stand in contrast to the historical shift during the 1980s and 1990s toward romanticization of the market, an emphasis on self-reliance as "freedom," and distrust or demonization of government—the latter epitomized in an oft-quoted 2001 statement by Grover Norquist, head of the antitax group Americans for Tax Reform: "I don't want to abolish government, I simply want to reduce it to the size where I can drag it into the bathroom and drown it in the bathtub."[61]

It is an irony of late–twentieth- and early–twenty-first-century American democracy that while the dismantling of New Deal safeguards and other contemporary forms of market fundamentalism benefit mainly large corporations and the very rich, proponents portray smaller government, deregulation, and shredding of the social safety net as the route to riches for ordinary citizens. In the name of "personal responsibility" and freedom, they tout a new "ownership society."

If individuals are to sink or swim on their own, Billionaire irony reveals that the same apparently is not true of corporations, which in the early 2000s enjoyed generous tax breaks, government subsidies, and much lower tax rates than those of the 1950s.[62] Nor were the large financial institutions whose high-risk investments precipitated a world economic crisis in 2008 left to bail themselves out; instead taxpayers did, and then saw those same financial institutions pay their employees huge bonuses and firmly resist regulation of the exotic financial instruments that caused the crisis. Corporate profits, as many observed, were privatized and risks socialized.

. . .

American political conservatism (rooted in what is elsewhere termed classical nineteenth-century liberalism) equates free enterprise or the market itself with democracy.[63] But contemporary neoconservatism in the United States differs starkly from the vision of Adam Smith—who is admired by many conservatives—in that it blurs the "distinction between a market *economy* and a market *society*, to the point where the latter seems to engulf life itself."[64] Beginning in 1980, the Reagan right recoded freedom so that it now "meant pursuing unlimited wealth, at least in one's dreams, and so identifying with the rich, their desire for low taxes and their aversion to 'big government.'"[65] By the early twenty-first century, however, even some Republican commentators in the United States observed that "[l]aissez-faire is a pretense" and that "[g]overnment power and preferment have been used by the rich, not shunned."[66] The trickle-down hypothesis and faith in privatization of government functions for several decades deeply influenced policy makers, though they have little evidentiary basis.[67] These and other "zombie economic ideas" (Quiggin's term) refused to die.

Decades ago economic historian Karl Polanyi warned against equating freedom simply with a market economy:

> The idea of freedom thus degenerates into a mere advocacy of free enterprise—which is today reduced to a fiction by the hard reality of giant trusts and princely monopolies. This means the fullness of freedom for those whose income, leisure and security need no enhancing, and a mere pittance of liberty for the people, who may in vain attempt to make use of their democratic rights to gain shelter from the power of the owners of property.[68]

Although a market economy can expand "juridical and actual freedom," Polanyi recognized that a moral obstacle arises when regulation, planning, and control—which "can achieve freedom not only for the few, but for all"—are "attacked as a denial of freedom" and when "the freedom that regulation creates is denounced as unfreedom."[69]

Indeed the idea that government regulation can *create* or protect freedom, rather than destroy it, was scarcely visible in American political rhetoric in the late twentieth and early twenty-first centuries. Instead politicians, business leaders, and pundits repeatedly pronounced all government spending to be wasteful and government agencies to be ineffective, a stance that risks becoming a self-fulfilling prophecy when legislators defund and deprofessionalize key agencies, such as the Federal Emergency Management Agency (FEMA).

By 2010, lights in many U.S. city streets began to be turned off; paved roads were returned to gravel; roads and bridges deteriorated; and teachers, firefighters, transit workers, and police were laid off as public coffers were depleted.[70] Trying to fill deep budget gaps, some states and municipalities began to sell off public assets such as highways, ports, and parking meters to sovereign wealth funds such as the Qatar Investment Authority or Abu Dhabi Investment Authority in the United Arab Emirates.[71] Meanwhile, though nearly three-quarters of citizens favored raising taxes on income above $250,000,[72] U.S. tax rates on the rich rested at historically low levels and the wealth of a fortunate few skyrocketed. Here was fertile ground indeed for satire.

Inheritance Tax Wars

The tax on inherited wealth is a lightning rod in American cultural politics. "Estate tax repeal," Graetz and Shapiro wrote, "is one important strand of a looming effort to strip from our nation's tax system the very idea that those who have more should shoulder a larger share of the tax burden."[73] Although opponents of the tax on inherited wealth imply that nearly everyone must pay it, only the very wealthiest Americans have paid any estate tax at all and many citizens have benefited from government programs the estate tax helped to fund.[74] In 2006, it is estimated that 99.7 percent of all people who died in the United States were able to pass on to heirs all of their assets, free of any estate tax.[75] Yet in the early 2000s, nearly half the respondents in a survey sponsored by the Kaiser Foundation believed that "most families have to pay the federal estate tax when someone dies," while only a third gave the correct answer of "only a few families," and an additional 18 percent reported they did not know—indicating that over two-thirds of respondents had incorrect information or no knowledge at all about this important tax.[76]

When opinion poll questions about the estate tax include accurate contextual information, however, support for the tax surges. In Robert H. Frank's 2005 study with the Survey Research Institute at Cornell University, respondents' *support* for the estate tax rose to a remarkable 80 percent when they were informed that repealing the tax on inherited wealth would "necessitate some combination of raising other taxes, borrowing more money from abroad and further cutbacks in government services."[77] In contrast, when the question excluded such a frame and simply asked whether respondents favored the proposal to abolish the estate tax, nearly 75 percent said they did—a likely reflection of pervasive antitax rhetoric in general as well as circulation of mis-leading talking points about the estate tax in particular. It is easy to sustain public confusion when U.S. journalists practice a common "he said, she said" reporting style rather than correcting specious statements or providing contex-tual information. Inaccurate perceptions of other federal taxes also are wide-spread; in the early 2000s, Krueger writes, "only 29 percent of people thought high-income people would benefit most from Mr. Bush's proposal to speed up and make permanent the previously enacted tax cuts," though data from of-ficial nonpartisan sources demonstrating precisely that were readily available to journalists.[78]

Many Americans in the early 2000s might have been surprised to learn that federal and local taxes in recent decades had been quite low, compared with those of other rich nations, and that the quality of public services they value had suffered as a consequence. "Small government" rhetoric crowded out dis-cussion of which public goods and services government can provide more ef-fectively than private entities or citizens themselves—such as fire and police protection; safeguards against contamination of water, food, and medications; and the safety of roads, bridges, dams, and airlines. In 2007, the Organisa-tion for Economic Co-operation and Development's annual survey of thirty countries in Europe, North America, and Asia showed that "the United States ranked 29th in national and local taxes as a share of Gross Domestic Product."[79] In addition to relatively low federal income tax rates, the wealthy had escaped much of the burden of Social Security taxes, since in 2012 that tax applied only to the first $110,100 of wage income (and excluded income from capital gains or dividends). Social Security taxes therefore hit the middle class and lower income groups hardest. During the 1980s, while millionaires' income tax rates dropped sharply, Social Security taxes on middle- and lower-income earners rose substantially.[80]

Furthermore, lower tax rates on capital gains than on wage income have favored the wealthy, who often earn substantial income from dividends and capital gains. That asymmetry led billionaire investor Warren Buffett to argue that the tax structure was unfair because the wealthy paid in federal income and payroll taxes a far smaller percentage of their income than did most middle class and poor workers.[81] Buffett famously declared that his secretaries paid higher tax rates than he did because the U.S. tax structure favored wealth, not work; hence the Billionaires' ironic slogans "Tax Work Not Wealth" and "Taxes Are Not for Everyone!"

False claims by opponents of the tax on inherited wealth that virtually all families had to pay it and that it posed a risk to family farms and small businesses helped to fuel popular support for repeal.[82] While the antiestate tax campaign sometimes acquired the aura of a grassroots force, it was initiated and bankrolled by elite antitax advocates. Countering their rhetoric was the man-bites-dog story of the so-called billionaire revolt, the progressive position on taxes taken by some actual billionaires.

Journalists pay attention (though perhaps only briefly) when Warren Buffett says, "I don't believe in dynastic wealth," and portrays inherited fortunes as a threat to democracy.[83] Buffett, who pledged to give to philanthropy about 85 percent of his fortune, said in 2001 that repealing the estate tax "would be a terrible mistake"—the equivalent of "choosing the 2020 Olympic team by picking the eldest sons of the gold-medal winners in the 2000 Olympics."[84] Yet when ultrawealthy individuals support the tax on inherited wealth, as Andrew Carnegie did in an earlier era, that stance attracts labels such as "class traitor." Banking heiress, art patron, and estate tax supporter Agnes Gund, for example, commented, "I've had a storm of people come at me saying, 'How could you be for this? You're so weird.'"[85]

Some journalists write about billionaires sparring across political party lines,[86] falsely equating the transparent political practices of ultrawealthy liberals such as George Soros with the secretive funding of many staunch conservatives.[87] In 2010, 90 percent of the political campaign funds spent without disclosure of their sources were from conservative groups.[88] Soros not only is transparent about causes he supports financially, but he "supports causes that are unrelated to his business interests and that, if anything, raise his taxes."[89]

Mainstream American journalists (unlike their European counterparts), often avoid making such distinctions, partly out of fear of appearing "biased" or of offending any segment of their audience.[90] Such news reporting practices help to explain the sticking power of inaccurate information about taxes and other matters. Thanks partly to strong early organizing by antiestate tax forces, media coverage of that issue often implied that the tax was suspect without explaining that only a small percentage of the population was required to pay it, or how much they paid, or how long the tax had existed and why.

Forces opposing repeal of the tax on inherited wealth entered the fray late, in the sense that the opposite side had already worked hard to offer a moral argument about why it was not fair to tax large accumulations of wealth. Advocates of repeal framed inheritance as a natural right, which government should not be able to tax, rather than a social privilege made possible by the society that had provided those who became wealthy with educated people to hire, as well as the "markets, the rules of law, the security, and the enforcement."[91] Progressive billionaires who held that an estate tax enshrines the core American value of equal opportunity faced an uphill battle in Congress even though they articulated positions that large percentages of citizens supported.

Proponents of reforming rather than eliminating the tax on inherited wealth, such as William Gates Sr. and Chuck Collins, offer both factual and moral counternarratives to "it's all my money, I did it alone, leave me alone." They encourage the very wealthy to critically assess how their wealth came to be, and to acknowledge help, luck, being in the right place at the right time, skilled employees, or—perhaps if they are religious—grace. Some owe their college and postgraduate educations to the GI Bill, and in that and many other ways, estate tax proponents argue, society made a substantial investment in their success. Hence they can be said to owe something back to society.[92]

That is the position of William Gates Sr., who remarked during my interview with him that it is acceptable in this country to acquire great wealth but that what is often overlooked is that today's American multimillionaire would not have found the same opportunities to cultivate his or her talents in Burkina Faso or Paraguay. Crucial here are the investments in social or human capital in the form of education and health care that enable the high productivity of U.S. workers, and thus their capacity to generate greater wealth for their employers than workers in countries such as Burkina Faso. Also crucial are U.S. investments in infrastructure, the legal system, and police and fire protection. Society's investments—the commonwealth—create the fertile ground, the conditions that enable individuals to succeed.[93] As Gates put it, since "the basic conditions of getting rich are conditions which society has created," he believes that the very wealthy have a substantial reciprocal obligation to society, "a sort of rebalancing, or the payment of a bill." The estate tax is "a way to say thank you," says Chuck Collins; "it's very patriotic."[94]

A number of other prosperous individuals support the "I didn't do it alone" narrative that counters the American myth of self-made wealth or the "great man" theory of wealth creation.[95] They include media mogul Ted Turner, Ben & Jerry's ice cream owner Ben Cohen, actor Paul Newman, George Soros, Warren Buffett, and members of the Roosevelt and Rockefeller families.[96] "If success is rooted in luck and privilege," write Collins, Lapham, and Klinger, "then perhaps we ought to either assure that luck and opportunity are more widely available, or be kinder to those without them."[97]

That behest of course requires the kind of government programs that are anathema to conservative antigovernment ideologues. William Gates Sr. recalls that when he was a guest on a talk show a man called in to criticize Gates for "being in favor of helping the government to steal his money." Such beliefs, Gates remarks, are often accompanied by "a very large misunderstanding about the way the estate tax works and who pays it."[98] Contributing to such misunderstanding was conservatives' determination to brand it as the "death tax"—which offered an opening for satirists.

"Heirs and Heiresses Unite! Death to the Death Tax!"

The political strategy to brand the estate tax as the "death tax" emerged from Republican pollster Frank Luntz's message research with focus groups, which "found that 'death tax' kindled voter resentment in a way that 'inheritance tax' and 'estate tax' didn't."[99] Republican leaders took Luntz's advice, adopted the term "death tax," and practiced tight message discipline. Lobbying firms and Republican offices on Capitol Hill set up a pizza fund (for pizza parties) to which one-dollar fines had to be paid by any staffer who referred to the "death tax" as the "estate tax" or by its correct legislative name, "Federal Estate and Gift Tax and Generation-Skipping Transfer Tax."[100] Dominant corporate news media, advertisers, and talk shows took their cue from conservatives and, at least initially, often adopted the "death tax" term as well.

Enter the satirists. To counter the brand label devised by estate tax opponents and to more accurately represent those who actually pay this tax, the satirical Billionaires dubbed it the "dynasty tax." They designed a poster bearing a color photo of Paris Hilton dressed in seductive denim, holding a pitchfork, with a farm in the background, and the caption "Repeal the Estate Tax! Save the Family Farm!"—deliberate irony, since family farms were not threatened by the estate tax. Another poster declared "Heirs and Heiresses Unite! Death to the Death Tax!" Indeed, "changing the face of the beneficiaries" of estate tax repeal—a tactic of serious as well as satirical supporters of the estate tax—was at least a symbolic success in that "the 'Paris Hilton Tax Cut' idea became so widely repeated in Congress, the media, and anti-repeal advertisements that on Christmas Day of 2005 the *New York Times* listed it as one of fourteen notable phrases that had entered the American lexicon that year."[101]

By 2005, opponents of estate tax repeal were gaining more traction, thanks in part to rebranding it the "dynasty tax." Though they were still "outmanned by pro-repeal advocates," the antirepeal forces "managed to get quite a bit of press coverage emphasizing the long-term fiscal costs" of both repeal and proposed legislative compromises.[102] Meanwhile, the Billionaires talked about how Bush "wants to make it possible for us to pass on our super-huge fortunes to our little lovelies Chad and Muffy, without a dime going to public schools, [or to] build hospitals or fix roads!"[103]

Ironic humor, as in rebranding the estate tax the "dynasty tax," sometimes registers widely in public culture and stimulates critical thinking, prompting a new look at familiar economic narratives. Yet we know it is difficult for satirists to simultaneously entertain, criticize, and instruct the same audience. Those who laughed at Kikki Baxx's quip—"Why is everybody so quiet? Times are good!"—are worlds apart from actual billionaires who might either sit in offended silence or laugh at her joke for quite different reasons.

Elite Reformists

That some billionaires and multimillionaires adopt progressive positions on wealth and taxes should not surprise us. Although scholarly analysis of moral economy has often emphasized subordinates' calls for fairer treatment by the powerful, the privileged too circulate deeply felt moral economy discourses.[104] Some of these are rhetorical defenses against claims on their wealth by the rest of society, while others are just the opposite. U.S. elites, as historians Fraser and Gerstle remind us, "have themselves grown up in a culture suffused by democratic and egalitarian traditions," including beliefs that while hierarchy can be expected to emerge from fair competition, "the government had to protect the general welfare against the predations of the irresponsible rich."[105] Democracy itself, they argue, "function[s] silently as a form of self-discipline, subtly informing the internal life of the powerful, establishing limits to their sense of entitlement."[106]

William Gates Sr. remarked to me that he "talk[s] to people every day who are well-to-do and who do feel like they ought to pay more taxes. . . . They are very comfortable with the notion." A couple of years before the 2008 financial meltdown, I asked Gates about elite attitudes toward escalating economic inequality.[107] His response:

> I think there is a rising concern but I don't think it is dramatic. I think it's modest. It's certainly not at the point where anybody is going to really do anything

about it. It may get there; I hope it does. The perfect reading on all this is what the Congress is doing with the tax structure; it's a perfect description of a society that doesn't care about who has the money.

Public advocacy for more progressive taxation was overshadowed in Congress by powerful organizing forces on the right, cultivation of what Sandra Morgen and her coauthors term "taxpayer identity politics,"[108] and tactics such as Grover Norquist's insistence that Republican legislators sign his pledge never to raise taxes. Progressives have nothing equivalent to the coordinated long-term funding of conservatism, with its capacity to shape public opinion through an array of well-funded think tanks, lobbyists, fund-raising, and public relations organizations.[109] In response, the satirical Billionaires set up a mock think tank called the Institute for the Preservation of Dynastic Wealth, and in 2007 mounted a "Trust Fund Kids for [Senator] Norm Coleman" campaign in Minnesota.

In the past, when elites have spearheaded democratic reform, popular dissent has helped to propel their initiatives—such as the antitrust movement, Greenback-Labor parties, Populists, 1877 railroad strike, Haymarket violence, the Wobblies, and the CIO.[110] At some moments of deep crisis, a fraction of elites has joined with progressive democratic forces, as in the New Deal, whose architects both supported the capitalist foundations of American society, and managed to reduce economic inequality substantially without negatively affecting economic growth.[111] Most crucially, during that era, intense social struggles created political space to debate alternative forms of capitalism and to devise legislative constraints on the powerful and wealthy in the name of social welfare, social justice, and democracy. By the late twentieth century, however, the freedom to pursue wealth had eclipsed freedom from poverty—one of Roosevelt's famous "Four Freedoms."[112] Here was a new Gilded Age that echoed the first Gilded Age and the 1920s as a time when "the rich in the United States slipped their usual political constraints."[113]

Why a Surge in Real Billionaires?

Historically, the politics of wealth in American democracy have been a dance, at times a battle, between plutocrats and economic populists. That dance has often been in the shadows. It took center stage briefly during the 1930s and 1940s as well as a century ago, when there were vigorous debates in Congress and the public arena about dramatic inequalities of wealth and power.

A thumbnail sketch of the rise and fall and rise again of the ultrarich could begin in the 1830s, when the United States had just a handful of millionaires. In the late 1800s Gilded Age, robber barons became multimillionaires from "railroads, manufacturing, and extractive industries such as oil and coal."[114] That era's ultrarich included men such as Andrew Carnegie, Henry C. Frick, and John D. Rockefeller—who in 1907 became the first billionaire in the United States.[115] A second historic surge in individual fortunes has occurred since about 1980, with the largest fortunes jumping to $50 or $100 billion by 2000. For only a brief period between the New Deal and the 1960s did the number of billionaires in the United States drop substantially.[116]

The vast gulf during the first Gilded Age between mansion owners and poor urban workers, as well as political corruption and large corporate mergers, contributed to wide concern that the nation had abandoned the antiaristocratic ideals of the Founding Fathers. Strong public sentiment against European-style inherited privilege contributed to reforms such as child labor laws, the introduction of an income tax and estate tax, and the direct election of U.S. senators.

Such measures (and successors such as the GI bill, Social Security, college loans and grants, federal assistance with home mortgages, and aid to small businesses) helped to build a strong middle class and to reduce economic inequality in the mid–twentieth century (though some racial and ethnic minorities benefited much less). As that equalizing trend reversed itself, anti–social-safety-net rhetoric heated up, and by the 1990s and early 2000s changes in U.S. welfare policy posed ever larger dilemmas for poor women trying to balance paid employment and family care.[117] In the early 2000s, attacks on the social safety net included calls from George W. Bush and others to partly privatize Social Security, though Bush dropped that initiative in the face of wide opposition. Billionaire slogans for that campaign are displayed in Figure 2.1, a 2005 demonstration in Washington, DC, organized by Ken Mayer (shown in photo), whose Billionaire name was Ivan Tital (as in "I want it all"). (Mayer was that city's Billionaire chapter leader.) By 2010, however, with the supposed "crisis" of Social Security and calls to privatize it again in the news, Obama played along and ignored the politically challenging but economically easy fix of raising the income cap on payroll taxes.

Who were the rich at the start of the new millennium? The top 0.01 percent of the population in income were sports and entertainment celebrities, information technology pioneers, and especially CEOs and other top executives who received lavish bonuses and stock options.[118] During the 1960s and

FIGURE 2.1 Billionaires for Bush, after participating with other organizations in a march against privatization of Social Security, Washington, DC. June 2005. Photo by author.

1970s, on the other hand, "companies tended to see huge paychecks at the top as a possible source of reduced team spirit, as well as a potential source of labor problems."[119] Most of the wealthiest Americans before the 1970s "were born into their money, which usually flowed from oil, chemicals, steel, real estate and commodities."[120] The rich of the early twenty-first century were younger than their counterparts of earlier generations, more divided politically, and more polarized economically as the gap between the haves and the have-mores widened,[121] thanks in part to a series of economic bubbles since the 1980s, and especially the explosive growth in unregulated markets in exotic financial instruments such as derivatives.

"Financial weapons of mass destruction" was billionaire investor Warren Buffett's description of derivatives, well before the 2008 financial meltdown.[122] Buffett's remark echoed one made a few years earlier by U.S. Treasury official Robert Altman, who termed derivatives the "economic equivalent of nuclear weapons because they are 'capable of obliterating governments almost overnight.'"[123] What is a derivative? A conventional definition is that "[a] derivative is a financial asset whose price is derived from, or based on, the performance of other equities or commodities, first used to hedge against future currency exchange risks, but increasingly traded speculatively for profit in the 1980s and 1990s."[124] Or, as LiPuma and Lee define them, derivatives are the "generic name for any security whose value is tied to an underlier" such as a mortgage, student loan, or credit card debt.[125] The market for derivatives more than quadrupled between 2002 and 2008, from $106 trillion at the end of 2002 to $464.7 trillion at the end of the first half of 2008.[126] In 2008, the total market in the type of derivative known as credit-default swaps, which are designed as a kind of insurance or hedge, was $55 trillion, more than the gross domestic product of all of the world's nations combined.[127]

Both Democrats and Republicans enabled the proliferation of financial derivatives, especially through legislation passed in 1999 and 2000 to prohibit most regulation of the derivatives market (through the Commodity Futures Modernization Act), even though the head of the Commodity Futures Trading Commission, Brooksly Born, had urged that these financial instruments be regulated. Deregulatory changes enabled creation of the investment banking sector and accelerated financialization of the economy, resulting in megafinancial institutions deemed "too big to fail" (which taxpayers bailed out in 2008), along with accounting tricks and exotic financial instruments that yielded scandals like those of the 1920s. Both Democrats and Republicans in 1980 deregulated the financial system in other ways, including repeal of federal interest rate ceilings and repeal of federal legislation prohibiting usury (thus enabling lending to people of modest means on terms that almost guarantee default). By 2008, many supported reversing this wave of deregulation, including the chairman of the United States Securities and Exchange Commission (SEC), Christopher Cox, who called for transparency and congressional regulation of the derivatives market.[128]

The 2008 financial crisis, with roots in the growing power of the financial industry, exposed American oligarchy as an open secret, and many worked hard to return that secret to the shadows of public life.[129] Much less threatening to the oligarchs than critique of "Wall Street-sponsored Democrats and Wall Street-sponsored Republicans" was the simple opposition between Tea Partiers, who wanted to drastically downsize government, and liberals, who criticized corporate excess.[130]

As in the earlier booms of the Gilded Age and Roaring Twenties, financial speculation and lax regulation fueled millennial economic inequality.[131] The 1990s dot-com boom and the real estate bubble of the early 2000s contributed to stunning wealth increases for those at the very top of the economic pyramid, as more and more capital moved into financial services rather than into factories or farms. Financial industry profits soared, as did that sector's share of the nation's income. In the early 2000s, celebrities accounted for only 3 percent of individuals whose net worth was $10 million or more; stock was the primary or initial source of wealth for more than 60 percent of these high-net-worth individuals.[132] Many reaped stock market gains from new forms of flash trading and leveraged buyouts, unlike an earlier era's investors in long-term blue chip stocks. Contrary to trickle-down economics theory, the stratospheric incomes on Wall Street—often based on the illusion rather than the reality of profit—contributed directly to the stagnation of ordinary workers' incomes.[133]

Parallels between the first Gilded Age and the early 2000s included not just extraordinary wealth inequality but also the undermining of democratic institutions through financial corruption or crony capitalism.[134] Bill Moyers articulates the historic loss:

> When the state becomes the guardian of power and privilege to the neglect of justice for the people as a whole, it mocks the very concept of government as proclaimed in the preamble to our Constitution; mocks Lincoln's sacred belief in "government of the people, by the people, for the people"; mocks the democratic notion of government as "a voluntary union for the common good" embodied in the great wave of reform that produced the Progressive Era and the two Roosevelts.[135]

It is this loss that helped fuel the anger of Occupy Wall Street participants, as well as the activism of the satirical Billionaires.

Seldom did media in the early 2000s spotlight these epochal shifts or the specific policy decisions that enabled the turn toward plutocracy, instability in financial systems, growing corruption, and economic hard times. Such avoidance contributed to a historical amnesia in American public culture.[136] Furthermore, citizens relied on increasingly segmented information sources that made it easy to inhabit "echo chambers" which simply reinforced prior opinions and preferences.

If democracy requires shared knowledge of basic "facts," those presumably would include recognizing that most scientists agree that humans have accelerated global warming, that President Obama was not born in Kenya, that tax rates on the very wealthy were at historically *low* levels in the early twenty-first century, that periods of much higher taxation in the past have coincided with strong economic growth (for example, the 1950s, 1960s, and 1990s), and that only a small fraction of the U.S. budget goes to foreign aid. Yet large numbers of citizens in the new millennium firmly believed the contrary.

"The Billionaires Will FIX the Economy! Trust Us!"

By 2008 the financial crisis had laid bare the very failures the satirical Billionaires' economic policy critiques had highlighted for nearly a decade. In addition to briefly shining a spotlight on the oligarchic face of American politics, the economic crisis exposed the public costs of huge tax cuts for the very wealthy, the drawbacks of loose regulation of large corporations, and declining material security for millions of Americans.

While contemporary robber barons, corporate elites, and corrupt government officials are the satirical Billionaires' targets, some scholars argue that a global economy driven by vast quantities of finance capital deployed in arcane transactions such as derivatives offers no recognizable object for social movement protest. Activists in September 2011 and earlier, however, decided that Wall Street itself was a fine object for their dissent. "Just because we can't see it doesn't mean it's not happening" declared a sign carried by an Occupy Wall Street protester in New York City in September 2011.

Although exotic financial instruments such as credit-default swaps, interest-rate swaps, and equity derivatives, which have fueled skyrocketing economic inequality, were ostensibly intended as instruments of risk mitigation, eminent economists agree that they have destabilized global finance. But as LiPuma and Lee ask, "How does one know about, or demonstrate against, an unlisted, virtual, offshore corporation that operates in an unregulated electronic space using a secret proprietary trading strategy to buy and sell arcane financial instruments?"[137] Such financial arrangements demanded new kinds of political struggle, as Bill Maurer argued in his studies of offshore finance: "the new economy . . . attempts to render questions of accountability moot . . . there is no easily identifiable subject on whom to place blame, no one whom we can take to task for a now nonlocatable structure of domination that is itself a part of us."[138]

Such changes, however, do not necessarily render dissent impotent. At issue are the consequences of governance—of national and international laws, norms, and institutional practices—which *are* worthy targets of critique and protest. These are simultaneously sites of the Polanyian "double movement"[139] or push-back against market expansion or one-size-fits-all economic policies—as evidenced by the late 2000s in growing international cooperation on regulating offshore banking havens via the Bank for International Settlements and other mechanisms.[140]

Actual agents of economic morality in this world of derivatives markets include a wide array of actors and institutions involved in transnational flows of finance capital—from the transnational banking system, to multilateral lending institutions such as the International Monetary Fund and the World Bank,[141] ratings agencies such as Moody's, companies that offer insurance against market-related risks, and governments that provide foreign aid, among others. None of these are impossible to target on specific policies and practices. The state itself, whose laws define the terms of economic competition for corporations and individuals, remains profoundly relevant to struggles over economic justice.[142] It is in principle still vulnerable to public pressure and has localizable targets of critique or protest such as government agencies (SEC, CFTC, Treasury) and elected officials who vote against regulation or transparency in the derivatives market—as well as little-publicized meetings, in places such as Switzerland, of international bankers who define capital standards for banks.[143] And the power of individual nation-states could be augmented if groupings of states acted together to redefine regulatory and tax policies in global finance through initiatives such as a tax on all international financial transactions, elimination of offshore tax havens, or wide adoption of a currency transaction tax (Tobin tax), as Patomaki argues in his book *Democratising Globalisation*.[144]

Those who suffer the most in global financial crises tend to be those who "had the least to do with producing the crisis."[145] The largest constraint on citizen participation in shaping policy is not the difficulty of identifying targets of critique or protest but rather the sheer power of the financial services industry and the dominance of vast corporate and personal wealth in politics. In a more robust democracy less beholden to the very wealthy, corporations would be less likely to escape tax obligations[146]; political candidates would not have to raise such vast sums of money in order to run for office; and federal regulators such as SEC officials would be more likely to fulfill their public mandates rather than cater to the financial interests of the industries they are supposed to monitor.[147]

Nonetheless, experiments are underway. An Occupy Wall Street working group on alternative banking, for example, included among its participants financial experts such as Carne Ross[148] and dissidents from inside Wall Street itself; they focused on how to develop democratic, transparent banks owned by employees and customers. Collective action has the potential to help build political support for requiring more transparent trading in the exotic financial instruments that destabilized the economy.

The Billionaires' public stance is that reform of democratic institutions could yield fairer rules of economic competition. Contrary to the myth of "free markets," there always are rules; at issue is who defines them, who benefits, and whether they can serve a broader public good (however difficult to define). Can democratic institutions foster the cooperation and social solidarity that have been critical to the survival of our species? Do citizens value what they can do for one another? While there are pitfalls in "idealiz[ing] the role of the state as the repository of community values and societal needs,"[149] the government's role in the economy need not stop at ensuring opportunities for private gain. The point is less the size of government than the character of its economic interventions and the interests it serves. Can Democratic as well as Republican politicians resist favoring the interests of Wall Street and address the concerns of citizens who elected them? How many corporations, as Robert Reich puts it, can "refrain from corrupting democracy" by staying out of politics?[150] These are the core concerns of the satirical activists who are this book's central players.

The dream of saving democracy through reforms such as public financing of political campaigns has inspired hundreds of thousands of activists, including a handful in Massachusetts who in the early 1990s already worked in serious jobs to assist those suffering the effects of unraveling social safety nets. To reach wider publics, they began experimenting with irony and humor. Out of those modest beginnings eventually emerged national media attention and a brilliant idea to brand themselves briefly in 1999—as "Billionaires for Forbes." The next chapter explores the 1990s pre-Billionaires' playful insurgencies and includes a close-up anatomy of a prank that changed everything.

3 Pre-Billionaires

Experiments in Satirical Activism, 1990s

SOAK THE RICH? That's what people did, literally, in the African kingdom of Barotse. Decades ago, drummers in a royal barge, traveling from the capital to an outpost with the king and his court during annual floods, were allowed to throw overboard great nobles "who had offended them and their sense of justice during the past year."[1] They particularly targeted magnates who had been stingy with gifts of food.

More often it is the poor who get soaked—both literally and figuratively—as illustrated in an audacious political spoof by the Billionaires' direct precursors, who are this chapter's focus. This 1990s Massachusetts network offers a rare glimpse of the embryonic stages of a national political mobilization.

Those drummers in the royal barge in an African kingdom, like this chapter's creative activists, were marginal subjects who enjoyed symbolic structural superiority for a day. In a gesture that was both pragmatic and sentimental, Barotse political overlords willingly forfeited their status during that annual spectacle. Allowing subordinates to blow off steam in such rituals of reversal (or status inversion) can contribute to political stability as well as signal elite empathy with the poor and marginalized. Indeed when joking itself is part of a ritual, it can express positive values of community and spontaneity.[2]

But can such rituals of "disorder within the rules"[3] be more than a mere safety valve? When they imply that something is awry—and thus potentially unstable—in relations between rulers and subjects, or between rich and poor, they can be dress rehearsals or provocations for actual insurgencies.[4] Rituals of reversal, as sites of symbolic manipulation and display of social tensions, may not only criticize but also imply alternatives to the current political order, and contribute to imaginings of new political possibilities, new political communities.[5] Those very risks encourage power holders to confine political rituals to choreographed events that are carefully designed to exclude symbols of inversion or dissent.

Surprise disruptions of political choreography became a hallmark of the social justice advocates who are this chapter's focus. These utterly unlicensed or unexpected intrusions onstage by dissidents who at first merely pretend to be part of the ritual are more directly threatening than ritualized subversions like those permitted annually in Africa on the Barotse royal barge. They are closer to "rough music," as when workers of an earlier era satirically teased or razzed someone on the print-shop floor while banging work tools and bleating like goats.[6]

Embarrassing the powerful, a technique pioneered by Saul Alinsky, is a key tactic in the repertoire of underfunded social movements that lack easy access to mass media: "[t]ypically CEOs or other high-ranking corporate officers are personally targeted . . . to hold them accountable for the policies and public actions of their organizations."[7] This tactic, Gamson remarks, "is relatively low risk and low cost," but it requires media coverage if it is to succeed, since otherwise no significant embarrassment is produced.[8] How proto-Billionaires adapted this embarrassment technique, wrapped it in humor, and attracted national media coverage is this chapter's little-known story.

To understand the antiritual actions that are the specialty of this chapter's satirical protagonists, Mary Douglas's notion of the joke itself as "anti-rite" is helpful: "The message of a standard rite is that the ordained patterns of social life are inescapable. The message of a joke is that they are escapable. A joke is by nature an anti-rite."[9] Counter to the "order and harmony" embodied in conventional ritual, a joke "disorganizes," symbolically "destroys hierarchy and order," and "denigrate[s] and devalue[s]."[10] The ethnographer's task, then, is to discern in antiritual the alternative values it celebrates as it subverts hierarchy or dramatizes its arbitrariness.

Douglas's "joke in the social structure" (introduced in Chapter 1) again provides a useful frame. Antiritualists, carnival revelers, jesters, and wise fools are bright reflectors of a social order's injustices and exaggerations. Such festive critique appealed to serious citizen activists working for social justice reforms in Massachusetts during the 1990s. Frustrated with the limitations of conventional conferences, rallies, leafleting, slogans, and press releases, they began to combine these traditional tactics with daring spoofs designed to bring joy, capture imaginations, charm spectators, and invoke a sense of the absurd. Posing as the very power holders they critiqued, they could slip undetected into the enemy camp and wreak symbolic havoc.

Here I invert two customary perspectives. First, I use the familiar spectacle of official rituals and the elites who perform them as a backdrop for close analysis of dramatic *antiritual* staged by ironic activists. Second, rather than focus mainly on antiritual as spectacle, I explore as well the personal experiences of direct participants. I rely in this chapter primarily on oral history, supplemented by media accounts. Oral history can humanize and democratize history by attending to voices that are effaced or marginalized in official archives. Furthermore, as Portelli's classic work illustrates, oral history is valuable precisely because it "tells us less about *events* than about their *meaning* . . . [T]he unique and precious element which oral sources force upon the historian and which no other sources possess in equal measure is the speaker's subjectivity."[11]

In talking today about their 1990s satirical activism, some participants distinguish present and past selves. In such cases, the narrator's historical perspective may tend toward irony because, as Portelli puts it, "two different ethical (or political, or religious) and narrative standards interfere and overlap, and their tension shapes the telling of the story."[12] By contrast, other oral historical accounts presented here more closely match what Portelli describes as epic narratives, where the consciousness of the person telling the story today appears to be quite close to that of the earlier historical moment being described. Most of the retrospective interviews on which this chapter is based were conducted in 2006—two years into the second term of George W. Bush—and that historical moment too shapes my interlocutors' views and descriptions of the past. By then, the conservative or market fundamentalist economic policies these activists criticized in the late 1990s had hardened; wealth inequality was extraordinary; and the country had shifted further to the right politically—making it even harder for their messages to register in public culture. Hence some narratives convey nostalgia for an earlier political moment that seemed to offer wider scope for dissent and progressive reform.

Grand initiatives often have small beginnings. During the early and mid-1990s, as wealth inequality and cuts in the social safety net accelerated, Boston activists staged tongue-in-cheek April Fool's Day press conferences ("celebrating" state budget cuts and tax loopholes), "Rallies for the Really Rich," and

"Half-Baked Sales to Save Human Services." They formed a fictitious Rich People's Liberation Front and performed skits posing as corporate executives in "Precision Cell Phone Drill Teams." In 1998, a bold political stunt catapulted them into the national media spotlight. That and subsequent media successes inspired still grander visions and paved the way for a national organization during the 2000 presidential campaign, and an even larger network in 2004 and beyond.

Antecedents: Protest as Play

The tongue-in-cheek activists who created the Billionaires are on the one hand daring innovators and on the other contemporary embodiments of satirically subversive forms with deep historical roots and connections to other forms of collective action. Such connections are often overlooked in analysis of social movements.[13]

The Billionaires' and proto-Billionaires' theatrical tactics contain resemblances to sixteenth-century carnival, charivaris, rituals of status reversal, spectacle, and "weapons of the weak."[14] Parody of the king "as a dupe of evil advisors who connived to tax, pillage, and steal all they could" featured in Mardi Gras in sixteenth-century France.[15] Carnival rites in an Andalusian town include a four-day celebration during which the rich leave town while the lower classes dramatically assert working-class moral codes that contradict those associated with elite domination.[16] Sixteenth-century European organizations called Abbeys of Misrule—festive and humorous "play-acting societies"—included roles such as the Prince of Improvidence and parades during which players distributed mock coins to spectators.[17] So too the Yippies in the 1960s and 1970s threw dollar bills from the balcony of the New York Stock Exchange, and the satirical Billionaires during the 2000s, as well as the Fat Cats in the 1990s, distributed mock currency to spectators. In short, protest as play has a long history.

Out of Massachusetts

For those who know the Billionaires only from media accounts, the contemporary part of our tale begins surprisingly early. It starts in Massachusetts in the early 1990s, a time of government budget cuts that unraveled the social safety net. The Billionaire lineage can be traced directly to a network of activists who held serious jobs in offices at 37 Temple Place in Boston. This was (and remains) an unassuming, narrow building on a busy commercial street; the lobby "wasn't posh . . . don't think marble," one of them remarked,[18] and in the early 1990s the building was not air-conditioned. Who was part of this early network? It included Chuck Collins, who had given away an inherited fortune when he was in his twenties, and who directed the Home Coalition (a statewide coalition of homelessness and housing groups). Collins had interpersonal skills and networks that allowed him to work effectively across class categories, including the homeless, mothers on welfare, activists, and wealthy elites. He worked, along with the late Steve Collins, for the Tax Equity Alliance for Massachusetts (TEAM), which later became the Massachusetts Budget and Policy Center. Also part of the proto-Billionaires' core network were Betsy Leondar-Wright and Deborah Weinstein, who worked at the Massachusetts Human Services Coalition (MHSC), a nonprofit progressive organization Weinstein and then Leondar-Wright directed.[19] Steve Collins (no relation to Chuck Collins) was a board member at MHSC during Weinstein's and Leondar-Wright's terms as director, and he later became director.[20]

In 1994, Chuck Collins and Felice Yeskel cofounded Share the Wealth, which became United for a Fair Economy (UFE) in 1995. The UFE group "Responsible Wealth," a *Boston Globe* article stated, had "become so well known within America's elite that members appeared on Oprah Winfrey's talk show earlier this year."[21] Chuck Collins hired Andrew Boyd in 1996 as UFE's creative action coordinator or "Minister of Culture." Boyd was a member of Reclaim the Streets and of Direct Action Network, both of which were later a source of recruits and ideas for the Billionaires. Boyd also headed a street theater troupe called Class Acts, which UFE helped to support.[22]

A "convergence of senses of humor," as Leondar-Wright put it,[23] among this network of early 1990s activists fed experiments with satire to attract media attention to issues of tax policy and drastic cuts to social services in Massachusetts. For the proto-Billionaires, the use of humor was a complement to, not a substitute for, traditional coalition-building, lobbying, and electoral politics. As Weinstein commented, "after . . . years of earnest activity . . . it seemed like it might be more likely to get press attention and the attention of state legislators if it were a little unusual and even funny."

And so the late Steve Collins and colleagues invented the Rich People's Liberation Front (RPLF), which Boyd's *The Activist Cookbook* says "can be used in many creative ways, including: guerrilla theater, media hoax, satirical event, or heckling that plays off a straight event."[24] The RPLF was described as a "wholly owned subsidiary of the Massachusetts Human Services Coalition," according to MHSC press releases.[25] Under the RPLF banner, Steve Collins created and played a well-dressed character he named Thurston Morton Beechcraft Collings-worth IV. The Rich People's Liberation Front name was used for a few years by activists from various organizations, such as MHSC, TEAM, Share the Wealth, and UFE. Under this label, they staged Rallies for the Really Rich, gave Silver Spoon Awards[26] to politicians who catered to the agendas of the ultrawealthy, and made surprise appearances at official events. On tax days (the April 15 IRS filing deadline) activists dressed as wealthy people and leafleted outside post offices, piggybacking on customary media coverage of deadline-day income tax filers. On these occasions, the faux-millionaire activists thanked "ordinary little people for our tax breaks," and for paying more than their fair share of the taxes.

Chuck Collins and others working for a progressive state income tax or-ganized mock protests against themselves; at their own informational picket lines they would have pseudo-wealthy protesters come to shout at them: "class war, taking away our money; how are we going to pass on millions of inherited wealth to our kids?"[27] Examples of their chants follow:

The rich, united, have never been defeated![28]
To hell with the needy, take care of the greedy!
Who needs day care, hire an au pair!

Declaring a "Save Our Loopholes Day," the Rich People's Liberation Front staged an April Fool's Day press conference and paraded at the Massachusetts State House, "thanking legislators for our loopholes," during the early 1990s (beginning shortly after William Weld became governor of Massachusetts and began cutting housing programs and other forms of relief for the poor).[29] Par-ticipant Leondar-Wright notes that the Save Our Loopholes Day forays by the RPLF were "pretty basic . . . it didn't have any of the high-tech aspects that the Billionaires got later and the humor was pretty crude, but it was a lot of fun."[30]

At least one legislator was fooled by the "save our loopholes" theme and asked in a helpful tone, "Well, exactly which loopholes are you concerned about? Tell me more."[31] The context, as Chuck Collins put it, was a state budget in which "everyone had to fight for every penny of spending, but if you could get a tax loophole it was the gift that kept giving."[32] To drive home that point, Steve Collins and Chuck Collins' group devised a compelling satirical image of back-door spending, which was captured, Chuck Collins notes, in "a TV clip with a scene of us taking a wheelbarrow of money out the back door of the State

House [to convey the message that] poor people . . . have to come here every year and lobby for their nickel and dime [while] we [rich people] get it built into the tax system and take our money out the back door of the State House." At the time, Chuck Collins says, "we were really getting clobbered . . . they were reforming the welfare state, they were cutting housing programs, they were ending our general relief program, they were not building any new housing."

Rallies for the Really Rich, created by Steve Collins and Deborah Weinstein, were connected to the April Fool's Day press conferences. Weinstein and others published a "Poor People's Budget," which analyzed the state budget by looking at programs that were important to low-income people, and highlighted the inequities of tax breaks for the wealthy and program cuts for everybody else. In conjunction with the Rallies for the Really Rich, Weinstein created and printed up a "Rich People's Budget" and had it delivered to state legislators on faux-silver trays. At the rallies, Weinstein said, "we would have people dress up in whatever we imagined rich people might wear."

Participants were volunteers of varying ages from church or religious groups, or staff from advocacy or service provider organizations. Some, Chuck Collins recalls, were low-income and homeless people, and some were welfare mothers—all of whom delighted in dressing up and spoofing the ultrarich. Steve Collins rented a tuxedo and made speeches at the Rallies for the Really Rich in his fictitious identity. A participant remarks wryly that apart from Steve Collins in his impressive rented tuxedo, many others in those early days purchased thrift-store gowns and furs and often "looked ridiculous" garbed in items such as a "ratty, fake fur thing."[33] Leondar-Wright said, "I was wearing a plastic tiara and a sort of moth-eaten fox stole over my Salvation Army prom dress, so we . . . didn't look like real rich people."[34] Costume quality improved markedly and signs became more professional later in the decade.

"Flakey policy pie" and "upside-down priorities cake" were offered at mock bake sales to save human services, in front of the Massachusetts State House.[35] A "half-baked sale to save human services" was designed to highlight the refusal of legislators in a wealthy state to even consider raising taxes in order to fund necessary services. Weinstein and other proto-Billionaires at the Massachusetts events asked friendly state legislators to put on an apron and help sell the cookies to passersby, and as a prop they had a giant thermometer on which were calibrated units of the millions of dollars the state needed to raise. With each sale of cookies for a few cents, Steve Collins would dramatically bend down to the bottom of the huge thermometer, make a tiny mark on it, and ring a gong.

After the mock bake sale, the organizers, Weinstein said, would "ceremoniously present" to the appropriate state House committee chair small sums of money as symbolic proceeds of the sale. The bake sale skit attracted press coverage, including NBC's *Today Show*.

Another mid-1990s creation of Chuck Collins and Andrew Boyd was the Precision Cell Phone Drill Team—self-described "corporate clones, the briefcase brigade"—dressed as prosperous corporate executives in business suits, power ties, and dark sunglasses, with cell phones at their ears as they marched in formation and performed satirical skits in public spaces such as a post office square or the financial district during the lunch hour. When the first estate tax debates occurred in the mid-1990s, Precision Cell Phone Drill Teams performed at United for a Fair Economy's workshops. During the 1999 WTO protests in Seattle, they performed their free trade skit.[36] Drill teams were invited by other organizations to liven up staid conferences and conventions by staging "interruptions"—for example, at the 1997 AFL-CIO convention in Philadelphia, and at a Ben & Jerry's annual corporate meeting. Title themes of Precision Cell Phone Drill Team scripts in the 1990s included "Free Trade SWAT Team," "Corporate Power," "Tax Cut Mutiny," "Welfare Reform," "Sweatshops," "Living Wage," and "Maximum Wage."[37]

The Class Acts theater troupe, headed by UFE's Andrew Boyd, during the second half of the 1990s created and performed dramatic theatrical illustrations of economic inequality.[38] Class Acts skits included "Fat Cat in the Hat" (performed during the 1999 WTO protests in Seattle) and "Corporate Soup Kitchen," which features a ladler serving "Department of Defense contracts, corporate subsidies, tax write-offs, Savings and Loan bailouts." UFE as the sponsor kept the theater troupe focused on issues of economic inequality and the corruption of the democratic process through big money, and the organization would, a UFE staffer noted, "pull the plug on certain skits" if they were off message or poorly executed.[39]

At popular education workshops and other venues, activists dramatically illustrated economic inequality through a performance called "Ten Chairs," which Andrew Boyd later recreated as a musical "100 Chairs" street theater event that was featured on the local news in Boston.[40] In performing the one hundred chairs version in an outdoor public space in Boston in the 1990s, they arranged for a man to arrive in a Mercedes with bodyguards and then claim the forty chairs that represented his share of the national wealth, while a theater troupe orchestrated chants back and forth.

Mike Lapham (United for a Fair Economy) found that theater such as the Precision Cell Phone Drill Team and Ten Chairs "is a terrific way to grab people's imagination. . . . People remember that stuff; it sticks with them and gets through to them." Visualizing inequality in such a way, Chuck Collins suggests, "hits you right in the chest, creates an emotional reaction."[41]

Creative actions such as satirical street theater are always a matter of experimentation, of trial and error. Actions that don't work as well as expected provide lessons on which to build. A former UFE staffer suggested that "for every stunt or skit or street theater thing that we did there was one that didn't work very well."[42] For example, in the mid-1990s, during the Boston Marathon, they tried out a version of the "Rat Race" skit, which is described in *The Activist Cookbook*, and which illustrates growing income inequality by having five individuals represent income quintiles, posing as characters suited to their class status, and then setting up a race such as a hundred-yard dash. A sports commentator would describe the action as a gun went off to start the race, and cheerleaders might also be present. The runners (or rats) in the two lowest quintiles would go backwards, the middle one or two would run in place, and the top quintile rat might race a hundred steps out in front.[43] Participants discovered from trial runs that the skit worked best not on street corners or sidewalks during an event such as the Boston Marathon, but in a long strip of space cleared out ahead of time for an audience gathered alongside it who can get the "most dramatic cross-section view of the different distances the runners travel."[44]

Creative approaches to activism, while quite varied, "draw upon a common pool of possibilities—humor, parody, surprise, hidden identity—which have political uses and limits," Boyd remarks.[45] *The Activist Cookbook* offers tips such as the following: maintain message discipline, use powerful metaphors and limited text, avoid laundry lists, focus on a compelling story and a vision, avoid lecturing or preaching, convey hope, offer doable alternatives, "balance art and message," "use the power of ritual," "anchor your story to an image," "publicize by creating an image," "involve your audience," "shock carefully and constructively," "use humor to undermine authority," "use the aura of theater," "stay in character," and "use music."[46] Leondar-Wright recalls that during her own street theater training she learned "to stick to one simple issue; dramatize it big and broad and humorous; make it carry its message visually (through the action or through written words) so that people who can't hear it still understand it; to involve the audience if possible; and to use traditional melodrama devices like villains, heroes, conflict, and resolution."[47]

The satirical tactics discussed thus far were embryonic forms of later Billionaire actions and semiotics. Eventually, UFE staff realized that while the Rich People's Liberation Front name "was funny in the liberal Massachusetts context,"[48] it was mostly a "left-wing in-joke . . . [and] wasn't politically strategic"[49] for a wider national audience. And so the RPLF was replaced with alternatives such as Big Money United in the late 1990s, and later the "Billionaires for [X]" concept. The Billionaires have other predecessors, beyond the immediate lineage traced here. Notable among them were the Western Massachusetts Fat Cats.

Fat Cats and Other Predecessors

"Whose idea was it to dress up and spoof the ultrarich?" I asked Chuck Collins in mid-2006. He replied:

> I think there's a creative commons here and we don't know where these things come from, that no single person does it. I think that Steve Collins and maybe Debbie Weinstein thought of this idea of dressing up in rich kids' drag, but I think that some of our cartoonists, like Dan Wasserman in Boston, [drew] . . . these funny images, the billionaire with his cup out: "we'll hire you for food" . . . we were taking the kinds of things that were just in the air . . . images of rich people are so prevalent; it is a stereotype . . . it's a very crude cartoon Daddy Warbucks kind of imagery.[50]

When I asked Andrew Boyd about what other activists had influenced him before his Billionaire days, he mentioned the Situationists as well as some groups that probably began in California in the 1980s, such as "Plutonium Players," "Reagan for Shah," and "Ladies Against Women."[51] In *The Activist Cookbook*, Boyd refers to M. A. Swedlund and the Fat Cats as a "sister group" to UFE's Rich People's Liberation Front.[52]

Particularly close to the later Billionaire approach, Boyd remarks, was the Ladies Against Women comedy troupe.[53] Ladies Against Women, a play on the name of the National Organization for Women, was based in San Francisco and spawned chapters on college campuses and elsewhere. Members dressed up like church ladies in pillbox hats and mesh white gloves and carried signs such as "I'd rather be ironing."[54] They posed ironically as unenlightened women who were oblivious to all the bother about feminism and staged events such as a mock bake sale for the budget deficit.

A 1985 article in the *Toronto Star* refers to Ladies Against Women as "a zany group of performers who poke fun at right-wing politics and male chauvinist attitudes" and notes the start of a Canadian Ladies Against Women (CLAW) chapter whose motto is "Close your eyes and do your duty."[55] A 1984 *Washington Post* article about events featuring conservative Republican women at the party's national convention in Dallas includes under the subheading "Outsiders" brief descriptions of protesters, among them Ladies Against Women members handing out their "Consciousness Lowering Manifesto" and carrying signs such as "Born to Clean."[56] It contrasts these and other "outsiders" (protesters) with the "insiders [who] have the clout," and asserts that "Inside, no one is listening to the outsiders."

With a less marginalizing narrative frame, a 1984 *New York Times* article about "careful orchestrating of a sober, pro-woman motif" at the Republican Convention describes Ladies Against Women as "demonstrators who spoke breathlessly and dressed coquettishly as they capered outside various events, mocking Phyllis Schlafly and other women unsympathetic to the organized feminist cause. 'Ban the poor!' they shouted . . . [T]hey held a bake sale to 'help Mr. Reagan with the deficit.'"[57] A Ladies Against Women member with a Billionaire-esque name—Mrs. T. Bill Banks—appears in the *Times* article as portraying a "chic disdain toward the environmental movement by draping herself elaborately in a baby harp seal skin with its eyes fixed open, waif-like." Playing along with the spoof, the article refers to another demonstrator "in white pillbox hat and yellow ruffled apron, [who] wore rouge in two clown-like dots. 'You're nobody till you're "missus," are ya?' she counseled some of the puzzled Republican women who passed by."

Ladies Against Women, Boyd said, made a lasting impression on him as a student when they visited the University of Michigan's Ann Arbor campus during the mid-1980s. He now sees that group's "meme of a fake organization" that had open membership and some star members as "embryonic"—whether consciously imitated or not—for the Billionaires. He appreciated their "high-level performances" and adoption of fictive names and characters, and terms their concept "provocative, pro-feminist in its intent but mocking the anti-feminist, button-down Republican women. Ladies Against Women was brilliant." Boyd says it "was good at modeling how a meme can convey a lot, a meme of a fake group." Ladies Against Women ended its activities in 1990, a few years before online organizing took off.

A satirical group who spoofed the rich and whose network of personal and work relationships intersected with the proto-Billionaires was the Fat Cats.

Based in Western Massachusetts during the 1990s, they used caricature and ironic protest and sometimes collaborated directly with the Eastern Massachusetts proto-Billionaires. M. A. Swedlund, who became a central organizer, describes the Fat Cats[58]:

> [Members] put on a set of ears, usually glued onto a hairband . . . , a big curly tail, and a suit that is as nice as possible and as big as possible, and it would be stuffed with pillows, and . . . you've usually got some black whiskers on your face . . . and almost always a big cigar, and they had money stuffed in their pockets. . . . They gave out $500 bills [inscribed with] some propaganda . . . [as] Fat Cat cash. [The bills bore slogans such as] "in exchange for favors" . . . and some organizing information was printed on the back.

The text of a sample Fat Cat $500 bill I examined (courtesy of Swedlund) reads: "This note is legal tender for all private contributions to Congress and is redeemable in Washington for special favors including subsidies, tax breaks, and weak regulation; 'Fat Cats of America Will Pay for Favors.'" The reverse side of the bill includes names of groups supporting the Massachusetts clean election law, main components of that law, a contact phone number for the Mass Voters for Clean Elections, and a call to "Get Big Money Out of Politics: Vote Yes on #2 Nov 3." Fat Cats also carried bags of money and champagne glasses, and waved signs such as "Have Pity on This Poor Kitty," "Fat Cats Against Change," and "Fat Cats Say No, No, No." A Fat Cats slogan—"Buy-partisan; we buy Democrats and we buy Republicans"—was used as well by United for a Fair Economy's satirical activists and was later adapted by the Billionaires; so too some of the Fat Cats' character names such as Phil T. Rich, which Andrew Boyd adopted as his Billionaire name. Fat Cats sang subversive lyrics to familiar tunes ("Deck the Halls with Boughs of Money" and "The Twelve 'Buys' of Christmas").

The first time Swedlund, a resident of Deerfield, Massachusetts, heard about the Fat Cats was when they appeared in a play performed in 1991 by the Pioneer Valley Pro-Democracy Campaign at a conference on money and politics that took place at Hampshire College under the auspices of the Working Group on Electoral Democracy. Among the members of the sponsoring group was Randy Kehler, founder of the nuclear freeze movement, which also called attention to the disproportionate influence of money in politics. The Pioneer Valley Pro-Democracy Campaign favored 100 percent public financing of federal elections and gathered signatures to put on the ballot a question about public financing of elections. Their picket signs at a September 1991 event on campaign finance law, outside the Sheraton Hotel in Boston, included "One Person, One Vote—Not One Dollar, One Vote!" and "The U.S. Needs a Pro-Democracy Movement, Too!" In 1992, the Pioneer Valley Pro-Democracy Campaign put on the ballot in the Western Massachusetts senatorial district (for the first time in the country) a measure calling for public financing of candidates who agreed to strict spending and contribution limits. The measure passed but was later repealed.

Fat Cats networks, as suggested, overlapped with those of the Massachusetts proto-Billionaires. Swedlund comments that they all knew one another, and "we were all working on similar things from different angles." Swedlund and her associates in the Pioneer Valley were also working in Boston by the time United for a Fair Economy was well established in that city. The Pioneer Valley Pro-Democracy Campaign, for example, worked with the Commonwealth Coalition, a statewide progressive coalition (based in Boston), on campaign finance legislation.

Fat Cats actions included appearances at political party conventions (both Democratic and Republican),[59] workshops, progressive political events, and political fund-raisers, where they might arrive in a limousine, attempt to enter the event, and usually be denied permission to do so. A Fat Cats skit in Washington, DC, in January 1993 toasted Bill Clinton as "the best president money can buy," a phrase later adopted by the Billionaires as well. In March 1995, Fat Cats performed an ironic skit before a legislative committee in Hartford, urging the honorable committee to "ignore the insanity that is demanding change . . . the system works for us . . . no public-financed elections!"[60] Swedlund recalls when they sneaked into the U.S. Congress, carrying costumes in a bag, changed into their cat attire in a restroom, and then "were glad-handing various people as they walked the halls of Congress." She reports that their appearances often "attracted good national coverage from TV and newspapers and we'd get interviewed; it was pretty effective that way too. You know, if you show up at a fund-raiser dressed as a cat in a limousine, people notice."

The Fat Cats, who numbered forty or so individuals over time, obtained modest funding from foundations that were working on the role of money in politics, such as a $10,000 grant in 1995 from the Northeastern Citizen's Action Resource Center. They experimented during the early and mid-1990s with attempts to set up chapters elsewhere, but in that pre-Internet organizing era they did not multiply into a national network of chapters as the Billionaires for Bush (or Gore) did in 2000. They conducted a few Fat Cats trainings in New Hampshire, Kentucky, and Massachusetts, and they "created some Fat

Cats litters here and there," Swedlund remembers. Pete McDowell, a member of the North Carolina Alliance for Democracy, organized a new Fat Cat troupe in Chapel Hill, North Carolina. In New Hampshire, Fat Cats members were sponsored in 1996 by the public interest group New Hampshire Citizen Action. Most of their activities wound up by the late 1990s.

A high point was Massachusetts governor William Weld's election celebration in 1994 at a Boston hotel. Two Fat Cats (Miss Kitty and Fat Cat) infiltrated the event in full costume, carrying a sign declaring, "Weld for Prez."[61] Both were professional actors,[62] and as Swedlund, who was not there, tells the story,

> They were dancing and giving interviews to the press and eating food and having a great old time. And they were there for probably forty-five minutes to an hour. More and more people arrived, and it was like a party . . . somebody finally realized . . . that maybe there was a hidden message with these two people and that maybe they shouldn't be giving interviews and talking and all this stuff at Weld's big party.

Having blended in well with the campaign party atmosphere, the two costumed Fat Cats kept up the lighthearted pose when approached by security officials, who "didn't want to make too big a scene" but eventually escorted them out politely.

That this 1994 event lives on in the group's oral history, and indeed has iconic status for members a decade later, is significant. Pride in the media coverage and the success of this kind of prank becomes a key element of group self-identity, morale, and solidarity. Humor, parody, surprise, and hidden identity were key elements of these activists' repertoire, and the satirical Billionaires' founders later drew on such experiences.

News coverage of Fat Cats also includes an August 2000 *New York Post* photo of two police officers escorting a person in a cat costume who carries a sign declaring, "Fat Cats for Bush (or Gore)." The photo caption reads: "Getting Carried Away: Miami police put a leash on a costumed 'fat cat' demonstrator during a speech by GOP presidential candidate George W. Bush (inset) yesterday." Other articles appeared in print media such as the *Cleveland Plain Dealer, Boston Globe, National Journal,* and *USA Today.*

How does Swedlund assess the effectiveness and limitations of the Fat Cats? She says "that satirical . . . on-the-street kind of thing is really good at pointing out the problem but not so good at presenting the solution." She found their approach most effective in crowded settings such as fairs or concerts, where the

Fat Cats' $500-bill play money attracted people to come up to them, ask them about their issue, read the text on the play money, and then put the $500 bills on their refrigerators. She comments that participating in satirical activism is much more fun than the serious variety; "it gets people's attention" and is a helpful "first step toward educating a particular group of people on an issue." She sees it as one of many tools for addressing issues such as public financing of elections.

When the Billionaires for [X] concept was launched in 1999 and 2000, organizers consulted Swedlund, and in 2004 she participated in a few Billionaire actions herself in Western Massachusetts. She wore a giant white top hat and tuxedo with a red and white striped vest that had belonged to her stepfather-in-law and which she thinks he must have worn in a Fourth of July parade.[63] As a satirical Billionaire she attended a 2004 Bush inaugural rally spoof in Northampton and in 2005 hosted a Billionaire fund-raiser for the organization MassVoters, which was attended by some New York and Massachusetts Billionaire members. Meanwhile, during the late 1990s, United for a Fair Economy's "Ministry of Culture"—its creative team, headed by Boyd—experimented with new forms of street theater and staged a 1998 event that won national media coverage.

Boston Tea Party, 1998

The most daring and widely publicized of United for a Fair Economy's pre-1999 political spoofs was their surprise appearance at an April 15, 1998, event on the Boston Tea Party Ship Museum, a floating tourist attraction in Boston Harbor.[64] Their "culture jamming" on this occasion—their first leap to a national stage—built on the theatrical repertoire just discussed, foreshadowed subsequent Billionaire activities, and provided powerful lessons for participants. The Boston Tea Party Ship event remains a vital part of this activist network's oral history, and members delight in recounting it. Indeed Boyd and others incorporate it into public presentations at conferences and in the classroom.

"Chuck [Collins] would come up with some crazy idea like this, and I was always the one who would say, 'oh that's not going to work for this, this, and this reason,'" recalled former UFE researcher, writer, and graphic designer Chris Hartman.[65] Hartman was one of five key participants who talked with me about the 1998 Tea Party Ship event. "I was the smart skeptical one who can poke all the holes in an idea," Hartman continued, "but I said, 'oh, I'll go along with this'. . . . I talked it over with my wife and we both said, 'oh, I don't know if this is going to work.'"

The story begins on a spring day in 1998 when Chuck Collins opened the *Wall Street Journal* and noticed that congressmen Dick Armey of Texas and Billy Tauzin of Louisiana were coming to Boston on tax day (April 15) to throw the entire U.S. tax code—thousands of pages—into Boston Harbor during a media event sponsored by Citizens for a Sound Economy (a recipient of substantial corporate funding). In 1998, a midterm election year, "tax reform" was a top Republican Party issue. The Armey-Tauzin event struck Collins as full of dramatic potential, so he gathered details about timing and plans by calling up the sponsoring organization, and asking excitedly, "Oh wow, I read about your event; how can I help out?"

Armey and Tauzin were proponents of abolishing the graduated income tax and replacing it with a flat tax and a national sales tax. (Steve Forbes, briefly a Republican presidential candidate in 1999, was also a proponent of a flat tax, and he later became the target of a different political spoof.) Armey and Tauzin framed their proposal as a tax revolt that favored ordinary citizens. Their plan to toss the U.S. tax code over the side of the Boston Tea Party Ship was intended as a symbolic echo of the 1773 Boston Tea Party, when revolutionary "patriots," dressed as Mohawk Indians with blackened faces, boarded three British ships laden with tea to be sold through loyalist merchants under a legal monopoly approved by the British Parliament, thereby undercutting American tea merchants. Led by men of wealth and power such as John Hancock and Samuel Adams, on the night of December 16, 1773, about 150 men from various walks of life boarded three ships, and for several hours opened cases of tea and dumped it overboard into Boston Harbor as a large crowd—including the British Royal Navy—watched. Tea parties in other colonies followed, political divisions hardened, and the stage was set for the Revolutionary War.

Although Armey and Tauzin's 1998 event—about a decade before a new form of "Tea Party" politics emerged in the United States—was meant to evoke metaphorical parallels to the 1773 Tea Party, the issues were quite different. The Revolutionary-era Boston Tea Party nonetheless offered evocative imagery and a frame with deep cultural resonance, and that is what mattered to them that April day in 1998.

To hijack Armey and Tauzin's Boston Tea Party Ship stunt and expose the disadvantages of a flat tax, Collins and his fellow UFE staff first considered having people dressed like billionaires appear in a cigarette boat, with others cheering them on. A UFE staff person suggested instead that they pose as a working family in a life raft that gets sunk as it paddles below where the congressmen would throw the trunk marked "Tea," which contained the tax code, into the water. They decided it would be a lot easier for them to get a life raft than a speedboat, and so they planned to have a man and a woman (two UFE staffers in their twenties) and a plastic baby doll hide in a life raft behind the prow of the ship where the politicians would be. Andrew Boyd, who was then a UFE consultant heading the Class Acts theater troupe, would arrange to be on the Tea Party Ship itself so he could signal the two in the life raft when the congressmen were on board. The first step was to arrange for colleagues to call up the organization sponsoring the Armey-Tauzin event, play the role of "goofy supporters," and sign up to participate, so they could be on the ship when the congressmen arrived.

The evening before the event, Hartman, along with Boyd and Kristin Barrali—a young financial manager at UFE who was in her first job since completing college—raced off to a discount store selling sporting goods to purchase a life raft. Barrali recalls that she was eager to do whatever it took to be part of the group, and so when Chuck Collins asked her if she wanted to go out on the life raft and get sunk in the harbor the next day, she said "definitely!"

Hartman and Barrali scouted out the harbor location, and Barrali approached the owner of a nearby houseboat moored in the polluted water near the ship. He turned out to be politically sympathetic and offered to let them use his houseboat as a staging ground and to take showers there afterward.

On that cool and cloudy April 15, Hartman got up early, met Barrali, and together they inflated their small rubber dinghy and reviewed their plans. Both were nervous about getting the timing right, and Barrali wondered about the life raft's flimsiness. Hartman and Barrali paddled into the harbor on the raft and positioned themselves just out of eyesight of people on the Tea Party Ship. They could hear people arriving on board, and they waited for Boyd to blow a whistle as a signal for them to move into view and stop right below the symbolic trunk that was to be dumped overboard.

Meanwhile, Mike Lapham, a UFE staff member, calmly strolled down the plank to board the Tea Party Ship with about five colleagues who were "dressed smartly in suits, ties, and sunglasses," posing as young Republicans. In contrast with the post–9/11 era, he recalls no security checks that day, and said he and his friends easily boarded the ship and "just kind of mingled in with the folks who were going in." The individuals on the Tea Party Ship included "a couple of congresspeople, a handful of staffers, and maybe supporters and press . . . and then about five of us sprinkled in right at the edge of the boat, so we were right there to do our chants and lean over and point." Lapham recalls that he and his colleagues had learned of Armey and Tauzin's Tea Party Ship plan less than forty-eight hours beforehand. "When Tauzin and Armey showed up with their entourage," he said, "we waited patiently for the right moment. . . . They were getting ready to toss off the tax code, which was really just a big cooler that still may have said 'tea' on it. . . . Normally people [tourists] were tossing off a box of tea symbolically, and it was on a rope so you could pull it back up."

Boyd, who also easily boarded the ship, was on edge as he watched for the right moment to blow his whistle to signal Barrali and Hartman to move their life raft into view. He had called Dick Armey's office and pretended to be a young Republican in order to get advance information, he said, "about where and when and what they were expecting to happen, so we could bring our group of young Republicans in to support them and look good to the media." Since cell phones were not widely used then, he had to run around a lot in order to track movement of Hartman and Barrali's boat and monitor what was occurring on the Tea Party Ship in order to time his signal precisely:

> So I show up early before Dick Armey and Billy Tauzin arrive and after Chris and Kristin have got themselves in a boat, but I don't know where the boat is and this is before cell phones . . . at least none of us have cell phones. And so I'm trying to find where these guys are so I can position myself well to give them the signal. . . . [I was] running along one side of the bank or up and down the ship looking for them. . . . I was very happy to find them [Chris and Kristin] . . . I would have been very upset at myself if I hadn't found them.

The success of their spoof demanded exquisite timing, and Boyd was worried:

> So then they [Armey and Tauzin] came on board, and the next very tense moment for me was when to blow the whistle. I positioned myself where I had a line of sight on the boat as well as Dick Armey and Billy Tauzin. I didn't want to do it prematurely, but I certainly didn't want to do it too late . . . ahhh! I felt I hadn't done very much to pull this action together compared to these other people, and here I was with the ultimate responsibility for it, [for being sure] the timing was perfect. . . . I was so unhappy; it was like not playing in the soccer game, being put in at the last minute, and then having to do the penalty kick.

Chuck Collins stood on a nearby bridge that offered a good view of the Tea Party Ship, and as he chatted with national reporters, he began telling them, "Something unexpected is going to happen." They were immediately interested: "Really? What?" When they asked who he was, he said he was with an organization (UFE) that opposed the tax cuts and he gave them his press release and encouraged them to "just watch." Collins waited with journalists on the bridge, and then,

> Sure enough, our boat comes around . . . the Working Family Life Raft. This is the working family that's going to be sunk by their flat-tax proposal. And then Andrew [Boyd] with . . . our [pseudo] rich guys start chanting, "Sink 'em with the flat tax! Drown 'em with the sales tax! Sink 'em, sink 'em, sink 'em!" they're chanting. Dick Armey and Billy Tauzin are standing there, and they do not know what to do. Their handlers are going crazy. So somebody just says, "Throw in the trunk!" Meanwhile, people who they think are their supporters are standing around saying, "Throw it in! Throw it in!" So they throw the trunk in—big splash—next to our little life boat, and on cue, Kristin and Chris topple the life boat, and now they're swimming and they're holding the little baby [doll] up.[66]

From the life raft, Hartman and Barrali had watched the surprise on Armey's and Tauzin's faces: "They just kind of stood there looking at us, fake smiles plastered on their faces. I think they weren't really sure what to do because they didn't want to throw this box on us while the cameras were rolling."[67]

No one requested Lapham and his colleagues to leave the ship or asked them what they were doing there, but he recalls that once they walked ashore again, "there was a sort of confrontation on the street where some people were angry at us for being there." When Tauzin and Armey "retreated to their limousine . . . [it] was surrounded by cheering members of the Rich People's Liberation Front—the UFE theater group—holding signs saying, 'We Love You, Armey and Tauzin!' 'Tax Cuts for Us, Not Our Maids,' 'Free the Forbes 400,' and 'We Rich Love the Flat Tax!'"[68] But when Andrew Boyd walked over to shake Dick Armey's hand, he felt a painfully hard grip as he addressed him in irony mode: "I remember . . . saying in character . . . 'Thank you for being our man in Washington; we'll be calling on you soon for some more favors; this is a great tax; we'll remember you.' . . . He was not happy and he was squeezing my hand really, really, really hard, and I remember following him back to his limo . . . which was nerve-wracking in its own way." Boyd's exhilaration mingled with dislike of being hated by the targets of the prank, even though he believes Tauzin and Armey's policy proposals justified UFE's action. Boyd describes the Tea Party Ship prank as "an incredible learning experience" and a valuable teaching case because it "was a beautiful example of how to reframe [an economic policy issue]—visually, conceptually, theatrically."

But two can play at the game of reframing. According to Boyd, after Hartman and Barrali had paddled away, Armey and Tauzin *restaged* tossing the trunk overboard, and some local television stations filmed it again and showed the second version rather than the first—a telling faithfulness to scripted political stagecraft:

> They have the case of tea on a rope. . . . There are a lot of media stunts on this damn boat, and so they yank it up, and by this point Chris and Kristin have paddled away, and they threw the stuff in again . . . and some of the local TV stations filmed it, and then they showed that second set of tapes. . . . So the lesson there is never leave the scene; it ain't over 'til the fat lady sings.

Most of the media coverage, however, focused on the life raft spoof, and Boyd terms it "a huge, massive success."

The story was broadcast on national radio and television networks such as CNN throughout the day, with captions such as "GOP Photo Op Backfires," and was reported by Reuters and the Associated Press. Collins describes the media coverage:

> The *Boston Globe* had a three-photo sequence: Working Family Life Raft, tipping, then the people in the water. . . . The TV stuff was the best; there was "GOP Photo Op Backfires," "Flat Tax Sinks Working Family." . . . We stole, we completely stole their act . . . and all afternoon I was doing interviews with different reporters. Rush Limbaugh went on and said, "I'm glad they fell into Boston Harbor." . . . In reflection on it, we spent fifty bucks to buy a raft; they spent fifty thousand bucks producing this event, hiring a professional media firm to publicize it . . . we completely devastated them.

Lessons learned from this event, Collins says, include focusing on "the visual you want: flat tax sinks working family"; culture-jamming (subverting) the message of your opponent; getting good advance information and planning carefully, which requires "precision and discipline" so that people know their roles, their places, and their arrival times, and they follow the plan. Particularly important, Collins remarks, is what you want to appear in the camera frame—in this case, a "pitiful working family life raft huddling below these guys who are going to drop a trunk that says 'Tax Code.' That's the picture . . . it's as good as it gets" (Figure 3.1).

FIGURE 3.1 "Your flat tax will sink the working family," shouted two demonstrators in their "Working Family Life Raft," as two congressmen prepared to dump the tax code, in a box marked "Tea," into Boston Harbor. April 16, 1998. Photo courtesy of *Boston Globe* and Getty Images.

Although Armey and Tauzin depicted a flat tax as a way to remove unjust tax burdens on ordinary citizens, Chuck Collins and his UFE colleagues' culture-jamming approach revealed what such rhetoric obscured. That meant reframing Armey and Tauzin's message by creating a compelling image to illustrate how their proposed tax code revision would actually benefit a privileged minority and harm poor and middle-class families.

During the mid-1990s, as media analysts Jamieson and Waldman observed, "Steve Forbes and his flat tax [proposal] were being criticized not only by Democrats but by most of the Republican establishment as well," including Newt Gingrich.[69] Because U.S. journalists "determine whether a proposal is considered 'reasonable' in public debate in large part by whether it is embraced by elite figures," the flat-tax proposal's rejection by key figures in both major political parties "increased the likelihood that it would be cast [by media] as outside the mainstream."[70] That same perception may have increased the likelihood that dominant news outlets would cover a political prank that satirized the flat-tax proposal.

Media Coverage of the 1998 Boston Tea Party Ship Prank

Some news media stories about the 1998 Boston Tea Party Ship prank played along with the tongue-in-cheek spirit of the UFE activists and the appeal of David-versus-Goliath stories.[71] A couple of accounts treated the capsizing of the Working Family Life Raft dismissively.

The *Boston Globe* carried the story on its front page, along with two photos of the "Working Family Life Raft."[72] The framing is "Republicans and anti-tax groups staged bits of Tax Day political theater across the country" on April 15 in order to dramatize their calls for a flat tax, national sales tax, lower taxes, or fewer taxes. The *Globe* also cites polls showing little public enthusiasm for such tax-change proposals, mentioning that those polled named health insurance as a top concern. The article mentions other recent Republican stunts such as "burying" the tax code by "staging a funeral procession" in Baltimore, and suggests that these staged Republican events have been ineffective: "Some politicians have taken on the tax code with stunts—and the tax code has won."

The last few paragraphs report that Armey and Tauzin "tried to replay the Boston Tea Party as a protest against the tax code. But they were forced to share the stage with a group of protesters." The reporter describes the UFE prank in detail, including the congressmen's surprise "when two protesters floated by in a dinghy labeled the 'Working Family Life Raft.'"

The *Boston Herald* also covered the story, opening with the scramble of last-minute tax return filers rushing to beat the midnight deadline on April 15, and then describing the Armey-Tauzin event and United for a Fair Economy counterprotest "by demonstrators who said Republican proposals were anti-working class."[73] Other articles appeared in the *Patriot Ledger* of Quincy, Massachusetts,[74] and the *Worcester Telegram and Gazette*.[75]

Rather than explore the substance of alternative tax positions, these news accounts mainly address theatrical aspects of the Boston Tea Party reenactment and capsized life raft. Since most of the articles did, however, at least mention the counterprotesters' "Working Family Life Raft" and one or more of their slogans, the media coverage confirms UFE staff members' assessment that having a strong visual message and a dramatic surprise, while piggybacking on an existing media event, can help to bring at least some media attention to a point of view that otherwise might have gone unmentioned entirely.

In addition to the 1998 news articles discussed here, at least one news account a couple of years later referred back to the Boston Tea Party Ship counter-protest. A July 2000 article (with photo) in the *Philadelphia Daily News* about the Billionaires' plans for that year's political party conventions includes four sentences describing the 1998 Tea Party Ship stunt, mentioning that United for a Fair Economy "first discovered the power of humor in 1998, when two Republican congressmen held a press conference in Boston to stump for the flat tax and a national sales tax."[76] Of course United for a Fair Economy staff members had "discovered the power of humor" years earlier, through experiments with "save our loopholes" days, bake sales to save human services, and Precision Cell Phone Drill Teams. For them, the 1998 Boston Tea Party Ship prank was a gratifying success that built on years of creative work and experimentation.

Rescued from Oblivion?

"To tell a story is to take arms against the threat of time," writes Portelli.[77] The retelling of stories such as the 1998 Boston Tea Party spoof, as with all oral history, is a process of creating meanings—a way to "preserve the tellers from oblivion" and to build a legacy for future action.[78] Such tales shape both individual and collective identities—effects that are profoundly important, even though they cannot be quantified. The pre-Billionaire activists' collective assessments of their 1990s tactical experiments with humor crucially shaped their subsequent political organizing. Their vivid recall in 2006 of an event that occurred eight years earlier reflects its affective and tactical salience. They had saved news clippings about the Tea Party Ship prank, watched television coverage of the story, and talked about it with their families, friends, and colleagues.

Shared elements of their five individual narratives include the spoof's eleventh-hour planning, relief that the Working Family Life Raft capsized on cue,[79] the pink baby doll floating in the water, faux-Republican infiltrators on the Tea Party Ship, wide media coverage, and postspoof exhilaration. For all of them, the national media coverage affirmed the event's success and marked the most intense such notice the young United for a Fair Economy organization had yet received. News media exposure, they assumed, helped to amplify circulation of their core messages about economic justice.

Hartman felt "exhilarated" that in spite of his initial concerns and their meager resources, their "little prank" succeeded against Tauzin and Armey's elaborate publicity stunt: "For our little organization that was only two and a half years old at that time, it seemed like a great coup . . . we felt that excitement of being a little bit on the edge . . . and maybe making people think a little bit." Although the spoof's concrete effects can't be assessed, Hartman said that as a day's worth of activity, he believes their prank afforded "a pretty good bang for the buck," compared to time they might have spent on other activities, such as working on a report, releasing it, and hoping it received press coverage. He sees such spoofs as one useful tool among many for "a growing movement" that relies on "a lot of different actions, modalities." The Tea Party Ship diversion was the kind of tactic to which the relatively powerless must resort, a David-versus-Goliath situation, because, as Hartman put it, "we just have hardly any resources to go onto the public stage and offer our view point-by-point with our political opponents."

Some of the satirical participants empathized with the pain and embarrassment of those whose political ritual had been undone, though such sentiments are partly overshadowed, Boyd admits, by the supportive glee and admiration of their peer group when they tell the story. When I asked Lapham what emotions he felt after the 1998 spoof, he replied that "mostly we were ecstatic that we were able to pull this whole thing off, from getting someone to allow us to launch the raft from their boat nearby to help us . . . infiltrating the event, having the boat come around at just the right time, and the media capturing it all and getting it up on national TV." At the same time, in 2006 he expressed ambivalence and empathy for those whose political stagecraft the spoof undid:

> I would say there is a little bit of questioning—OK we hijacked this event be-
> cause we think they're doing something bad; how would we feel if we were
> doing a publicity event and someone else hijacked our event? Is it fair? . . . They
> were engaging in theater to dramatize their point, and we decided to engage in
> superimposed theater that reinterpreted what they were doing. It's in a public
> place; maybe in some way that's all fair game.

If the prank was morally justified and a fair use of public space, Lapham suggests, it was because he and his colleagues believed Armey and Tauzin's flat-tax proposal was harmful and UFE as a small organization had much less opportunity to call public attention to its message than Armey and Tauzin did: "Certainly for an organization that's trying . . . to get inequality into the spotlight, and has a hard time getting the press to pay attention to inequality and the unfairness—the way rules are tilted to favor the wealthy—we're looking for whatever opportunity we can to make a point."

Whatever the limitations of such forms of political action, elation about a short-lived, symbolic status reversal can boost morale, create a new sense of the possible, and thus help to sustain activists' energies for more conventional work on legislation, voting, and electoral research. Other indirect and difficult-to-measure effects of such pranks include the possibility that they change the minds of nonparticipating observers or inspire them to become politically active or to think more critically and carefully about the issues.

These small political openings and fleeting insurgencies might be termed "dramas of citizenship."[80] Through such symbolic displays of social tensions, as Kertzer argues in a different context, "we recognize who are the powerful and who are the weak, and through the manipulation of symbols the powerful reinforce their authority. Yet, the weak, too, can try to put on new clothes and to strip the clothes from the mighty."[81]

In 2006, Hartman told me he looked back on their late 1990s satirical actions with some "wistfulness for the freedom" of that time. He expressed nostalgia as well for the 1960s (before he was born): "I think that one thing that's missing in our culture that maybe was more present in the 1960s was a culture of protest and also an optimism or a sense of whimsy about politics that would do a lot in our present moment . . . [when] a lot of people are just turned off by politics, and that includes earnest, progressive, demonstration-attending people." As an antidote to such political alienation, Hartman sees "clever, funny tactics" as adding a necessary "balance" to an activist repertoire that also includes "serious" activities such as electoral and legislative research, and writing reports and press releases. In the years after the Tea Party Ship prank, he enjoyed participating—as a private citizen rather than a UFE employee—in an occasional satirical Billionaires action.

Although Hartman and his colleagues in United for a Fair Economy for a time straddled the worlds of satirical and serious forms of political critique, by the early 2000s some of them (including Hartman and Collins) were focused mostly on serious modes of shaping public policy and becoming credible economic policy spokespeople for the media. UFE staff directed their professional attention toward issues such as the racial wealth divide, CEO pay, and the estate tax, and UFE eventually broke off its connection with the satirists who later became known as the Billionaires. UFE began to collaborate actively with actual wealthy people who shared their view that the estate tax should be preserved. For example, UFE and Public Citizen published a study of the eighteen wealthy families who had been bankrolling efforts to repeal the estate tax, and Hartman says that was often mentioned in news stories about the estate tax. When UFE was associated with Big Money United and later the Billionaires, their spoofs targeted candidates of both major political parties. The point, as one interviewee put it, was the "corruption of the democratic process" through big money from corporations and individuals, not the failings of one particular party.[82]

Political Antiritual

Unlike earlier African nobles with foreknowledge of a possible ritualized dunking by their subordinates, Armey and Tauzin were caught completely by surprise, embarrassed, and angered by the satirical infiltrators at their political ritual on Boston's Tea Party Ship. The visual message of the capsized Working Family Life Raft was so unmistakable, and potentially so damaging to their cause, that the Armey-Tauzin group reenacted tossing the trunk overboard after the life raft and its crew had exited the scene. UFE staffers, exhilarated by their success, were emboldened to try even more daring actions during subsequent presidential campaigns.

Subversions such as the 1998 Boston Tea Party prank are antirituals that have a destabilizing potential, whether by inviting retribution from those satirized or by stimulating wider protest or critical thought that can shape political change. These are difficult outcomes to trace through social scientific methods.

Actual rituals of reversal, such as the Barotse scene that opens this chapter, in Turner's view, accommodate both paradox and exultation: the subversive message and the successful caricature.[83] The absurdity of such reversals, he argues, has the effect of affirming regularity and hierarchy, illustrating the "reasonableness of everyday culturally predictable behavior" between individuals of different status.[84]

But such affirmation was not the outcome for participants in the 1998 Boston Tea Party Ship subversion, which was an unexpected rather than ritualized reversal. The politicians who were targeted, together with their staff, were very angry at the protesters. Boyd remembers Dick Armey's painful handshake, and Collins remarks that Armey's and Tauzin's political handlers "were going crazy." Barrali recalls that Armey and Tauzin "looked incredibly shocked and they appeared even more shocked by people dressed in suits all around them saying 'go ahead, sink 'em! . . . they're just the working poor. Who cares? Go ahead and sink 'em!'" In these respects, the 1998 Boston Tea Party was not a ritual that smoothed out tensions between power-holders and their opponents. Oral history interviews render these tensions legible in ways media accounts do not. Heartened by their 1990s feats, these Massachusetts activists turned their attention to a new presidential campaign.

4 Branded

Billionaires for Bush (and More)

"HEY! IT'S A BILLIONAIRE!" people on the street called out to the
Billionaires' musical maestro Clifford Tasner, who was wearing
his top hat and tuxedo as he walked back to Manhattan's Union Square around
3:00 A.M. after the Billionaires' 2004 Coronation Ball at the Frying Pan. Someone on Twenty-third Street called out to him, "Billionaires for Bush!" and he
chimed back, "Four More Wars!" "One great thing that all the New York Billionaire street actions had done," Tasner says, "was really communicate our *brand*
all around the City—so much so that even people hustling late at night knew
who we were and were amused by it."[1]

What's in a brand? Though the question is more likely to be asked of corporations than of protest groups, the tongue-in-cheek activists who call themselves Billionaires, as illustrated in this chapter and the next, became savvy
brand strategists, masters of "iconic image marketing" and "image-based difference."[2] With a red, white, and blue piggy bank as their logo, the Billionaires
built a brand around glossy graphics and attractive costumes, names that conveyed their core message, well-researched policy positions, website, buttons,
T-shirts, music CDs, and singing troupe (The Follies). The self-described
branding strategy of Billionaires for Bush (B4B):

> B4B has developed strong brand recognition. Every element of the campaign
> (from button to action to TV spot to website) is part of a deliberately crafted
> identity. Each element contains a consistent look and feel, and also bears our
> name, website and catchy logo. In this way we not only build the profile of the

organization but we engage in guerrilla political persuasion, because embedded in our very name and identity is a strong political argument: Billionaires are for Bush; Bush is for Billionaires; Bush caters to the interests of large corporations, not you.[3]

While other social justice activists are attentive to their public image, the Billionaires are especially purposeful in shaping these perceptions.[4] Their members include individuals with professional experience in public relations, and their leaders state they have "borrowed heavily from the mythmakers of Madison Avenue."[5] Striving to be polished, professional, glamorous, sexy, and witty, they style themselves as counter-traditional protesters and borrow legitimacy from the very worlds they critique.

At each stage—the 1999 Billionaires for Forbes, 2000 Billionaires for Bush (or Gore), and 2004 Billionaires for Bush—their organizational culture changed; their numbers and media coverage multiplied dramatically; and their "production values" (polish, professionalism, quality of signs and costumes) increased. By 2004 their national organization embraced the flashy, clean aesthetics that appeal to the MTV generation.[6] In that year, the Billionaire brand meant effervescence, wittiness, glamour, lightheartedness, and a hip, ironic sensibility. "Brands could conjure a feeling," Klein writes, and many found the Billionaires utterly charming.[7]

Behind every brand "success," however, is a story of careful timing as well as competing visions, surprises, conflicts, and ambivalence about particular tactics. The Billionaires are no exception. Their style did not blossom effortlessly but rather emerged from years of experimentation, especially the pioneering activities of predecessors discussed in the previous chapter. The discipline and hierarchy required in order to achieve a lustrous image sometimes clashed with the grassroots ethos of social movement activists, and some Billionaire events had a more ragtag appearance than others. Protecting their brand, as illustrated in this chapter and the next, required internal organizational discipline and monitoring. As one of the training documents distributed to members across the country puts it, "Brand identity is very important to Billionaires for Bush. One way to strengthen the Brand is to keep the look of Billionaires' projects consistent."[8] That document also reminds members to stay on message and to coordinate their activities with the organization's national leaders.

Since social movements in general have only weak control over participants, it is difficult for them to implement "any coherent or coordinated framing strategy at all."[9] Billionaire leaders had to mediate the tension between their desire to control the message and protect the brand image but at the same time expand "virally" or horizontally and tap the energy and creativity of DIY (do-it-yourself) techniques. Leaders of the organization's flagship New York City chapter hoped that new chapters would adopt the messaging and appearance standards they recommended. Yet, as Gamson comments, social movements usually "rely heavily on those whose commitments are normative and voluntary. If some participants are unwilling to follow directions, one can try to persuade them but there is little to prevent them from trying their own version of what they think will be more effective."[10]

The Billionaires—style mavericks in the protest world—mirror the corporate quest for brand magic. Following a brief consumer shift toward "brand blindness" and a sharp drop in advertising budgets in the late 1980s and early 1990s, corporate brands made a striking comeback.[11] "A new breed of companies," Naomi Klein writes, "saw themselves as 'meaning brokers' instead of product producers."[12] As production moved offshore into the hands of overseas contractors, companies have competed in what Klein terms "a race toward weightlessness: whoever owns the least, has the fewest employees on the payroll and produces the most powerful images, as opposed to products, wins the race."[13] Ad agencies since the late 1940s have pursued "brand essence," shifting attention away from products and "toward a psychological/anthropological examination of what brands mean to the culture and to people's lives"—generating "brand equity mania" and "logo inflation" by the 1980s.[14]

Intangibles—warmth, community, romance, sense of purpose—are the advertiser's quest.[15] Starbucks doesn't win customers just for its coffee; as the company's CEO, Howard Shultz, puts it, "It's the romance of the coffee experience, the feeling of warmth and community people get in Starbucks stores."[16] Political activists in turn should take lessons from advertising, which "circumvents reason, working with the magical, the personal, and the associative," argues media and culture scholar and Billionaire board member Duncombe.[17]

The Billionaires are "meaning brokers" who project an image of panache, urbanity, élan, and wit—more urban hipster than "heartland" farmer or machinist. They are cultivators of "attitude" who are plugged into the cultural zeitgeist, in sync with currents of popular culture such as *The Daily Show*, *The Colbert Report*, and *The Onion*. *Washington Post* reporter Hanna Rosin includes the Billionaires among political groups that exemplify "downtown cool and hipsterism" and are part of a new "cool frenzy" on the left.[18] The Billionaire known as Thurston Howell IV (Kurt Opprecht), a New York writer who appears in Richard Avedon's *New Yorker* photo of nine Billionaires, commented in 2008 that acquaintances implied he had earned "cool credits or kudos" when they discovered that he was a member of Billionaires for Bush in 2004.

Most striking is how the Billionaires deploy this branding strategy to pioneer a symbolic segmentation in the world of protest itself—a move that parallels in some respects a conspicuous divide in the corporate world since the 1990s. The corporate split, as Klein describes it, is between the "extra-premium 'attitude' brands that provide the essentials of lifestyle" (Nike, Reebok, Benetton, Calvin Klein), and the "deeply unhip big-box bargain stores that provide the essentials of life and monopolize a disproportionate share of the market (Wal-Mart et al.)."[19] Similarly, the Billionaires premise their brand on a distinction between their glamour on the one hand and popular cultural stereotypes of scruffy "angry liberal" protesters or 1960s holdovers on the other. The Billionaires themselves manufacture "image-based difference."[20] That's why they pose as counterprotesters and practice mock dismissal of so-called traditional protesters but at the same time view themselves as morale boosters and media magnets for "traditional" protestors when they show up as faux opponents at the same events. Their strategy is to turn media stereotypes to their advantage, and therefore to the advantage of the causes they espouse. Media relations specialist Lisa Witter termed the Billionaires for Bush "head turners" who are "ahead of the curve," because they "get culture" and they "make the whole progressive movement look good."[21]

Paradoxically these satirical hipsters have resurrected a forgotten brand image of conservatism as the domain of robber barons and failed economic policies, harkening back to the era eclipsed by the New Deal. Their satire works to reverse the great historic shift in the popular image of conservatism by rebranding it and associating it with economic injustice, the corruption of democracy, and the erosion of middle-class security, which in turn opens a political space for rebranding and reviving American progressive politics.

The Billionaires' debut in presidential campaign politics occurred in the winter of 1999 in New Hampshire. Here tactics of the creative activists featured in Chapter 3 were reborn.

Billionaires for Forbes, 1999

The 1999 presidential primary season in New Hampshire saw a commingling of protesters in furs, gowns, tuxedoes, and top hats carrying banners declaring, "Trillionaires for Trump," "Millionaires for Gore," "Billionaires for Bush," "Billionaires for Forbes," and "Tax Cuts for the Wealthy."[22] United for a Fair Economy staffers wanted "to spoof all the candidates beholden to big donors and corporations"—from any political party.[23] Extending their "nonpartisan educational parody," they experimented with names such as "Big Money United," a fictive coalition in support of all the candidates, with slogans such as "Because inequality is not growing fast enough."[24] And they recycled the Fat Cats' slogan "We are buy-partisan: we buy Republicans and we buy Democrats."[25] A Big Money United sign displayed the names of candidates Bush, Gore, Forbes, Trump, and "any of the above," with a box to check beside each option. The only box checked was "any of the above."

In March 1999, Steve Forbes's presidential candidacy and his advocacy of a flat 17-percent federal income tax caught the attention of Chuck Collins and his colleagues at United for a Fair Economy. Andrew Boyd said they viewed Forbes as particularly emblematic of the "rule of money eclipsing equal-access democracy." When they learned that Steve Forbes would announce his presidential candidacy on the steps of the State House in Concord, New Hampshire, on March 17, 1999,[26] Collins, Boyd, and colleagues deployed the same kind of careful advance planning, discipline, and precision practiced in their 1998 Boston Tea Party Ship spoof.

Describing that day in detail as we talked during lunch at New York's Algonquin Hotel, Collins said, "I remember thinking we have no idea what is going to happen."[27] As people assembled for Forbes's presidential candidacy announcement on the State House steps, he noticed that there seemed to be more media than ordinary citizens. A *New York Times* reporter estimated that about fifty people were present.[28] The reporters seemed bored, a participant remembered; journalists wondered how they were going to survive such activities for five months.

Well-dressed young people standing directly in front of Steve Forbes at Concord's State House cheered and waved signs and a banner declaring, "We Love You, Steve!" (with heart symbols) and "Run, Steve, Run!" As Forbes began to speak, those same enthusiasts interrupted him with applause and amped up the crowd, chanting, "Run, Steve, Run!" Then a secret signal and they flipped the banner over to reveal another: "Billionaires for Forbes, because inequality is not growing fast enough." New signs appeared along with chants such as "Tax Cuts for Me, Not My Maid."

When Steve Forbes's campaign manager saw what was happening, he walked over to Chuck Collins and the supposed young Republican fans and, as Collins put it, he "pulls my sign out and then they muscle us out, literally physically move us out of the frame." Boyd remembers "dagger eyes" from a Forbes campaign manager.

But it wasn't over. Collins had selected as their spokesperson one of their office interns, whom a staff member describes as a "golden boy . . . with beautiful blond hair, beautiful teeth . . . he looked like a college Republican, wore a suit . . . and he just glowed."[29] They had positioned this intern directly behind Steve Forbes. After the "Billionaires for Forbes" banner was unfurled, UFE's "golden boy" staffer held his own press conference. Since the press already had copies of the presidential candidacy announcement Forbes was making at that very moment, they pulled their cameras out of their tripods and turned their attention to the infiltrators. Golden Boy, as Collins recalls, told the reporters, "we don't understand why he's upset; we love Steve Forbes. Why do we love him? Because he's the only one who understands the real needs of us rich kids." Journalists asked Golden Boy, "Who are you?" and he said, "I'm Steve Newcombe [a pseudonym] and I want to work for Steve Forbes." "But who are you really?" the reporters asked, and he stuck to his ironic script saying, "I love Steve Forbes." When a journalist asked, "Well, are you attacking his policies?" Golden Boy replied, "Why would we attack him? He's our hero!"

Stepping out of his pose as a Forbes supporter, Collins then handed out a press release announcing, "Billionaires for Steve Forbes," which included on it the UFE phone number (which some reporters later called). Collins answered reporters' questions and told them he and his colleagues were forming an organization that would follow the Forbes campaign wherever it went, an idea journalists appeared to find quite interesting. "Everywhere he goes, we're going to be there to cheer him on," Collins repeated during his interviews, though he and his colleagues lacked the capacity to accomplish that. The Forbes campaign, he said, "took that [assertion] quite seriously, and they thought we were the Democratic Party. . . . 'Is James Carville behind you?' 'No, we love Steve Forbes so much, we want to be with him; he's the only one who understands us, the only one who understands the needs of true billionaires in our country.'"

"A SWAT operation" was Collins's assessment of UFE's stunt at Forbes's 1999 candidacy announcement. He had chosen as the faux young Republicans individuals in their twenties and thirties who could project a well-groomed image, and he screened out the "guys who looked like hippies, untrimmed beards . . . we just picked our crew."[30] They appeared to be business students and faculty from a nearby college. Andrew Boyd, who had participated in their brainstorming for the Forbes event, credits Collins with inventing the "Billionaires for [X]" moniker.[31] Collins then elaborated the concept with Boyd and members of the Class Acts theater troupe in Boston. This test run of the Billionaires for [X] meme was a media hit that paved the way for a vast expansion on a national scale.

"If Steve Forbes had played along," Collins said, there would have been no problem: "If he could have been funny, he could have laughed this off, but he's *irony-deficient*. Do we want a president who is irony-deficient, who cannot take a joke?"[32] Euphoric after the Forbes spoof, a participant said, "we completely hijacked" Forbes's presidential candidacy announcement."[33] "Again, the lesson," Boyd remarked, was "you can get away with a lot of stuff. We're not professional spies or anything, you know."[34]

As with the 1998 Boston Tea Party Ship prank, exhilaration over the success of their satire was mixed with ambivalent feelings of sympathy for those whose event they had upended. Boyd reflected:

> You feel bad about it too . . . because here it's his campaign and you know how difficult it is to run a campaign, and we're like totally f*** it up. And we're lying to them. . . . I mean, you know the guy is lying to the people and he's a billionaire and he's trying to make more money for the superrich, so it's justified, but that doesn't mean you feel good about it. I don't."

I then asked, "How long do those feelings last, and how do they mix with feelings of exhilaration and triumph?" Boyd replied that the peer group's admiration overpowers ambivalent empathy:

> Your peer group is much more powerful than some campaign manager who gives you dagger eyes or some thug of the campaign manager who shunts you out of the way or something. But your peer group is like, "Man, that's so cool!" and you tell those stories and people say, "Dude, that was rad!" you know . . . so all that . . . actually becomes much more powerful, much stronger reinforcement.

Ambivalence resurfaced when Boyd later met Forbes's campaign manager at another New Hampshire event the Billionaires tried to subvert. Boyd said the campaign manager "was just hating me," and that made him uncomfortable even though he thought his colleagues' actions were completely justified.

Mike Lapham, another participant in the spoof at the Forbes presidential candidacy announcement, also expressed ambivalence: "I did stop and think about it a little bit, and considered whether it is a fair tactic."[35] Yet again he was motivated by the difficulty of getting the press to "pay attention to inequality . . . [and] the way rules are tilted to favor the wealthy" without using tactics such as street theater. Steve Forbes, he said, was "all about helping rich people get richer," and his candidacy announcement offered an opportunity to make that point.

The Billionaires for Forbes debut, like the 1998 Boston Tea Party Ship prank, generated national media coverage. Even brief mentions of the Billionaires for Forbes in news accounts delighted members, who knew that their message could be conveyed by simply mentioning their organization's name. The *New York Times* reported that "Mr. Forbes's remarks were disrupted by a few hecklers, some wearing fur coats, who called themselves Billionaires for Forbes."[36] The *Boston Globe* mentioned United for a Fair Economy, Billionaires for Forbes, and their banner's slogan, "Because inequality is not growing fast enough," along with their point that "Forbes's flat tax would shelter rich investors and sock middle-class wage earners."[37] The *New Hampshire Union Leader* also named the Billionaires for Forbes and referred to them as "a group of young people . . . dressed in expensive suits and dresses," heckling the candidate.[38] Two days later another article in the same paper referred to "Billionaires for Forbes" as "social-ist wealth redistributors . . . a bunch of frustrated mimes" and the same "rabble" who "crashed" the 1998 Armey-Tauzin event on the Boston Tea Party Ship.[39]

Newspaper accounts, in short, varied from playing along with the satire—neither condemning nor praising the Billionaires' message—to disparaging the protesters and depicting them as marginal leftists, although the Billionaires' position accorded with centrist democratic impulses that have a long history in the United States. A brief televised account of Forbes's candidacy announce-ment on Fox News included the following words from correspondent Carl Cameron: "But the flat tax has critics. A brief scuffle occurred when protesters unveiled a 'Billionaires for Forbes' sign, accusing Forbes of supply-side eco-nomics to help the rich."[40]

The Billionaires for Forbes appeared again about a month later at a Ports-mouth event, where Forbes was to bury the U.S. tax code on tax day in sym-bolic allusion to a similar Revolutionary War action in which "New Hampshire farmers held a mock funeral for one of King George's tax decrees."[41] Here the Billionaires for Forbes staged a New Orleans-style funeral in celebration of the burial of the tax code and all the government programs likely to be cut thanks to the $200 billion "shortfall Forbes's flat tax would create—public education, Social Security, environmental protection . . . we toasted the demise of public education."[42] Collins says that here "again it was taking his [Forbes's] message but just taking it over the top."[43] That day, as they had done at Forbes's candidacy announcement, Collins said, the Billionaires assembled a very photogenic group, with women "dressed to the nines in elegant evening gowns, and we all had little champagne glasses and we actually had New Orleans-style musicians." By this time Collins was getting to know Forbes's campaign manager a bit, and the latter "just tried to wall us off; they wouldn't let us in; again we did our own press conference. During Steve's speech we were toasting and yelling, you know just being rowdies and cheering him on: 'Yay, Steve!' We were like the over-the-top gang." Their actions caused Forbes's campaign manager "a lot of stress," according to Collins, and the campaign later shifted to indoor events, at which attendees were screened. The *New Hampshire Union Leader* reported that the Billionaires for Forbes staged their own "pretend funeral . . . [with coffins, one of which had a notice that read 'The Flat Tax Will Bury Working Americans.'"[44]

There were just three Billionaires for Forbes actions, and that was enough to show participants the potential of the new brand and approach. Collins recalls that "the testing with Forbes was where we really saw that this has potential for chapters, and "we could see the viral potential" for organizing.[45] A member of the Class Acts theater troupe who participated in the Forbes events (Andy Hermann) found the approach tested in 1999 to be much more effective and pleasing to the public than traditional street theater: "First, crashing someone else's event gives you something to shape your own performance around, and it builds in an inherent sense of drama that is difficult to achieve when people are shuffling past you on the street. Second, the presence of the media allows you the possibility of reaching a far wider audience."[46] While he too is critical of dominant news organizations, he added that "If the other side can get the media's attention, then your side had better be able to as well, or your message is going to get drowned out." In sum, the 1999 presidential primary season offered a testing ground for a Boston network of satirical activists who attracted national media coverage when they used ironic humor and polished visuals to convey a sharp countermessage at official political events. Out of these experiments emerged a much larger vision of the political potential of the Billionaires for [X] approach.

Billionaires for Bush (or Gore), 2000

In 1999 and 2000 the Billionaires "rode the wave" of the lively global social justice movement, as one of their lead singers, Fonda Sterling (Victoria Olson), put it.[47] The 1999 Seattle WTO protests marked the larger global movement's appearance in the United States. By the early 2000s, such activism was "seeing a renewal unparalleled since the thirties," writes Naomi Klein.[48] The Billionaires avoided the giant puppets that were popular at such protests, but they embraced the economic justice agenda.

The 1999 Seattle WTO protests occurred about eight months after the 1999 launch of the short-lived Billionaires for Forbes and just a few months before the debut of Billionaires for Bush (or Gore). Some of the proto-Billionaires described in the previous chapter (who included Billionaires for Forbes participants) marched against the WTO in Seattle in 1999, or later joined protests at meetings of the World Bank, IMF, and World Economic Forum, as well as demonstrations targeting outsized corporate mergers or media consolidation. In 1999 the Billionaires' parent organization, United for a Fair Economy, had an outpost office in Seattle, and they and various affiliates organized workshops on globalization and the WTO, trained speakers, and worked on neighborhood organizing.[49] United for a Fair Economy staged a march behind a "Big Money United" banner during the large legal protest in Seattle, and the Precision Cell Phone Drill Team performed skits there as well. Boyd recalls a group marching under a "Billionaires for [various presidential candidates]" banner in the WTO protests.[50] "We briefly saw action at the Battle in Seattle, where we bravely stood up for the right to own genetically modified organisms," he said during his oral history "homily" at the Billionaires' "Last Huzzah" celebration in Manhattan in January 2009.

In 2000, Andrew Boyd and his associates decided to focus on the key theme that had worked in the 1999 Seattle WTO events organized by United for a Fair Economy, namely democracy versus corporate power. They hoped to "link up with efforts to reform the campaign finance system and combat domestic economic inequality."[51] In January 2000, they joined other protesters in New Hampshire outside a presidential debate, called themselves "Big Money United," and chanted "Bush, Forbes, Trump, Gore, we don't care who you vote for!"[52]

Once it became clear that George Bush and Al Gore would be presidential nominees in 2000, the Billionaires' cofounders made two key decisions. First, they decided to target candidates of both major political parties by naming their network Billionaires for Bush (or Gore). Second, they sensed the potential for massive expansion and decided to allow "viral" grassroots growth of the organization[53] rather than opting for a strongly centralized and hierarchical structure, and rather than confining themselves to the image-conscious screening of participants and the close management that had been practiced at the key 1999 Billionaires for Forbes events and the 1998 Boston Tea Party Ship diversion. Both decisions proved controversial. Yet success, measured by a rapid multiplication of local chapters and a growing media profile, overshadowed objections until after the 2004 election.

Why target both Bush and Gore? United for a Fair Economy answered as follows in an August 2000 press release: "Even though Bush and Gore differ on some policies and sometimes wear different-colored power ties, both candidates are deeply committed to ignoring economic inequality."[54] Both candidates, stated the press release, "oppose raising the minimum wage to the cost of living," support keeping wages low in order to keep profits high, and "support corporate-managed trade through bodies like the WTO and IMF." For similar reasons, Ralph Nader dismissed politicians from both major parties in 2000 as "Republicrats."[55]

The Billionaires "created a stylish logo by splicing together a donkey and elephant [symbols of the Democratic and Republican parties] and a 'candidate' by digitally morphing photos of Bush and Gore into a single eerie image."[56] That technical feat, a UFE staffer remarked, was enabled by Boyd's "incredible talent for gathering talent around him; he would get these people who had unbelievable skills that we certainly didn't have on staff," such as digital face-morphing technology.[57]

The debut of Billionaires for Bush (or Gore) occurred at the massive April 16, 2000, demonstrations during the annual meeting of the World Bank and International Monetary Fund in Washington, DC. Boyd helped organize their appearance and also worked with Reclaim the Streets members and others to mobilize the satirical IMF Loan Sharks, who formed an affinity group for the April 16 protests.[58] The IMF Loan Sharks wore shark noses and fins atop their heads, dressed in grey tuxedos,[59] and were accompanied by the Hungry March Band. Duncombe describes his participation in that April 2000 march with the IMF Loan Sharks, who got to know one another's politics and "strengths and weaknesses . . . fears and hopes" as they held meetings in New York to discuss the politics and economics of the World Bank and IMF before going to Washington, DC.[60] He recalls that they "form[ed] kick lines in the street while belting out our version of 'Mack the Knife.'"[61] One glimpses the logistical challenges and resourcefulness required for such events by considering how Andrew Boyd and a fellow activist friend managed to acquire one hundred tuxedoes for the Loan Sharks to wear during the April 16, 2000, march in Washington, DC. Boyd obtained all the shark noses and organized people to cut out the shark fins from blue and gray material, and then he and his colleague Lois Canright arranged a barter deal to trade her canoe for one hundred tuxedoes from a community youth center in New York.[62]

Billionaires for Bush (or Gore) was "such a hit" at the A16 (April 16) demonstrations that Boyd decided that for the next four or five months he would "work like a maniac" on that organization, create a website, and stage a "Million Billionaire March" at the two national political party conventions.[63] Boyd became the de facto leader of the Billionaires for Bush (or Gore) in 2000 and of Billionaires for Bush in 2004. In 2000, he assembled "a team of talented volunteer designers, media producers, and veteran street theater activists," as he co-organized Billionaires for Bush (or Gore) with help from networks such as Reclaim the Streets, Lower East Side Collective, attendees of Burning Man festivals,[64] volunteers from Wesley Clark's and other presidential campaigns, and initial support from United for a Fair Economy.[65] They created posters, bumper stickers, buttons, and an award-winning website (http://www.billionairesforbushorgore.com). Boyd and his team also made mock radio ads and compiled political materials such as "a political platform, a full campaign speech, and a candidate product comparison chart," all of it adding up to a polished look and coherent multimedia message.[66]

By June 2000, "wildcat chapters were springing up," Boyd writes, and by the time of the Republican convention in late July that year, the Billionaires "were already a minor sensation" and their "website was getting one hundred thousand hits a day (twenty thousand unique page views)."[67] Those numbers shot up to two hundred thousand hits per day during the Democratic convention in Los Angeles in August.[68]

"The idea of a large-scale mobilization of Billionaires, a real battalion of Billionaires," Chuck Collins recalls, became a reality in 2000, when they appeared at both the Democratic and Republican national party conventions (in Los Angeles and Philadelphia) to continue their "nonpartisan educational parody."[69] Their Million Billionaire March at both political party conventions attracted national media coverage.[70] At the 2000 Democratic convention in Los Angeles, the Billionaires for Bush (or Gore), as announced in a UFE press release, "crown[ed] their two-headed candidate BushGore, as members play[ed] 'Hail to the Chief' on hundreds of kazoos."[71] The Billionaires performed in the streets and at parallel political party conventions cosponsored by UFE with groups such as Common Cause, Sojourners, and Public Campaign.

During the 2000 Republican convention in Philadelphia, the Billionaires for Bush (or Gore) held a vigil for corporate welfare and—echoing their Yippie ancestors—"attempted to levitate the interest rate by linking arms around the Federal Reserve and conducting a séance."[72] Boyd writes that "[n]early a hundred Billionaires in full dress joined us in the streets, chanting, singing, burning [fake] money, smoking cigars. We . . . auctioned off merchandising rights to the Liberty Bell. . . . The media were all over us. . . . My Billionaire character, Phil T. Rich, became a hit on the radio interview circuit. . . . An editor at *The Nation* called us 'the sea turtles of the convention protests.'"[73] The "sea turtles" comparison invokes a famous bit of street theater in the huge 1999 anti-WTO demonstration in Seattle, when environmentalist protesters dressed as sea turtles formed a counterintuitive alliance with teamsters, marching together amid shouts of "Turtles love teamsters!" and "Teamsters love turtles!"

The Billionaires confronted competing humorists in the streets during the 2000 Philadelphia convention protests. Boyd spoke of "pitched battle with the Radical Clown Front, who tried to throw us off our guard with their Dada chants . . . but we kept our nerve and prevailed."[74] The Revolutionary Anarchist Clown Bloc showed up in street protests "in rainbow wigs, others fiddling around with four-foot-high bicycles, playing makeshift instruments, singing songs."[75] Examples of Dada chants include "Three Word Chant! Four Words Are Better! Hey-hey! Ho-ho! Hey-hey-ho-ho-has-got-to-go. Hey-yey! Ho-ho! Haa-ha-ha-ha-ha-ha!"[76]

As the Billionaire network burgeoned in 2000, its founders modified the original "viral" model and it evolved into a hub-node structure that included some message control and central coordination.[77] The Billionaires' website had a place for new chapters to register, though not all of them did so; some were what Boyd terms "wildcat chapters." While UFE played a coordinating role in the early months, eventually the Billionaires' New York City chapter took on that role as UFE delinked from the Billionaires in the early 2000s.[78] Initially, as Boyd describes it, "UFE became the organizational hub of an ad hoc network of Do-It-Yourself movement grouplets . . . UFE was providing funding, infrastructure, research capacity, media contacts, and mainstream legitimacy. The grassroots injected energy, street smarts, and creative elaboration of core ideas."[79] Participants debated the merits of controlling the message; as one chapter head put it, "they really hoped that if they did a slam-dunk job on signs and having everything so user-friendly that you could just go to the website and get an action off the website that they wouldn't have as much problem with message wandering. And I've been out on the streets with the Billionaires, and it still wanders [laughs]; it's hard to control, there's no doubt about it."[80]

Recognizing the risks in the "viral" strategy, the organization's founders decided the best approach would be to put together a good handbook and website with tips on how to stage Billionaire actions, "and then let many flowers
blossom."[81] Their 2000 website included a "Be a Billionaire" section from which
members could select satirical names for themselves, pick up fashion tips, and
download posters, slogans, and sample press releases.[82] Ideally, as chapters tried
out new materials, they would "fix bugs and add features," and "best practices"
would be "integrated into version 2.0, and the process repeats."[83]

Coordinating such feedback from local chapters, however, required national
staff and resources that often exceeded the organization's actual capacities. Such
challenges—together with calls from some for closer monitoring of brand conformity or message discipline and quality (of press releases, signs, costumes)
among local chapters—were the focus of much deliberation (and occasional
minor conflict) within the organization for several years. These tensions in part
reflected long-standing differences between building decentralized, grassroots
social movements on the one hand, and establishing organizations or institutions on the other.[84] In addition, they emerged from the particular relationship
between the "loosely-affiliated Billionaires grassroots base and United for a Fair
Economy's mission which required building organizational muscle and clout
in order to pursue a broad social justice agenda over the long haul."[85] Unlike
the Billionaires, a UFE consultant remarked, UFE "is not really a membership
organization; instead its forte is providing analysis and value-added popular
education to other organizations."[86] Frictions over these competing missions,
however, were accompanied by "a great deal of synchronicity" and synergy.[87]

During the 2000 presidential campaign, the satirical Billionaires' network
grew to about fifty-five chapters.[88] How did it do so? A UFE staffer was amazed
at how fast Billionaires for Bush (or Gore) spread across the country even
though UFE put "no staff on that" and could offer few resources.

On the one hand, the Billionaires' approach "demonstrate[d] the potential
of the web for disseminating not just information, but ready-made organizing
and message-making tools" that do not require much bureaucracy or hierarchy.[89] On the other hand, as a member of the Billionaires' governing board
commented, it is difficult to control a grassroots network of activists, and it was
sometimes hard for the organization's leaders "to rein people in if the quality
was bad or the politics were wrong." Staying on message, the board member
continued, meant staying away from controversial "cultural" issues, by which
they meant abortion and religion (which are in any case difficult to address

through ironic humor), and focusing instead on the core issue of "growing economic inequality and the corruption of the democratic process through big money, big corporate money and rich people's money."[90] The wider the network, the more challenging it became to maintain control of the message and the image—to protect the brand.

The national network's New York leadership tried to protect the Billionaire brand by dissuading other chapters from departing markedly from the organization's intended focus on economic fairness. At the same time, Boyd remarks, "everyone has a different vision" and there needs to be space for innovators with good ideas. The ideal, he said, was to "lead by example."[91] "If you give people a fun and seemingly effective and easy-to-enact way to participate," Boyd said, "then people leap at it; that's a central lesson."[92] He saw the role of a flagship chapter as one "where you're pushing the envelope, and then people can follow that lead and you create a lot of space; you create a strong concept that makes intuitive sense and that is inspiring to replicate, but then you create enough space for people to give it their own stamp, their own personal flavor."[93]

Some Billionaires had roots in the direct action community[94] and others in more conventional political campaigns (or both), and they did not always agree about organizational tactics or identity. Yet Billionaires for Bush (or Gore) effectively brought together individuals from the direct action left who, as Boyd put it, have a lot of "moxie and . . . cultural savvy and willingness to do anything," and more mainstream advocates of campaign finance reform. Boyd suggested that he was able to recruit members from both communities because he "had one foot in each of them," given his prior experience with United for a Fair Economy, Reclaim the Streets, and Direct Action Network.

The strategic capacity of a social movement is enhanced when leadership teams include "insiders" and "outsiders," when leaders' sociocultural networks include both strong and weak ties to diverse constituencies, and when leaders' collective action repertoires are diverse, Ganz argues.[95] The globalization movement in 1999 and 2000, for example, combined anticorporate and anticapitalist activists.[96] Furthermore, as Ganz writes, "[p]ersons with 'borderlands' experience of straddling cultural or institutional worlds" are often able to make innovative contributions to social movement strategy.[97]

Many new members of the satirical Billionaires joined as self-recruits after encountering media coverage of a Billionaire event, visiting the organization's website, or witnessing a street action. Boyd and others at the organizational hub would receive emails or phone calls from people in other parts of the country saying they had started to put together a local chapter and were looking for suggestions on how to piggyback on events such as a local visit from the nation's president or vice president. In addition to self-recruitment, membership multiplied through mobilizing structures rooted in existing organizations.[98] Interpersonal ties—those "created by or within the movement itself"—are particularly vital for retaining members and are underplayed in "structural" analyses of social movement organization.[99] Such relationships played a key role in the expansion of the Billionaires' network in 2000 and 2004.

Billionaires Between Elections, 2000–2003

The Billionaires are an episodic organization, intensifying during national presidential campaigns and then reappearing, in various guises, in intervening years. While about a half dozen New York Billionaire members were particularly active between the 2000 election and mid-2003, many had to curtail commitments to the organization to make up for hours lost in their jobs and professional activities during the height of the 2000 campaign. Robin Eublind remained an active organizer as Andrew Boyd scaled back his involvement to an advisory role after the 2000 and 2004 elections. Between the 2000 and 2004 national elections, even without the immediate motivation of a presidential campaign, members remained in contact through listservs, social gatherings, other forms of activism, and the staging of an occasional Billionaire event (especially in New York, Los Angeles, Portland, and Boston). Some remained networked via websites such as ArtandPolitics.com.[100]

Billionaire activities were in sync not only with presidential election cycles but also with wider social movement currents. The late-1990s wave of protests hit a trough after the September 11, 2001, attacks and then surged again in the United States beginning in 2002 and during the lead-up to the 2003 Iraq invasion, peaking during the 2004 presidential campaign, and then rising again in 2011 during global antiausterity protests and the emergence of Occupy Wall Street. The Billionaires drew energy between the 2000 and 2004 presidential campaigns from public outrage over the Enron scandal, antiwar protests, more lenient rules about media mergers, and meetings of the World Economic Forum.

By 2002, a participant in her twenties said, "the messaging was improving, the costumes were improving and it was a lot more targeted, like focusing on Enron, taking that very, very hot topic and creating this theater around

Enron—amazing!"[101] New York Billionaires posed as counterprotesters at events such as the February 2002 World Economic Forum meetings in New York (appearing as Billionaires for Bush or Bloomberg and as WEF Billionaires: Wasn't Enron Fun); a March 2002 protest against the FCC's approval of media mergers, in Washington, DC (Billionaires for More Media Mergers); an October 2002 national march for peace in Washington, DC; the February 2003 worldwide demonstration for peace; and a March 2003 United for Peace and Justice march against the Iraq war (Billionaires for Bush's War). In the early 2000s, Los Angeles Billionaire Clifford Tasner (Felonious Ax) wrote subversive lyrics to familiar tunes and produced Billionaire music CDs (*The Billionaires Are in the House, Never Mind the Rabble,* and *Stay the Course*), which helped to energize The Follies singing troupe and others.

When George W. Bush became president—thanks to the Supreme Court's 2000 ruling in his favor—and implemented even more conservative policies than many had expected, and when Ralph Nader's role in the 2000 election attracted growing criticism from non-Republicans, some faulted the Billionaires for Bush (or Gore) for having targeted candidates of both major political parties. For example, a West Coast Billionaire reports that at a community meeting of Democrats in 2000, when the topic of Billionaires for Bush (or Gore) came up, "a guy was fuming about it and screaming" at her because he thought the organization's focus on both candidates contributed to Gore's loss by blurring the distinctions between Bush and Gore.[102] Debates about whether or not to focus on presidential candidates of both major parties proved especially divisive for the Billionaires in 2004. In addition, some were displeased with the 2004 shift toward a more hierarchical, centrally governed organization that contrasted with the more decentralized, consensus-driven approach of the Lower East Side Collective and Reclaim the Streets networks from which a number of early Billionaires had been recruited.

Late 2003 marked a sharp change in the Billionaires' strategy and sponsorship, as leaders made the contentious decision to spotlight Bush alone during the 2004 presidential campaign. When the Billionaires changed their focus to Bush, they delinked from United for a Fair Economy—a 501(c)(3) nonprofit, nonpartisan organization—which had been the parent organization of Billionaires for Forbes in 1999 and Billionaires for Bush (or Gore) in 2000. In 2003, the organization incorporated as Billionaires, Inc., "a nonprofit, nonpartisan corporation, organized under Section 527 of the I.R.S. tax code."[103] In 2004 the Billionaires established modestly paid positions for a webmaster (Matthew

Skomarovsky, aka Seymour Benjamins), CEO/Schmoozer-in-Chief (Andrew Boyd, aka Phil T. Rich), and national field coordinator (Alice Meaker, aka Iona Bigga Yacht)—three key positions which a member described as the "heart-beat of the organization."[104] Executive council members estimate that possibly $150,000–$200,000 were raised to support the Billionaires for Bush during the first half of 2004, about ten times the funds raised in the Billionaires' 2000 campaign. Even so, it was difficult to fund salaried positions, and those occupy-ing them worked many unpaid hours as the organization expanded and activi-ties intensified. In July 2004, a news account quoted the Billionaires' head of public relations, Pam Perd, as saying their need for more funding is "the irony of the Billionaires."[105] Another source, quoting PoliticalMoneyLine's website, states that the Billionaires had raised $37,575 by August 2004, and that their top donor, Michael Kieschnick (president of Working Assets), gave $12,000.[106] The Billionaires raised money through merchandise sales (CDs, buttons, books, T-shirts, bumper stickers), parties and balls, and networking with pri-vate donors. At the January 2005 Billionaire "Convergence" (a national meeting in Washington, DC, during the week of the presidential inauguration), Alan Greenspend presented a document with fund-raising tips, titled "Stuffing the Pig: Fundraising and the Joys of Schmoozing." The Billionaires did not keep all of the proceeds of their fund-raising for their own organization; in August 2005, for example, they donated part of the money from a fund-raiser to the Poor People's Economic Human Rights campaign.[107]

Comparing the 2000 and 2004 Billionaire organizations, Boyd commented in 2004, "We sort of went on instinct last time [2000] . . . it's more conscious now."[108] Whereas in 2000 the Billionaires for Bush (or Gore) had mobilized just a few months before that year's presidential election, for the 2004 campaign they began about a year in advance, built a "stronger infrastructure" (Boyd's term), and were able to take full advantage of the Internet and text messaging on mobile phones.[109]

The supercharged anti-Bush sentiment in 2004 boosted Billionaires for Bush membership numbers and energies. During the 2004 presidential cam-paign, political scientist Ken Sherrill (Hunter College, NY) commented to a *New York Times* reporter: "I haven't seen this kind of passion and activism in this country since 1968 or '72. The sheer intensity of the anger is really extraor-dinary, the kind of thing you usually associate with the religious right."[110]

Furthermore, during the 2004 campaign season, dissent that had been "staved off" in post–9/11 America could be "contained as part of our business as usual," cartoonist Art Spiegelman writes.[111] In 2004, dissenting messages carried new force as they entered a public arena enlivened by the launch of the progressive Air America radio (featuring Al Franken), Jon Stewart's satirical televised news program on Comedy Central's *Daily Show*, Michael Moore's film *Fahrenheit 9/11*, advocacy groups such as MoveOn.org and America Coming Together, the documentary *Outfoxed: Rupert Murdoch's War on Journalism*, and critical best-selling books by former Bush administration insiders such as Treasury secretary Paul O'Neill and counterterrorism adviser Richard Clarke.[112]

The decision to become Billionaires for Bush—rather than Billionaires for Bush (or Kerry)—mirrored a broader shift in public opinion and political party identities. A larger share of the population now perceived sharp differences between the two major parties: "Republicans cut taxes on the rich and try to shrink government benefits and undermine the welfare state. Democrats raise taxes on the rich while trying to expand government benefits and strengthen the welfare state."[113] (By 2010, however, many Democrats too seemed increasingly reluctant to raise taxes on the superrich.) An early Billionaire participant said: "In 2004 ... we realized our mistake, that Bush and Gore were not similar in politics, that Bush was much more extreme than we had known, and we were aware of this problem as early as 2003 when we started talking about [how] ... it's not going to be 'Billionaires for Bush or whoever the Democratic nominee is.'"[114]

"I think what we learned from 2004," Boyd explains, is that "you can make the ... broader critique as you try to throw your weight behind a particular outcome, you can ... critique corporate capture of government by still saying that one party is a lot more captured than the other party [chuckles]. ... So that's what we tried to do in 2004, and I feel like it worked pretty well"[115]; "I'm very glad we didn't go 'Billionaires for Bush or Kerry' at that moment, but I'm not unhappy that some other groups sprouted up to do that."[116] Similarly, the "Naderite insight that both parties are corrupted by wealth," another member (Jeremy Varon) commented in 2004, "is provisionally true, but we can't afford the luxury of systemic critique right now."[117] He felt a sense of "heightened stakes" in the 2004 election, which "had the aura of Armageddon."[118]

In short, even though both Democrats and Republicans were part of an apparatus that stymied campaign finance reform and other changes, Billionaire organizers saw Bush as the more dangerous man who should be the target of critique in 2004. Varon (Merchant F. Arms) remarked on how widespread and intense that sentiment was: "It's really amazing how big a tent Kerry has— through no virtue of his own—that people are that upset at Bush." Energizing the Billionaires for Bush in 2004 was a presidential administration criticized by many for starting a war in Iraq, and for discouraging public debate through practices such as censoring scientific studies about climate change that did not reinforce the administration's own stance, screening out critical citizens from the president's "town meetings," and controlling critical journalists' access to the president.

Some members nonetheless opposed the Billionaires' decision to alter their two-party focus, drifted away from the organization after that, and joined other activists such as Greene Dragon[119] or Critical Mass bike rides. A woman in her thirties who had participated since 2000 criticized the Billionaires' decision to focus only on the Republican candidate as a missed opportunity to highlight the corrupting role of big money in politics in both major political parties:

> [The decision] squandered so much of the momentum and political depth the project had in the first place . . . because the whole vision of Billionaires for Bush (or Gore) in the beginning was that we were really going to be able to explain that corporate money in politics . . . corrupted both sides of the aisle, that yes, Republicans got more corporate money but the corporate money the Democrats got was nothing to sneeze at and really had negative influences over politics. . . . When we were first doing the Billionaire stuff in 1999 and 2000, we were talking about plutocracy, rule by the rich; that's the real issue, not one party we don't happen to like at the moment.[120]

She added that in 2000, when reporters would often get the group's name wrong and omit the "or Gore" component, members would correct them: "We're buy-partisan; we buy both parties."

In addition to the divide between those who favored targeting both major political party candidates and those who did not, some Billionaires in 2004 talked about two cultures within their organization. They described a "cultural clash" equivalent to "Burning Man meets MoveOn.org"—referring to a membership contrast between artists who frequent events such as Burning Man on the one hand, and others rooted in more conventional political and professional worlds on the other, including corporate professions such as public relations and law. A slightly different interpretation came from a man on the New York Billionaires' executive council who said to me in early July 2004 that the clash was more like "Burning Man meets DNC" (Democratic National Committee), in the sense that he thought the Billionaires were moving (or should move) toward a more mainstream or (though he said he didn't like to use the term) "legitimate" organizational identity than MoveOn, which he termed "marginal" compared to the DNC.[121]

While the Billionaires for Bush appeared to have a "countercultural" or "neo-Yippie vibe," Merchant F. Arms (Jeremy Varon) said, "the trappings are more radical than the actual message or goal." As a historian who specializes in the 1960s, an author of a book on that era's social movements,[122] and a coeditor of a journal called *The Sixties*, Varon is well placed for such observations. The Billionaires, he said, are "really in the service of completely above-board establishment, democracy-by-the-books electoral strategy"—progressive reformism rather than radicalism. Theirs was "a politics of make America fairer, redistribute the wealth, make the American middle class viable, and vote George Bush out of office." The Yippies, by contrast, "thought the entire political establishment was corrupt . . . they didn't even believe in McCarthy in 1968; it was a politics of smash the system."[123]

In 2004, the intense focus on defeating Bush softened such divides, which became topics of friendly jokes rather than polarizing debate among the Billionaires. When members were informally mingling before a planning meeting in New York, for example, I heard a man in his early forties who sought "mainstream" status for the Billionaires gently tease an experienced activist in his thirties about being an "anarchist."[124]

The (Karl) Rove Action, 2004

An escapade known as the "Rove action," carefully planned and executed by a small group of insiders in February 2004, was a turning point for the Billionaires for Bush.[125] About one hundred protesters from various groups had gathered outside a Republican fund-raising reception at a Manhattan nightclub where Karl Rove was the guest speaker (an event that raised $400,000 for the Bush-Cheney campaign).[126] A witty *New York Times* article recounts the tale, which begins as follows[127]: "As hundreds of guests with invitations waited to pass through velvet barriers to enter the club, a small group of men in bowler hats and women in gowns marched up, chanting, 'Four more wars' and 'Re-elect Rove.'" Participant Andrew Boyd recalls the Billionaires marching toward the entrance of the club where Karl Rove was to speak and chanting, "'Karl Rove is Innocent! Karl Rove is Innocent!': People stopped to look, and behind their curious faces, you could almost hear the mental gears clicking: 'Innocent? . . . hmmmm . . . so, wait . . . what's he not guilty of?' And we had a long list of all that he was 'not guilty of' (push-polling, misinformation, Machiavellian dirty tricks, etc.) laid out in a leaflet, which we handed them."[128]

At first, security agents and other protesters mistook the Billionaires for Bush for a pro-Rove group when they marched over to join Republican supporters, on the opposite side of the street from Sierra Club protesters and other anti-Bush groups—who then heckled the Billionaires: "'We want the truth and we want it now!' the Sierra protesters shouted. The Billionaires shouted back, 'Buy your own president!'"[129] The police eventually caught on and then escorted the Billionaires to the same pen as the Sierra Club protesters. That was only a prelude to the drama that followed:

> A black town car pulled up and out stepped a man whom the crowd assumed to be Mr. Rove. "There is Karl Rove," people shouted. Reporters, photographers and television cameramen swarmed the man, but the police pushed them back. Another man lifted the velvet rope to let him enter. But the would-be Mr. Rove walked over to the crowd of protesters and began shaking hands, when finally, again, this was seen to be a joke. It was not Mr. Rove, but an actor playing the part.[130]

A woman who participated in the protest said to me that the Rove action "was fantastic; we not only fooled security and the counterprotesters, but we also fooled our own people because they didn't realize that our Karl Rove was actually our friend Tony [Rip Torn's son Tony Torn, who had a small part playing one of the husbands in the remake of the movie *Stepford Wives*]."[131]

Sheer delight appears on Billionaires' faces when the Rove event is mentioned. They "scrambled reality for a brief shining moment," as Varon put it. For him, the Rove action was the organization's "apogee," its "best action." "What was cool," he says, "was that we really pulled off the most Situationist action insofar as it was about five minutes of confusion among everybody as to what exactly was going on."[132] "The police were confused and the protesters were confused and I was confused and thought that 'Karl Rove' was really Karl Rove and started yelling at him because I wasn't in on the joke ahead of time . . . CNN was fooled, *Time* was fooled, the *New York Times* was fooled."[133]

The Billionaires experienced the "Rove action" as an exhilarating success that helped to establish their public identity (at least among readers of publications such as the *New York Times*) during the 2004 campaign season as clever, witty, lighthearted protesters. As a member in her thirties put it, "The Karl Rove action, I think, really put us on the map."[134] A few months after the Rove event, a

New York Times article about novel protest tactics referred to the Billionaires for Bush as "one of the better known of the theatrical protest groups."[135] Such external portrayals of the group were quickly absorbed into their self-representations and self-images. Mainstream media coverage, for most members, indexed success for the organization.

"I Sleep in My Tuxedo"

Their "golden hour" is how Phil T. Rich described the 2004 Billionaires when he addressed their 2009 "Last Huzzah" celebration in Manhattan. The launch had been modest. In early January 2004, a half dozen or so people gathered in a SoHo loft for the first meeting of Billionaires for Bush. They included Andrew Boyd (Phil T. Rich), Robin Eublind, Victoria Olson (Fonda Sterling), Olive Oilfields, Pam Perd, and an attorney. Several knew one another previously through Lower East Side activist, artistic, and performance networks. At least one (Pam Perd) had substantial public relations expertise that was instrumental in the group's media success.

The organization grew to a national network of one hundred chapters by the fall of 2004. Participants in the New York City network likely numbered more than 150. Smaller chapters in other cities sometimes had six to twelve core members and another several dozen who participated in some actions. Large events such as the Million Billionaire March in Manhattan in August 2004 drew at least two hundred Billionaire participants from across the country.

Who were they? Artists, actors, musicians, photographers, lawyers, writers, academics, corporate professionals, students, and recent college graduates. Fonda Sterling suggested that artists were a "natural, though often unconsidered" source of recruits for socially progressive political groups.[136] She remarked, "As the proverbial 'canary in a coal mine,' an artist trying to survive economically harsh times is among the first to feel the pinch of decreased funding for the arts, as well as across-the-board slashing of funding for social services." Boyd recruited a woman in her thirties because he knew she liked to sing, and he invited her and another early participant to organize a Billionaire ball and Follies choir as a performance troupe that might tour the country (though its main activities turned out to be in New York City). Another early participant, writer Kurt Opprecht, met Andrew Boyd through a mutual friend. Opprecht (who became Thurston Howell IV) so enjoyed the January 2004 Billionaires' Ball, which attracted media attention, that he decided to attend a

Billionaire planning meeting. He became one of the most active participants and contributed his writing talents to various Billionaire projects, including editing their tongue-in-cheek 2004 book, *Billionaires for Bush: How to Rule the World for Fun and Profit.* (Widely traveled and a certified professional life coach as well as a writer and writing instructor, Opprecht published in 2012 the e-book *The Billionaires' Manifesto.*)

From the spring of 2004 until the November election, the Billionaires for Bush sustained a fast pace of events. Some were national days of action such as Cheap Labor Day (on Labor Day), while others were local. In addition to musical performances by the Billionaire Follies and events noted earlier, examples of their activities during this period included bird-dogging the Bush-Cheney motorcade in Pennsylvania; "tabling" in Union Square to offer information and merchandise to passersby; "Cheney Is Innocent" candlelight vigils; a Coronation Ball; a "Widen the Healthcare Gap" mock counterprotest against the Service Employees International Union (SEIU); "Education Is Not for Everyone Day"; a "Drunk on Power" Ball; and a fund-raiser featuring cartoonist Art Spiegelman.

Monet Oliver de Place (Marco Ceglie)—whose Billionaire attire was a skipper's cap, ascot, and crested navy blazer—led the Billionaires for Bush "Limo Tours" through states where the election was too close to call. A 2006 "mockumentary" film (*Get on the Limo*) by Megan Kiefer chronicles those travels.[137] Ceglie terms the Limo Tours a "permanently life-marking experience that, win or lose, nobody regrets doing." The Limo Tours took mostly New York Billionaires to twenty-five cities in fourteen states—twelve of them swing states such as Ohio, Pennsylvania, and Florida—for a total of 13,500 miles.[138] They departed from the Democratic National Convention in Boston in July 2004 and returned triumphantly to Manhattan the day before the Republican National Convention opened in New York in August 2004.

By Halloween of 2004, as Owen Dwight Howse recounted at a New York chapter meeting a few weeks after the election, the Billionaires had "become so iconic that people dress up as Billionaires just for Halloween"—one of them without even realizing that there was an actual organization called Billionaires for Bush. Owen Dwight Howse shared a personal anecdote: he was at a Halloween party in a bar and saw a guy wearing a tuxedo and carrying a "Billionaires for Bush" sign. Owen Dwight Howse didn't recognize him and went over and introduced himself and said "I don't think I've seen you before. Have you come to our meetings?" The man looked at him as if he had no idea who he was. Owen Dwight Howse continued talking with him and found out that the man had just dressed up like a Billionaire for Halloween: "I honestly don't even think he had any idea what we were about other than obviously we were a joke." Meg A. Bucks then called out, "There is an actual organization!" and Owen Dwight Howse quipped, "There is an actual organization; it's not just a bumper sticker."[139]

During the final weeks before the 2004 presidential election, Billionaires also stepped out of fictive character mode and engaged in more traditional political activities with other organizations. Boyd encouraged such activity, saying at a mid-October 2004 meeting, "Doing the basic grunt work of knocking on doors, phone calling, things like that are equally important to the continuing persuasion effort that we're doing in Billionaire character; this is absolutely critical and shouldn't be seen as secondary . . . it's all about turnout, and it's probably all going to be about voter protection as well." He said that for those activities "you don't have to put the stupid tuxedo on," to which Owen Dwight Howse immediately quipped, "I sleep in my tuxedo."

Polishing the Brand

"Well, if I wear this boa, I can get away with wearing my rock-and-roll T-shirt."[140] Such attire worked in 2000 but was definitely forbidden for 2004 Billionaires, said a participant in her early thirties. "Super ragtag" is how Chuck Collins described the Billionaires of 2000 by comparison with their polished successors in 2004. Breaking with conventional left aesthetics, the Billionaires for Bush aimed for high "production values," precisely because, as Merchant F. Arms (Varon) put it, "the left is often kind of shaggy and amateurish and makes a sort of fetish about being earnest and . . . kind of antiprofessional."[141] The Billionaires became "obsessive" about details of costume and consistency of messaging, he said, so that a certain look, a critique, and a set of slogans and images would proliferate virally through virtual organizing. Thurston Howell IV (Kurt Opprecht) remarked, "If you don't dress up well enough or if you shout the wrong things . . . it just sort of makes us some bunch of loonies."[142]

Sierra Club protesters, by contrast, "didn't have matching outfits, and their signs were hand-scrawled, unlike our perfectly lettered placards," said Boyd of comrades at the 2004 Rove event.[143] The woman who joked about wearing a T-shirt and boa in 2000 said that was when "we were just trying to find our identity."[144] "But at the time, we were doing something that hadn't really been done before, and that attracted a lot of people." She laughed as she said the "costumes in 2000 were just terrible . . . [but] for the time they were funny and cool, and they worked and they got the idea across." Then in 2004, "we have the ball gown, we have the pearls, and there was slight extravagance but not so much that it wasn't believable on the street, and that's why the Rove action was so successful."[145]

Their polish and performance quality, combined with their command of political and economic issues, attracted media, she said. For example, after the Billionaires' huge party in January 2004, which followed their attention-grabbing Karl Rove impersonation, she comments that a *New York Times* photographer "[did] a photo shoot of us holding the sign in the loft where the party happened . . . they were just lapping it up. They thought, 'God, this is amazing; look at these people; they've got the shtick, they've got something that works.'"[146] Another woman in her thirties, a writer for progressive media who was a Billionaire participant in the early 2000s, commented that even though costumes were of poorer quality in 2000, "we were really focused on content; whenever we did an interview, we were very focused on tons of economic data, tons of connections between individual companies and individual politicians and large parties and . . . legislation . . . we were really focused on being funny, and the coverage took off from there . . . we were just visual enough that the spoof worked, the satire worked, we were always being photographed."[147]

Through their dress and style the Billionaires appropriated stereotypical symbols of corporate America and the contemporary right (projecting images of wealth, clean-cut respectability, and professionalism) in order to advance an agenda now associated with the left (reducing the disproportionate political influence of the ultrarich and large corporations). When the Billionaires and more traditional protesters share a public space, they sometimes engage in mock heckling of one another; "angry liberal" protesters bearing handmade signs and clad in casual clothes become "straight men" in glitzy Billionaire street theater. Emma Chastain, writing about the Billionaires for Bush in the *New Republic Online* after accompanying their Million Billionaire March on the eve of the 2004 Republican National Convention, lightheartedly counterposes the Billionaires' effervescence, bonhomie, and "sunny good humor" on the one hand, and the "unseemly anger and earnestness of left-wing protesters," "liberal fury rut," "bitterness," "scruffy lefty protesters," and a political "Left [that] takes itself too seriously" on the other.[148]

How this genre-bending protest was produced and how it played on the streets invite closer attention. What else lies behind the shiny surfaces of their brand magic?

5 Humor's Workshop, Humor's Witnesses

THE BILLIONAIRES' MANHATTAN ASSEMBLIES, said Merchant F. Arms (Varon), were "kind of a trip; I mean, they're almost like a performance in themselves."[1] At the height of the 2004 presidential campaign, weekly planning meetings I attended were imbued with the same kind of theatrics as their public performances. "Whose media?" called out Meg A. Bucks. "Our media!" roared the Billionaires at the start of a summer 2004 Manhattan chapter meeting. "Whose Constitution?" "Our Constitution!" Soon a round of self-introductions: "Ivy League Legacy, chair of the Speakers' Bureau, and I sing with The Follies." "Alan Greenspend, Minister of Special Operations and schmoozer." "Special Operations" is the Billionaires' "prank and information-gathering" wing, he adds. "Phil T. Rich, also a schmoozer." "Dr. DeBooks, Follies." Announcing their real names was optional, as in "Riggin de Polls (Mark), infomercial." "Betty Berkowitz, no real name yet" [laughter]. "Ivan Aston Martin, messaging." "I am Ken. I'm from Brooklyn, and I think that's part of America" [laughter]. His joke indirectly referenced Republican talk of the "real America." When I introduced myself near the start of one Manhattan chapter meeting—giving my Billionaire name, real name, academic affiliation, and researcher role—someone called out, "Whose academia?" and attendees answered, "Our academia!"

Fast-paced and exuberant, the 2004 meetings often drew more than fifty Billionaires at a time, as well as print and broadcast journalists and videographers. Gatherings were announced in advance on the Billionaires' website and were open to anyone. Most were held in an airy Lower East Side loft belonging to an absent sympathizer. Here Billionaires dressed casually in what they dub "angry liberal attire"—jeans, T-shirts, sweaters. These planning sessions were occasions for pep talks; gossip; briefings on legal rights and what to do if arrested; reports and videos of Billionaire actions and media coverage; role-playing; improvisation workshops; singing by The Follies; trying on donated ball gowns; and brainstorming new slogans, events, and talking points.

In the amped-up language that characterized such events, Andrew Boyd declared during a September 2004 planning session, "The next eight weeks could change the history of the universe!"[2] Everyone cheered that evening when Boyd reported that now if one typed "Bush" in a Google search, "Billionaires for Bush" came up as number six. Boyd read aloud a letter of complaint from a radio station listener who had missed the Billionaires' irony and took them as actual Bush supporters: "Shut up! You are not helping the president get re-elected. You are making the Republican Party look like a bunch of out-of-touch elites!" Hilarity and enthusiastic cheers punctuated the showing of a video of Billionaires on the roadside cheering and waving to George Bush and Jeb Bush as they passed by in their campaign bus in Pennsylvania while Andrew Boyd in his gray suit and bowler hat, with a huge plastic cigar in his mouth, grinned, bowed, and waved at the presidential motorcade.[3]

· · ·

When protest as play is this much fun, can participants still judge its effective-ness? A risk of any protest is that it is likely to feel "good" to the actor but not necessarily win over audiences. The theatrical exuberance of a meeting, like singing in church, excludes the skeptic. Satire is not necessarily funny to those who are its targets, and it can backfire if an audience perceives it to be sadistic or inappropriate. Such were the Billionaires' occasional demons—usually dis-placed by a self-confident buoyancy.

Newcomers to Billionaire meetings were occasionally abashed by the sheer intensity, theatricality, and quick wit on display in these gatherings. While chatting outdoors with several of us after her first meeting (spring 2005), one woman in her twenties said she had found it "intimidating" for its emphasis on fast one-liners and coming up with good ideas quickly.[4] The moderator had cut her off at one point when she was speaking. It was the responsibility of the or-ganization's Ministry of Love to welcome such newcomers,[5] find out how they wished to contribute, and put them in touch with committees or subgroups where their talents could shine.

While jocular exuberance infused the Billionaires' planning gatherings, these meetings also inevitably encompassed the hard, and often tension-ridden, work of planning the next street action. It was in such work that the internal debates and personal ambivalences that accompanied changes in organizational strategy and focus revealed themselves.[6] Performing protest as play, winning favorable media coverage, and persuading the public was work. Performative intensity in Manhattan Billionaires' meetings, then, modeled the actual energy and commitment demanded of the network's most engaged participants.

The Manhattan meetings, however, were a revved-up version of what happened elsewhere. The Washington, DC, chapter meetings, according to their leader Ken Mayer, "were never as regular nor as animated as the New York City meetings that I have heard about." They were smaller (three to ten people), and they had a "core group of passionate Billionaires with great stage presence."[7] Meetings centered on planning an action a week or two hence, Mayer says, "so we were focused on developing messaging for signs, shouts, and slogans . . . we did come up with funny lines, evaluate them, praise or critique them." They usually met in a café or bar, and Mayer reflected in 2012 that he had focused on "one-off events instead of on team building" or "setting up regular meetings to develop a group ethos and élan."

In this chapter, I explore what goes on behind the scenes to train and mobilize participants nationally and to project a polished brand image, and I also spotlight bystander responses, including spectators whose subtly dissonant voices are missing from media accounts and from most Billionaires' personal experiences as performers on the street. A key theme here is performance, a "display of verbal artistry for an audience that evaluates the performers in some way."[8] At their best, the Billionaires command attention through clever wordplay and displays of personal magnetism. Charisma, as Max Weber tells us, signals unusual "gifts of the body and spirit," a "creative power," "an extraordinary quality of a person," and a "non-lasting or unstable authority."[9] Such gifts both helped the Billionaires to recruit new members, and captivated news media as well as spectators who said they usually ignore protesters. Charisma, however, was not the only quality valued, and finding ideal Billionaires was a challenge.

Play Well and Be a Ham

When Andrew Boyd persuaded his friend Lois Canright to start a Billionaire chapter in Seattle, she targeted people, she said, who were "kind of theater-oriented, which is really a different bent from your average earnest lefty."[10] Canright (Ivana Reitoff), then in her midforties, had prior political experience working for United for a Fair Economy, Citizens Trade Campaign, and Hands Off Washington. She said that many people, herself included, "are not really the world's best Billionaires because we are too serious; we actually don't know how to play that well, and you really have to be a ham to do it well." Furthermore, "you've got to be unafraid, you can't have stage fright . . . and you've got to know how to push yourself forward in other people's faces a little bit, which is what we learned when we really did our actions." The ideal Billionaire, she said, was a rare blend of experienced activist and thespian.

Canright personally experienced the thespian challenges during her own Billionaire debut. It was a tax day event she organized at her city's main post office, for which New York Billionaires had sent her press release material and a leaflet just a day earlier. On the street, when she repeated a prepared line such as, "Billionaires for Bush, thanks for paying our taxes," people would look at her blankly. So then she stepped out of her Billionaire persona and tried to explain what she meant "fairly quickly, over and over." A lot of people did appreciate it once they understood it, and a few Bush supporters were offended. Canright at first wondered if the Billionaires' New York material might be "too satirical for the people on the street" in her city, since a lot of observers did not realize they were being ironic. Yet she soon saw that "it was an education to realize just how slick and assertive you have to be . . . we were really green." They were just "getting their legs about being their character, about how they felt pretending to be rich, about accosting people on the street." At that early stage, she said, they weren't thinking, "Our prime goal today is to win media." She went on to organize "rallies" at the state capitol in Olympia, thanking legislators for tax policies that favor Washington state's ultrarich.

This West Coast chapter organizer's assessment of her first Billionaire street appearance is a reminder that what appeared as easy bystander and media successes for the Billionaires actually required much advance preparation and theatrical practice. In addition to memorizing slogans and talking points and understanding underlying policy debates, participants had to master the subtle metacommunication that signals a joke: "humor is created by establishing a 'play frame'" that is signaled by "voice quality, a body movement or posture, a lifted eyebrow—any of the various things people do to indicate fantasy to one another."[11] All of that had to become second nature in rapid-fire street theater.

Spirit Possession: Learning How to Be a Billionaire

Billionaires had to transform what they knew about great wealth into embodied knowledge—conveyed through bodily expression—in order to perform their political dissent convincingly. Improvisation and performance workshops, therefore, were part of the Billionaires' Manhattan chapter meetings. Participants learned how to make desirable impressions on audiences or deal with hecklers (don't take the bait and don't step out of character) or with overly enthusiastic spectators who joined in shouting slogans with them—and thereby disrupted the Billionaires' carefully crafted media image.

General Lee Greedy drew on his college acting and improvisation training to lead a discussion at a June 2004 Manhattan meeting to help members, as he put it, "work on character issues, performance issues, have people discuss when they hit snags, dry spots, lose character." Attendees talked over what to do when Billionaires performing in public yelled over one another, or did disparate chants at the same time, or made too much noise when a member was being interviewed by a journalist, as well as how to handle the "juggling act" required to stay in character while discussing serious issues during a news interview. Energized Follies members diverted that serious discussion as they arrived, singing (to the tune of "The Caissons Go Rolling Along"): "We're so rich that it's zany, Billionaires for Bush and Cheney. We will give you the stars and the moon. . . ."[12] They had just come from a fund-raiser for an opponent of Tom DeLay, and they revved up the meeting, eliciting very loud cheers, clapping, and whistles.

Coached by thespians in their midst, Manhattan Billionaires in July 2004 meetings practiced impersonating the ultrawealthy and chatting with one another in character. Leading them in such exercises was Ivy League Legacy, actress Melody Bates, who had recently completed an MFA in acting at Columbia University and who has since been working as an actor, director, and theater instructor. Bates offered tips about mannerisms, voice, carriage, posture, costumes, and the importance of not being so condescending as to anger people, or so aloof that people on the street ignore them, or so appealing that the parody loses its bite. As Billionaires began a practice session, here is how Bates instructed them to adjust their bodies, to "come into your own billionaire shape"[13]:

Picture for yourself your billionaire self, and . . . figure out how that billionaire self stands, how they fit in your body . . . what's different about the way they hold this body from the way you hold it. . . . Some of the things to play with are

. . . a sort of generic idea of high class with a very straight spine and excellent posture, sort of an old-fashioned sense of the word. . . . Now as you are coming into your own billionaire shape, I want you to just experiment with small moves; don't move your feet too much yet, just . . . see if you're looking around, what happens, how you hold your head, how you might hold your hands.

Next she had them imagine small props—top hat, clutch purse, cane—for their Billionaire personas, and asked them to walk around the room, "taking care of each other," without speaking. "Really self-focus, which shouldn't be hard for all of us," she said, prompting laughter.

How do Billionaires feel as they impersonate the ultrarich? "I channel . . . the people I knew at the tennis club" during childhood vacations on Cape Cod, said a middle-class Seattle woman. It was a strange experience for Billionaires as political progressives to sense their own simultaneous "envy and hatred" of the corporate master class when they dressed up and performed as Billionaires, said Boyd.[14] Most Billionaire participants, he continued, have some "emotional distance" from the painful side of the economic system and rely on an abstract understanding of it. While they are committed to "greater social justice," he said, participating in the Billionaires' organization offered them a way to "indulge our fantasies of being rich beyond imagining and play at that, but play at it in a way that was obviously critical of a society that allows some people to be that way while infant mortality rates are huge in inner cities and there are sixty million uninsured Americans, many of them children. . . . So we were able to sort of have our cake and eat it too, and also have a very effective or potentially effective campaign."[15] He suggests, "psychically we're sort of working off our guilt or something."[16]

Each Billionaire projects a fictive character with a distinctive personality and a back story. Merchant F. Arms (Varon) claims to represent the "dark side of impossible wealth," while Thurston Howell IV (Opprecht) describes himself as a more lighthearted character: "I do sort of feel a little bit like Thurston Howell III," a *Gilligan's Island* character named by *Forbes Magazine* as one of its top fifteen fictional billionaires.[17] "I'm the fourth; and he's just . . . a little silly but generally you know not a bad fellow . . . a little bit goofy but kind of friendly, although he's more of a curmudgeon than friendly." Iva Fortune talks about her Billionaire persona as "looking for a husband, inebriated, decadent, martini-swilling . . . someone who's never earned any of her wealth . . . usually off sailing." The risk of such poses was that spectators might conflate the present with the past and resent the enactment of privileged aloofness.

Some Billionaires are more comfortable than others breaking character and engaging with spectators during their street actions. But stepping in and out of character can be a challenge, a male Billionaire in his early twenties commented; sometimes people on the street "want to talk to you one-on-one, and just switching from the slogans to an actual nuanced discussion and staying in character is like a juggling act."[18] Their website in 2004 advised members to "use irony as a Trojan Horse . . . to win the attention of the media or a voter and then break character to explain our message in plain terms. Speaking from the heart is often a better way to reach swing voters, particularly when speaking through the press."[19]

The power of their street performances hinged on split-second reactions that bypass conscious awareness, as hinted in Lois Canright's description of her first street performance as a Billionaire in Seattle: "You've got about three seconds . . . it's so quick! . . . The real impression that you make is the visual, and whether or not they even listen to anything you say is based on your visual."[20] The "visual" here encompasses not just costumes and signs but poise, gaze, affect, grace, and magnetism. Voice quality and locution are pivotal. At play in Billionaire encounters with the public are subtleties of affect, "intensities that pass body to body . . . resonances that circulate about, between, and sometimes stick to bodies and worlds . . . affect and cognition are never fully separable."[21] Thus an ideal Billionaire performance would entice someone to pay attention and to feel a psychic connection, followed by an "aha!" moment when political cognition is triggered—not necessarily just recognition by those who already agree but also enlightenment or even transformation.[22]

Might Billionaire performances resemble spirit possession—wherein an individual is possessed by the soul of a very wealthy person, as imagined worlds of wealth are embodied in a Billionaire's fictive persona through mimesis or imitation of the ultrarich? A society that constantly cultivates imaginings of wealth readily produces social knowledge that enables such mimesis. The possibility that mimicry of the powerful is experienced not only as celebration but also as critique animated anthropological studies of spirit possession, which sometimes includes elements of satire and burlesque "as witty and historically perceptive metacommentaries [that] . . . challenge the dominant social order and regime of truth."[23] In a society that offers little real opportunity to "tame" the very rich, a satirical Billionaire then becomes a medium through which the superrich and the "99 percent" encounter one another, symbolically denaturalizing or contesting the authority of the wealthy.

One particular spirit inspired Andrew Boyd when he put on his suit and performed as Phil T. Rich (see Figure I.1). The suit was made by his immigrant (maternal) grandfather, a Jew who came to the United States from Romania in 1914, and worked as a tailor on New York's Lower East Side for fifty years. Soon after his parents married, his grandfather, to their complete surprise, dropped off a custom-fitted suit that fit his father perfectly. He had taken no measurements and had done it all by eye, without telling anyone. Boyd's father died in 2000, and in 2004 when he needed a suit, his mother suggested he try that one. It fit him nearly perfectly, and it became his Billionaire costume for that entire campaign year. Boyd says, "When I rode into battle against the forces of plutocracy, hypocrisy, and irony-deficiency, I felt like my ancestors were with me."[24]

When they take political satire to the streets, performers try to sustain spectators' psychological collaboration throughout the performance, a process that includes, as Beeman puts it, a crucial but fragile and constantly shifting phatic connection that "keeps all parties engaged with each other."[25] The dynamics are anything but predictable, and displays of quick-witted connection with spectators (including journalists) are prized. But who gets convinced of what? It takes great skill for the performer to separate her own self-appraisal (my puns are funny!) from what she actually triggers in her interlocutors.

In activists' street performances, contexts are emergent, open-ended. Both performers and observers "position themselves . . . and are simultaneously positioned by others according to factors such as class, ethnicity, and gender,"[26] as well as less observable individual consciousnesses. Individuals hear Billionaire performances in different registers. Whether a Billionaire street performance resonates powerfully with a *Washington Post* reporter as well as a Verizon technician or toy store doorman, then, depends on artistry, context, and luck.

Satire and Pearls on the Street

"Is it a joke? I can't figure out if it's a joke," said a woman encountering the Billionaires for the first time at their 2004 tax day event outside New York City's central post office. A man who was a bystander at the same event at first wondered, "But are they for or against Bush?" As passersby linger and watch, they usually realize that the "campy, spoofy" (as one observer put it) Billionaire impersonations are meant to be ironic.

Satirical cues can misfire, however, and not everyone gets the joke or appreciates it even if they do understand it. Sometimes observers respond as much to the Billionaires' performance of conspicuous leisure as to the content of their play, perhaps especially when they attempt to cross class or race categories. Unfriendly responses from likely sympathizers, even if uncommon, return us directly to the paradoxical risk of "pulling off the parody a bit too well" or becoming what one spoofs—in this case, as a Billionaire put it, "clubby elites who are screened off from the rest of the world."[27] The Billionaires' challenge as street performers is to denounce inequality through empathic humor that reaches across the country's growing economic divide even as they enact a caricatured aloofness, self-admiration, and foppery.

Billionaire street performances play on uncertainties and unsettle ideas about political categories—as the Yippies also did in the 1960s when Jerry Rubin dressed up as Uncle Sam when called to testify before the House Un-American Activities Committee (a leftover from the 1950s McCarthy era). Thus a passerby at the Billionaires' street event outside New York's main post office on George Bush's birthday may at first think the giant birthday card for the president is a kind gesture, then consider the context (final months of a presidential campaign), look more closely at the staging, slogans and over-the-top impersonations of the ultrarich, and finally rethink the intentions behind the birthday display. A birthday cake sat next to a large white cardboard cutout of the state of Ohio gift-wrapped with a red ribbon bow. The Billionaires called out: "What do you give the man who has everything? The election!" and "We are giving the state of Ohio to the president along with all the other swing states!" If they are confused at first, some spectators delight in catching on to the ruse, while others never fathom it. Witnessing the event, one young man exclaimed, "They lost their mind!" Clearly he had not gotten the message.

Indeed, spectators—whether they get the joke or not—become active co-producers as well as consumers of meanings in Billionaire street performances, which sometimes include lively interchanges with bystanders.[28] Occasionally Bush opponents who missed the irony of the Billionaires' messages became furious and shouted comments such as "That's disgusting!" And Bush supporters who had mistaken the Billionaires for Republicans and taken their slogans literally either joined them in chanting slogans such as "Four More Wars!" or reacted with embarrassment ("We appreciate your support, but can you tone it down?") or became angry and said the Billionaires were hurting the Republicans' image when they called out "Leave No Corporation Behind!" or "Four More Wars!" When a hostile passerby in Seattle shouted, "So you blame Bush for everything?" the Billionaires stayed in character and replied, "No, we think he's the best president money can buy!" If a Bush supporter shouted something positive about the president, the Billionaires cheerily replied "Huzzah!"—after which the heckler was likely to walk away quickly.

Decoding the Message[29]

Like all parody, that of the Billionaires is constituted by a "dense web of allusion," or what some theorists term intertextuality.[30] Such intertextuality, which varies from the deliberate or explicit to the generalized, entails the "constant and inevitable use of ready-made formulations, catch phrases, slang, jargon, clichés, commonplaces, unconscious echoes, and formulaic phrases . . . linguistic echoes and repetitions . . . [which] are accented in variously evaluative ways, as they are subjected—or not—to overt ridicule, or mild irony."[31] Spectators of course have unequal familiarity with precursor texts such as the Bush administration's education policy slogan "Leave No Child Behind"—the unspoken referent for the slogan "Leave No Billionaire Behind!"

Hence whether or not members of the public comprehend the Billionaires' ironic humor depends not only on picking up oral cues such as shifts in linguistic style or register but also on audience ability to recognize the humor's allusions or intertextual links—for example, the linguistic intertexuality of the fictive name Alan Greenspend and former Federal Reserve chairman Alan Greenspan, or the connection between "four more wars" and "four more years," or that between the Billionaire name Lucinda Regulations and the politically conservative drive toward loosening economic regulations, or that between the Billionaire name Thurston Howell IV and the *Gilligan's Island* television character Thurston Howell III.[32]

The invention of names and creative reworking of catch phrases—enabled especially by the social circulation of media phrases and discourses in popular culture[33]—is the Billionaires' core intellectual enterprise. That is the focus of brainstorming sessions in their planning meetings, discussion and debate via email, and informal discussion elsewhere. Once that work is accomplished, the alchemy of content and delivery comes into play.

Humor presents a message within a cognitive frame that is suddenly removed, "revealing one or more additional cognitive frames which audience members are shown as possible contextualizations or reframings of the original content material."[34] When a joke succeeds, the audience understands the contrasting frames so that, as Beeman writes, "[t]he tension between the original framing and the sudden reframing results in an emotional release recognizable as the enjoyment response we see as smiles, amusement, and laughter."[35] But if amusement is observable, who gets convinced of what is much harder to assess. It takes great skill for the performer to separate her own self-appraisal from what she actually triggers in her interlocutors. Most Billionaires had little direct knowledge of the latter. That is where an anthropologist might step in.

I found that some spectators delighted in the Billionaires' wit and playfulness, while others envied the ostensible leisure and privilege of the satirists themselves. One might assume that the Billionaires' street parody would build solidarity with non-elites, especially union members or those struggling to pay their rent. But I sometimes discovered the opposite—especially when I talked with bystanders during Billionaire Christmas caroling on Fifth Avenue, and their satirical counterprotests to union picketing at Verizon near Times Square. On the streets, what Boyd describes as the Billionaires' "hipster, ironic, college-educated"[36] ethos had unpredictable effects.

Christmas Caroling on Fifth Avenue, 2004

On a chilly Christmas Eve in 2004, when many New Yorkers still felt demoralized by Bush's victory, nine Billionaires for Bush members met near St. Patrick's Cathedral and strolled up Manhattan's Fifth Avenue singing their versions of Christmas carols. The men wore handsome wool coats with top hats or Santa caps, and the women furs and long gowns. To the familiar tune of "Joy to the World," they sang: "Toys for the world are made by kids, and not by elves at all! We work them night and day, for very little pay And little tiny hands make all your favorite brands, that fill up the shelves in every shopping mall"[37]—obviously invoking Third World sweatshops that employ child labor to produce toys. Other carols included "Rest Easy Wealthy Gentlemen" to the tune of "God Rest Ye Merry Gentlemen," and "Prison Cells" to the tune of "Jingle Bells." I joined them with tape recorder and notebook. The group walked to Cartier, Tiffany's, the Disney Store, Trump Tower, FAO Schwarz, and the Plaza Hotel.

When the Billionaires entered the festively decorated lobby of Trump Tower, a white woman in her midforties who was assisting shoppers greeted them warmly and encouraged them to sing next to the Christmas tree. As they began singing softly, she was at first too far away to hear the words. After a few songs she walked over and told them they needed a microphone, so then they sang in louder voices, "Toys for the world are made by kids, and not by elves at all. . . ."

As she heard the lyrics, her smile disappeared and she shook her finger from side to side, saying, "No, they're not going to allow you to do that . . . you can't do that. I'll have to call security." One of the Billionaire men said cheerily, "We're done," and then they sang as the Trump Tower employee politely escorted them to the door. She was still friendly as I walked with her across the lobby; I smiled and asked, "They can't do this because . . . ?" She replied, "Because they're singing for a cause." I asked, "What's the cause?" She replied, "Billionaires for Bush, whatever. You can't do a cause in here. If they were just singing Christmas carols, they could sing Christmas carols." I thanked her and wished her a good holiday.

Once outside of Trump Tower, the Billionaires were exuberant. One of the men said to the others with a huge smile, "I love you guys!" Another replied, "Oh, that was so wrong but so fun!" A bystander on the street joined us for a while and said he wanted to sing too. Then, as we walked up Fifth Avenue, I asked one of the Billionaires—an executive committee member in her thirties who had years of activist experience—what she thought about the Trump Tower episode:

> You just realize you and your community are participating in something unprecedented and lovely [laughs]. It's like taking that moment of confusion and taking it to its *n*th degree almost, because there's so many layers. There's the true spirit of Christmas, the commodification of Christmas, but taking Billionaire songs to the lobby of Trump Tower and having a woman at Trump *insist* that we sing—assuming of course that we're going to be singing lovely Christmas carols, and we do—only we're not on message with Trump philosophy.

I laughed and said, "But you look like you're on message!" She replied, "We do! We're on message for ourselves!" The Billionaire known as Cassius King added, "I mean, how perfect: Billionaires in a billionaire's place with a Billionaire choir invited by a billionaire's employee [to sing]!" Meg A. Bucks: "A billionaire who's in Chapter 11 bankruptcy, I believe." Cassius King: "Well no . . . it's just his Trump Casino."

As they walked up Fifth Avenue singing, people often stopped to listen and picked up phrases such as, "O come, let us exploit them" (to the tune of "O Come, All Ye Faithful"), or lines from "Prison Cells" about spending more on prisons than on schools, which a teacher and other passersby appreciated. Some listeners seemed puzzled, and a few did not like what they heard. "Oh, in front of Cartier [jewelry store], come on!" said one woman, and her male companion added, "I don't care for it." A woman who told me she is from South Africa and lives in New Jersey said, "I think it's fantastic; maybe they'll bring the real message of Christmas back and not just make it a consumer's holiday." When I asked a man nearby what he thought of the songs, he said, "Interesting . . . all I heard is 'oil and plunder.' They're making fun of Bush?" A woman said she assumes the message is that we should not have reelected George Bush. Another woman said, "I love them; I've seen them once before . . . I couldn't agree more." When one of the male Billionaires called out their slogan "Four More Wars!" a woman on the street repeated that to her friend and laughed, "No, they're not for Bush . . . that makes me happy." A foreign couple told me they don't like Bush. Another man said, "They need a mic" since it was difficult to catch the lyrics.

When the Billionaires reached the FAO Schwarz toy store plaza, an African American man dressed in a red Nutcracker soldier suit and hat was greeting customers at the door. He watched them sing and smiled. When I walked over and asked his opinion, he replied,

> Oh, I'm not even listening . . . I don't listen to that kind of thing . . . I gotta pay my rent . . . I don't have time for that; if you're poor, you don't get nothin'. That's for people who got money . . . my rent is due tomorrow. Now if they give me money for my rent, I'll go over there and stand there all night and write the words down, but in the meantime if they're not gonna help me to pay my rent, they're outta here. I don't have time for it . . . I think they're cute, though.

Here he imitated them as he raised his voice, and then as the Billionaires finished singing "Prison Cells," he said, "Only in America is it tolerated." He did not add how unlikely it would be that an African American man singing such lyrics on that same street would garner warm or amused responses. Shortly after that, I heard a security person saying to the doorman, "Be advised . . . they're not allowed inside the store to take any kind of photographs."

I heard very few critical remarks from bystanders during the Billionaires' Christmas caroling, but the comments of the costumed African American doorman at FAO Schwarz are revealing. He perceives an economic gulf between his world and that of the singing satirists. Terming the Billionaires "cute," he mimics their voices humorously, subtly inverting the status differential he detects by gently mocking them in a conversation that occurred out of earshot of the Billionaires themselves.

In contrast to these Christmas Eve episodes on Fifth Avenue, I heard much more pointed criticism about the Billionaires while chatting with people on the street a few weeks earlier at a counterprotest with Verizon workers.

Billionaires Counterprotest Verizon Union Picketers, 2004

"'Billionaires for Bush' to Support Verizon Wireless CEO Ivan Seidenberg Against CWA Union Protest" read the advance press announcement, which described a photo op of "Billionaires, dressed to the nines in tuxedoes and evening gowns," arriving in a limousine.[38] On a cool and windy day in December 2004, about ten Billionaires stepped out of a stretch limousine outside Verizon's offices a few blocks from Times Square. Dressed in tuxedoes, evening gowns, and furs, they chanted: "No Jobs? No Problem!" "What's Outrageous? Union Wages!"[39] One of their signs read, "What Are We Trusting? Union Busting!" "Tex Shelter" passed out a mock job application and read aloud questions on the form: "Do you think that $5.15 is (a) too low for a minimum hourly wage; (b) as much as CEOs can be expected to pay; or (c) a fair day's wages?" Some Billionaires replied that it was a fair day's wage, and one proposed a toast to Verizon's CEO, prompting cheers and boos.

This was a mock counterprotest staged in collaboration with the Communications Workers of America (CWA), who were holding a lunch-hour rally in support of Verizon Wireless workers' unionization efforts. (Verizon workers, but not those at Verizon Wireless, already had a union.) A couple of dozen CWA protesters—confined in a pen of barricades set up in advance by the police—gave speeches and chanted criticisms of their CEO. When the Billionaires stepped out of their limousine, some of the workers at first took the Billionaires' words literally and shouted at them angrily. A Billionaire told me, "There was a woman there when we arrived who . . . was furious, and she was screaming at us, and even making obscene gestures; she was upset . . . it was like a face-off as we were getting out of the limousine: 'Don't you have anything better to do? Bush is an evil man, get out of here, we don't want you on our sidewalk,' that kind of thing." "We tried to be charming and smiling and giving our usual quips and somewhat ignoring her," she continued,

> and the union members behind her seemed to sort of understand that this was a bit of a set-up and that we weren't really who we pretended to be; so they were kind of quietly watching, and then I think people noticed that we were talking to the union folks and that it was a genial atmosphere, and more people caught on, and then I saw her come up to some of my fellow Billionaires, apologizing and saying, "I'm so embarrassed, I'm so sorry, I didn't realize who you were!"[40]

Pedestrians observing the Verizon event were also confused at first. A middle-aged tourist asked the Billionaires if they were with Donald Trump, a question Meg A. Bucks repeated to the crowd. I caught up with that spectator and her companion once they had walked past the Billionaires, and one of them, speaking in a Southern accent, said they thought the Billionaires were trying to raise money on the street as part of Donald Trump's television program *The Apprentice*, which often did send contestants out to New York's streets and businesses as part of the show. Her friend asked, "Is that a play they're advertising there?" and the other woman said, "No, they're for a politician, they said." In short, the Billionaires' message seemed to have been utterly lost on these tourists.

Among spectators watching the Billionaires more closely, critical observations came from an African American woman in her thirties or early forties and an African American man—both of them unionized Verizon employees on their lunch break—and from a blond woman with whom they were chatting. The latter worked at Verizon Wireless and thought the unionization efforts there, which had been going on for years, were fruitless.[41] None of them had heard of the Billionaires for Bush. The white woman said, "I'm assuming they're making fun of people . . . I guess it's a joke? The union was just out here protesting. . . . We were trying to figure out what Bush had to do with it." The African American woman asked me, "So what are they, I mean, who are they, where are they from?"

"They are people who have nothing better to do with their lives, and they don't actually work . . . the millionaire and his wife . . . I'm working, and they have time to get into costumes and do this kind of stuff on a work day," said the male Verizon employee. The African American woman (who later told me she was not a Bush supporter) also commented that she had to work for a living whereas the Billionaires obviously could take time off during the middle of the day to dress up and perform at such an event.

Unlike the FAO Schwarz Christmas caroling, here I had a chance for longer conversation, and so after listening to their comments, I briefly explained who the Billionaires were and noted that many of them had full-time or part-time jobs. "Well, at least that's good," said the white woman. I said that some of the Billionaires for Bush struggled to make ends meet, and their organization did not have a lot of money. The women wondered if the union had paid for the Billionaires' limousine. It did—an expense a Billionaire executive committee member later acknowledged to be ironic, and yet he remarked that unions also pay for props like giant inflatable rats. "It's just a tool," he said, and then added, "if there's one thing I've discovered in this crazy year or so, it's that irony has absolutely no bounds or any limits anymore, so I think we have to redefine the word entirely—maybe 'super-irony.'"[42] Here the core irony that political activists posing as billionaires were actually struggling to keep their organization afloat financially after the presidential election was coupled with the irony of having a labor union fund a limousine for satirical activists who sided with workers trying to unionize while the satirists pretended to take the side of a corporate CEO. At that time the Billionaires were experimenting with new forms of modest fund-raising as a political entertainment troupe for hire by sympathetic groups they thought they could assist through live performances.

As the African American woman looked at the limousine, she said, "That's what they use my union dues for; that's interesting." To the three Verizon employees I said that usually the Billionaires take the subway or walk or take a taxi. I asked, "What if they bring media attention to the issue and help the cause of the union? That's what they are trying to do." The white woman replied, "Yes, but if this is for [Verizon] Wireless, they've been refusing to be union for how many years?"

When I next chatted with three white male Verizon employees wearing business suits, they told me they had not heard of Billionaires for Bush. One said, "I like Broadway; that's about all I took from the protest; they're very theatrical, but I'm not really sure what their message is." "Nice fur coats," another offered. When I walked over to another white man and asked what he thought the Billionaires' message was, he replied: "Well, obviously they're upset about jobs being outsourced and obviously they hate Bush [laughs]; I haven't heard much about this Seidenberg guy." I asked him if he thought this style of protest was effective. He answered, "It's entertaining, it's humorous, and it's a good idea." He asked if they were all actors (I told him most were not), and he said they look "rich and educated but not very moral." Another man commented that New Yorkers tend to walk by "because this stuff [occurs] on most every corner," and that it was lunch hour and people wanted to be on their way.

I spoke with a more enthusiastic male employee of the Communications Workers of America who said he had heard of the Billionaires for Bush during the presidential campaign and appreciated their willingness to assist the union:

> I think it's a great thing; using humor to make a point is very effective and very helpful . . . I think it's great that they are willing to be helpful to things like this; I mean, it's one thing to poke fun at George Bush and try to make a point about his constituency; it's another thing to translate that into an understanding of organizing, which I think is uncommon really for a lot of people who are not directly connected to labor.

When I asked him to assess the effectiveness of that day's Billionaire appearance for getting the message out to people passing by, he replied, "I can't tell; I think it's great." He laughed as he said, "Our folks [CWA], when they first showed up, thought they were for real and somebody said, 'I was going to start pinning them!'" Signaling the importance of audiences beyond immediate passersby, he said he thought that working with the Billionaires helped the union "send a message to Verizon Wireless that we are going to keep the pressure on them until they stop firing workers for organizing, that they should allow workers to exercise their rights." He remarked on the challenges of union organizing now, as compared to an earlier time when middle-class people understood that "unions were a force for good and for justice."

A national staff member of the Communications Workers of America (not a Verizon worker) praised the collaborative effort between the union and the Billionaires and the value of humor to communicate a social justice message. I asked him how he thought passersby perceived the event, and he replied, "It's New York, so everyone wants to pretend that they've seen it all before, but some people are really looking—'What is going on?'—so this is a good thing."

I later let some Billionaires know that their Verizon event had sparked frank and critical remarks from spectators with whom I had conversed. An executive committee member said that what she found most interesting about street re-actions I reported was the Bush angle—the women on the street who wondered what Bush had to do with the union cause that day. She suggested that the Bil-lionaires for Bush name—a brand she and others wanted to keep after the 2004 election—would work much better "when we're talking about issues like priva-tizing Social Security and eliminating the dynasty tax, they are issues that'll get played out in Congress and Bush is very much identified with them."[43] Leaflets or more explicit messaging at the Verizon event, she thought, would have clari-fied how the union's issues were linked to Bush administration policies. Collab-oration with unions, for many Billionaires, was an intensely felt commitment that went beyond political party identity, and they were eager to try new tactics, even if some events proved more successful than others.

Overall, the Verizon event "seemed slightly out of context" during that post-election moment, remarked a Billionaire executive committee member.[44] In ad-dition, in a country where fewer than 8 percent of private-sector workers now belong to unions,[45] and where antiunion rhetoric is pervasive, the context for satire about antiunionism is challenging, especially since in 2004 it was not a widely circulated fact that the steady decline during recent decades in union membership and workers' pay and benefits had been accompanied by rising worker productivity, skyrocketing CEO pay, huge corporate profits, minimal corporate tax payments, and a sharp decline in the share of total national income earned by the middle class. The public obscurity of those structural changes in the early 2000s contributed to a spectator paradox: an assumption that the satirical Billionaires themselves were wealthy and privileged undermined the very solidarity the Billionaires intended to communicate.

Billionaire Fandom

In stark contrast to spectators' responses during the Billionaires' Christmas caroling and Verizon events shortly after the 2004 election, a Boston Billionaire encountered almost overwhelming enthusiasm from spectators during the August 2004 Million Billionaire March down Manhattan's Fifth Avenue.[46] After joining their march at the Plaza Hotel, he and a handful of other Billionaires became separated from the rest of the group and merged with the thousands of other protesters in the street that day before the start of the Republican National Convention. When they reached Union Square, he and his companion Billionaires "were mobbed with Billionaires for Bush fans who said, 'We love you guys, where are the rest of you?'" They were pinned up against a wall, surrounded by people asking them questions, and television crews from Reuters, the Sundance Channel, and other outlets showed up to interview them. They proceeded to Forty-second Street, and television crews converged on them again. He said the Billionaires seemed like "the most popular outfit there."

During the 2004 presidential campaign, when the Billionaires were birddogging the president's campaign bus in Pennsylvania, a Manhattan Billionaire in his thirties observed the delight of other protesters when the Billionaires showed up; he suggested that "[we] lend a certain kind of legitimacy to protest if we show up . . . they were so thrilled: 'Oh my God, the New York Billionaires!' . . . People applauded, 'Oh, there's the Billionaires! Oh, there's the Billionaires!'"[47]

The Billionaires' flashy visuals (tuxedoes, evening gowns, silk ascots, tiaras, money-print ties, elbow-length gloves, professionally printed banners, and brightly colored placards) and lighthearted style attracted attention from passersby who said they might ignore more "traditional" protesters or would resent loud, angry speech. A man remarked as he watched the July 2004 Billionaire street action in New York to "celebrate" Bush's birthday: "It could be just another table with a bunch of hippies at it, and you'd just walk by and say, 'Yeah, whatever—hippies.'... But this is totally entertaining." A man at the New York Billionaires' 2004 tax day street action commented, "I think they're really funny. I think that protests and that kind of stuff can be kind of boring." Another observer of the same event said, "I think it gets people to turn their head and question reality, which is great."

A well-dressed Republican couple in their early forties, who planned to vote against Bush, observed the Billionaires for Bush at their July 2004 New York street action celebrating George Bush's birthday, and commented:

> I think the key to protest now is not to alienate people, because you scare the crossovers like we are; we're Republican, lifelong Republicans, but we're voting for Kerry. But we don't want to go back to the sixties, where they're so radical and they're so obnoxious, if you will, that you scare away the crossover people.... You know, I think this type of thing is good because it appeals to people like us.... And the more protesters are like the rest of us, the more influence you'll have.[48]

These Republicans were the kinds of spectators the Billionaires wanted to win over.[49] Doing so required an organizational emphasis on visual unity or stylistic conformity to protect the brand, and that meant a discipline and direction from the top which made some uneasy.

Ironies of Governance

"We're a meritocracy," said a Billionaire executive committee member with years of activist experience. The Billionaires try to be as transparent as a meritocracy can be, he said, but they must be hierarchical, and the "totally consensual" model he had seen in some organizations "drives me nuts." Another Billionaire who had participated since 2000 said the organization "makes no real pretence about being a participatory or democratic nonhierarchic organization in the way that some of the antiglobalization groups aspire to be"[50]— and which Occupy Wall Street later adopted. Earlier he had been a member of the Direct Action Network, which he said strove to be "rigorously nonhierarchical and . . . have almost no leadership principles whatsoever, for better and for worse." The Billionaires, by contrast, "while certainly soliciting and encouraging the participation of everybody and trying to cultivate leaders, does have implicitly or explicitly a set of tiers and then . . . 'surprise, surprise!'—people who do the most work have the most power." For example, individuals who were in charge of components such as the speaker's bureau or media relations or special operations or national chapter coordination were part of the national executive committee, which sometimes appeared to function as a powerful (albeit very hardworking) group of insiders. Such hierarchy, a member said, "becomes potentially a problem when people who don't have as much time or experience and don't know how to buy into the concept or have a strong sense of ownership . . . then feel left out and kind of drift away."[51]

At the same time, when a core group works very hard, "there is a danger that they . . . martyr themselves and become burned out," he added. Furthermore, the existence of that core group, he suggests, can "give the impression that there is an organization inside the organization inside the organization," whereas greater transparency might create a higher "comfort level" for all who join. When the organization's limited transparency is added to the "costumes and funny names . . . the whole thing can also feel a little weird . . . and ingroupy," he said, because "you've established this private language and literally kind of renamed yourself, and . . . a kind of clubbishness comes with that." An organization that parodies the ultrarich risks reproducing their aloofness: "This is one of the great ironies of spoofing the superrich; if you adopt their affect, you at some point send a negative set of signals that is part of the problem with the culture of elites. . . . So it's a tricky pantomime, and if you pull off the illusion too well, you become what you're spoofing."[52] After the 2004 presidential election, the Billionaires experimented with new governance structures, and when Merchant F. Arms led a mid-2005 "strategery" session, he explicitly addressed lingering tensions: "We want . . . to model a new Billionaire style, which is inclusive, participatory, and democratic, which are three words that have not been at the top of everybody's mind and what they feel about the group." Although they discussed these contradictions and ambivalences openly during their mid-2005 "strategery" meetings,[53] during the fast-paced 2004 Billionaire campaign activities they usually surfaced only in private conversations.

Building a "National Movement"

Behind what a Billionaire termed an "emphasis on fun and glamour"[54] was a serious political network of people with passionate political commitments and a willingness to offer many hours of their time to build a national network of Billionaires. Only a handful received any salary. Among those who held a full-

time paid staff position for the first ten months of 2004 and who made the Billionaires for Bush nearly her primary occupation was the national director of
field operations, Iona Bigga Yacht (Alice Meaker, now Alice Varon; Figure 5.1).
In 2004, she was an experienced activist in her mid-thirties, who had a B.A. in
philosophy from Reed College and an M.S. in management and urban policy
from the New School for Social Research. Meaker had worked on several political campaigns, once served as policy adviser to the chair of the New York City
Council's Economic Development Committee, and had been active in several
grassroots organizations, including the Lower East Side Collective, which she

FIGURE 5.1 Iona Bigga Yacht (Alice Meaker), national director of field operations
for Billionaires for Bush, 2004. Photo by Carl Skutsch.

cofounded. She was in charge of identifying and working with heads of Billionaires for Bush chapters across the country so that they could, as she put it, "build a movement." She updated chapter listings on the website and put local chapters—which varied widely in size and activity levels—in contact with New York media teams, creative teams, and experts on costuming, props, and graphics. Meaker said she helped them "think through when to do an action and how to execute it, [and] how to bring in new people." National executive committee members assisted, such as an experienced activist who prepared talking points for a West Coast Billionaire to memorize in preparation for a public appearance by a senior Cabinet official in the Bush administration. While visiting her city, the executive committee member worked with her on lines, delivery, media training, and attire. She was to carry no signs since they are confiscated by security, and to put on her Billionaire "bling" (flashy jewelry and accessories) once inside the room, seated in front of the press corps. He was pleased that the resulting media coverage included a "picture of [the Billionaire] in the audience in full bling . . . sitting right in front of the press corps."[55]

The mounting tally of new chapters became a keen point of interest at each 2004 Manhattan planning meeting, where Meaker displayed a poster-board U.S. map with pins marking Billionaires for Bush chapters in red and blue states, and pink or light blue battleground states. Her mid-October announcement that in just over nine months they had expanded to ninety-eight chapters brought applause and cheers of "Huzzah!"[56]

In that pre-Facebook time, Meaker encouraged participants to post photos and descriptions of Billionaire actions on blogs in order to build a sense of national organizational identity. "It's really powerful," she told Manhattan meeting attendees, "to see, 'Look those are the folks in San Francisco doing what we just did last week, and in Des Moines and Iowa City' . . . it's good to *develop that sense like this is a national movement*, but we need the images, we need that on the blog." She also invited volunteers to call people in other chapters and ask how things were going, so that "people in Iowa City . . . know people in New York care what happens there."

Since New York was not a state any Democratic presidential candidate was likely to lose, Billionaires there were having fun, Meaker said, while those in other states were "reaching the voters that are going to decide this election."[57] To assist them, the New York Billionaires developed a "rapid deployment force" of members who could travel to battleground states. Meaker invited volunteers for road trips centered on candidates' campaign appearances, so they could "mak[e] sure when Bush-Cheney come to town in battleground states [that] we have Billionaires there to celebrate."

Billionaires on the Limo Tours, headed by Marco Ceglie (Monet Oliver de Place), covered thousands of miles; helped to seed chapters in places such as Toledo and Madison; and generated media coverage as well as poignant encounters between New York Billionaires and people they met elsewhere in town squares, restaurants, and coffee shops. "A reason I was passionate about the Limo Tours," said Ceglie, "stems from my desire to get our heads out of New York. I am very suspicious of group-think and the bubble effect, and know that we cannot speak to, say, the Cleveland experience as well as someone who lives there."[58] "Local people who live in these areas are much more equipped to come up with slogans, strategy, and messaging that speaks to the local experience," Ceglie added. Pittsburgh chapter founders, for example, created the locally resonant slogan "More Stogies, Less Perogies."

Chapter heads sometimes thought that New York attempted too much control or that there was a lack of clarity about who had to "approve or 'green-light' an action before they [could] take the Billionaire brand and run with it—or they're frustrated about not being able to get things green-lighted when going through official channels," Boyd remarked to those assembled for a mid-2005 Billionaire "strategery" meeting in a public building not far from Times Square. Some chapter heads with whom I spoke complained about local initiatives delayed because they were told to wait for input from New York in coordinating logistics, scheduling, and budgeting. One chapter head said that she had only two days' notice to prepare for a visit and event featuring a New York Billionaire.[59]

When such tensions between local autonomy and national coordination were debated during the Billionaires' mid-2005 "strategery" meetings, some favored "empowering" local chapters to change flyers, messaging text, and so on to suit their needs. They disagreed about the extent to which New York leaders should comment if other chapters were on or off message.

New York's assistance nonetheless was often welcome. A West Coast chapter head Boyd had recruited in early 2004 said that when she was deciding whether or not to take the job it was persuasive to hear that the New York headquarters chapter "thinks up the themes, thinks up the slogans, makes the signs, makes everything" so that the main responsibility of a chapter head is to "organize your people, get your characters together, get your props, your place, [and] work it all out" locally.[60] She laughed as she said that of course it didn't always work out easily, and the start-up work was time-consuming, including "pummeling all the email lists" from various activist groups.

I know of at least one chapter that sprang up without New York coordination, and used hand-lettered signs and a beautiful handmade banner rather than professionally printed placards. If that embarrassed some New York leaders, others saw such initiatives as success stories. After all, a chapter leader said, the Billionaires for Bush in 2004 were deliberately "creating something that they don't own, and they want it that way; they want groups . . . to pick it up and run with it and do whatever they do and not be accounting to anybody."[61] For the brand bearers, however, the signals from New York could not be clearer.

Visual Unity

"Appearances are everything," the Billionaires' website advised participants. "Formal dress is required. . . . We really must insist that you dress the part. . . . Visual unity is very important to us. Remember, it takes conformity, not individuality, to become a Billionaire for Bush. So don your black suits and evening gowns, and hit the streets!"[62] Seattle Billionaires were not to imitate that city's casually dressed Microsoft multimillionaires. Instead their chapter head said they were to think of images of wealth from New York's Upper East Side, or British royalty.[63] The website advised Billionaires to dress to "preserve the traditional image of the billionaire in America."[64] Showing up in jeans and a tuxedo shirt was frowned upon; those who didn't dress the part "bring us down," a Billionaire said.[65] Many Billionaires, however, were on tight budgets, and they searched thrift shops for their elegant attire. At one 2004 Manhattan Billionaire meeting I attended, a member brought a bag of donated evening clothes, which women tried on and modeled for one another.

Wealth differences among the Billionaires were keenly felt by some but seldom discussed. While most Billionaires held college degrees and many had full-time jobs, some worked part-time and some were underemployed, struggling to make ends meet and wondering if they would lose their New York apartments. One Billionaire told me she had been disheartened because she could not afford to travel with them to a national political party convention in a distant city in 2000, when she was just getting started in her career.[66] She occasionally felt frustrated listening to activists talk about low-income people, "but they didn't get that they weren't talking about other people." This wasn't just a problem with the Billionaires, she said. She was part of another activist organization whose members often went out for food and drink at an expensive restaurant bar after their meetings. She knew those social occasions were "where the group actually jelled" and made important social connections and plans for the next meeting. She described how she would have to "pay twenty bucks for a burger or just sit there and be hungry." When she suggested going to a diner or coffee shop, members said, "Oh, but we like it there," even though "this was a really progressive group." When they talked about how the organization could diversify to "bring in more leadership of color and low-income leadership," she would suggest they "start by not having the postmeeting in places that are alienating to people who don't have money." When I asked how we might understand or explain this, she said, "I think it's about people of privilege not understanding privilege even when they talk about it." Nonetheless, she said, "I really respect the political work of these groups." Though she eventually left the network, hers was just one example of affective solidarity persisting in spite of tensions, bruised feelings, and ambivalences.

Limited ethnic and socioeconomic diversity characterizes many activist networks, and this was an issue the Billionaires' leaders cared about deeply. Their members tended to be white, well educated, and middle class or upper middle class, yet committed to the challenges of building cross-class and cross-race coalitions. For example, the New York chapter staged "counterprotests" in collaboration with picketers supporting the right to unionize and improve working conditions of Starbucks and Verizon employees. At a July 2004 Manhattan chapter meeting, Boyd announced links to a Latino network through the Coney Island Mermaid Parade a few weeks earlier, as well as to a multicultural group at New York University. He said he had met a Native American Billionaire in Los Angeles who adopted the fictive name "Dances with Stock Options."

Billionaire Talking Points

Being a Billionaire was "not a free-for-all," remarked Merchant F. Arms (Varon).[67] A West Coast chapter leader said she felt like the teacher who's trying to get students to do their homework—"Come on, read the [policy] documents on the website!"[68] Participants were to stay on message, focus on the economy and corporate takeover of democracy, avoid "culture war issues (gun control, gay marriage, abortion) because they're not germane to what we're doing," and avoid being so "condescending that you really rile people."[69] Sample talking points distributed to Billionaires preparing for the 2004 Republican National Convention in New York included how to respond if someone asked, "Isn't John Kerry a billionaire?" The suggested response: "Kerry may *be* a billionaire, but President Bush has been a great *friend* to billionaires. He's the best politician Big Money can buy. After all, why rent when you can own?" The "Guide to the RNC" also offered one-liners about Kerry such as, "He's a flip-flopper: Clean air? Clean water? Which is it, John?" and "He wants to repeal tax cuts for those making more than $200,000 per year." If asked, "Aren't most actual billionaires against President Bush?" the suggested answer was, "We all hear about a few renegade class traitors like George Soros and Warren Buffett who are against President Bush, but if you check the stats, of the nation's 277 billionaires, 121 have given money to President Bush but only 39 have given money to Kerry. We know a sure thing when we see it."[70]

Additional tips from the 2004 convention guide: memorize and repeat three to five facts,[71] attend to your visual message, stick together, don't mix with non-Billionaires, don't break the law by telling anyone whom to vote for, don't make fun of the flag, don't be a mock racist, and hardwire the word "billionaire" to Bush by repeating the full name of the organization. The aim was witty, concise messages with a surprise twist—an emperor's new clothes factor—that captured an unspoken truth.

The New York Billionaires' emphasis on economic messaging was resisted by only a few, some of whom felt they should be free to "lampoon religion and greed."[72] A rare instance that elicited strong New York executive committee intervention was a move by the head of the Billionaires' Anchorage chapter to spoof religion and cultural issues after the 2004 election. His chapter was expelled from the network since it was Billionaire policy not to take positions on "God, guns, gays, and abortion." The assumption was that humor about "culture wars" issues would alienate people and be ineffective. Because the Anchorage chapter head did not follow that policy, the New York national field coordinator told him (by email) that the organization appreciated his "passion and conviction" but that "we'll no longer consider ourselves to have an official Anchorage chapter and you'll be unsubscribed from the B4B chapter leader discussion list as well." That decision prompted the Anchorage chapter head to complain on a radio program in Alaska, arguing that "the satirists have become what they satirize."

"The Billionaire persona is a little too two-dimensional for grappling with God and gays," a Billionaire chapter head in another East Coast city wrote in an email to his colleague in Anchorage.[73] He suggested that if the Anchorage chapter head wanted to engage those issues he would be "better served finding some other vehicle for expression." On this point, the Billionaires I knew were confident they had understood public sentiment and the limits of ironic humor in millennial America.

Conclusion

It is not at all unusual for activist networks to inadvertently alienate or neglect some of the very constituencies whose interests they claim to represent, as scholars of social movements have shown.[74] Some Billionaires were keenly aware of such risks, even if most were unlikely to have direct conversations with individuals thus affected. Such knowledge is precisely what Andrew Boyd told me in mid-2006 he hoped to gain from my research—"something about ourselves that we don't already know."[75] Indeed, one of the most useful contributions of academic researchers to social movements, argues Marc Edelman (building on John Burdick's work), "may be reporting patterns in the testimony of people in the movement's targeted constituency who are sympathetic to movement objectives but who feel alienated or marginalized by [an] . . . aspect of movement discourse or practice."[76] I offer such material in a spirit that is simultaneously sympathetic and analytically critical.

This chapter has looked behind the scenes at the work required to perform protest as play and to sustain the Billionaire brand. We have heard participants' own frank self-assessments and concerns, as well as the voices of both skeptical and enthusiastic spectators at live street performances. The Billionaires, however, were also players on a much larger stage, and that is the subject of the next chapter.

6   Media Players

"WE CRACKED THE CODE OF AMERICAN MEDIA CULTURE. For a brief, shining moment, we outsmarted the system."[1] So claimed Merchant F. Arms. Photographed by Richard Avedon for the *New Yorker*, and featured in Art Spiegelman's cartoon in that same magazine, as well as in hundreds of other print and broadcast media accounts, the Billionaires had surely mastered corporate news media. Or had they?

For a social movement, media attention is an "ambiguous gift."[2] The news media spotlight can help to publicize messages of dissent, mobilize followers, and influence target constituencies, thereby broadening political contestation beyond established players with abundant resources. On the other hand, dominant news organizations often ignore or trivialize protesters' agendas while focusing on spectacle or entertainment value. And many protests get no media attention at all. That risk of invisibility prompts some activists to adopt ever more spectacular approaches. The Billionaires, as we have seen, have been at the leading edge of such innovation. But do they use the media—sneaking in substance through satire—or do media use them, as convenient entertainment? Is the relationship parasitic or symbiotic, or perhaps both? What does media coverage of the Billionaires tell us about the public political sphere and "struggles for visibility"[3] in early twenty-first-century America?

The Billionaires played to both the superficiality and the power of the media world's glittering surfaces. In jockeying for media visibility, the Billionaires participated in broader processes of creating new forms of nonstate political activity during a time of increasing "concentration of economic and symbolic power."[4]

This chapter explores the Billionaires' media tactics, along with underlying changes in the political economy of journalism. It then examines how the Billionaires' live performances, words, and actions were portrayed in dominant news media, thereby shaping their identity in the public sphere. How did the Billionaires, in turn, assess the limitations and potential impact of media coverage?

The Billionaires' Media Strategy

"Coaxing media to cover something is not just a walk in the park," said the Billionaires' "speakers' bureau" chair, Ivy League Legacy (Bates).[5] From a standard public relations playbook, a skeletal explanation of how the Billionaires drew media attention might read as follows.[6] First, they appeal to emotions (the conscious and unconscious allure of celebrity, beauty, glamour, fun) and link these to facts about the president's policies—such as George Bush's huge tax cuts for the wealthy, risky deregulation, two unfunded wars, and absence of public advocacy for campaign finance reform.[7] Second, the Billionaires simplify their message for easy media consumption: Republican policies favor the ultrarich and hurt the middle class and poor. Or, both major political parties are too beholden to wealthy funders of their campaigns. They repeat and elaborate their central message with a variety of effective sound bites, slogans, and songs, as well as during interviews while they are "in character" and speak in irony mode, or when they break character and shift to what they term "angry liberal" mode. Third, they offer journalists a story that is "different": their satirical street theater is part of a "new" (or newly revived) form of political protest that is more polished, witty, and appealing than conventional protest. The Billionaires offer high production values—attractive costumes and professional banners backed up by clever fictitious names, slogans, chants, songs, exchanges with passersby, and mock heckling of more "traditional" or "angry liberal" protesters.[8] Crucially, they circumvent media hostility to "traditional" protesters.[9] And their irreverent humor helps to attract younger participants, tapping into the hip, ironic sensibility that characterizes Comedy Central's popular "fake" news programs, *The Daily Show* and the *Colbert Report,*[10] and the satirical newspaper *The Onion*.

Fourth, the Billionaires have savvy public relations specialists among their own members and an effective media response team (who do some of the work for the media). They offer journalists press kits and issue well-written, witty press releases announcing their events. They provide members with background policy information and talking points so they can be engaging and well-informed interviewees. "Have a couple of people on hand who are ready to talk" and who can perform the role of "media star," the Billionaires' website advises those organizing actions.[11] Their website included a "Pressroom" section designed both to assist journalists and to update members and the public about news media articles about the Billionaires.

Fifth, the Billionaires create synergy by staging some of their appearances at public events that already attract media, such as a film premiere, political party fund-raiser at which prominent politicians appear, national political party conventions, or even the tax day rush at a large urban post office. Such venues allow the Billionaires to join someone else's bandwagon, attach their own ironic messages, and engage journalists at events where "they were likely to be bored and not to have much to do . . . but every media outlet has somebody there, so that's fantastic."[12] During the 2000 Democratic National Convention, a public relations person from United for a Fair Economy sent a runner every day with "a hand-delivered Billionaire press release to where all the media were camped out."[13] Finally, the organization's David-versus-Goliath stance appeals to journalists and the public: a small (but rapidly growing) activist network confronts the vast wealth and power of corporations, lobbyists, and politicians.

Such strategies suit news reporters' and editors' everyday constraints of budget, time, and content. The Billionaires were welcome subjects for journalists under pressure to make news entertaining—as long as journalists did not feel the joke was on them. Reporters often played along with the spoof. In addition to offering news reporters a touch of glamour, wit, and charm, the Billionaires likely suited many journalists' preference for reformist rather than revolutionary movements.[14] Even so, the Billionaires had to work hard to counter media tendencies to trivialize, obscure, co-opt, or commodify dissident messages.[15]

How to disrupt conventional news frames and expand support for alternatives has long been a part of social movement theory. Since a news frame defines an issue and the range of permissible debate, and shapes public opinion, simply attracting media coverage is not enough. The challenge for any social movement, Gitlin remarks, is "to achieve publicity for its analysis and program on its own terms [even though] the frames remain powerful [and can process] opposition into hegemonic order."[16]

While the Billionaires' novelty attracted public attention, their media strategy also built on a 1960s playbook. Since activists during the 1960s were learning, as Gitlin put it, "that they could not determine which of their words, if any, would end up on the air," some began to experiment with potent visual images that would convey their messages.[17] For example, Jerry Rubin, when called to testify in 1966 before the House Un-American Activities Committee, wore an American Revolutionary costume so that any news coverage would capture that image and the public would recognize the contradiction about freedom of speech.[18] Gamson, in a brief mention, praises the satirical Billionaires' media strategy and includes them among a few "movements [that] have found ways of making the media interest in celebrities and spectacle work for them as part of a larger media strategy."[19] Performing or embodying a news frame through drama, guerrilla theater, costume, and props can be particularly effective, he observes.

Activist spectacles offer what Andrew Boyd terms a "bell curve of meaning": multiple interpretations shaped by bystanders and participants, some of whom stay "on message" while others are renegades.[20] Protesters, spectators, and journalists coproduce meanings and interpretations of their events.[21] But the Billionaires hoped to turn to their advantage what media critics such as Moyers and coauthors Jamieson and Waldman describe as journalists' tendency to repeat what officials say without investigating the truthfulness of talking points, correcting misstatements, or offering crucial historical contextualization.[22] That meant devising names, slogans, and sound bites that were pithy enough to stand alone—to deliver their messages in news stories that would quote them with little or no historical or policy background information. Even if a news account only reported the Billionaires for Bush name or a slogan such as "Leave No Billionaire Behind," their message was conveyed.[23]

In addition to preparing press releases and hoping that journalists would pick up their cues, Billionaires circulated through their own print and electronic networks news stories in which they themselves featured, as well as members' photographs and reports of their street actions in multiple cities. They posted counts, videos, and links to press coverage on their website, which also instructed those who organized actions to "post a review of the action on the B4B Action Blog, and be prepared to share a brief report at the next B4B general meeting."[24] Participants' narratives of what happened (or an idealized—hyperreal—version of what happened) included plot lines, character definition, and street dialogue journalists might have missed. Such websites served at once as direct media outlets for members of the public curious enough to access the information, and also as a convenient source for journalists wishing to add detail to the stories they were producing.

An example that pleased the Billionaires was a Yahoo news report on a 2006 Billionaire event in Washington, DC, that followed almost verbatim the press release given to the news agency by their Washington, DC, chapter head, Ivan Tital (Ken Mayer).[25] A member's report on that to a Manhattan chapter meeting prompted the quip, "We recite, you report."

New Media, Old Media

"New" media—emergent information-communication technologies—became a tool for Billionaires to organize actions, boost their exposure, and create their own public representations of their organization as a means of influencing audiences. "New" media can embody novel forms of citizenship and activism.[26] Yet they may also reproduce market logics and are neither inherently progressive nor conservative. The Billionaires, like other new media users, build on what Kahn and Kellner term the "prehistory of internet activism" since the 1960s, which includes a "community media movement [that] . . . has promoted alternative media such as public access television, community and low-power radio, and public use of new information and communication technologies."[27] Alternative media such as Indymedia and Wikipedia are often assumed to challenge mass media conventions and representations and to "appear more democratic and socially inclusive," but Atton cautions against a "celebratory approach to alternative media" because that obscures their connections to "other aspects of social and cultural life."[28] Although I refer to dominant, corporate, and mainstream media as roughly equivalent categories that are usually contrasted with independent, community, or alternative media, I recognize the limitations of such terms and the heterogeneity they mask. In the early twenty-first century, distinctions between "mainstream" and other media producers have become increasingly blurred, as have boundaries between media consumers and producers.

While my focus here is the dominant corporate news organizations (principal television, radio, and print journalism outlets) that were the Billionaires' primary media targets, they were also on friendly terms with alternative news outlets such as Indymedia, as well as Internet political groups such as MoveOn (www.moveon.org). Yet the Billionaires especially, as Andrew Boyd commented to a journalist, "use corporate media as an ally. . . . We do something, it gets media attention, people hear about it, and then they want to do something too."[29]

Billionaires as Media Players

The Billionaires are players *in* as well as *of* the media—neither wholly compliant nor resistant.[30] Frankfurt School theorists Adorno and Horkheimer might see them as exemplars of the dictum that "Anyone who resists can only survive by fitting in."[31] From that perspective, once their "deviant" brand—glamorous (rather than scruffy) protester—wins attention from the culture industry, they become a part of it. After all, the Billionaires craft self-representations that are intended to counter negative images of protesters that have been created and circulated by the very same profit-centered media organizations on which the Billionaires themselves rely. That strategy, if successful on the Billionaires' own terms, is simultaneously a means of claiming cultural legitimacy and of challenging hegemonies, of "subverting and rewriting dominant images."[32] The Billionaires, in short, are an example of groups that try to "challenge media power, whether implicitly or explicitly, through becoming active themselves within the media frame."[33]

When they become media players or subjects of broadcast or print journalists' accounts, the Billionaires cross a social boundary; they are "elevated" from the realm of banal or "ordinary" life to the "larger-than-life."[34] Like most citizens, the Billionaires are attracted by the "magic" of media, even if they are critical of journalistic practices and sometimes satirically protest outside the Federal Communications Commission as Billionaires for More Media Mergers.

Anthropological studies of mass media often deconstruct or fault media representations of cultural "others," or explore how those who create, consume, or feature in media products in other parts of the world "manipulate these technologies to their own cultural, economic, and ideological ends."[35] In the United States, protesters themselves are often depicted as "cultural others"—as exotic, curious, marginal, or threatening. Yet some of them, such as the Billionaires, design rhetorical tactics and modes of self-presentation intended to bend media technologies and proclivities to suit their purposes, in order to reach imagined publics. For *Washington Post* reporter Hanna Rosin to deem the Billionaires part of a new "cool frenzy" on the left, and to include them among political groups that exemplify "downtown cool and hipsterism,"[36] delighted them. Such stories fashioned the Billionaires' public identity and helped to enhance their popularity. But how constrained was the Billionaires' space for tactical play in corporate media worlds?

Corporate News Journalism

The Billionaires faced a corporate news journalism landscape characterized by many as one of increasing concentration of media ownership, shrinking resources for investigative journalism, treatment of news as profitable commodity rather than public service, conservative media bias, credulousness toward official sources, the false balance or false equivalencies of he-said/she-said reporting styles, a tendency to recycle official talking points rather than correct misleading statements, neglect of historical context, and an emphasis on politics as spectacle and on the "horse race" (who's up or down today) rather than substantive public policy issues.[37] On the latter point, for example, when Paul Krugman monitored media reports ("major cable and broadcast TV networks") during the 2004 presidential campaign, he found ample coverage of Mr. Kerry's haircuts but not his health care proposals.[38]

Some assume that the market can and should provide the forms of mass communication necessary to sustain democracy, but others argue that market forces favor "oligopoly control and the depoliticization of content, that are far from the liberal ideal of a free market place of ideas."[39] Still others refute entirely the link between democracy and an informed public and suggest that only a small fraction of the population "deliberate on public issues," and that most people consume news not to "become well informed about public issues" but to be entertained, comforted, or informed of facts immediately relevant to their own lives.[40] However one perceives the relationship between media and democracy, many argue that media history tells a story of the "naturalization of inequality" with respect to "who can effectively speak and be listened to."[41] Challenges to media power are usually delegitimated by the very institutions critics target. However trenchant Bill Moyers's critiques of dominant news organizations, and however deep his expertise, not many media consumers are likely to be exposed to his views.

The political economy of U.S. journalism changed profoundly in the late twentieth and early twenty-first centuries. As ownership rules were loosened, a wave of mergers followed and the number of major media corporations in the United States plunged from fifty in 1983 to a mere five by 2004.[42] This consolidation is a heavy counterweight to the democratic potential of technological innovations that have enabled multiplication of media outlets.[43] Indeed the latter have not fulfilled their promise, according to a 2011 federal study of media, which found—according to a *New York Times* summary—that the recent proliferation of online news sources "has not found a corresponding increase in reporting, particularly quality local reporting. . . . [which] has receded at such an alarming pace that it has left government with more power than ever to set the agenda and have assertions unchallenged."[44] A scarcity of investigative reporting shifts coverage away from citizens' concerns and brings heavier reliance on news releases from public relations experts.

The first wave of media deregulation (including the demise of the Fairness Doctrine) during the 1980s in the United States brought cuts in foreign news bureaus, investigative reporting, and in-depth documentary programming.[45] Further deregulation under the Telecommunications Act of 1996, a product of enormous lobbying by print and broadcast media, was passed by a Republican Congress and signed by President Clinton. There was wide (bipartisan) public opposition to such moves, clearly evidenced in public FCC hearings across the country during the early 2000s when former FCC chairman Michael Powell tried to change the rules to allow even more consolidation of media ownership.[46] But these public voices seemed to carry far less weight with the FCC and U.S. legislators than did corporate lobbyists.

With investments in multiple media (newspapers, magazines, movie studios, radio and television stations, and book publishing), a handful of corporations and their leaders—even if not assumed to be monolithic—have enormous power. If the choices major media corporations offer consumers are narrow, that is not the result of conspiracy, says Bagdikian.[47] They don't need to operate as an OPEC-like cartel since they already share with one another "too many of the same methods and goals"; they pursue "possibilities for mutual protection"; and they have intersecting boards of directors.[48] Furthermore, media power itself is naturalized as it is reproduced, albeit unevenly, in everyday life.[49]

Networks increasingly hired marketing consultants to assess the popularity of topics, and as news has become entertainment, profit assessments—more than public service obligations—have shaped decisions about coverage. Well before the 2008 financial meltdown, in the 1990s and early 2000s, Wall Street pounced on newsrooms, slashing budgets for staff writers and sometimes eliminating researchers entirely, even as owners negotiated lucrative personal deals with private equity firms.[50] Contributing to cuts in foreign and other news bureaus were the declines in advertising revenues that accompanied the rising popularity of online news sources.

The 2008 financial crisis brought more closings and bankruptcies of daily newspapers and huge cuts in news staffs, leaving far less coverage of political corruption, campaign finance law loopholes, and municipal budget cuts at precisely a time when watchdogs were much needed. Some of the bankruptcies were the result of large debt assumed in earlier mergers and acquisitions (as when Chicago investor Sam Zell bought the Tribune Company).[51] Such deals yielded large fees for the banks that arranged them, and some of those bankers reportedly had expressed prior doubts about the associated financial fundamentals of those deals.[52]

Some argue that what is killing newspapers is not necessarily the popularity of free online news sources per se but the way newspaper executives have cut costs and quality in response to such changes and to Wall Street demands on publicly held media companies for higher profits and stock prices.[53] Entertainment conglomerates risk sacrificing the public interest and information needs of a democracy as they compete for ratings and profits. Former *New York Times* editor Bill Keller observes a "retrea[t] from the hard labor of journalism under grinding commercial pressure, the steady downsizing and dumbing down, the pandering, the substitution of dueling blowhards and celebrity gossip for actual reporting."[54] His prescription is for more investigative journalism on tough subjects.

In addition to Wall Street investors "hobbling" the press by pumping up profits "at the expense of reporting," Moyers observes that journalists in the early 2000s also faced intimidation, harassment, and misrepresentation of their work from some political conservatives and corporations—practices that contribute to a *conservative* media bias, even on the part of liberal reporters.[55] The latter strive to avoid appearing to have lost their objectivity, even when this results in falsely balanced reporting that gives equal weight to arguments that are not equally defensible or supported by evidence. Attacks by conservative ideologues, Jamieson and Waldman argue, help to tilt reporters' news stories *away* from their "favored candidates and policies" and to make them "tougher on Democrats."[56]

To agree with such a stance is not to endorse a view of news media as a "conspiracy of bosses,"[57] or to demonize press barons, but rather to call attention to crucial dimensions of the contemporary political economy and norms of journalism, and to institutional constraints and subtle forms of power journalists experience in their own workplaces.[58] This era of media consolidation and digitization, anthropologist Dominic Boyer observes, has brought a speed-up in the work of journalists, job insecurity, the "congestion of news access," a "hollowing out" of journalists' critical engagement with the news, widespread imitation, and a "pack mentality."[59]

American journalistic norms that encourage reporters to pursue false balance or false equivalencies led Krugman to joke that "if one party declared that the earth was flat, the headlines would read 'Views Differ on Shape of Planet.'"[60] That both sides of an argument do not necessarily have equally valid claims, or that not all issues are reducible to two opposing sides, are assumptions more often expressed in the work of European than U.S. reporters.[61] Thanks in large part to compliant U.S. journalists who did not correct Bush administration misstatements linking Saddam Hussein to the September 11 attacks, two years later "almost 70 percent of the public still thought it likely that Saddam Hussein was personally involved in the terrorist attacks of that day."[62] Journalistic norms in other countries are more likely to assume that the reporter has a responsibility to arbitrate competing claims, investigate the underlying evidence, and offer the audience enough information to allow reasonable inferences or conclusions. A striking example from Ireland caught Jon Stewart's attention.

American viewers who had grown accustomed to a deferential presidential press corps were shocked, Frank Rich writes, when a television reporter on the Irish network RTE (in June 2004) interviewed President Bush in a very different style, "challenging him repeatedly about the failure to find weapons of mass destruction and his claim that the war in Iraq has made us safer."[63] That news story led Jon Stewart to ask during a *Daily Show* program, "Where can we get a journalist like that?" It was precisely the paucity of that kind of reporting in dominant U.S. news organizations that opened space for satirists such as Stewart and Colbert. Indeed one was more likely to see on Stewart's *Daily Show*, than on mainstream network or cable news, clips of archived footage to help place the day's news stories in context, correct misleading narratives, or document an individual's contradictory statements—whether of a Democrat or a Republican.

In 2004, an "angry Bush-hater" news frame shaped coverage of political party conventions, sometimes misleadingly. Cable news coverage of the 2004 Democratic National Convention in Boston, for example, favored "a script portraying Democrats as angry Bush-haters who disdain the military."[64] Contrary to that frame, Krugman observes, Democrats at the convention cheered the portions of John Kerry's speech where he talked about a strong America, while a Fox News reporter falsely "asserted that conventioneers . . . were silent when he [Kerry] called for military strength." So too false images of protesters spitting on returning troops or calling them baby-killers in the Vietnam era were part of a "myth of liberals disrespecting troops" in earlier eras.[65] Journalists who rely on epithets such as "Republican haters" or "Bush haters" often miss the opportunity to explain exactly what policies the supposed haters oppose and why.

Dominant news media during the 2004 presidential campaign tended to adopt a Republican politics-of-envy frame that ignored the ways Bush's policies distinctly favored the very rich.[66] News accounts often mentioned that Senators Kerry and Edwards were multimillionaires without using those labels for President Bush or Vice President Cheney, playing along with Republican characterizations of Kerry as being out of the mainstream. During the 2012 presidential campaign Mitt Romney, whose economic policies seemed to favor the ultrarich, also portrayed talk of economic inequality as rooted in "envy" and "class warfare."[67] Again, the constricted space for serious public discussion of wealth inequality leaves a wide opening for satirists.

In corporate media worlds, would the Billionaires too be treated as "alternative celebrities"[68]—well informed, witty, attractive, and articulate—whose interventions in the public sphere would generate lighthearted accounts of their street theater rather than news stories exploring the policies they criticized? As protesters, what media frames awaited them?

Protest and the Media

Dominant U.S. news organizations seldom probe the fundamental issues of social and economic justice that are the focus of protest. Moyers writes, "the question of whether our political and economic system is truly just or not is off the table for investigation and discussion by our dominant media elites."[69] Common media frames of social protest in the United States during the 1960s, as Gitlin remarks, included trivialization, polarization, emphasis on internal dissension, marginalization, undercounting or disparagement by numbers, and disparagement of the movement's effectiveness.[70] He connects some of these patterns to journalism's technical and institutional characteristics: recruitment, promotion, reporter assignments, occasional intervention by political elites, and tendencies on the part of reporters and editors to "adapt and reproduce the dominant ideological assumptions prevailing in the wider society."[71] While there were conflicts within news organizations about how to cover 1960s social movements, media often conveyed the impression that "extremism was rampant and that the New Left was dangerous to the public good."[72]

Decades later, mainstream U.S. media coverage of anarchist protest, McLeod and Hertog found, "emphasizes the actions rather than the issues of a protest in a way that protects the illusion of objectivity," tends to rely on official sources and official definitions, and often depicts protesters as violating norms of dress and behavior; whereas the alternative press focuses on social norms violated by the institutions or agencies that are the targets of the protesters.[73] Similarly the media watch group FAIR found that corporate news organizations focused on police viewpoints instead of protesters' messages about the Afghanistan war and other issues during the May 2012 NATO summit in Chicago.[74]

Even as mainstream journalists sidestep activists' messages about social and economic justice, their coverage of protest implies a pluralist society that is "full of political vitality . . . [and where] opinions and interests contend freely."[75] Protests become a "carnival" of diverse groups and interests, and media depictions of demonstrators have comic overtones. Yet reporters, protesters claim, often underestimate crowd size and deem demonstrators' underlying messages unintelligible or irrational or unworthy of attention. Furthermore, dominant news organizations seldom announce political demonstrations in advance or provide information on how to contact organizers.[76] If a small minority of demonstrators engage in violence in the form of attacks on property (such as smashing a Starbucks window), those images are endlessly replayed in place of any serious media attention to the substance of issues advanced by the vast majority of peaceful protesters.[77] Coverage of national events such as political party conventions in turn focuses on the possibility of protester violence, often quoting police and other officials about security precautions and again ignoring the substantive issues that are expected to drive large numbers of protesters into the streets.

That tendency frustrated the Billionaires' musical producer, Clifford Tasner (Felonious Axe), when he joined the large 2004 anti-Bush demonstration on the eve of the 2004 Republican National Convention in New York. He wrote in his journal that August day that the "aggressive tactics" of protesters who favor direct action "feed the media's love of a sensational story and sometimes steal the focus from those of us working so long and hard on creative activism."[78]

Meanwhile, some protesters directly expressed the same concern to the *Washington Post*'s Robert Kaiser during that August 2004 march in New York City. Kaiser wrote that when "more than a few" people in the "vast crowd" that day saw his *Washington Post* press pass, they "made pointed remarks about how 'the mainstream media' didn't care about their anti-war, anti-Bush message, but only covered them to see if a riot might happen."[79] Kaiser terms the anger in those comments "a sign of the times," though he does not analyze that anger. Neither does he trivialize the protest. Indeed he found it remarkable: "I have covered a lot of demos in my long reporting career—the first was the March on Washington in 1963 for civil rights. But this felt like one of the very biggest I'd ever seen. Seventh Avenue was jammed with marchers, a larger percentage of them looking like ordinary people from across the country."[80] Kaiser's description of the marchers as "high-spirited" at least hints at their energy, sense of solidarity, and exhilaration that day. How did the Billionaires fare with corporate media?

How Dominant News Media Cover the Billionaires

Media coverage of the Billionaires grew dramatically between 2000 and 2004. Between January 2000 and June 2007, more than 550 articles about the Billionaires appeared in print.[81] The largest share was published in the election years 2004 (45%) and 2000 (22%). While media coverage dropped, as would be expected, between national elections, many more articles about the Billionaires were published between the 2004 and 2008 elections than between the 2000 and 2004 elections.[82] The approximately five hundred articles published between January 2000 and May 2006 came from forty states (plus Washington, DC) and a half dozen foreign countries.[83] Articles focused on Billionaire activities connected to presidential debates, candidate appearances or rallies, national Democratic and Republican party conventions, shadow conventions, presidential inaugurations, antiwar rallies, G8 summits, antiwar demonstrations, tax filing day, the estate tax, police spying on protesters, and performances by The Follies (Billionaire choir). Media coverage in 2008 included the Billionaires who posed as "Lobbyists for McCain" during that year's presidential contest and as "Billionaires for Bailouts" in Wall Street demonstrations during the 2008 financial meltdown. Thurston Howell IV, still an active Billionaire in 2008, remarked that Wall Street was a media-rich environment as the financial crisis intensified in the fall of 2008, but it offered reporters little to film; the satirical Billionaires for Bailouts, he said, successfully took advantage of that opportunity.[84]

As gatekeepers who decide which protest groups should be considered important players, mainstream journalists enhanced the Billionaires' visibility by mentioning them prominently, and usually quite favorably, in their articles about political protest. The Billionaires were sometimes subject to mild trivialization or marginalization but seldom placed in polarizing frames. I saw little or no journalistic disparagement of the group's effectiveness or numbers, and no mentions of internal dissension.

Most strikingly, mainstream media images of the Billionaires emphasized their polish and glamour, mirroring the organization's own image-crafting strategies and reproducing the emphasis on surfaces and icon-making that so strongly defines American politics and journalism in the late twentieth and early twenty-first centuries. Merchant F. Arms (Varon), again, argues that the Billionaires were able to "reengage . . . real political economy through the realm of the surface."[85] Without thus adapting to the visibility game of a society of spectacle, he and other Billionaires felt they had little possibility of getting any part of their message circulated in corporate news media.

News stories about the Billionaires were often tongue-in-cheek, entertaining accounts, with headlines such as "Tuxedos, Pearls, and Satire Fill the Streets," "Billionaires Take the Time to Thank 'the Little People,'" "The Birth of the Meta-Protest Rally?" and "Billionaires for Bush? Well, Yes and No." Opening with vivid descriptions of their costumes, slogans, and fictive names, news articles often presented the Billionaires in a theatrical narrative that simulated the response of spectators on the street: initial surprise and confusion, then gradually catching on to the joke and appreciating the irony of the slogans and names. "There was a fraction of a moment when no one knew how to react," begins a *Boston Globe* article about the Billionaires and other anti-Bush protesters outside the Park Plaza Hotel in March 2004.[86]

Examples of U.S. and foreign journalists' descriptions of the Billionaires follow:

> "One of the better known of the theatrical protest groups whose snappily-dressed members picket Republican events shouting slogans like 'Blood for oil' and 'Corporations are people too!'" (*Newsday*)[87]

> "Billionaires for Bush has quickly become the 'dah-ling' of the convention. Part street theater, part satire group, the Billionaires get smiles from police officers and their photos taken by bemused tourists." (*The Record*, Bergen County, NJ)[88]

"They looked like overflow from Jay Gatsby's garden party: pearls, top hats, gloves up to the elbow." (WBUR)[89]

Andrew Boyd wore "an elegant Old World suit made many decades ago by his immigrant grandfather . . . top hat [and] tie emblazoned with images of hundred-dollar bills . . . [and] brandishing his plastic cigar" (*The American Prospect*)[90]

"A political street theatre group whose ironic fox-furs, tuxedos and clinking martini glasses have been cropping up across New York all summer, to either entertaining or irritating effect." (*Financial Times*, London)[91]

"[W]earing a flapper-era dress and elbow-length gloves . . . a lengthy cigarette-holder in hand." (*New York Times*)[92]

"[A] crowd of bluebloods of questionable pedigree" (*St. Petersburg Times*)[93]

"[A]ctivist street-theatre group . . . dressed in tuxedoes and flowing evening gowns . . . pseudo-bluebloods." (*Ottawa Citizen*)[94]

A "whimsical" protest group "whose members mock Republican economic policy." (*Salt Lake Tribune*)[95]

Depicting the Billionaires as iconic of a "new" form of protest, one journalist termed them "the antithesis of window-smashing anarchists."[96] A 2004 *New York Times* article by Jack Hitt counterposed the Billionaires for Bush to "typical" protesters "in high dudgeon" who "carried the usual placards" and who included a Sierra Club member who "wore a doormat decorated with tufts of glued fuzz to resemble, she said, 'Mothra, the giant moth that defeated Godzilla.'"[97] Comic overtones in his depiction of Sierra Club protesters eclipse their environmental message. He depicted the Billionaires in appealing language ("surprisingly organized," "handsome," "stunning") that countered his characterizations of the traditional protesters as angry, absurdly costumed, and predictable. Hitt wrote, "Amid the hand-drawn placards [of other protesters], the Billionaires unsheathed their professionally printed, brightly colored laminated posters."

A CNN reporter also favorably contrasted the Billionaires with "anarchists" on the eve of the 2004 Republican National Convention in New York: "While the Billionaires for Bush promised they'll play croquet and sip three-martini lunches, it's the anarchists who police are really worried about."[98] A 2004 *Chicago Sun-Times* article carried a photo with the caption "Not all the protesters are pierced or angry: 'Billionaires for Bush' and others keep the atmosphere light outside the convention."[99] And a 2004 *Boston Globe* piece referred to the Billionaires as "the fancy-dressed group" and "part of a well-organized, liberal-leaning protest machine calling itself Billionaires for Bush," who "stag[e] swanky protests in which they enthusiastically defend tax loopholes for the rich and war contracts for friends of the president."[100] In many articles about demonstrators at national political party conventions in 2004, the Billionaires were mentioned in the lead paragraph or received more attention or more favorable coverage than other groups.

The Billionaires themselves are keenly attuned to such journalistic distinctions, as vividly described by a participant in her thirties: "[Journalists'] point of reference was protestors wearing scarves around their mouths, throwing rocks or bottles, or just spitting or being, you know, confrontational. And here we are with our ball gowns and long gloves and pearls, and we're just so polite. But at the same time we're saying: 'What are you guys doing to the economy? What are you doing to the people who live here?'"[101] She assumed that reporters would note their sharp economic message as well as their attractive appearance.

Journalistic framing of the Billionaires after the 2004 presidential election continued to depict them as more charming than other liberals and other protesters, and as evidence that irony was still alive. *New York Times* reporter Haberman interviewed a half dozen Billionaires in a Greenwich Village apartment shortly after the election, and featured them in a column about the impact on political humor of Bush's return to office. He favorably contrasted their satire with the grumbling of "liberals draped in sackcloth," mentioned their "dynasty tax" label for the estate tax, and wrote that "they assumed that campaign financing, Social Security's future and tax reductions for the rich would inevitably be part of their [postelection] agenda."[102] Briefly noting their positions on a few issues, he followed the conventions of dominant frames for such stories by not analyzing their policy substance and instead simply wrote, "Agree with them or not on the big issues, the Billionaires are proof that irony in New York has a strong pulse, no matter how quick some were to pronounce it dead right after Sept. 11."[103] Haberman contrasted the Billionaires with traditional protesters he termed "Starbucks trashers" and said that unlike the latter, the Billionaires "understand that a message—especially one not universally popular—can be more effective if delivered with a smile, not a scream."[104]

Even a journalist who did mention the economic policy issues that are the Billionaires' focus[105] conformed to a pattern noted by Jamieson and Waldman,[106] when he wrote that a Billionaire "news conference" inside a stretch limousine was "supposed to highlight what Democrats charge is the inequity of Bush's tax plan." Instead of independently quoting or analyzing recent economic data available from official nonpartisan sources such as the Congressional Budget Office, the reporter simply said "Democrats charge" that the Bush plan is inequitable, and he quotes a statistic offered by the Billionaires. Many articles did not even go this far—they did not mention any relevant statistics or policy arguments offered by the Billionaires or by others. Policy differences, if mentioned at all, were framed as he-said/she-said charges by Democrats or Republicans, as if all such issues could be reduced to partisan bickering and as if the supposed bickering was the only story the press was obliged to tell the public.[107]

A rare example of a journalistic piece about the Billionaires that went beyond he-said/she-said reporting illustrates Pedelty's point about differences between U.S. and European news frames.[108] It is a 2004 article in *The Independent* (London), which offered contextual information about the Billionaires' economic policy issues. After describing the Billionaires in the opening paragraph, the reporter wrote: "Like all good satire it works because it is *dangerously close to the truth*. It's not hard to see why America's billionaires love Bush. Two thirds of his massive $350bn programme of tax cuts has gone to the richest 10 percent of Americans."[109] The article went on to analyze why the poor often supported Bush in spite of his policies that harmed their economic interests and security.

While the Billionaires usually fared well in journalistic accounts, they were occasionally placed in marginalizing news frames, as in a 2004 Agence France-Presse article headlined "Cranks and Jokesters Take U.S. Protest to the Streets." Though the reporter's framing marginalized all protesters, he still depicted the Billionaires more favorably than other groups, described them as "hard to top," and remarked on their "swanky suits, bowler hats and ties printed with 100-dollar bills."[110]

Similarly, a July 2004 *New York Times* article about political groups setting up tables to publicize their issues in Union Square during the height of the presidential campaign recycled a common journalistic frame—citing an "almost circuslike atmosphere."[111] But here too the reporter shined a flattering spotlight on the Billionaires and included a photo of them.

The Billionaires fared well even when caught in a marginalizing frame such as the one that opened an article in the conservative *Washington Times*.[112] The piece featured anti-Bush counterinaugural festivities in January 2005 and the lead sentences read: "Loyal Republicans, esteemed statesmen, satin-wrapped ladies and country music luminaries have their place in the spectrum of inaugural festivities. But so do guerrilla poets, die-hard Democrats, punk rockers, hip-hop artists, disc jockeys and assorted noisemakers who will people alternative celebrations to mark President Bush's second term in office." The Billionaires for Bush were the subject of four paragraphs in this article, far more than any other group. The *Washington Times* reporter quoted Ivan Tital (Ken Mayer)—head of the Billionaires' Washington, DC, chapter—breaking character to comment succinctly on the economic issues that are the group's focus: "We believe the issues of class and economics which are central to American policies have been muted in American politics. Social issues like guns, God, and gays are used by politicians of both parties to distract the public from real issues of class and wealth." Reporter Jennifer Harper mentioned the Billionaires' upcoming "auction of an Arctic National Wildlife Refuge" at the Franklin D. Roosevelt Memorial.

A minority of news articles about the Billionaires adopted a disavowal framing that conveyed a negative or openly skeptical message. Some, like a *Washington Times* piece, questioned the equation of Republicans with billionaires and pointed to counterexamples such as George Soros or the wealth of John Kerry's wife, Teresa Heinz-Kerry.[113] Under the headline "Protesters' Messages Miss Mark," a reporter described an array of protesters at the 2000 Republican National Convention in Philadelphia and concluded that "With low unemployment, a booming stock market and no major international crises to galvanize public attention, demonstrators had difficulty finding a large audience for their long and colorful list of complaints."[114] The same article quoted protesters complaining that the thousands of corporate news media journalists in the city that week gave too little attention to the efforts of peaceful protesters, and that many citizens were probably unaware that protests were occurring at all.

Television coverage too highlights political protest as theater or spectacle, and as potential danger—as in a *CBS Evening News* story about protests at the Republican National Convention in 2000.[115] Correspondent Susan Spencer began: "The 'Unity 2000' march seemed to unite every cause that's ever had a T-shirt. It snaked its way through Philadelphia streets peacefully—part street carnival, meet the Billionaires for Bush." At that point an "unidentified male" Billionaire said on camera, "We've been running this country for too long from behind closed doors." Such locutions were the product of careful advance preparation on the part of the Billionaires, who designed them precisely for fleeting media coverage. Spencer also talked about police crowd-control training and said, "There was no trouble today, but there are whispers about civil disobedience once the convention actually starts. And city fathers are holding their breath." She did not reveal the source of the "whispers," and nowhere in this piece was there any discussion of why people were protesting, aside from simply naming the Free Tibet movement. The Billionaires for Bush accomplished more in this brief CBS news account than any of the other groups depicted because Spencer both mentioned the name of their organization—a message in itself—and quoted a member.

In 2007, their environmentalist message penetrated news filters when they posed as Billionaires for Coal. An *International Herald Tribune* article referred to the Rainforest Action Network dismissively as "a scrappy little advocacy group" and said this about Billionaires for Coal protesting outside Merrill Lynch in Texas: "Dressed in top hats, carrying bags of coal and calling themselves 'Billionaires for Coal,' the group was protesting what it felt was the hypocrisy of a giant investment bank that proclaims a devout commitment to 'environmental excellence' even as it provides financing for dirty power plants."[116] A Fox News account carried the heading "Have a lump of coal, Merrill Lynch" and described the protesters' opposition to Merrill Lynch's role in financing a Dallas utility company's "plan to build 11 new coal power plants" in Texas.[117] Here again, the point of the protest was captured in the group's name itself and in short accompanying descriptions, allowing satire to seep into a news frame that instead had comic overtones. The comic incongruity of people in top hats carrying bags of coal helped to protect them against complete dismissal.

Overall, U.S. mainstream media coverage of the Billionaires and other protesters gives little attention to the substance of their arguments and focuses instead on what they wear and do at particular demonstrations. Protecting the "illusion of objectivity,"[118] U.S. journalists tend to report on protest as street theater, carnival, threat, or spectacle.

Billionaires Reflect on Media Attention

There has been little research on how news coverage affects protest groups themselves, though media attention "may affect group dynamics such as internal solidarity, boundary maintenance and coalition formation."[119] There is no question that media attention boosted the Billionaires' morale and helped them to retain members and attract new ones. A news story about the Billionaires might prompt a reader to look at their website and then to start a new chapter or join a local chapter. (I myself first learned of the Billionaires for Bush from Jack Hitt's 2004 *New York Times Sunday Magazine* feature article.)

A woman who had participated in Billionaire activities during both the 2000 and 2004 election campaigns replied as follows when I asked her about the rapid rise in the number of Billionaires for Bush chapters in 2004[120]: "*Because of the media we would get more and more people* and . . . we'd get more and more people who had different skills who kept raising the production value, so it was incredible."

Especially during the height of the 2000 and 2004 presidential campaigns, the Billionaires basked in the media spotlight: "There was a time when we could curl our diamond-crusted finger; we could bat our pretty eyes . . . and they [journalists] would flock to us and write stories about us," said Merchant F. Arms to Billionaires gathered for a mid-2005 "strategery" meeting in Manhattan.[121] That changed after Bush's 2005 inauguration, when the Billionaires noticed a drop in media attention and had to rethink their aims. For a time in 2005, they felt lost. As Merchant F. Arms put it, "We've sort of lost our shadow, and in losing our shadow, we've kind of lost our soul." The Billionaires later rebounded, but media coverage was always vital to their morale. The rise and fall and rise again in the volume of coverage mapped the organization's emotional arc.

"We can't will our shadow back," Merchant F. Arms said, "but [it's a matter of] reengaging the world to give us, in a sense, our shadow and our soul back."[122] How to redefine the organization and restore its "soul" was the focus of long Billionaire "strategery" meetings in mid-2005. When the Billionaires bounced back in new forms such as Billionaires for Wealthcare, Lobbyists for McCain, Billionaires for Bailouts, Billionaires for Coal, and Billionaires for Tar Sands, media attention followed. The *New York Times* covered their widely viewed "No You Can't" video spoof in 2008.[123] Even several years after Bush's second inauguration, they found welcome reminders of their iconic status: Zakes Mda's 2007 novel *Cion* mentions the Billionaires for Bush, which prompted a member to email the organization's listserv to announce that "The Billionaires have made it into yet another province of the culture-scape."[124]

Yet the Billionaires' accomplishments did not necessarily confer journalistic standing in the sense Gamson describes more generally, that is as "serious players in any policy domain . . . whose comments are directly or indirectly quoted . . . [rather than] object[s] being discussed by others."[125] Billionaire membership per se did not lead journalists to seek them out as sources on economic policy issues. Instead, as we have seen, reporters described Billionaire glamour and street theater, quoted their slogans and talking points, photographed them, and allowed the Billionaires' own press releases to shape news stories—without publishing probing interviews about the economic policies they critiqued.

Yet as the Billionaires reflected on their public image during a mid-2005 "strategery" meeting, singer and musician Fillmore Barrels (Dave Case) suggested that they took themselves too seriously. Offering to play devil's advocate, he said it was unrealistic to expect that the media would do much with the Billionaires' economic messaging research. After all, he said, "we're the jesters . . . the clowns."[126]

If seen as bit players in a corporate news media game, the point for the Billionaires is that they *are* players and that mainstream media at least captured their core message, which was embedded in everything they did—organizational name, slogans, individual names, songs, and costumes.[127] Since journalists tended not to disembed the Billionaires' messages or use them to explore underlying economic policy issues and debates, did Billionaire tacticians assume that audiences would "see through" news coverage? Yes, argues the organization's cofounder Andrew Boyd: in 2000, the Billionaires had learned that the mainstream media "could be seduced to 'play along' with the literal, tongue-in-cheek meaning, letting the public decode the implied and subversive meanings for themselves."[128]

"The reason the media loves us is because we're like sexy copy, we're interesting, we're that kind of quirky weird story that editors love, so we fit, we work very well with the media, we fit that paradigm that they want because that's what we're supposed to do, that's what we're engineered to do," said Billionaire Ken Mondschein, head of their Meme Team in 2004 and at that time a doctoral student who was in his late twenties.[129] Mondschein, an expert on the Middle Ages and Renaissance, later became a Fulbright Scholar in France and an expert swordsman who teaches historical fencing. I asked him as we sat on the floor at the end of a 2004 Manhattan chapter meeting what he thought about the Billionaires drawing legitimacy from the culture of wealth and celebrity they critique, and he replied: "We do and we don't because . . . we only tap into as much as a parody does. We really are a piece of burlesque; we're charivari . . . the whole idea of carnival. . . . We take . . . politics and we further carnivalize it, and in a sense we're speaking truth to power but in a more palatable way than angry activists shaking a fist in the street."

I then asked him to talk about the extent to which news media cover the substance of the Billionaires' issues. Having charmed the media, the Billionaires' further challenge, I assumed, was to capitalize on the media's attraction to their *style* of activism by focusing public attention on the *substance* of their messages about Bush's policies. So I mentioned media superficiality, sound bites, and a culture of celebrity. His reply:

> Well, "superficial" of course is a loaded term. . . . I'm working on that. . . . [We offer a] candy-coated shell—it's fun, it's a party, and you go inside and there's a real message there and the message is potentially subversive. . . . As for Billionaires for Bush breaking out of the media paradigm, I don't think so; we're so created to work in that paradigm, we're also trapped in it. . . . There is no room for nuance, not in an academic sense, not us like sitting around a seminar today and talking about nuance, because we are geared toward sound bites.

And so the Billionaires are simultaneously designed to work within a corporate news media paradigm and are also trapped in it. While Billionaires can break character—take off the Billionaire top hat—and build more nuanced arguments, he says, that is not necessarily effective:

> Most of them [ordinary citizens] have so much stuff on their plate; they have to take the kids to soccer practice, they must go buy groceries and this and that . . . and they don't need some intellectual from New York going on about finer points of the budget, the educational system, and all that. The reason why we've had so much success is that we do have a shtick that works. . . . I know again I'm just toeing the party line, but the party line is in its own way a really good statement of how people communicate with each other these days. . . . I don't want to put a value judgment on the sound-bite culture, because it is its own thing, its own creature . . . it's better to light a candle in this case than to curse the darkness.

In his view, and perhaps that of most members, their success indeed is affirmed by media mentions of their name, slogans, and chants, since these embody their dissenting messages. They deliberately offer a "candy-coated" shell around a message that is serious and "potentially subversive."

Media attention affected internal group dynamics, both boosting feelings of solidarity as well as contributing to subtle shifts in individual status accorded to members journalists quoted or photographed. Jokes about media access were sometimes leveling mechanisms, such as referring to a member as a "media hound" or gently chiding or teasing individuals who appeared too eager for the camera's gaze. One member in her twenties, however, said she felt uncomfortable with all the reporters and cameras at their Manhattan planning meetings during the height of the 2004 presidential campaign. That became "nerve-wracking" for her, and she said she wouldn't speak her mind in such an environment.[130]

For many Billionaires, delight in media attention was not just a matter of individual ego but also the gratification of having the organization's messages in the spotlight for public consumption. Thurston Howell IV (Kurt Opprecht) described his pleasure in having cameras pointed at him and his "Small Government, Big Wars" sign as he posed next to the U.S. Treasury Building during a September 2005 antiwar rally in Washington, DC[131]:

> Well, at one point I got up on the banister; there's a sort of a patio and then a railing on that patio at the Treasury Building Annex. . . . It's like twenty feet above the street level so anyone could see me and they were all marching past, and I held up a big sign that said "Small Government, Big Wars." And of all the signs that were there, that one was the one I chose to hold up, and it was so fun to see so many cameras pointed at me for so long, not because I wanted to be on camera—that's sort of worn off—but it was sort of fun to see . . . people seeing our message, seeing me as a Billionaire. It was reaching some people, and it was just fun. . . . I was in the yachtsman outfit.

He and other activists who reveled in such occasions knew, as Gamson put it, that "a demonstration with no media coverage at all is a nonevent, unlikely to have any positive influence either on mobilizing followers or influencing the target. No news is bad news."[132]

When a Billionaire friend teased Opprecht about being a "camera hound" during the January 2005 presidential inauguration protests in Washington, DC, Opprecht said to him: "Look, what do we do with Billionaires for Bush? We try to influence the world. How do we do that? By getting on TV." He said his friend had become so accustomed to all the television coverage that he had "forgotten that this was a major part of what we do."

"We felt totally like rock stars," Opprecht said, when other protest groups were stuck in the activist pen during the 2005 inauguration demonstrations in Washington, DC, while the Billionaires were sought out by the media and treated differently.[133] At a subsequent Manhattan chapter meeting he mentioned that day's CNN interview with the Billionaires and said that "it was really a testament to how hard we worked and what we'd done." He contrasted the Billionaires' star quality with what he saw as pointless political activity in the pen to which other protesters were confined on Inauguration Day, and where the Billionaires stayed for no more than twenty minutes. That sense of being media celebrities was double-edged; some members felt it risked going too far and worried that other groups perceived the Billionaires as exclusive or snobbish, though this appeared to be a minority opinion.

Most Billionaires offered euphoric assessments of how mainstream media accounts portrayed them. They described their media coverage in one of the organization's internal documents in early 2005 as follows: "We generate more press, dollar for dollar, than almost any other grassroots organization."[134]

Faustian Contract?

The Billionaires' relationship with dominant news organizations might strike some as a "Faustian contract."[135] They convey their dissent, with flair, through conventional journalistic channels, and they do not immediately threaten the very existence of current hierarchies of power and wealth. Yet they do chip away at those edifices in ways few historians would discount. Such ideological and practical struggles, as James C. Scott argues, can "create political and economic barrier reefs of their own"—much as "millions of anthozoan polyps create, willy-nilly, a coral reef."[136] The creative activism of the Billionaires and the publicity their festive protest generates can help to inspire more political engagement.

All political advocacy networks can at least toy with hegemonic processes that use power to organize consent and to secure political projects. The effectiveness of modest activist initiatives should not be discounted since the work of securing hegemony is always uneven and incomplete, and, as Gavin Smith puts it, there are "crucial unstable moments when organized collective action can be effective within a field of uneven power resources."[137] Furthermore, change must be imagined before it can be enacted, and thus activists whose aim is to reframe issues or to illustrate contradictions between ideological claims and actual political practice can have profound effects, however subtle or difficult to measure they may be.

7   After Satire?

"**W**E SHOWED AMERICA WHAT PLUTOCRACY LOOKS LIKE," declared the Billionaires' cofounder Andrew Boyd.[1] George W. Bush himself let this truth slip out in a provocative joke at the Alfred E. Smith Memorial Foundation dinner in October 2000, as he told the audience: "This is an impressive crowd of the haves and have-mores. Some people call you the elite, I call you my base."[2] By the end of the 2000s, that was not the kind of joke most politicians would want ordinary citizens to overhear.

To recap the Billionaire tale: The return of plutocracy sends to the streets objectors who impersonate imaginary plutocrats. These protesters against extreme wealth inequality carefully avoid the semiotics of poverty because they have concluded that public culture in their country effaces the working poor. They don costumes intended to defy images of "traditional" protesters because they believe that influential voices in the media disparage the latter. Since wealth itself is an object of popular admiration, they assume that elegantly attired protesters pretending to be billionaires will be objects of attraction. They are mostly middle class, but as they parody the ultrarich, some admit they fantasize about joining them. They wrap their economic and political critique in ironic humor because they have learned that otherwise journalists and many ordinary citizens will not listen. And their beliefs are likely shared by many in a country whose most trusted source of "real" news in the 2000s was a comedian, Jon Stewart, the host of a satirical news program.[3]

Why had satire become such an influential medium in American critical politics? Political satire and irony flourish especially when other forms of political critique are curtailed, or when conventional political categories, modes of expression, and organization seem inadequate—an apt description, many would argue, of early–twenty-first-century America. Some emphasize growing corruption and the rise of a powerful "shadow elite" in U.S. politics as fuel for parody such as Jon Stewart's,[4] while scholars of mass media and performance studies locate explanations in the "highly choreographed nature of current political debate,"[5] as well as structural transformations in dominant news media. Critical media scholars have observed a decline in investigative reporting, emphasis on news as profitable commodity rather than public service, consolidation of corporate ownership, homogenization of content due in part to growing reliance on a few news agencies such as AP and Reuters (and sometimes public relations firms), and emphasis on play-by-play accounts or the political "horse race" rather than substantive political and economic issues.[6] American politics, many argue, increasingly resembles "a kind of professional performance culture" in which politics is "depoliticized" through an emphasis on "event staging, spinning, and images above political ideas and dialogue."[7] The heavily scripted or ritualized qualities of contemporary political debate and news reporting can make political satire seem more sincere, authentic, and incisive.[8] Sometimes parody itself appears almost real, as in Tina Fey's impersonations of 2008 vice presidential candidate Sarah Palin, where Fey drew laughter by repeating Palin's own words verbatim.

Americans, however, have long been more accustomed to political comedy that blandly targets personal idiosyncrasies rather than barbed satire. When comedian Steve Bridges impersonated President George W. Bush as the two of them stood at twin podiums during the 2006 White House Correspondents' dinner, the audience laughed appreciatively. But they responded coldly to Stephen Colbert's satire of the president a few minutes later on that same stage. While Bridges spoofed the president's faulty syntax, mispronunciations, and rhetorical style, Colbert satirized Bush's low approval rating (32% in early 2006); implied that the president ignored facts and did not read books; and reminded the audience about warrantless wiretapping, the Valerie Plame CIA scandal, and failure to find weapons of mass destruction in Iraq. Colbert also scathingly satirized media tendencies to parrot officials' talking points. Initially, mainstream media ignored Colbert and touted instead Bush's good-humored participation in the Bridges segment.[9] Colbert's lampoon, however, became a

YouTube hit, and then dominant news organizations covered the story. It remains a cultural touchstone, an illustration of how satire can shift national political discourse and of how "fake" news parody feeds off perceived limitations of "real" news coverage.

Such limitations include a constriction of media's contributions to imagining new social vistas and constructing community—a theme media ethnographers inspired by Marshall McLuhan and Benedict Anderson have explored.[10] If today's media elites seem averse to exploring social justice issues,[11] that is a reminder of Habermas's classic narrative about an earlier broad historical shift in democratic societies from a "culture-debating" to a "culture-consuming" public. Habermas laments that with the loss of critical discourse, "the world fashioned by the mass media is a public sphere in appearance only."[12] Others dispute the claim that rational-critical debate has declined, why it has declined, or whether it was ever much more than an ideal.[13] What Habermas views as the erosion of public rational-critical argument accompanies a "sentimentality toward persons and corresponding cynicism toward institutions."[14] Whatever the limitations of Habermas's arguments (such as idealization of the bourgeois public sphere, or neglect of the plebeian public sphere, or overstating the manipulative power of the cultural industries, or too sharply dichotomizing information and entertainment),[15] in the early twenty-first century many Americans would instantly recognize expressions of the trends Habermas traces. Observers lament a contemporary American politics of personality more than issues, style more than substance, and tactics more than context. In this political public sphere, a would-be battle of ideas becomes a war of images and sound bites. From such a perspective, mass media has foregone its public service obligations and undermined the public sphere's political functions[16]—among them a capacity to engage deeply issues of dissent and protest.

Hence we see wide spaces opened for satirists who perform the function of the Shakespearean fool. The Billionaires, Yes Men, Jon Stewart, and Stephen Colbert all hold a mirror up to society. We have seen them use irony and satire to destabilize—to open to scrutiny and critique—conventional political and media narratives. Billionaire Ivan Tital (Ken Mayer) says, "Like Lear's fool jester, we use humor to present otherwise unpalatable, unspeakable ideas in an accessible, digestible way."[17]

The "unspeakable ideas" or elephants in America's living room that have been the Billionaires' focus center on two key themes: the morality or fairness of the economy in an age of astonishing wealth for a few, and the dominant role of big money—from both corporations and individuals—in politics. As the economic crisis deepened and the effects of the Supreme Court's 2010 Citizens United decision played out during the 2012 presidential campaign, it became more difficult to confine the elephants in the room. By the end of the 2000s, the Billionaires' core critiques of runaway wealth and corporate power resonated widely. The economic crisis made people on the streets of New York City much quicker to understand the Billionaires' point, observed Thurston Howell IV (writer Kurt Opprecht).[18]

In a time of precariousness and fear, this book recaptures political domains of conviviality and play. If play is a vital form of citizenship, how can we assess the wider significance of the Billionaire brand of satirical political activism?

Parody Is Serious Business

The effects of political advocacy networks or social movements are notoriously difficult to determine.[19] One can interview consumers of activist messages and track outcomes of legislative or electoral battles, but many consequences are quite subtle. "Changing the terms of debate or official policies in national or international arenas may be the key battles," Fox writes, "yet such victories often translate with great difficulty into tangible improvements on the ground."[20] Nonetheless, political categories may be destabilized, debates reframed, new ideas and norms introduced, political participation expanded, individual subjectivities altered, and social networks mobilized in ways that shape later political movements, policies, and institutions. As Sidney Tarrow observes, the effects of social movements can be fleeting but powerful.[21]

So too the effects of political jokes. Focusing on the parodic genre known in Russia as *stiob* (which originated in the 1970s), anthropologists Boyer and Yurchak observe parallels in "discursive and ideological conditions" in late-socialist and contemporary capitalist contexts, and suggest that the florescence of a particular parodic aesthetic "during late socialism in Eastern Europe . . . contributed significantly to the disenchantment of the dominant discourse and thus to socialism's sudden and spectacular end."[22] Again, parody is serious business; it can "mak[e] that which is invisible and unthinkable, suddenly recognized and apprehended."[23]

Theorists of political humor have long debated whether it serves as a dress rehearsal for other forms of rebellion or as a safe release for aggression against concentrations of power. Whatever the effects, political culture-jamming, as this book illustrates, can disrupt politicians' branding messages (about job creators, freedom, big government) and destabilize dominant corporate and discursive frames by exposing contradictory meanings. When the Billionaires perform in public, they unsettle ideas about political categories: What's wrong with being rich? Are those well-dressed people really protesters? Satirical activists, when they attract public and media attention, can step out of character to discuss political issues in depth, inform voters, and, perhaps in small ways, help to reframe public discourse.

Part moral conscience, part safety valve for dissent, and part therapy for the politically disaffected, the Billionaires' ironic humor fuels a serious political campaign that has offered a running commentary on a decade that has seen America's largest financial institutions falter or collapse, its economy nosedive, and its legislative politics near paralysis. To assess the significance of such humor, we must go beyond measurable impacts of activism on concrete matters such as votes or legislation and consider less tangible but no less profound consequences, including the reimagination of political possibilities and alternatives.

The Billionaires attracted many individuals to political activism for the first time and helped them to develop skills for future mobilizations; built a national organization of one hundred chapters in several dozen states at its peak in 2004; altered the thinking of at least some voters (members claim); energized their base and their own members, many of whom participated simultaneously in more conventional forms of activism; and through flashy visuals, wit, and irony attracted corporate news media attention (however fleeting) to extreme wealth inequality and the role of big money in politics. While the particular stakes of the 2004 presidential election led them to focus on Bush, their foundational issues are nonpartisan in that they target financial corruption of the political process, which they see in both major political parties. The Billionaires penetrated corporate news media filters in a way that left much interpretive work up to audiences; mainstream media coverage exposed the public to the group's name and slogans on placards, often without using such text as a springboard for explicit analysis of alternative positions on the moral economy and policy issues to which the group calls attention. Yet even mentioning the name "Billionaires for Bush" or "Billionaires for More Media Mergers" or the slogans "Corporations Are People Too!" and "Leave No Billionaire Behind" communicated their argument. The Billionaires played the visibility game on corporate media terms.

Satirical activism of course is just one of many tactics for dissent—a tool that can complement or actively support other initiatives. While their resources are more modest than those of conservative think tanks, serious organizations that address the economic fairness issues which are the Billionaires' core focus include Public Citizen, Democracy 21, the Institute for Policy Studies, Common Cause, United for a Fair Economy, and Poor Peoples Economic Human Rights campaign.[24] The Institute for Policy Studies in Washington, DC, for decades has provided research and policy resources for social justice movements ranging from the civil rights movements of the 1960s to contemporary environmental, peace, and global justice movements.[25] United for a Fair Economy also issues carefully researched reports on the growing wealth divide and sponsors participatory workshops and other activities such as grassroots organizing on fair taxation.[26]

Some individuals bridge both worlds or work on creative activism through multiple organizations. The Billionaires' cofounder Andrew Boyd, who was United for a Fair Economy's "Minister of Culture" during the 1990s pre-Billionaire years, crafted experiments in creative activism that later provided a foundation for the Billionaires during the 2000s. Today he codirects The Other 98%, and he and John Sellers operate Agit-Pop Communications, "an award-winning net-roots subvertising agency . . . that delivers cutting edge videos, widgets, and boots-on-the-ground guerrilla marketing to progressive campaigns."[27] They have coordinated actions with the Yes Men, US Uncut, and other networks. Boyd's collaborators for the 2012 book *Beautiful Trouble* included the Yes Men, The Other 98%, Code Pink, Ruckus Society, and other organizations and individuals who worked together to compile "best ideas and practices and ideas" in creative political actions—"principles, practices, theories, case studies."[28] Other Billionaires work in nonhumorous organizations on environmental issues, antitorture campaigns, voter registration, estate tax, and media reform. Some find satirical and serious tactics to be complementary and mutually energizing, as did the Billionaires' Massachusetts precursors, discussed in Chapter 3, who experimented with humor to draw media and public attention to attacks on the social safety net and other economic justice concerns in their work on state budget policy and health, social, and human services programs. These current and former satirical activists display not the cynical apathy some attribute to those who embrace irony but instead a deep political engagement and commitment.

The impact of any single organizing effort, satirical or not, is limited; effective challenges to the status quo require multiple mobilizations. And as Tarrow remarks, if collective action succeeds, the political openings that shaped the constituent movements (which may be "complementary, competing or hostile") in turn "produce broader cycles of contention that spread from movement activists to those they oppose, to ordinary interest groups and political parties, and inevitably, to the state."[29]

By the end of the 2000s, as the global economic crisis deepened, these wider social and political fields were enlivened by ever more vocal and widespread opposition to austerity policies and the politicians who supported them. Could the world economy, many wondered, be made to work for everyone rather than just a few? Is a "human" economy possible, one where "economic action is directed towards the well-being of whole persons and communities, not a mechanical and one-sided individualism"?[30] Questions of economic fairness, wealth inequality, and political corruption took center stage among a new wave of dissidents who felt no need to wrap their messages in satire or to don elegant protest attire. Were the satirists of the 2000s and earlier years portents, or had they in small ways prepared the way for the serious demonstrations that followed? Or, just as likely, perhaps more sustained offensives against the status quo require humor as well as earnestness.

Humor, after all, can spawn the deep sense of social connectedness or human kindness that Victor Turner describes as "communitas."[31] And that social poetry brings us close to the ethos of Occupy Wall Street.

From Billionaires to Occupy Wall Street[32]

At the end of the 2000s the streets were alive with global protests against austerity programs that demanded deep sacrifices from the middle class and poor yet asked little or nothing from the megarich and financial institutions. "Occupy Wall Street" protests that began in New York in September 2011 and sparked joint actions in cities around the world were inspired in part by Wisconsin's massive demonstrations in 2011 against state austerity programs and attacks on workers' collective bargaining rights,[33] as well as the "Arab Spring" protests against Middle Eastern dictators and European antiausterity demonstrations. "Occupy" participants staged peaceful demonstrations calling for Wall Street to be held accountable for its role in the financial crisis and for banks and huge corporations to pay their fair share of taxes and help to restabilize the housing market, end the foreclosure crisis, and invest in American jobs.[34] Among the signs protesters waved in New York were "Honk If You Can't Afford Lobbyists!" and "Democracy

Not Corporatization" and "Revoke Corporate Personhood," the latter of course a nonironic echo of the Billionaires' slogan "Corporations Are People Too!"

Occupy Wall Street's aesthetics and media strategy ran counter to the Billionaires' elegant dress code and mainstream media branding tactics. Yet the Billionaires have promoted messages of economic justice that Occupy Wall Street participants would cheer. Some Billionaires left their elegant attire behind and joined Occupiers, while others donned tuxedoes and ball gowns and appeared in New York's Zuccotti Park as Billionaires for Plutocracy and Billionaires for the One Percent. Their signs: "Buy Your Own Democracy!" "It's a Class War and We're Winning!" "Thanks for Paying Our Fair Share!"

Although Occupy Wall Street, like the Billionaires, was a response to a perceived crisis in representative democracy, Occupy differed from the Billionaires by distancing itself from electoral politics and constituting itself as a form of direct action or direct democracy.[35] Occupy Wall Street practiced participatory decision-making by consensus in its general assembly, was decentralized, and "refuse[d] to recognize the legitimacy of the existing political authorities by making demands of them,"[36] though there was contestation within Occupy on the latter point. Occupiers have worked to prevent home foreclosures, and "Occupy the SEC," as mentioned earlier, carefully researched proposed financial industry reforms and sent a lengthy comment document to the Securities and Exchange Commission and other federal agencies in early 2012.[37] Soon after Hurricane Sandy struck the eastern United States in October 2012, "Occupy Sandy" quickly mobilized hundreds of volunteers to help New Yorkers who needed food, clothing, blankets, and other assistance.

For many, Occupy's ethos centered on crafting everyday practices that embody new political forms and solidarity in spaces beyond state control, which some participants assumed would undermine existing power structures in ways that might eventually cause their collapse. The Billionaires' aim, by contrast, was social democratic reform within the confines of electoral or representative democracy: a better social safety net, more progressive taxation, and campaign finance reform. In addition, their organization was more hierarchical—or meritocratic, as some members put it—and their decision processes were therefore less decentralized and consensual than was common in earlier social justice activism[38] or in Occupy Wall Street.

A mere two months after the Occupy movement began, news media mentions of income inequality had quintupled.[39] Occupy Wall Street and the 2012 presidential campaign seemed suddenly to place wealth disparities into the limelight. Furthermore, though "We are the 99 percent!" branded a movement and (for a time at least) shifted national political discourse, when this book went to press it remained unclear whether Occupy's vast mobilization would inspire progressive legislation on campaign finance, taxes, the social safety net, or financial industry regulation.

The 2008 financial crisis had dramatized the dangers of a deregulated economy, and even those who considered a market economy to be legitimate were now more likely to believe that "a market economy that knows no limits poses a threat to democracy."[40] Occupy Wall Street, like the satirical Billionaires, gave voice to citizens' distaste for excessive corporate power and their deep concerns about accountability, inequality, and economic fairness.

What Occupy had accomplished, Jedediah Purdy argued, was a revival of the idea that "economic life has moral and political dimensions that we can't afford to surrender to market logic," as well as "a sense that stronger democracy is possible."[41] Both, he said, were powerful counterexamples to the assumption that "political hope is futile."[42] At the same time, Purdy says that Occupy's success "is a glimpse of larger and more complicated goals, not a program or a strategy, or even the beginning of either."

Social movement scholar Todd Gitlin asserts that Occupy cannot be politically effective if it renounces formal political processes and institutions: "Its euphorias are its own. . . . The result is not a change in the way institutions operate. The result is the movement itself."[43] Similarly, Yale philosopher Matthew Noah Smith terms Occupy Wall Street "all play and no power."[44] Occupy's "joyous street theater," he said, "was politically meaningless." Gitlin agreed with Smith that effective "left resistance to inequality . . . remains in the hands of established movement organizations" such as labor unions.

Yet Smith also acknowledges that Occupy Wall Street's "energy and open-faced joy . . . probably has reinvigorated" unions and experienced organizers whose energy had flagged in the face of both the economic downturn and "intense challenges from the Right."[45] These are by no means inconsiderable consequences, and they mimic what I saw and heard repeatedly with respect to the Billionaires and other ironic activists such as the Yes Men. When asked what they accomplish through their ironic activism, Mike Bonanno—one of the three principal Yes Men—made no large claims about trying to build a social movement or even necessarily making much of a difference in the world.[46] He simply said he saw himself helping to build morale for those who really are in the trenches doing the hard work of organizing for change.

Occupy's playful theatricality, which Gitlin and Smith count among its limitations, is precisely what the Billionaires and Yes Men see as their own strength. "The euphoria of its existence," in Gitlin's view, was Occupy's focus, and that was certainly part of what captivated the Billionaires about their own organization. But that joyfulness also was contagious and energized other activists—as was clear during their visits to Billionaire meetings and during the Billionaires' mock counterprotests of groups with which they sympathized, such as the Sierra Club, Code Pink, and many more.

Occupy's theatrics engaged the same "latent strain in popular sentiment" that was the Billionaires' target—namely, "disgust with plutocracy and an enabling government, distrust of the political classes, and *eagerness to see something happen*."[47] Yet Occupy struck a chord in popular culture at a historical moment that allowed it to blossom and enter public culture and consciousness much more fully than the Billionaires. To what extent that difference reflected historical timing versus tactics is uncertain. But the Billionaires themselves welcomed Occupy's "rebel yell, the full-throated claiming of outrage," as Andrew Boyd put it.[48] At the same time, Occupiers told me they too found humor to be a personal restorative and morale booster.[49] Indeed a Clown Brigade was part of the movement's flexible repertoire.

Tactical diversity is a strength in social movements. The civil rights movement used freedom rides, bus boycotts, sit-ins at segregated lunch counters, and marches—while Occupy borrows tactics from global protests against the war in Iraq as well as alter-globalization movements.[50] Culture-jamming and ironic humor are long-standing tactics in broader protest repertoires. Parody and sincerity, humor and earnestness are friends rather than foes in social movements.

An even stronger argument is plausible: it is play that keeps political life healthy. Cultural historian Johan Huizinga wrote in his classic study that "fair play" and a "spirit of fellowship" helped legislators to act "without prejudice to the interests of the country which they serve with all seriousness."[51] Indeed, "it is the decay of humor that kills."[52] If life, Huizinga says, is to be "lived as play," then that is to accept the wisdom of Plato "when he called man the plaything of the gods" and to know deeply that "none of our pronouncements is absolutely conclusive."[53]

"This Land Is Our Land"

Social movement scholars since the mid-1980s have challenged instrumental metaphors of rational economic calculation and purposive formal organizations, pointing to the value of a "cultural perspective" that recognizes that protestors' motivations are not confined to pursuit of "material advantages for individuals or groups."[54] In addition, resource mobilization theorists eventually acknowledged that their framework insufficiently addressed "'enthusiasm, spontaneity, and conversion experiences' or the 'feelings of solidarity and communal sharing' that rewarded movement participants."[55]

It matters that the Billionaires not only are cyber-networked activists who recruit and mobilize members electronically but enjoy as well crucial forms of social connection (meetings, social events, street actions). Their effectiveness depends not just on mediatized images but also on live performance. Their audience includes not only street spectators and media but fellow activists and, importantly, one another. More than a play of symbols or invocation of an imaginary world, the satirical Billionaires constitute social relationships and organizational modes that energize their own and others' political activism.

Sentiments of solidarity were felt powerfully by participants during the events that opened this book—the August 2004 Croquet in the Park and Million Billionaire March on the eve of the Republican National Convention in New York. A deep sense of social connectedness moved participants as well during the Billionaires' 2008 election night celebration. That night of Barack Obama's electoral victory the Billionaires performed political vaudevilles in a program that concluded with singing Billionaire lyrics ("we own America") to the tune of the famous Woody Guthrie song, "This Land Is Your Land."

But midway through the song, their leading troubadour, Ivy League Legacy (Melody Bates), broke in and said, "OK, this time we take off our top hats and tiaras [that is, break character] because what we've always been about is making this song true." And so for the first time—"repossessing the meaning of the words"—the Billionaires sang the original rather than ironic lyrics of "This Land Is Your Land."[56] Merchant F. Arms described that experience as "profoundly cathartic," a moment when he and others believed once again that "some of the hideous and crippling inequalities of our economy and political system can be undone."

Later that night in Union Square, the Billionaires joined in an ecstatic, spontaneous celebration, where Latinos, African Americans, and whites were all dancing in the streets. Celebrants reappropriated patriotic sloganeering from which they had "felt so profoundly alienated," Merchant F. Arms said. They chanted "USA, USA," sang "The Star-Spangled Banner," raised the American flag, and chanted Obama's name along with "Yes we did, yes we did!" in exhilaration over how oft-excluded identities "were at last represented in the American political process." Here was communitas—though the mood proved transitory and change more difficult to accomplish than many had hoped.

In spite of the personal rivalries and tactical disagreements that characterize any political organization, affective solidarity is a hallmark of the Billionaire network. Thurston Howell IV had remarked in late 2005 that "the fellowship, the bonds that we have . . . are still very strong."[57] The sense of solidarity was evident years later at gatherings such as Reverend Billy's "canonization" of the Billionaires in 2011 and their 2009 "Last Huzzah" party in Manhattan, where members placed mementos of their Billionaire years in a "time capsule" and Andrew Boyd presided over ritualized acts, such as the "hanging-up of the unknown tuxedo."

"The Little Kid with the Slingshot"

"In the end it is the little kid with the slingshot who brings down the giant— let that be us," said Ivy League Legacy (Bates) to the sad Billionaires who had gathered to reassess their strategies the night after Bush's 2004 victory.[58] The sheer power of the Billionaires' targets—megacorporations, media, political lobbyists—is daunting, producing in the Billionaires contradictory feelings of potency and powerlessness. Merchant F. Arms (Varon) remarked that "[we] believed powerfully enough in our own parody that we're prevented from feeling genuinely optimistic that the kind of power that we've been satirizing can be as easily undone as a lot of people would like to think."[59]

That complex sensibility is quite close to what Kathleen Stewart writes about everyday life in America:

> This is the daydream of a subject whose only antidote to structural disenfranchisement is a literal surge of vitality and mobility. . . . It's a facility with imagining the potential in things that comes to people not despite the fact that it's unlikely anything good will come of it but rather because of that fact. It's as if the subject of extreme vulnerability turns a dream of possible lives into ordinary affects so real they become paths one can actually travel on.[60]

Rather than undermine individuals' rationality, such a stance recognizes the unpredictability and frustration of all human agency.[61]

The dream of shaping public sentiments about wealth and democracy— how to fund presidential campaigns; redress extreme wealth inequality; protect the environment, health care, and Social Security; and democratize corporate media—energized individuals in dozens of states to commit their time and talents to satirical activism. Some savored performing in public, while others preferred the background research from which the organization's wordsmiths crafted ironic slogans, talking points, and songs. They teased a few about being "media hounds," only to be reminded that the organization could have little impact without media coverage.

The Billionaires remained critically reflective about their own organization—concerned, for example, with how easy it was to get caught up in the charm of the joke and become self-absorbed, to take media attention too seriously. Admitting doubt about their political efficacy, the Billionaires' Washington, DC, chapter head, Ken Mayer, said, "Sometimes I feel it's just doing something to make us feel good that we're doing something."[62] And yet, reinforcing the insights of both Huizinga and Stewart, he said in 2004, "I love putting on a mask; putting on a tuxedo gives me confidence as well as a lot of fun. . . . Right now I'm unemployed and I don't have an identity. When I put on a tux, I do have an identity; I'm a Billionaire." (Since then Mayer has been employed as a teacher of classics and a writer, and in 2012 he donned his Billionaire tuxedo and top hat to speak in front of the Maryland state capitol during a 2012 protest against the Supreme Court's Citizens United decision.)

One New York Billionaire in his twenties, who was active as well in nonsatirical political campaigns, reflected shortly after the November 2004 election that it was unrealistic to expect the Billionaires "to create this massive culture shift in the next four years. The process of reeducating the masses is not on our shoulders."[63] He added: "We take ourselves very much too seriously in a lot of cases, and we're not that big and important . . . this [Bush election] is not our failure; it's also not our burden." He expressed appreciation for what they had accomplished on a small scale and believed they should now focus on local elections and capitalize on their "ability to use humor . . . rallying the troops . . . to reach people on personal levels and talk to people one-on-one and work our networks."

Others found that participating in the Billionaires softened the pain of past political engagement as nonsatirical activists. As we chatted after a July 2004 Manhattan chapter meeting, a New York Billionaire in his early forties commented, "No one can be sincere about politics anymore." His Billionaire companion replied, "When you do, it hurts, I say from experience. . . . when you are sincere about politics and you put everything into it, it is so dangerous that it hurts when your man loses!" Her companion responded, "which happens most of the time . . . so we protect ourselves with irony." He added that the Billionaires' organization "is very strategic and meaningful, and it's focused, and it's not just mouthing off, and it's not just like doing weird libidinal things in the street and stuff like that, but it's actually well-thought-out politics . . . this is a way to . . . almost operate within the system without seeming to operate within it."[64]

Billionaires' experiences on the streets reinforced the organization's founding assumption about the palatability of dissent as humor. A Seattle man in his late forties said to me in July 2004 that he joined the Billionaires because "there is not nearly enough fun in political activism" and he enjoys the Billionaires because it's more politically effective when "people are laughing as they're learning . . . it's easier to listen to somebody when they're making you laugh, when they're having a good time; you feel less weighted down by what might otherwise be heavy information; it's an easier way to reach past people's potential defenses, and I think it gives people more hope too." Lois Canright found her Billionaire activities to be a good antidote to "years of earnest fact-mongering" and says she is more convinced than ever of the effectiveness of this kind of theatrical messaging.[65]

Not least important was the hope satirical street theater gave to the Billionaires themselves, including some of the most critically reflective among them. During the height of the 2004 presidential campaign, Merchant F. Arms remarked that "the surprising thing is the unbelievable kick you get" when you don Billionaire attire, "put on a character," and offer an "elegant presentation . . . everybody responds to something well done."[66] Reflecting in 2005 on his Billionaire experiences, Merchant F. Arms said, "Looking back, it was a magical ride." A well-educated Manhattan Billionaire in her thirties, who had participated in the Billionaires' network since 2000, said the 2004 campaign had been "dizzying . . . it was so easy to just get caught up in it and focus on it and not do anything else . . . it was fantastic; I was so happy to be part of it."[67]

Thurston Howell IV talked of the exhilarating sense of "dressing up, playing the role of someone else, someone that's really different from your own persona." He said he had recently realized that such performances had a psychological function:

> I think when . . . all of us are out as the people we normally are, we're repressing so much of ourselves because it doesn't necessarily fit that image. I don't wear tights, I don't dance, I don't . . . laugh out loud. All these things that part of you

wants to do but most of you doesn't, so you get to dress up and play this [Billionaire] role where you can be loud or obnoxious or hoity-toity or conservative or whatever. It somehow serves the whole psyche by exorcising—or it's not just a catharsis but bringing them out and letting them air themselves—aspects of your personality that somehow make you feel more whole, make you feel more calm, and I think that's part of why it's so much fun. I really had underestimated that until I started being a Billionaire.

In short, participants viewed their Billionaire activities as a source of joy, social connection, affective solidarity, and a path to self-knowledge and psychic well-being. Without exaggerating their political effects, participants found it personally meaningful to be able to express their political opinions publicly and playfully.

"I Dedicate Myself to an Impossible Cause"

Belief in any activism was severely tested for some Billionaires in November 2004. Two days after George W. Bush was declared winner of the 2004 election, about fifty Manhattan Billionaires gathered to take stock and to comfort one another. That evening the lights in the Lower East Side loft were low; wine, pizza, brownies, and other snacks were served; and people shared tears and hugs and mingled until Andrew Boyd called the meeting to order. "I think a primal scream is in order," Boyd announced. A loud collective roar filled the room for several seconds. It helped to suspend (temporarily at least) political alienation. Boyd's comoderator at that meeting then asked, "How's everybody feeling?"—which produced another uproar as people shouted words such as "great!" "pissed!" and "sucky!" Boyd said he wanted to share a couple of funny things, since they were supposed to be the funny wing of the left wing. "Who's feeling funny?" he asked. "Not!" someone called out.

A form of postdefeat group therapy, that gathering had been billed in the listserv announcement as "a chance to debrief, check in, and just mull over where we're at and where we're headed. . . . Hugs, commiseration, solidarity, and fierce primal screams of defiance, mixed with some light conversation about our plans for the future." During this meeting, bodies were more casually positioned than in any other I had witnessed, with some Billionaires lying on their backs on the floor as they addressed the group. Some talked briefly, others in long, reflective soliloquies. While few might interpret the outcome of a presidential election as a test of satirical activists' effectiveness, a few Billionaires felt they and their organization had failed because Bush was returned to office. A group photographer described the meeting as "very emotional."

"Hopelessness Can Change the World" was the passage Andrew Boyd that evening chose to read aloud from his 2002 book *Daily Afflictions*. As he concluded, he asked those assembled to repeat in unison the selection's final line, which they did amidst laughter: "I dedicate myself to an impossible cause." Here is part of the passage Boyd read:

> A lapse of faith should not be feared. On the contrary, you should welcome it as a revelation. Our situation *is* hopeless. Our cause *is* impossible.
>
> You are faced with a stark choice: Do you dedicate yourself to an impossible cause? Or do you look after your own, making do as best you can? The choice is clear: You must dedicate yourself to an impossible cause. Why? Because we are all incurable. Because solidarity is a form of tenderness. Because the simple act of caring for the world is itself a victory.[68]

However Sisyphean the political challenge, the message was to join others in making a political commitment, since "the simple act of caring for the world is itself a victory."

Irony's Gift

The comedic media narrative of dinosaur topiary in Provençal-style gardens surrounding palatial California homes—analyzed in this book's Introduction—encourages comforting fantasies of great wealth. If wealth is framed as comedy, differences between the ultrarich and the rest seem natural and reconcilable, and governments should let markets run "free."[69] Unlike classical comedy's reassuring plot resolutions, however, the humor of the Billionaires highlights the avoidable suffering that occurs when unrestrained markets do run wild. Their satire points to the need for deep structural change to reverse injustice. The Billionaires scramble everyday understandings of the world, highlighting how extreme wealth differences are created through deliberate political decisions, not processes of nature. These are the differences between comedy and satire, and they mark profound contrasts in American moral visions. Dominant political and media discourses favor the comedic vision that downplays or accepts extreme wealth disparities—an imbalance the satirical Billionaires, in a modest way, try to disrupt.

Do irony and parody—satire's weapons—signal despair, in contrast to comedy's rosy optimism? No, say theorists of humor. Even when it ridicules its target, satire's aim is positive change.[70] Irony opens spaces of hope. Humor's gift, writes Zijderveld, is to show us that today's world can be made differently: "alternatives, as unreal and absurd as they may seem to be, are not unthinkable. Humor shares this with utopias and it is up to the audience to decide, by a laughing response, whether a utopia is nothing but a joke."[71] It is up to the Billionaires' audiences, and the reader, to decide if their vision of a fairer economy is simply a joke.

REFERENCE MATTER

Acknowledgments

Warm thanks go to the satirical Billionaires for so generously accommodating an anthropological researcher in their midst. I have had hundreds of conversations with friends and colleagues about this project, and their insights have shaped this manuscript in more ways than I can enumerate. A few among many who deserve special thanks are Laura Ahearn, Ulla Berg, Catherine Besteman, Andrew Boyd, Matt Buckley, Arpita Chakrabarti, Chuck Collins, Jane Collins, Micaela di Leonardo, Kathryn Dudley, Marc Edelman, Matt Feifarek, Eric Gable, Ajay Gandhi, Lesley Gill, Daniel Goldstein, David Graeber, Carol Greenhouse, Mary Hawkesworth, David McDermott Hughes, Omotayo Jolaosho, William Kelly, Frederick Klaits, Bruce Knauft, Catherine Lutz, Fran Mascia-Lees, Leita Luchetti, Melanie Hughes McDermott, Noelle Molé, David Nugent, Marian Sackrowitz, Louisa Schein, James C. Scott, Parker Shipton, Kurt Spellmeyer, Natalie Tevethia, Jeremy Varon, Debra Vidali, Art Walters, David Watts, Wendy Weisman, Brett Williams, Eric Worby, Diana Wylie, members of my spring 2005 political anthropology seminar at Rutgers University, participants in a 2004 miniconference and 2005 workshop on constructions of political space and political agency at Princeton University, and participants in colloquium presentations of this work at American University, Brown University, City University of New York Graduate Center, Columbia University, Emory University, Rutgers University, and Yale University. Particular thanks for insightful suggestions go to the anonymous readers of the prospectus and book manuscript, and to Michelle Lipinski, Joa Suorez, and Kate Wahl at Stanford University Press.

I thank those who provided permission to draw on material I first published in "Satire and Dissent in the Age of Billionaires," *Social Research: An International Quarterly* 79(1):145–68 (www.socres.org); and in "Neoliberalism, Satirical Protest, and the 2004 U.S. Presidential Campaign," in *Ethnographies of Neoliberalism*, edited by Carol J. Greenhouse, University of Pennsylvania Press, 2010.

Appendix

Research Methods

This book is based on data I collected between 2004 and 2012 through participant-observation, semi-structured and informal interviews, searches of media archives and organizational websites, membership on listservs, and reviews of documents in the Boston office of the nonprofit organization United for a Fair Economy (UFE). To trace the Billionaires' origins and history, I conducted oral history interviews with current and former UFE staff members and others who were part of a network of proto-Billionaires during the 1990s. I also interviewed individuals who had participated in the 2000 Billionaires for Bush (or Gore) but who did not join the 2004 Billionaires for Bush, as well as leaders of related organizations. I have talked with some Billionaire members at length on multiple occasions, and I have conducted in-depth interviews with many more about their personal backgrounds and experiences with the Billionaires and other activist organizations.

During the height of the 2004 presidential campaign (April to November), I attended weekly internal planning meetings of the Billionaires for Bush Manhattan chapter (the organization's largest), as well as frequent street actions and social and fund-raising occasions (such as one that featured cartoonist Art Spiegelman). During the 2004 campaign, I also spent time with the Boston, Seattle, and Washington, DC, chapters of Billionaires for Bush, observing public events and talking with participants. I interviewed chapter heads and members from other states as well when they visited New York or attended the January 2005 national Billionaire "convergence" in Washington, DC. In 2005, I attended a series of summer "strategery" meetings, Manhattan chapter planning meetings, and street actions. Thereafter I continued conversations and interviews with the Billionaires and attended key events such as the January 2009 "Last Huzzah" party in Manhattan, and the May 2011 Reverend Billy "canonization" of the Billionaires in New York City.

At the Billionaires' planning meetings and street actions I always identified myself as a researcher. On the street I visibly carried a tape recorder, notebook, and camera, and interviewed (on audiotape when interviewees agreed) bystanders and Billionaire participants. I also spoke informally with print and broadcast journalists and videographers who covered the Billionaires. In 2004, Arpita Chakrabarti, Noelle Molé, and Wendy Weisman (all doctoral students at Rutgers University at that time) assisted me with street-intercept interviews of spectators at Billionaire events. I have named them whenever quoting from one of their interviews.

When I quote from my own conversations and interviews, I sometimes use real names for individuals who are accustomed to speaking for public attribution, if they confirmed that to be their preference. Even in those cases, I shift to anonymous attributions when material quoted is personal or sensitive or might be embarrassing to others. And in the rare instances where someone requested that I not report a particular remark made in a conversation or interview, I of course have honored that request. Much of the Billionaires' activity, like that of other political activists, was deliberately public and "on the record."

Figures on media coverage in Chapter 6 are based on database searches conducted by Noelle Molé, as follows: (1) using key words "Billionaires for Bush," LexisNexis—regional news sources, state sources, general news, major papers, magazines and journals, world news, North/South American news, European news sources, Asia/Pacific news sources, Middle East/African news sources; (2) using key words "Billionaires for Bush," Google and Google News; (3) Billionaires for Bush website; and (4) using key words "Billionaires for Bush," Access World News. Duplicate or nearly duplicate articles by the same author that appear in more than one publication are counted when such articles are given new titles.

I have referred in endnotes to the dates of my conversations and interviews with Billionaires, without defining boundaries between these discursive forms, since both encompass wide variation in structure and degree of formality.

Notes

AH 00.00.00 = author's conversations or interviews and date of event (as in AH 06.15.10 = author's conversation or interview on June 15, 2010).

Introduction

1. In 2012, *Forbes* magazine, which publishes annual data about the world's billionaires, counted 1,153 billionaires in the world (http://www.forbes.com). A billion is a thousand millions, in U.S. terminology. In 2005, Bill Gates was worth $46 billion, Warren Buffett $44 billion, and the family of Walmart founder Sam Walton about $90 billion (Reich 2010b:viii). By contrast, the GDP of Kenya in 2006 was $14.4 billion, that of Cameroon $12.5 billion, Zimbabwe $17.8 billion, Lithuania $18.2 billion, Vietnam $39.2 billion, and Morocco $43.7 billion (*Economist* 2006a). Another telling datum: in the mid-2000s, "The world's 500 richest people [had] an income of more than $100 billion, not taking into account asset wealth. That exceeds the combined incomes of the poorest 416 million" (United Nations. Human Development Indicators 2006:269).

2. Media attending the Billionaires' Croquet in Central Park that day included (among many others) the *Washington Post, Newsday, Der Spiegel*, the *Denver Post*, CNN, the Newark-based *Star Ledger*, the *Philadelphia Daily News*, the *American Conservative*, WFUV (public radio at Fordham University), NY Channel 1 (Spanish television station), and Direct Listen Channel 9.

3. Phillips 2002b:5. For overviews of contrasting approaches to democracy, see Dunn 1992; Shapiro 2003; and Tilly 2007.

4. Blow 2011:A23; Bartels 2008.

5. DeParle 2011; Reich 2010c:A21.

6. Shiller made this comment during a televised interview with Charlie Rose (Public Broadcasting Service, *The Charlie Rose Show*, July 30, 2009).

7. Phillips 2002b:xiii–xiv.

8. Twain 1897.

9. From Trudeau's appearance on the PBS program *Charlie Rose*, October 11, 2004.

10. Kakutani 2008. Jon Stewart is anchor and managing editor of *The Daily Show* on the cable network Comedy Central, which is owned by media giant Viacom. See http://www.thedailyshow.com.

11. Kakutani 2008.

12. Yarwood 2004:12–13. On speech play, see Sherzer 2002. See Huizinga's (1955) classic analysis of the play element in culture.

13. Tilly 2004:ix. Recent overviews of social movements include Della Porta 2011; Edelman 2001; Goodwin and Jasper 2003; Johnston 2011; Melucci 1996; Nash 2005; Snow, Soule, and Kriesi 2007; and Tilly 2004.

14. Hitt 2004.

15. Roubini and Mihm 2010.

16. Rosen 2012.

17. Rosen 2012:29.

18. Rosen 2012:2.

19. Rosen 2012:1.

20. A willingness to ignore open secrets or uncomfortable truths—a "fundamental tension between knowledge and acknowledgment"—is how sociologist Eviatar Zerubavel (2006:3) characterizes "elephants in the room."

21. See Bartels 2008; Croll 2012; Johnston 2003; Wedel 2009.

22. The U.S. Supreme Court's 2010 decision (5–4) in *Citizens United* vs. *Federal Election Commission* removed earlier restrictions on direct corporate donations to political campaigns. It also allows such donations from labor unions, though their resources are much more meager. The decision rested on the claim that corporations—like people—have First Amendment rights.

23. Eggen 2010.

24. Dworkin 2010.

25. Some argue that the United States has always been plutocratic (Holland et al. 2007:188).

26. Stein 2006.

27. Jurgensen 2004.

28. J. Warner 2007:18, emphasis in original.

29. Klein 2002:281–82. For examples of culture jamming, see the Canadian journal *Adbusters* (www.adbusters.org), the Culture Jammers Encyclopedia (www.sniggle.net), and Subvertise (www.subvertise.org).

30. Material quoted in this paragraph is from Waxman 2006.

31. On contemporary forms of conspicuous consumption and competitive displays of wealth among the ultrarich (such as megahouses they rarely inhabit), see Conniff 2002. See also Offer (2006) and Veblen's classic study (1899).

32. Duncombe 2007a:205, n.11.

33. Sperber and Wilson (1981:198) review semantic and pragmatic approaches to irony in linguistics, and propose a "mention theory of irony," an approach that requires

no reliance on a notion of figurative meaning. According to their use-mention distinction, in speech expressions such as "what lovely weather," irony-as-mention "expresses an attitude to the content of an utterance [e.g., ridicule, disbelief], whereas [irony-as-use] expresses an attitude to the weather" (302–3).

34. Jamieson and Waldman 2003; Pedelty 1995.

35. Linguists term such interpretive indeterminacy *textual polysemy*.

36. White (1973) draws on Northrop Frye's (1957) archetypes of comedy, satire, tragedy, and romance as narrative plot modes. The boundary between comedy and tragedy is often fuzzy, as scholars have noted (see Zijderveld 1983:23).

37. A sentiment expressed by some of America's Founding Fathers, such as James Madison in the *Federalist* (Wootton 2003:xxii).

38. T. Frank 2012:67–68.

39. Schutz 1977:50.

40. Schutz 1977:50.

41. White 1973:7. However limiting such typologies may be, and however masterfully some writers meld them, echoes of these classic plot modes are detectable in the writings of historians and anthropologists, as well as in journalists' accounts. Master historians, White (29) observes, are not confined by common affinities or patterns of relationship across standard modes of plot, argument, and ideology; such historians achieve instead a "dialectical tension" among these categories as they combine them in unexpected ways.

42. See Donham (1990:Conclusion) on the implications of Northrop Frye's (1957) classic typology of plot types for "the archetypal stories anthropologists tell." See also Krupat (2001:135), who writes: "what Hayden White (1973) brilliantly demonstrated for histories would hold for ethnographies as well: that it was their 'emplotment' rather than their data or 'facts' which carried their 'explanatory affect,' and so their 'truth-effect.'"

43. White 1973:8.

44. The metahistorical element of historical texts, for White (1973:ix–x), centers on their "deep structural content which is generally poetic, and specifically linguistic . . . and which serves as the precritically accepted paradigm of what a distinctively 'historical' explanation should be." White (1973:x) distinguishes his approach from "other analysts of historical writing" in that he does "not consider the 'metahistorical' understructure of the historical work to consist of the theoretical concepts explicitly used by the historian to give to his narratives the aspect of an 'explanation.'"

45. White (1973:10). For a critique of White on this point, see Krupat (2001:134), who concludes that "'the ultimate inadequacy of consciousness' need not be the reference point for happiness or comprehension."

46. Donham 1990:192.

47. DeMartino 2000:43.

48. Greenhouse 2010; Haugerud 2010.

49. Democracy Now, February 24, 2012. http://www.democracynow.org.

50. Other tools of satire include antithesis, colloquialism, anticlimax, topicality, parody, obscenity, violence, vividness, and exaggeration (Schutz 1977:50).

51. As Donham (1990:192–93) put it in a different context. That position implies not a naive positivism as epistemology but rather the positing of connections that make objects of contestation newly visible.

52. See also Miyazaki 2004; Crapanzano 2003; and Harvey 2000, on hope.

53. Purdy 2000:213. Irony is associated with the Socratic dialogues of Plato during a historical moment of growing cultural insecurity in ancient Greece (Colebrook 2004).

54. Boyd 2002a:153.

55. See Anderson 1983.

56. S. Hall 2002 [1981]:192.

57. As G. Smith (2004:217) writes, "Regarding the powerful, we may speak of hegemonic processes when power is used to organize consent, and when consent is used to facilitate the securing of a political project." On varying approaches to hegemony, see Comaroff and Comaroff 1991; Gramsci 1971; Scott 1990, 1985; Williams 1977; and Willis 1977.

58. See Jamieson and Waldman 2003; McChesney 1999; Moyers 2008.

59. Yarwood 2004:11.

60. On theoretical approaches to power, see Gledhill (2000) and the collection edited by Lukes (1986).

61. Carter and Stelter 2010.

62. See Boyer and Yurchak 2010; and Hanser 1952.

63. Collins 2012.

64. April 2011 *Washington Post* and Maris/McClatchy polls showed 70–80 percent of Americans support higher taxes on the rich and corporations. See Pew Research Center, "The Deficit Debate: Where the Public Stands" (http://pewresearch.org). Large percentages of citizens in the early 2000s believed the wealthy are asked to pay *less* than they should in federal taxes, and that the poor are asked to pay *more* than they should, according to 2002 and 2004 National Election Study surveys (Bartels 2008:140).

65. Stewart 2007:86.

66. The color photo was published as part of a posthumous portfolio on democracy in the November 1, 2004, issue of the *New Yorker*.

67. Communitas, according to V. Turner (1995 [1969]:177), is a society of "concrete idiosyncratic individuals, who, though differing in physical and mental endowment, are nevertheless regarded as equal in terms of shared humanity . . . [and who] confront one another integrally, and not as 'segmentalized' into statuses and roles."

68. Published in the *New Yorker*, September 20, 2004.

69. Newman 2004.

70. This account of Chris Hartman's experiences is based on my interview with him on June 21, 2006. Hereafter my conversations and interviews are coded with my initials and the numeric date, as in AH 6.21.06.

71. http://www.billionairesforbush.com/nyc.eventlist.php (accessed August 28, 2004).

72. Reich 2011. See also Murray Edelman (2001) on why belief in democracy itself is a premise that should be questioned.

73. Cf. Bakhtin 1984 [1968]:467–68.

74. See Boyer and Yurchak 2010; and Yarwood 2004.

75. Goldstein 2003; and Boyer and Yurchak 2010.

76. Boler with Turpin 2008; Day 2011; Gray, Jones and Thompson 2009; Klein 2002; Riegert 2007.

77. Graeber (2009) and Juris's (2008) ethnographic studies of the global social justice movement include groups that adopt whimsical approaches. The Billionaires' cocreator Andrew Boyd (2002a,c) has written articles about the 2000 network Billionaires for Bush (or Gore). One of the Billionaires' governing board members (Duncombe 2007a)—a specialist on media and culture—includes brief discussion about them in his work on ironic humor and spectacular dissent. Activist and performance studies scholar Larry Bogad (2005) discussed the Billionaires for Bush in an essay on the 2004 Republican National Convention protests. Performance studies scholar Amber Day (2011), drawing exclusively on published sources, includes the Billionaires in her comparative study of satire as political critique. Political scientists Farrar and Warner (2008), drawing on secondary data from media accounts and the Billionaires' website, analyze their role as political culture jammers.

Chapter 1

1. AH 7.16.04.

2. Naughton 2001.

3. See Hastings 2009; and Buffett 2011.

4. Quoted in Rich 2010c:WK11.

5. For autobiographical accounts by those who have given away a fortune, see Mogil and Slepian, with Woodrow 1992.

6. Duncombe with Boyd 2007b:44.

7. The organization's website between 2004 and 2008 was http://www.billionaires-forbush.com. In 2008, Clifford J. Tasner (a Hollywood producer whose Billionaire name is Felonius Ax and who led their Los Angeles chapter) set up a new website (http://www.thebillionaires.org; accessed December 28, 2012). Tasner produced satirical Billionaire music CDs such as "Never Mind the Rabble: Here Come the Billionaires" (2000) and "The Billionaires Are in the House" (2004). Both feature songs with ironic lyrics set to familiar tunes.

8. Billionaires for Bush 2004.

9. The Billionaires' motto. See http://www.billionairesforbush.com/overview.php (accessed March 19, 2012).

10. Their ad: http://www.bushin30secconds.org/view/14_large.shtml (accessed June 25, 2012).

11. Kaiser 2004.

12. On satirical activists' use of flashmobs, see Boyd and Mitchell (2012:46–47).

13. Dwyer 2008.

14. Both videos are available on YouTube and on the Billionaires' website (http://www.billionairesforbush.com; accessed December 28, 2012).

15. Gamerman 2008.

16. Segal 2008:C01.

17. Video of *The Rachel Maddow Show* segment in October 2009 was posted on the Billionaires for Wealthcare website: http://www.billionairesforwealthcare.com (accessed August 9, 2010).

18. See Krugman 2007.

19. Leonnig 2010.

20. http:agit-pop.com (accessed May 21, 2011). Agit-Pop describes itself on its website as "an award-winning net-roots subvertising agency."

21. See http://www.RepubliCorps.us (accessed May 21, 2011).

22. See http://other98.com (accessed May 21, 2011).

23. Brave New Foundations helped to organize that May 2011 Lincoln Center action with The Other 98% and other organizations. For video and write-ups, see http://other98.com/david-koch-theater-rebranding (accessed May 21, 2011).

24. http://other98.com/citizens-united-anniversary-we-lit-supreme-court-with -giant-dollar-signs (accessed January 27, 2012).

25. On its website, US Uncut describes itself as "a grassroots movement taking direct action against corporate tax cheats and unnecessary and unfair public service cuts across the U.S." http:/www.USuncut.org (accessed June 4, 2011). A sister organization— UK Uncut—started in October 2010 and opposes austerity economics as "the policy of the powerful." http://www.ukuncut.org.uk/about/ukuncut (accessed June 11, 2011).

26. Sturr 2011.

27. Quotes and other material in this sentence and the one that precedes it are from http://www.theyesmen.org/usuncut (accessed June 4, 2011).

28. Goodwin 2012.

29. *Ibid.*

30. Gates and Collins 2003. William Gates Sr., Collins's coauthor, is the father of Microsoft founder Bill Gates, who was the richest man in the world for more than a dozen years.

31. Responsible Wealth, a project of United for a Fair Economy: http://faireconomy .org/responsible_wealth (accessed December 28, 2012).

32. Data from public disclosure records examined by Public Citizen and United for a Fair Economy, cited by Johnston 2006.

33. Shapiro 2003.

34. Critchley 2002:3–4.

35. On phenomenology and anthropology, see Desjarlais and Throop 2011.

36. AH 8.22.04.

37. N. Smith 2005:10.

38. As Harvey (2003:190) writes, "much of what passed for finance capital was in fact unredeemable fictitious capital supported by scandalous accounting practices and totally empty assets."

39. Harvey 2003:13, 16–17, 211. See also Hacker 2006; Krugman 2007; Reich 2007; Roubini and Mihm 2010.

40. http://www.insidejob.com (accessed December 28, 2012).

41. *New York Times* 2011.

42. Baym 2005; and J. Warner 2007.

43. Hanser 1952:51, quoted in Yarwood 2004:14.

44. Pomorska 1984:xi.

45. M. Douglas 1968:365.

46. M. Douglas 1968:373.

47. Bakhtin 1984 [1968]:49.

48. Orwell 1968:284.

49. A position that contrasts with those in the preceding paragraph is found in Speier 1998:1358–60.

50. Freud 1960. Zijderveld (1983:39) remarks that "Freud . . . was rather cautious in his argument in favour of the aggressive nature of humour and laughter. It was his followers who gave it an all-embracing quality."

51. Schutz 1977:8.

52. See, for example, Kertzer 1988; Scott 1990; and discussion in Chapter 3.

53. Stallybrass and White 1986:14; Scott 1990:177–79, 186.

54. Bakhtin 1984 [1968]:11–12.

55. Mbembe 1992; Scott 1985.

56. Yarwood 2004:14.

57. Smith 2009.

58. Quoted in the original 1656 version as follows: "An Irony is a nipping jeast, or a speech that hath the honey of pleasantnesse in its mouth, and a sting of rebuke in its taile" (from Reyner 1657).

59. Booth 1974:ix.

60. Attardo 2001:166.

61. Colebrook 2004; Fernandez and Huber 2001a,b; Fussell 1975; Harvey 1989.

62. Oxford English Dictionary online, http://dictionary.oed.com (accessed July 7, 2004).

63. Baldick 1990:114, quoted in Fernandez and Huber 2001b:2–3.

64. Colebrook 2004:15.

65. Colebrook 2004:14.

66. Fernandez and Huber 2001b:4–5.

67. Fussell 1975.

68. Kirkpatrick 2001.

69. *Ibid.*

70. Quoted in Kirkpatrick 2001.

71. Beers 2001.

72. Fernandez and Huber 2001a:263.

73. Clifford 2001:255.

74. Zimmer 2010:22.

75. Suskind 2004.

76. Rich 2006:87.

77. Fernandez and Huber 2001b:18.

78. A. Newman 2008.

79. Didion 2008.

80. As K. Stewart 2007:93 writes in a different context.

81. In Britain in 2010–11, the conservative government's slogan "we're all in this together" became a focus of rhetorical irony and contestation as austerity programs were implemented.

82. Hutcheon 2000:xiv.

83. Hutcheon 2000:xiii.

84. White 1973:167–68, emphasis in original.

85. White 1973:232.

86. See Klein 2002:282–83 and Duncombe 2007a:129–30 on Guy Debord and the Situationists in relation to contemporary protest as spectacle.

87. AH 7.02.06.

88. A working group called the "Ministry of Love" was also part of the Lower East Side Collective in Manhattan (Duncombe 2007a:91). Some early Billionaires were recruited from the Lower East Side Collective.

89. Cf. Fernandez and Huber 2001b:26.

90. Boyd 2003, 2002a, 2002c; Boyd and Mitchell 2012.

91. Boyd 1999b and 2002b.

92. Fernandez and Huber 2001b:22.

93. Marcus and Fischer 1999 [1986].

94. Marcus 2001:220, 211, emphasis in original.

95. Marcus 2001:211.

96. See Ahearn's (2001) review of the concept of agency.

97. Larson 1984.

98. October 19, 2004, Billionaires for Bush Manhattan chapter meeting.

99. AH 7.2.06.

100. Portelli 1991.

101. Holmes and Marcus's (2005:248) term for anthropologists' paraethnographic interlocutors.

102. Here Boyd means juxtaposing different versions of the same event, as in Akira Kurosawa's 1950 Japanese film *Rashomon*, which centers on different accounts of an "encounter in the forest between a bandit and a samurai and his wife." The phrase just quoted is from Heider (1988:74), who analyzes ethnographic implications of the Rashomon effect.

103. AH 7.2.06.

104. AH 3.11.12.

105. Edelman 2001:310.

106. Holmes and Marcus 2005:249–50.

107. Edelman 2001:309.

108. Gledhill (2000) and Burdick (1998) represent excellent examples.

109. Cf. Debord 1988.

110. For examples, see Duncombe 2007a; Graeber 2009; Juris 2008; Klein 2002.

111. See Gitlin 1993.

112. Duncombe 2007a:141.

113. See Graeber 2009.

114. Duncombe 2007a:129.

115. Duncombe 2007a:130.

116. Debord 1988:2.

117. Debord 1988:13.

118. Duncombe 2007a:5.

119. Duncombe 2007a:7.

120. Foucault 1979; Adorno and Horkheimer 1989 [1947]; Duncombe 2007a.

121. Duncombe 2007a:8. See also Lakoff 2004.

122. Duncombe 2007a:148.

123. Duncombe 2007a:155.

124. AH 12.3.08.

125. Klein 2002:283.

126. See Shepard and Hayduk (2002) on ACT UP and related groups.

127. Duncombe 2007a:136–37; see also Klein 2002:315–16.

128. Duncombe 2007a:137.

129. Klein 2002:ch.13. The "situation," as a participatory and possibly transformative event, was distinguished from the "spectacle," which Situationists condemned for its spectator passivity and acquiescence rather than intervention. Duncombe and other organizers of Reclaim the Streets tried to "turn spectators into producers" (Duncombe 2007a:73).

130. Duncombe 2007a:67.

131. Duncombe 2007a:73; Graeber 2009:382.

132. Leonnig 2010. This protest was also mentioned the next day in the *New York Times* (Lichtblau 2010).

133. For examples of their actions and public attention, see the Yes Men website (http://www.theyesmen.org/; accessed December 28, 2012), as well as their book (Yes Men 2004) and movie (*The Yes Men*). A *New York Times* article describes one of their early hoaxes and its consequences (Feder 2001).

134. Yes Men 2004:11.

135. Yes Men 2004:8.

136. http://www.theyesmen.org/hijinks/dow/ (accessed March 12, 2006).

137. http://www.theyesmen.org/hijinks/dow/ (accessed March 12, 2006).

138. Boyer and Yurchak 2010:203.

139. Yes Men 2004:9.

140. Yes Men 2004:160.

141. *Ibid.*

142. Yes Men 2004:161.

143. Yes Men 2004:169, 172.

144. AH 3.15.06.

145. Duncan 2011.

146. http://revbilly.com/events/billionaires (accessed May 13, 2011).

147. Duncombe 2007a:164.

148. Music by Jay Gorney (1931), lyrics by Yip Harburg.

149. The David Koch reference was new; a previous version of the Billionaire pledge substituted "George Bush" for "David Koch."

150. Grote 2002:361.

151. *Ibid.*

152. Grote 2002:368.

153. At that protest, Reverend Billy was arrested and released twenty-four hours later—as he mentioned during his Theatre 80 performance. See Mayer's (2010) profile of the Koch brothers.

154. See Coffey 2011.

155. Carr 2011a.

156. McGrath 2012.

157. McGrath 2012:23.

158. Stelter 2012.

159. McIntire and Luo 2012:A14.

160. Jones, Baym, and Day 2012:50.

161. Carr 2011b.

162. Jones, Baym, and Day 2012:57.

163. Rosen 2012:16.

164. Rosen 2012:16.

Chapter 2

1. Haidt 2012. See also YourMorals.org (accessed December 28, 2012).

2. Gledhill 2004:347.

3. See Hart, Laville, and Cattani 2010.

4. Based on data from official nonpartisan sources such as the Federal Reserve, National Bureau of Economic Research, Bureau of Labor Statistics, Tax Policy Center, and World Health Organization.

5. Tim Mitchell 2002; Polanyi 1957 [1944].

6. Rose 1999:197.

7. Slight changes in a question's wording can affect results (Johnston 2003:83). Opinion poll questions invoke or trigger in respondents particular frames for issues, implying what is at stake in the way they link images and ideas (Gamson 2007). Here I use professional opinion surveys from sources such as Gallup and Harris polls along with studies done by scholars and by the *New York Times*.

8. Murray Edelman 2001:106.

9. http://billionairesforbush.com/diy_v2_ch4.php (accessed June 20, 2012) is the source of messaging tips quoted in this paragraph, unless otherwise noted.

10. AH 7.8.05.

11. Unless noted otherwise, quotes in this paragraph are from http://billionairesfor bush.com/diy_v2_ch4.php (accessed June 20, 2012).

12. December 12, 2005, on WBAI New York. http://billionairesforbush.com/diy_v2_ch4.php (accessed December 28, 2012).

13. Hacker 2006:24. See *Economist* 2006b:29; Fraser and Gerstle 2005; Krugman 2007; Reich 2007.

14. *Economist* 2006b:29.

15. Gates and Collins 2003:112; United for a Fair Economy 1997.

16. See Reich 2010a; Krugman 2006, 2007; Hacker 2006. See Dudley 2000; Goode and Maskovsky 2002; Gusterson and Besteman 2010; Newman and Chen 2007; and Williams 2004 on precarity and poverty in America.

17. Hacker 2006:5–6.

18. Hacker 2006.

19. Author's interview, August 8, 2006, at the Gates Foundation office in Seattle. Unless otherwise noted, all quotes of William Gates Sr. in this chapter are from this interview.

20. See Gates and Collins 2003.

21. Krugman 2002:63. See Gates and Collins (2003:13–16) for summary statistics comparing wealth and income in the 1880s–1890s Gilded Age with the present era. See also Bartels 2008. See http://elsa.berkeley.edu/saez/ (accessed December 28, 2012) for current data on U.S. income inequality.

22. Reich 2006.

23. Reich 2010b:v.

24. Phillips 2002b:xiii.

25. Congressional Budget Office data cited by Pear 2011.

26. Hacker and Pierson 2010:16.

27. *New York Times* 2006.

28. Keister and Moller 2000:63–64; wealth here is defined as net worth or the "value of assets owned by the household."

29. Offer 2006:274; Krugman 2002:76.

30. AH 7.26.05.

31. Cited in Gilson and Perot 2011.

32. Bartels 2008:146.

33. As observed by di Leonardo 2008, 1998; Fussell 1983; Marcus with Hall 1992; Ortner 2003; and Sennett and Cobb 1993, among others.

34. Comaroff and Comaroff 2001:14–15.

35. Fraser and Gerstle 2005.

36. Manza 2011; see also Wright 2005.

37. Krugman 2002, 2007.

38. R. Frank 2007b:39.

39. Krugman 2007:43, 48.

40. Reich 2010c:A21.

41. Krugman 2007:47.

42. Madrick 2007:32; Hungerford 2012.

43. Leonhardt 2008.

44. Krugman 2007:264.

45. Hacker and Pierson 2010.

46. Phillips 2002b.

47. See Offer 2006; Keller 2005; Scott and Leonhardt 2005.

48. Keller 2005:xii.

49. Wilkinson and Pickett 2009.

50. Phillips 2002a:12.

51. Fraser and Gerstle 2005:290. See also Collins et al. 2008.

52. Krugman 2007:268; Jacobs and Skocpol 2005; Leonhardt 2011.

53. Moyers 2008; Reich 2010a.

54. Moyers 2008:196.

55. *Ibid.*

56. Krugman 2007:268, 176–77.

57. Krugman 2007:176–77, 268.

58. Krugman 2007:175.

59. Jacobs and Skocpol 2005:219.

60. Zinn 2003:650; *New York Times* 2005.

61. R. H. Frank 2010.

62. Johnston 2003:43. Although official U.S. corporate tax rates in the early 2000s were "among the highest in the industrial world . . . the taxes that corporations pay [were] among the lowest," according to the nonpartisan Government Accountability Office (*New York Times* 2008a).

63. Cf. Hayek 1994 [1944].

64. Gledhill 2004:340; see also Edelman and Haugerud 2005.

65. Willis 2006:19.

66. Phillips 2002b:xiv.

67. Quiggin 2010.

68. Polanyi 1957 [1944]:257.

69. Polanyi 1957 [1944]:256.

70. *New York Times* 2010.

71. Taibbi 2010:ch.5.

72. Leonhardt 2011.

73. Graetz and Shapiro 2005:4.

74. Gates and Collins 2003.

75. In 2006, individuals received a $2 million exemption and couples received a $4 million exemption. Assets above those levels were taxed at 45 percent. The standard individual exemption was set to rise in succeeding years and then to be reset by Congress in 2011 (Public Citizen et al. 2006:6). In 2011, the tax was extended for two years, with a $5 million exemption for individuals ($10 million for couples), and a rate of 35 percent. By comparison, John D. Rockefeller's heirs paid an estate tax of 70 percent when he died in 1937.

76. Allan B. Krueger (2003), citing a study by economist Larry Bartels that was later included in Bartels 2008:207.

77. R. H. Frank 2007.

78. Krueger 2003.

79. Gardner 2007:11.

80. Phillips 2002a:12.

81. Buffett 2011.

82. Gates and Collins 2003.

83. L. Thomas 2006:C1.

84. Johnston 2001.

85. Naughton and Thomas 2001.

86. For example, Robert Frank (2007a)—not Robert H. Frank—wrote in his *Wall Street Journal* blog on wealth that he "started thinking about how politics has become a battle of billionaires versus billionaires."

87. Mayer 2010.

88. Center for Responsive Politics and Public Citizen, as reported in Bauerlein and Jeffery 2012.

89. Rich 2010a.

90. Jamieson and Waldman 2003; Moyers 2008.

91. Graetz and Shapiro 2005:7.

92. Collins, Lapham, and Klinger 2004.

93. An argument Chuck Collins, William Gates Sr., and others codeveloped (see Collins, Lapham, and Klinger 2004; and Gates and Collins 2003).

94. AH 6.8.06.

95. A point made by Collins, Lapham, and Klinger 2004:1.

96. Narratives by a number of wealthy individuals who support the tax on inherited wealth are included in Collins, Lapham, and Klinger 2004.

97. Collins, Lapham, and Klinger 2004:3.

98. Gates and Collins's 2003 book on the estate tax carefully reviews false claims made by opponents of the estate tax, such as exaggerations of its effects on family farms and businesses.

99. Unless otherwise noted, points about the "death tax" labeling strategy included in this paragraph are drawn from Gates and Collins (2003:58–59). See also Johnston (2003:82–83) and Graetz and Shapiro (2005:326–27) for references on how the "death tax" label affected public opinion.

100. Gates and Collins 2003:290.

101. Graetz and Shapiro 2005:282.

102. *Ibid.*

103. http://billionairesforbush.com/diy_v2_ch4.php (accessed December 28, 2012).

104. And indeed these are mutually constituted, since moral economy notions held by the poor "found support in the paternalist tradition of the authorities" (E. P. Thompson 1993:188); see also Scott 1976, 1985.

105. Fraser and Gerstle 2005:291.

106. Fraser and Gerstle 2005:289.

107. I asked Gates: "Has there been a shift in the degree of concern [among elites] in recent years? Is there rising concern compared to ten or twenty years ago, or is there no alarm?"

108. Morgen et al. (2012, in the abstract) argue that "taxpayer identity politics are a strategy to build popular consent for deKeynesinization."

109. Graetz and Shapiro 2005:ch.9; Hacker and Pierson 2010.

110. Fraser and Gerstle 2005:287; and Phillips 2002b.

111. Krugman 2007:213.

112. The others were freedom of speech and expression, freedom of worship, and freedom from fear—as outlined in Franklin Delano Roosevelt's address to Congress on January 6, 1941 (*Congressional Record*, 1941, Vol. 87, Pt. I).

113. Phillips 2002b:xii.

114. Krugman 2007:18.

115. In 1918, Rockefeller's wealth equaled 1.6 percent of the nation's economy, while that of Andrew Carnegie was equivalent to 0.3 percent of the national economy. By comparison, Bill Gates's 2006 wealth was equivalent to 0.4 percent of the national economy and that of Warren Buffett 0.3 percent (*New York Times* 2007:A1, A20–21). See Myers (1910) on the history of early American fortunes.

116. Krugman 2007:18.

117. Collins and Mayer 2010.

118. Krugman 2007:130.

119. Krugman 2007:143–44.

120. R. Frank 2007b:6.

121. R. Frank 2007b:7.

122. Quoted in Goodman 2008.

123. LiPuma and Lee 2004:196, n.3.

124. Downey and Fisher 2006:9.

125. LiPuma and Lee 2004:192.

126. Goodman 2008:A1.

127. Cox 2008; see also Williams 2004.

128. Cox 2008.

129. See Financial Crisis Inquiry Commission 2011; and Roubini and Mihm 2010.

130. Taibbi 2010:246.

131. Phillips 2002b; Krugman 2007; Roubini and Mihm 2010.

132. R. Frank 2007b:45.

133. Krugman 2007.

134. Fraser and Gerstle 2005.

135. Moyers 2008:4.

136. Rich 2010b; and Jacoby 2008.

137. LiPuma and Lee 2004:2.

138. Maurer 1995:138, 141.

139. Polanyi 1957 [1944].

140. http://www.bis.org/ (accessed March 14, 2012).

141. The World Bank, unlike the World Trade Organization, has emphasized accountability (at least rhetorically) in recent years.

142. See, for example, Sawyer 2004.

143. Taibbi (2010:246) makes the latter point.

144. Patomaki 2001:172. James Tobin in 1972 "internationalized an earlier suggestion by John Maynard Keynes . . . [for] taxing currency transactions for global benefit," the aim being to "reduce the instability and volatility of international financial markets" partly by discouraging highly destabilizing speculative movements of money (Patomaki 2001:ix, xiv, xv).

145. Patomaki 2001:xviii.

146. *New York Times* 2008a.

147. For example, credit-rating agencies responsible for assessing corporate risk "are paid by the issuers of the bonds they rate" (Lewis and Einhorn 2009).

148. Ross 2011.

149. Panitch 2000:7.

150. Reich 2007:216.

Chapter 3

1. Gluckman 1965:104, quoted in V. Turner 1995:110.

2. Douglas 1968:370.

3. Scott's (1990:177) phrase.

4. Scott 1990:178.

5. As argued by Davis (1975:123), Kertzer (1988), and Scott (1990:177–79, 186), among others. See also Babcock (1978) on symbolic inversion.

6. Darnton (1984), describing episodes from eighteenth-century France.

7. Gamson 2007:258; Alinsky 1972.

8. Gamson 2007:258.

9. Douglas 1968:370.

10. Douglas 1968:369.

11. Portelli (1991:50, emphasis in original). See also Abrams's (2010) overview of oral history.

12. Portelli 1991:53.

13. Koopmans 2007:19.

14. On carnival, see Davis (1975) and Bakhtin (1984 [1968]). The history of such forms can be traced back centuries earlier (Davis 1975:ch.4). Charivari is "a noisy, masked demonstration to humiliate some wrongdoer in the community" (Davis 1975:97). On weapons of the weak, see Scott (1985).

15. Kertzer 1988:146.

16. Kertzer (1988:149–50), citing research by David Gilmore (1975).

17. Davis 1975:99–100.

18. AH 6.21.06.

19. At that time, she was Betsy Wright.

20. In addition, Jane Collins worked at MHSC as a staff writer. The three individuals who share the Collins surname are not related to one another. MHSC folded in 2006, about a year after Steve Collins's death.

21. Lewis 1997.

22. Others who advised or participated in proto-Billionaire satirical actions included Carol Brill, director of the Massachusetts Association of Social Workers; lobbyist Judy Meredith; and retired social worker Ginny Burns from the Massachusetts Association for the Prevention of Cruelty to Children (Leondar-Wright, personal communication, July 11, 2006).

23. AH 5.30.06.

24. Boyd 1999a:52.

25. Betsy Leondar-Wright, personal communication, July 11, 2006.

26. An echo of former senator William Proxmire's Golden Fleece awards to public officials judged to have wasted taxpayers' money.

27. AH 6.8.06.

28. Parallel to composer Sergio Ortega's famous political song "El Pueblo Unido."

29. AH 6.8.06.

30. AH 5.30.06.

31. AH 5.30.06.

32. AH 6.8.06.

33. AH 6.21.06.

34. AH 5.30.06.

35. Deborah Weinstein, AH 6.21.06.

36. Andrew Boyd, AH 7.2.06.

37. From files viewed by the author in May 2006 at United for a Fair Economy's Boston office.

38. See Boyd 1999a.

39. AH 5.30.06. Off-message topics included issues such as the Israel-Palestine conflict, abortion, and religion.

40. See Boyd (1999a: 67–88) for a full description of both.

41. AH 6.8.06.

42. AH 6.15.06.

43. See Boyd (1999a:56–58 and subsequent information sheets) for scripts, variations, and instructions.

44. Boyd 1999a:58.

45. Boyd 1999a:12.

46. See Boyd 1999a:12–16.

47. Email message from Leondar-Wright, July 3, 2006. Some members of this network (such as Chuck Collins and Betsy Leondar-Wright) were among the hundreds, eventually thousands, of activists who received training in street theater, public speaking, and other skills from the Movement for a New Society in the late 1970s and 1980s. Some MNS trainers had prior experience with the antinuclear, anti–Vietnam War, and civil rights movement. In addition, as Boyd (2002a:155) notes, the Art and Revolution Collective during the 1990s, "which was inspired by RTS [Reclaim the Streets] and the diverse Do-It-Yourself (DIY) alternative youth cultures of the hip hop, punk, and rave music scenes . . . organized 'Convergences' throughout the United States to train activists and artists in nonviolent tactics, prop and puppet-making, and decentralized decision-making."

48. AH 5.30.06.

49. AH 9.14.04.

50. AH 6.8.06.

51. AH 9.14.04 and 6.22.06. The San Francisco-based Plutonium Players originated Ladies Against Women, which performed a satirical stage revue, subtitled "An Evening of Consciousness-Lowering."

52. Boyd 1999a:52.

53. In addition to those noted below, media references to this group include (among others) *New York Times* (1989), *Atlanta Journal and Constitution* (1993), Slinger (1988), Harris and Mintz (1986), Bilodeau (1985), and Brazaitis (1998).

54. Brazaitis 1998.

55. Crew 1985.

56. MacPherson 1984.

57. Clines 1984.

58. AH 7.14.06.

59. Fat Cats's slogans at the 1992 Democratic Convention in New York included the following: "The Futures Market in Politicians is Here!" "We Turn Financial Clout into Political Clout!" and "We Deal in Hard Cash, Soft Money, and Political Favors!"

60. Original script from files of M. A. Swedlund.

61. R. Turner 1995.

62. Josh "Waffles" Dostis and Suzy "Kitty" Polucci.

63. AH 7.14.06.

64. There are at least two brief published accounts by participants at this event: Collins and Yeskel (2000:193–94) and Leondar-Wright (2005:218–19). Unless otherwise noted, my account is based on my 2006 oral history interviews with participants.

65. AH 6.15.06.

66. AH 6.8.06.

67. Hartman (AH 6.15.06).

68. Collins and Yeskel 2000:194.

69. Jamieson and Waldman 2003:170.

70. *Ibid.*

71. Other activities sponsored by United for a Fair Economy and its Responsible Wealth group were mentioned as well in newspaper articles in the late 1990s and 2000s: *Boston Globe* (Lewis 1998), *Washington Post* (Smart 1999), *New York Times* (Gold 1999), and *Salt Lake Tribune* (Boulton 2000). Some of these stories covered UFE's role in recruiting shareholders to file resolutions with major corporations to examine the growing gap between the pay of average workers and chief executive officers, and to cap CEO pay (either at a flat rate or as a multiple of average employee compensation).

72. Zitner 1998.

73. Heaney 1998.

74. *Patriot Ledger* 1998.

75. *Worcester Telegram and Gazette* 1998.

76. DiFilippo 2000:7.

77. Portelli 1991:59.

78. *Ibid.*

79. Lapham remarked that later they "auctioned off the life raft at a UFE event as a souvenir, so someone has that life raft somewhere."

80. Holston and Appadurai 1999:14, cited in Goldstein 2004:5.

81. Kertzer 1988:5.

82. UFE staff member (AH 5.30.06).

83. Turner 1995 [1969].

84. Turner 1995 [1969]:176.

Chapter 4

1. Excerpts from Clifford Tasner's journal entry (emphasis added) on September 1, 2004, emailed to me August 27, 2008. I thank him for permission to quote from it.

2. The phrases in quotes are from Naomi Klein (2002:13, 6), writing in a different context.

3. From a three-page document distributed at the Billionaires' national "Convergence" in January 2005: "Billionaires for Bush 2005–2006: Using Numbers to Get Serious About Unchecked Corporate Power."

4. Cf. Shepard and Hayduk (2002) and Prokosch and Raymond (2002) on attention to public image in social movements.

5. Duncombe with Boyd 2007b:44.

6. These terms for MTV generation aesthetics are from Klein 2002:286.

7. For example, see Kaiser (2004) in the *Washington Post.* The phrase quoted is from N. Klein 2002:6.

8. "Billionaires for Bush, Hot Brief," one-page handout at Billionaires' for Bush national "Convergence," January 21–22, 2005, Washington, DC.

9. Gamson 2007:253.

10. *Ibid.*

11. Klein 2002. Since the late 1960s, the United States has spent a much larger share of its GDP on advertising than have the United Kingdom, Sweden, Japan, West Germany, and France (Offer 2006:122).

12. Klein 2002:21.

13. *Ibid.*

14. Klein 2002:7, 28.

15. Offer 2006:49.

16. Quoted in Klein 2002:20.

17. Duncombe 2007a:98.

18. Rosin 2004.

19. Klein 2002:16.

20. Klein's (2002:6) term.

21. Lisa Witter, speaking at national Billionaire "Convergence," January 21–22, 2005, Washington, DC. Witter then was chief strategy officer of Fenton Communications, a public relations firm that assists nonprofit organizations and progressive causes.

22. I reviewed photos and news clippings of such events in United for a Fair Economy's Boston office files.

23. UFE staff person (AH 5.30.06).

24. Created by Andrew Boyd, this also became a slogan for the Billionaires for Bush in the 2004 presidential campaign.

25. See Boyd 1999a:54.

26. While Forbes claimed to be the first U.S. presidential candidate to announce his candidacy on the Internet, the New Hampshire State House event described here was his first public appearance to announce his candidacy (Berke 1999).

27. AH 6.8.06.

28. Berke 1999.

29. AH 6.8.06.

30. Chuck Collins (AH 6.8.06).

31. AH 7.2.06. In 1999, the Billionaires for [X] concept was registered as a trademark.

32. AH 6.8.06.

33. AH 6.8.06.

34. AH 7.2.06.

35. AH 11.16.06.

36. Berke 1999.

37. Kiernan 1999.

38. DiStaso 1999.

39. Lessner 1999.

40. Fox News Special Report 1999.

41. Hermann 1999. Hermann was a member of the Class Acts satirical theater troupe then affiliated with United for a Fair Economy.

42. Hermann 1999.

43. AH 6.8.06.

44. M. Reed 1999.

45. AH 6.8.06.

46. Hermann 1999.

47. Victoria Olson, email, June 15, 2005.

48. Klein 2002:336.

49. During the 1999 WTO meetings they shared an office in Seattle's Belltown with the Alliance for Democracy.

50. AH 7.2.06.

51. Boyd 2002a:157. Some hoped as well to address the "prison-industrial complex, the death penalty, police brutality, and the threatened execution of [journalist] Mumia Abu-Jamal" (Boyd 2002a:157).

52. See Radin's (2000) *Boston Globe* account.

53. See Boyd 2002a,c.

54. http://www.zmag.org/Bulletins/pbfbogu.htm (accessed September 13, 2004).

55. Krugman 2007:155.

56. Boyd 2002a:157.

57. AH 5.30.06.

58. See Graeber (2009:288–91) on affinity groups, defined as "small groups of people who feel they share something important in common, and decide to work together on a common project" (2009:288). He notes their roots in a 1920s Spanish anarchist confederation and their use during the 1980s antinuclear campaigns, as well as the more recent global justice movement.

59. See photo in Boyd 2002a:152.

60. Duncombe 2007a:111.

61. *Ibid.* "Mack the Knife" was composed by Kurt Weill and the original lyrics in German were by Bertolt Brecht. It was popularized in the United States in the 1950s and 1960s and has been sung and spoofed by many performers since then.

62. AH 7.2.06.

63. AH 9.14.04.

64. See http://www.burningman.com (accessed August 17, 2011) for an overview of this annual Black Rock Desert, Nevada, event and its history.

65. Boyd 2002a:157.

66. *Ibid.*

67. Boyd 2002a:158. Some "wildcat chapters" were "sister campaigns, such as Billionaires for Closed Debates which addressed the monopolizing of the Presidential debates by the two major parties, and Billionaires for More Media Mergers which protested growing media concentration at the National Association of Broadcasters in San Francisco" in the fall of 2000 (Boyd 2002a:374).

68. Boyd 2002a:158.

69. AH 6.8.06.

70. See Chapter 6.

71. Press release, United for a Fair Economy, August 9, 2000. http://www.zmag.org/ Bulletins/pbfbogu.htm (accessed September 13, 2004).

72. Press release, United for a Fair Economy, August 9, 2000. http://www.zmag.org/ Bulletins/pbfbogu.htm (accessed September 13, 2004).

73. Boyd 2002a:158.

74. Part of Boyd's "homily" at the Billionaires' 2009 "Last Huzzah" party in Manhattan.

75. Graeber (2009:411). See also the websites of the cofounder of the Clandestine Insurgent Rebel Clown Army, Larry M. Bogad: http://www.clownarmy.org/ and http:// www.lmbogad.com (accessed December 28, 2012).

76. For examples of the dada chants, thanks go to Andrew Boyd (AH 8.13.11). On the Radical Clown Front, see Graeber 2009.

77. The hub-node terminology is borrowed from the Rand Corporation's classification of types of activist networks, as outlined in a study commissioned by the U.S. Army, in order to assess how to fight them (Ronfeldt et al. 1998:11–14). See also Rheingold (2002) on "smart mobs."

78. The process of delinking from UFE as the Billionaires shifted their legal status to that of a 527 organization for the 2004 campaign created some bruised feelings and

puzzlement at first, but these were resolved with time. Several interviewees mentioned a somewhat bumpy transition.

79. Boyd 2002a:158.

80. AH 8.22.04.

81. AH 6.8.06.

82. Boyd 2002a:159.

83. From a three-page document distributed at the Billionaires' national "Convergence" in January 2005, "Billionaires for Bush 2005–2006: Using Numbers to Get Serious About Unchecked Corporate Power."

84. Boyd 2002a,c.

85. Boyd 2002c:378.

86. AH 8.22.04.

87. Boyd 2002c:378, 2002a:159.

88. They did all this in 2000 on a modest start-up budget that included a small salary for Boyd and an intern, though Boyd (and others) ended up working many unpaid hours during the 2000 campaign. Boyd estimates that the total budget for the 2000 Billionaires for Bush (or Gore) may have been around $20,000 and that his salary may have been around ten dollars an hour. For a while, in 2000, he also had a codirector and an intern assisting him.

89. Boyd 2002a:160.

90. AH 5.30.06.

91. AH 6.22.06.

92. AH 7.2.06.

93. AH 7.2.06.

94. See Graeber 2009.

95. Ganz 2003:289.

96. Graeber 2007:377.

97. Ganz 2003:289.

98. See Goodwin and Jasper (2004:21) for a summary of theoretical debates on this subject.

99. Goodwin and Jasper 2004:21.

100. ArtandPolitics.com (accessed September 1, 2004) included many photos and accounts of early Billionaire activities.

101. AH 7.8.05.

102. AH 8.22.04.

103. The website states further that "Contributions to Billionaires, Inc. (or to 'Billionaires for Bush') are not tax-deductible as charitable contributions and are part of the public record. There is no limit on the amount an individual can contribute to Billionaires, Inc. Billionaires, Inc. will not accept contributions from candidates or candidate committees." "History and incorporation of Billionaires for Bush," http://www.billonairesforbush.com/diy_v1_ch6.php (accessed July 12, 2004).

104. AH 8.31.05.

105. McKelvey 2004.

106. Herman 2004.

107. AH 8.31.05.

108. AH 9.14.04.

109. Activists used text messaging to stage spontaneous rallies, to alert others to police crackdowns and clashes, and to direct volunteer medics to those in need of help.

110. Rosenthal 2004.

111. Spiegelman 2004.

112. Suskind 2004; and Clarke 2004.

113. Krugman 2007:158–59. "By 2004," Krugman (2007:159) observes, "76 percent of Americans saw significant differences between the parties, up from 46 percent in 1972."

114. AH 5.30.06.

115. It worked well in terms of public and media appeal, though the 2004 election outcome bitterly disappointed the Billionaires and other progressives.

116. AH 7.2.06.

117. AH 7.16.04.

118. As he remarked during a presentation at the Billionaires for Bush "strategery" meeting, June 14, 2005, Manhattan.

119. Greene Dragon terms itself "a band of modern-day patriots celebrating the American Revel-ution against corporate tyranny." http://greeenedragon.net (accessed December 28, 2012).

120. AH 11.22.06.

121. Conversation at a Billionaire street event (AH 7.6.04).

122. Varon 2004; see also Varon 2005.

123. AH 7.16.04.

124. In this context, he meant an advocate of direct action; see Graeber (2009) on that approach.

125. The account presented here draws on multiple conversations with Billionaire members, as well as press coverage. See, for example, Slackman and Moynihan's (2004) account in the *New York Times*.

126. The club was Eugene, on Twenty-fourth Street, between Fifth Avenue and Avenue of the Americas.

127. Slackman and Moynihan 2004.

128. Raphie Frank and Mindy Bond, interview with Andrew Boyd, *Gothamist*, October 29, 2004. http://www.gothamist.com/archives/2004/10/29/andrew_boyd_cultural . . . (accessed May 1, 2005).

129. Slackman and Moynihan 2004.

130. *Ibid.*

131. Some Billionaire members knew Tony Torn previously through their participation in the Reverend Billy choir.

132. See Graeber (2007:394–95) on links between contemporary direct action and the Situationists, who use "art as a form of revolutionary direct action."

133. A CNN television broadcast on February 19, 2004, describes the Rove event: "Some lively political theater on the streets of New York may be a preview of what we'll

see during this summer's Republican convention. About 100 protesters dressed in top hats and tuxedoes, calling themselves 'Billionaires for Bush,' and they were greeted yesterday by an actor imitating Bush political advisor Karl Rove. The real Karl Rove was speaking nearby at a fund-raiser that netted, by the way, about $400,000" (CNN 2004).

134. AH 7.8.05.

135. Archibold 2004.

136. Victoria Olson, June 15, 2005.

137. Film by Oddly Honest Productions.

138. AH 12.6.04.

139. Meeting of New York chapter of Billionaires for Bush, November 23, 2004.

140. AH 7.9.05.

141. AH 12.3.08.

142. AH 12.29.05.

143. Raphie Frank and Mindy Bond, interview with Andrew Boyd, *Gothamist*, October 29, 2004. http://www.gothamist.com/archives/2004/10/29/andrew_boyd_cultural ... (accessed May 1, 2005).

144. AH 7.9.05.

145. AH 7.8.05.

146. AH 7.8.05.

147. AH 11.22.06.

148. Chastain 2004.

Chapter 5

1. Jeremy Varon, July 16, 2004.

2. September 14, 2004, New York City chapter meeting.

3. July 13, 2004, meeting of Manhattan chapter of Billionaires for Bush.

4. May 17, 2005, New York chapter meeting.

5. "Ministry of Love" was borrowed from the Lower East Side Collective (see Duncombe 2007a:91).

6. Earlier social movement scholarship tended to obscure "the disputes, the divisions, and the dropouts" (Edelman 1999:185).

7. AH 6.28.12.

8. Ahearn (2012:162). For an overview of theoretical approaches to the study of performance and performativity, see Ahearn (2012:160–83). See Bauman and Briggs (1990) on poetics and performance.

9. Weber 1973 [1946]:245, 262, 249.

10. AH 8.22.04.

11. William Fry (1963:138, quoted in Yarwood 2004:9).

12. The song title is "Billionaires for Bush"; it is included on the CD *Here Come the Billionaires!*, with lyrics by Clifford J. Tasner (aka Felonious Ax) of the Billionaires Los Angeles chapter.

13. Billionaires for Bush Manhattan chapter meeting, July 13, 2004 (author's transcription). Anthropologists will hear echoes of Bourdieu (1977:94–95) on *habitus*.

14. AH 7.2.06.

15. AH 7.2.06.

16. AH 7.2.06.

17. Forbes.com describes the fictional Thurston Howell III as "eccentric Harvard grad [who] fled U.S. . . . . Rumored to be living on private island in Pacific with wife Lovey and skeletal staff. . . . Known for his bare-knuckled boardroom style, despite socialite manners." http://www.forbes.com/2002/09/13/400fictional_print.html (accessed January 2, 2006).

18. Comment from a man in his twenties during June 29, 2004, Manhattan chapter meeting.

19. http://billionairesforbush.com/diy_v2_ch4.php (accessed December 28, 2012).

20. AH 8.22.04.

21. Seigworth and Gregg 2010:1–2. In this context, bodies are "defined not by an outer-skin envelope or other surface boundary but by their potential to reciprocate or co-participate in the passages of affect" (Seigworth and Gregg 2010:2). "[A]ffect is persistent proof of a body's never less than ongoing immersion in and among the world's obstinacies and rhythms, its refusals as much as its invitations" (Seigworth and Gregg 2010:1).

22. Thanks go to Melanie Hughes McDermott for ideas on this point.

23. Boddy 1994:423. Thanks to Eric Gable for suggestions on this theme.

24. AH 7.6.12.

25. Beeman 1993:386.

26. Farnell and Graham 1998:419.

27. AH 7.16.04.

28. See Ahearn 2012; and Duranti and Brenneis 1986.

29. Some portions of this section draw on Haugerud 2010.

30. See Bakhtin 1981; and Dentith 2000:ch.1.

31. Dentith 2000:5.

32. On intertextuality in speech play, see Sherzer 2002:10, 154.

33. Analyzed by scholars such as Debra Spitulnik (1997), now Debra Vidali.

34. Beeman 2000:103.

35. *Ibid.*

36. AH 7.2.06.

37. Songs mentioned in this paragraph are available on the CD, *Here Come the Billionaires!* (2000 and 2001), with lyrics by Clifford J. Tasner (aka Felonius Ax).

38. December 1, 2004, "media alert" distributed by email.

39. This event occurred on December 2, 2004, and had been discussed at a previous Billionaires for Bush planning meeting I attended. Unless otherwise noted, all quotations in this discussion are from my conversations on the street that day.

40. AH 1.6.05.

41. A shorter account of this event is included in Haugerud (2010:119), and portions of this discussion quote from that account.

42. AH 12.4.04.

43. AH 1.6.05.

44. AH 12.4.04.

45. Reich 2010b.

46. AH 5.27.06.

47. AH 7.16.04.

48. I thank Noelle Molé, who assisted me with street intercept interviews at that event, for this interview (on audiotape).

49. A woman on the executive committee said the Billionaires for Bush hoped that by adopting an image that distinguished them from "traditional" protesters they would reach people who are "definitely not automatically going to jump into a protest or necessarily even appreciate if a protest showed up on their main street" (AH 1.7.05).

50. AH 7.16.04.

51. *Ibid.*

52. *Ibid.*

53. "Strategery," again, was a Bush malapropism popularized by comedian Will Ferrell, among others.

54. Email to author, 6.15.05.

55. AH 10.1.04.

56. October 14, 2004, Manhattan chapter meeting. Billionaires for Bush had eighty-eight chapters in mid-September 2004 and a couple of dozen chapters in March 2004.

57. June 29, 2004, Manhattan chapter meeting.

58. AH 8.31.05.

59. A comment I heard during the January 2005 "Convergence" in Washington, DC.

60. AH 8.22.04.

61. *Ibid.*

62. http://billionairesforbush.com/diy_v2_ch1.php (accessed December 28, 2012).

63. AH 8.22.04.

64. Under "Suitable Attire," "Becoming a Billionaire": http://www.billionairesforbush.com/diy_v1_ch1.php (accessed December 28, 2012).

65. AH 12.29.05.

66. AH 11.22.06.

67. AH 7.16.04.

68. AH 8.22.04.

69. AH 7.16.04, and Billionaire handout prepared for the 2004 Republican National Convention in New York.

70. "Guide to the RNC [Republican National Convention]," Billionaires for Bush, two-page flyer, August 2004. Robert Frank (2007b:8–9) writes that individuals with a net worth of 1–10 million dollars are more politically conservative than those with a net worth of 10–100 million dollars.

71. Examples of such facts listed in the document: "Bush supported legislation eliminating overtime pay for 6 million workers. 52% of Bush's tax cuts will go to the richest 1% (those whose income in 2010 will be $1.5 million). The number of Americans without health insurance stands at 45 million. The average American family is paying $2700 more in health care premiums than they were four years ago. . . . George Bush gave a tax break

of $986 million to the WalMart heirs and $300 per person to most ordinary people." From "Guide to the RNC," Billionaires for Bush, two-page flyer, August 2004.

72. AH 12.6.04.

73. Email copied to author, with recipient's knowledge, March 15, 2005.

74. Edelman 2005; Escobar 2008; Riles 2001.

75. AH 7.2.06.

76. Edelman (2009:257) here is paraphrasing Burdick (1998).

Chapter 6

1. Jeremy Varon, addressing a Billionaire "Strategery" meeting, Manhattan, June 14, 2005.

2. Gitlin 2003:307.

3. Thompson 1995:247.

4. Thompson 1995:241.

5. June 7, 2005, Manhattan chapter meeting.

6. In this paragraph I build on suggestions offered in "The Media Rules Manual: The Science of Media Seduction," by Mathis Media, LLC. This handbook was distributed to anthropologists during a media training workshop at the 2002 annual meeting of the American Anthropological Association.

7. Bush did sign the 2002 McCain-Feingold legislation, but without any signing ceremony or Rose Garden press conference (Kroll 2012). Shortly thereafter, conservative challenges to the bill's constitutionality began.

8. A common pattern in Latin America as well (Ulla Berg, personal communication). See online archives of the Hemispheric Institute for Performance and Politics at http://www.hemi.org (accessed December 28, 2012).

9. Gitlin 2003; Graeber 2009; McLeod and Hertog 1999.

10. A point made by Phil T. Rich (Andrew Boyd) in an interview quoted in the *Boston Globe* (Slack 2004).

11. http://www.billionairesforbush.com/nyc/actionguide.php (accessed November 27, 2004).

12. So said a media coordinator who was involved in the 1999 Billionaires for Forbes and the 2000 Billionaires for Bush (or Gore) parent organization, United for a Fair Economy (AH 5.30.06).

13. AH 5.30.06.

14. See Gitlin 2003:171, 310.

15. On the commodification of dissent, see Frank and Weiland 1997.

16. Gitlin 2003:311. See also Goffman (1974) on frame analysis.

17. Gitlin 2003:304.

18. *Ibid.*

19. Gamson 2007:253.

20. Duncombe 2007a:140 and fn.23.

21. An emphasis in British cultural studies (Hall et al. 1980). Earlier, Frankfurt School theorists such as Max Horkheimer and Theodor Adorno had analyzed the "cul-

ture industry" as a vehicle of "mass deception" and obstacle to independent thought (Adorno 1991). Later the focus of media studies shifted from media producers to consumers who appropriate texts and produce meanings (see Askew 2002), though some media and cultural analysts caution about the risk of romanticizing resistance and exaggerating "the meaning-creating agent and the possibilities of cultural bricolage" while ignoring what Bourdieu (1977) terms the misrecognition that helps to uphold hierarchies of power, authority, and wealth (Garnham 1992:372–73).

22. Moyers 2008; Jamieson and Waldman 2003.

23. Boyd 2002c:373.

24. "Guide to Organizing an NYC Billionaires for Bush Action," http://www.billion airesforbush.com/nyc/actionguide/php (accessed November 27, 2004).

25. From the May 11, 2006, Manhattan chapter meeting of Billionaires for Bush. The member's quip echoes Stephen Colbert's "roast" of journalists a few days earlier at the White House Correspondents' Association dinner.

26. Boler 2008.

27. Kahn and Kellner 2006:705.

28. Atton 2008:216.

29. O'Brien 2004. See Graeber (2007:379) on his engagement with corporate news media in spite of opposition from some anarchists.

30. Such a perspective reflects the nondichotomous character of domination and subordination, resistance and power, complicity and contestation (cf. Mahon 2000:475; Gledhill 2000; Mitchell 1990; Ortner 1995).

31. Adorno and Horkheimer 1997 [1947]:132.

32. Mahon 2000:470.

33. Couldry 2000:181.

34. Cf. Couldry 2000:47.

35. Askew 2002:1. On anthropology and media studies, see Askew 2002; Dickey 1997; Ginsburg, Abu-Lughod, and Larkin 2002:3; Postill 2009; and Spitulnik 1993.

36. Rosin 2004:D1.

37. See, for example, Bagdikian 2004; Bird 2010; Fallows 1997; Henry 2007; Jamieson and Waldman 2003; McChesney 2006; and Moyers 2008.

38. Krugman 2004b.

39. Garnham 1992:363. Schudson (1992:153) writes that "the commercial model of journalism that dominates general, public discourse today and grew out of the penny press of the 1830s seeks a market, not an association or community."

40. Posner 2005:9.

41. Couldry 2000:192.

42. Bagdikian 2004:16. The five dominant media companies by the early 2000s were Time Warner, Walt Disney Company, Murdoch's News Corporation (based in Australia), Bertelsmann (based in Germany), and Viacom (Bagdikian 2004:3).

43. Baym 2005:261. Technological change includes vast expansion in the number of channels offered through cable and satellite systems; the speed of information transmission; Internet delivery of "high-resolution images and video"; the multiplication of

online blogs, newspapers and magazines; and "emergence of hand-held and computer-based video and editing systems . . . [that] lower the threshold to production, in terms of both required capital and technical skills" (Baym 2005:261). As Posner (2005:8) remarks, "[t]hirty years ago the average number of television channels that Americans could receive was seven."

44. Peters and Stelter 2011.

45. Moyers 2008:345.

46. Moyers 2008:325.

47. Bagdikian 2004:7.

48. Bagdikian 2004:8–9.

49. Couldry 2000:5.

50. See Moyers 2008:341.

51. *New York Times* 2008b.

52. Carr 2011b.

53. See Burrough 2011.

54. Keller 2005:xviii.

55. Moyers 2008:308; see also Jamieson and Waldman 2003:170.

56. Jamieson and Waldman 2003:170.

57. A position Warner (1992:389–90), among others, warns against.

58. On Foucauldian power and discipline in journalistic workplaces, see Pedelty 1995.

59. Boyer 2010.

60. Krugman 2011.

61. Pedelty 1995:9–12.

62. Moyers 2008:321.

63. Rich 2004.

64. Krugman 2004a.

65. Krugman 2007:185.

66. Krugman 2004b.

67. Davidson 2012.

68. Couldry's (2000:17) term.

69. Moyers 2008:322. See di Leonardo (2008) on the "neoliberalization of consciousness" that has contributed to obscuring in the public sphere rising inequality and eroding democracy.

70. Gitlin 2003:301.

71. *Ibid.*

72. Gitlin 2003:302.

73. McLeod and Hertog 1999:314.

74. Hollar 2012.

75. Gitlin 2003:309.

76. Schudson 1992:152.

77. McChesney 1999.

78. Clifford Tasner, journal entry, August 30, 2004 (quoted with permission).

79. Kaiser 2004.

80. *Ibid.*

81. These numbers include articles that focused on the Billionaires for Bush, the Billionaires for Bush (or Gore), or the Billionaires for Forbes, as well as those in which they were mentioned briefly. About 10 percent of the articles appeared on page A1 of a newspaper. See Appendix (Research Methods) for details about data sources.

82. Just 2 percent of the total articles were published in 2001, 2002, and 2003 combined, while 15 percent appeared in 2005, 7 percent in 2006, and 8 percent in the first half of 2007. These percentages are based on the following raw counts by Noelle Molé: 121 articles in 2000, 4 in 2001, 4 in 2002, 5 in 2003, 254 in 2004, 86 in 2005, 37 in 2006, and 43 in the first half of 2007—for a total of 559 articles.

83. Australia, Belgium, Canada, England, France, Ireland, and Singapore.

84. AH 12.11.08.

85. AH 12.3.08.

86. Slack 2004.

87. Foley 2004.

88. Klein 2004.

89. *WBUR Here and Now* 2004.

90. McKelvey 2004.

91. *Financial Times* 2004.

92. Cave 2004.

93. Trigaux 2004.

94. *Ottawa Citizen* 2004.

95. Helm 2004.

96. O'Brien 2004.

97. Hitt 2004.

98. Feyerick 2004.

99. Sneed 2004.

100. Slack 2004.

101. AH 7.8.05.

102. Haberman 2004.

103. Jamieson and Waldman (2003:167) write that when candidates trade accusations about their opponent's harmful proposals on Social Security, for example, journalists are likely to focus on tactics and avoid assessing the accuracy of the candidates' claims—whether out of fear of appearing "biased" or because they lack the necessary knowledge to sort out the facts, or both.

104. Haberman 2004.

105. Johnson 2000.

106. Jamieson and Waldman 2003.

107. Cf. Jamieson and Waldman 2003:168.

108. Pedelty 1995.

109. Hari 2004, emphasis added.

110. Carnegie 2004.

111. Cave 2004.

112. Harper 2005.

113. Gray 2004.

114. McIntire 2000.

115. CBS 2000.

116. *International Herald Tribune* 2007.

117. Donaldson-Evans 2007.

118. McLeod and Hertog 1999:314.

119. McLeod and Hertog 1999:323–24.

120. AH 7.08.05.

121. Manhattan, June 14, 2005.

122. Varon addressing Billionaires during a "Strategery" meeting in Manhattan, June 14, 2005.

123. Dwyer 2008.

124. Billionaires for Bush listserv email, October 24, 2007.

125. Gamson 2007:251.

126. "Strategery" meeting, Manhattan, July 5, 2005.

127. Boyd 2002c.

128. Boyd 2002c:372.

129. September 7, 2004, Manhattan chapter meeting.

130. AH 10.30.04.

131. AH 12.29.05.

132. Gamson 2007:252.

133. Unless otherwise noted, all Opprecht quotes in this paragraph are from AH 6.17.05.

134. From a document distributed in January 2005 to attendees of the national "Convergence" of Billionaires for Bush in Washington, DC, January 21–22, 2005.

135. Ginsburg 1991. A term later used as well in Ginsburg, Abu-Lughod, and Larkin (2002:10) in their discussion of indigenous media as a possible "Faustian contract with the technologies of modernity, enabling some degree of agency to control representation under less-than-ideal conditions."

136. Scott 1985:xvii.

137. G. Smith 2004:217.

Chapter 7

1. During his speech at the Billionaires' "Last Huzzah" party in Manhattan, January 25, 2009.

2. http://www.pbs.org/newshour/bb/politics/july-dec00/alsmith_10-20.html (accessed August 19, 2007). This Bush quote later circulated widely (e.g., on YouTube) and was included in Michael Moore's film *Fahrenheit 911*.

3. According to a July 2009 *Time* magazine poll, http://www.timepolls.com/hppolls/archive/poll_results_417.html (accessed January 7, 2010). Stewart also polled well in a 2007 Pew Research Center survey (Kakutani 2008).

4. Wedel 2009.

5. Day 2011:back cover.

6. See Boyer and Yurchak (2010) and Chapter 6 in this volume.

7. Boyer and Yurchak 2010:208–9.

8. Boyer and Yurchak 2010; Day 2011.

9. Media Matters for America 2006.

10. Askew 2002:7; McLuhan 1994; Anderson 1983.

11. Moyers 2008.

12. Habermas 1989 [1962]:171.

13. See Schudson (1992) for a discussion of these issues in the context of American history, and Calhoun (1992:1–50) for an overview of debates about Habermas and the public sphere. See Garnham (1992) and Warner (1992) on Habermas's analysis of media and the public sphere. Calhoun (1992:33) suggests Habermas may have "overestimat[ed] the degeneration of the public sphere. The revitalization of a critical public during the 1960s (and its refusal to quite go away since then) lends further credence to this view." Calhoun (1992:4) also recommends "keep[ing] fully in mind Habermas's two-sided constitution of the category of the public sphere as simultaneously about the quality or form of rational-critical discourse and the quantity of, or openness to, popular participation."

14. Habermas 1989 [1962]:172.

15. Such criticisms are summarized in Garnham (1992:359–60).

16. Others, as Calhoun (1992:4) writes, fault Habermas's work for "illusions and dangerous tendencies of an Enlightenment conception of democratic public life, especially in mass society . . . [and] for an inadequate grasp of everyday life (including mass media) in advanced capitalism, and for exaggerating the emancipatory potential in the idealized bourgeois public sphere."

17. Public copresentation with the author at the Department of Anthropology, American University, Washington, DC, March 15, 2005.

18. AH 12.11.08.

19. See Giugni, McAdam, and Tilly 1999; Snow, Soule, and Kriesi 2007; Tarrow 1998.

20. Fox 2009:491.

21. Tarrow 1998.

22. Boyer and Yurchak 2010:181, 213.

23. Boyer and Yurchak 2010:212.

24. Lessig (2011:Appendix) provides additional information on such initiatives. See, for example, OpenSecrets.org, FollowTheMoney.org, OpenCongress.org, MapLight.org, and Rootstrikers.org.

25. Institute for Policy Studies: http://www.ips-dc.org/ (accessed December 28, 2012).

26. United for a Fair Economy: http://faireconomy.org (accessed December 28, 2012).

27. http://agit-pop.com/ (accessed December 28, 2012).

28. http://beautifultrouble.org (accessed December 28, 2012).

29. Tarrow 1998:23–24.

30. Hann and Hart (2011:170); see their discussion of the notion of a human economy, which is also the focus of the edited collection by Hart, Laville, and Cattani (2010).

31. Turner 1974.

32. Portions of this section draw on Haugerud 2012.

33. Collins 2012.

34. See Writers for the 99% (2011); and Taylor et al. (2011).

35. See the Federalist and anti-Federalist papers compiled by Wootton (2003) for early American debates about direct democracy and "large, unchecked assemblies" versus a Federalist constitution that relies on representation rather than direct democracy.

36. Graeber 2011.

37. Democracy Now 2012.

38. On the latter, see Graeber 2009; and Juris 2008.

39. Byers 2011.

40. Hart et al. 2010:9.

41. Purdy 2012.

42. *Ibid.*

43. Gitlin 2012.

44. M. N. Smith 2012.

45. *Ibid.*

46. Lesley Gill (email, March 17, 2011) describing a presentation by Bonanno at Vanderbilt University on March 16, 2011.

47. Gitlin 2012, emphasis in original.

48. Haberman 2011.

49. Author's conversations in Zuccotti Park, October 2011 and March 2012.

50. Hedges 2012; see Juris (2012) and Razsa and Kurnik (2012) on tactical borrowing and innovation in Occupy movements.

51. Huizinga 1955:207.

52. *Ibid.*

53. Huizinga 1955:212.

54. Jasper 2003:153; Goodwin, Jasper, and Polletta 2001.

55. Edelman (2001:290) here quotes Zald (1992:330–31).

56. Quotes in this section from Merchant F. Arms about that evening are from AH 12.3.08.

57. AH 12.29.05.

58. November 4, 2004, Manhattan chapter meeting.

59. AH 12.3.08.

60. Stewart 2007:116.

61. The latter phrase closely paraphrases Moore and Sanders 2006:11.

62. AH 11.17.04.

63. He made these comments and those quoted in the sentences that follow during a group discussion at the November 4, 2004, meeting of the Manhattan Billionaires.

64. Planning meeting of Manhattan Billionaires (AH 7.13.04).

65. AH 7.5.12.

66. AH 7.16.04.

67. AH 7.8.05.

68. Boyd 2002b:62.
69. Again, the notion that any markets are "free" of rules or regulations is a myth.
70. Schutz 1977:50.
71. Zijderveld 1983:58.

Works Cited

Abrams, Lynn. 2010. *Oral History Theory.* New York: Routledge.

Adorno, Theodor W. 1991. *The Culture Industry: Selected Essays on Mass Culture,* edited by J. M. Bernstein. London: Routledge.

Adorno, Theodor, and Max Horkheimer. 1997 [1947]. *Dialectic of Enlightenment.* New York: Verso.

Ahearn, Laura. 2001. "Language and Agency." *Annual Review of Anthropology* 30:109–37.

———. 2012. *Living Language: An Introduction to Linguistic Anthropology.* Malden, MA: Wiley-Blackwell.

Alinsky, Saul. 1972. *Rules for Radicals.* New York: Random House.

Anderson, Benedict. 1983. *Imagined Communities: Reflections on the Origin and Spread of Nationalism.* London: Verso.

Archibold, Randal C. 2004. "Hey Hey, Ho Ho, Those Old Protest Tactics Have to Go." *New York Times,* June 1, 45, 47.

Askew, Kelly. 2002. "Introduction." In *The Anthropology of Media: A Reader,* edited by Kelly Askew and Richard R. Wilk, 1–13. Oxford: Blackwell.

Atlanta (GA) Journal and Constitution. 1993. "Party Beat: Arts Festival of Atlanta." September 19, L3.

Attardo, Salvatore. 2001. "Humor and Irony in Interaction: From Mode Adoption to Failure of Detection." In *Say Not to Say: New Perspectives on Miscommunication,* edited by L. Anolli, R. Ciceri, and G. Riva, 166–85. Amsterdam: IOS Press.

Atton, Chris. 2008. "Alternative Media Theory and Journalism Practice." In Boler 2008, 213–27.

Babcock, Barbara A., ed. 1978. *The Reversible World: Symbolic Inversion in Art and Society.* Ithaca, NY: Cornell University Press.

Bagdikian, Ben. 2004. *The New Media Monopoly.* Boston: Beacon Press.

Bakhtin, Mikhail. 1981. *The Dialogic Imagination*, translated by C. Emerson and M. Holquist. Austin: University of Texas Press.

———. 1984 [1968]. *Rabelais and His World*. Cambridge, MA: MIT Press.

Baldick, Chris. 1990. *The Concise Oxford Dictionary of Literary Terms*. New York: Oxford University Press.

Bartels, Larry. 2008. *Unequal Democracy: The Political Economy of the New Gilded Age*. New York: Russell Sage Foundation.

Bauerlein, Monika, and Clara Jeffery. 2012. "Occupied Washington: Grotesque Income Inequality Is Just a Symptom of Our Larger Political Disease." *Mother Jones*, January/February. http://motherjones.com/print/148941 (accessed March 10, 2012).

Bauman, Richard, and Charles L. Briggs. 1990. "Poetics and Performance as Critical Perspectives on Language and Social Life." *Annual Review of Anthropology* 19:59–88.

Baym, Geoffey. 2005. "*The Daily Show*: Discursive Integration and the Reinvention of Political Journalism." *Political Communication* 22:259–76.

Beeman, William O. 1993. "The Anthropology of Theater and Spectacle." *Annual Review of Anthropology* 22:369–93.

———. 2000. "Humor." *Journal of Linguistic Anthropology* 9(1):103–6.

Beers, David. 2001. "Irony Is Dead! Long Live Irony!" Salon.com, September 25. http://archive.salon.com/mwt/feature/2001/09/25/irony_lives/ (accessed January 1, 2013).

Berke, Richard L. 1999. "Forbes Declares Candidacy on Internet and the Stump." *New York Times*, March 17, 19.

Billionaires for Bush. 2004. *How to Rule the World for Fun and Profit*. New York: Thunder's Mouth Press.

Bilodeau, Paul. 1985. "Thousands Take Part in Anti-Nuclear Rallies." *Toronto (Ontario) Star*, October 27, A2.

Bird, Elizabeth S., ed. 2010. *The Anthropology of News and Journalism*. Bloomington: Indiana University Press.

Blow, Charles. 2011. "Empire at the End of Decadence." *New York Times*, February 19, A23.

Boddy, Janice. 1994. "Spirit Possession Revisited: Beyond Instrumentality." *Annual Review of Anthropology* 23:407–34.

Bogad, Larry M. 2005. "A Place for Protest: The Billionaires for Bush Interrupt the Hegemonologue." In *Performance and Place*, edited by Leslie Hill and Helen Paris, 170–79. New York: Palgrave Macmillan.

Boler, Megan, ed. 2008. *Digital Media and Democracy: Tactics in Hard Times*. Cambridge, MA: MIT Press.

Boler, Megan, with Stephen Turpin. 2008. "*The Daily Show* and *Crossfire*: Satire and Sincerity as Truth to Power." In Boler 2008, 383–403.

Booth, Wayne. 1974. *A Rhetoric of Irony*. Chicago: University of Chicago Press.

Boulton, Guy. 2000. "Visiting Activists Aid Fight for Consumer Watchdog." *Salt Lake (UT) Tribune*, August 12, B4.

Bourdieu, Pierre. 1977. *Outline of a Theory of Practice*. New York: Cambridge University Press.

Boyd, Andrew. 1999a. *The Activist Cookbook: Creative Actions for a Fair Economy*. Boston: United for a Fair Economy.

———. 1999b. *Life's Little Deconstruction Book: Self-Help for the Post-Hip*. New York: Norton.

———. 2002a. "Billionaires Crash the Extreme Costume Ball." In Prokosch and Raymond 2002, 152–61.

———. 2002b. *Daily Afflictions: The Agony of Being Connected to Everything in the Universe*. New York: Norton.

———. 2002c. "Truth Is a Virus: Meme Warfare and the Billionaires for Bush (or Gore)." In *Cultural Resistance Reader*, edited by Stephen Duncombe, 369–78. New York and London: Verso.

———. 2003. "The Web Rewires the Movement." *Nation*, August 4. http://www.thenation.com/article/web-rewires-movement (accessed January 1, 2013).

Boyd, Andrew, with Dave Oswald Mitchell. 2012. *Beautiful Trouble: A Toolbox for Revolution*. New York and London: OR Books.

Boyer, Dominic. 2010. "Making (Sense of) News in the Era of Digital Information." In Bird 2010, 241–56.

Boyer, Dominic, and Alexi Yurchak. 2010. "American Stiob: Or, What Late-Socialist Aesthetics of Parody Reveal About Contemporary Political Culture in the West." *Cultural Anthropology* 25(2):179–221.

Brazaitis, Tom. 1998. "Schroeder Dared to Do It All—And Congress." *Cleveland* (OH) *Plain Dealer*, April 26, 3D.

Buffett, Warren. 2011. "Stop Coddling the Super-Rich." *New York Times*, August 15, A20.

Burdick, John. 1998. *Blessed Anastacia: Women, Race, and Popular Christianity in Brazil*. New York: Routledge.

Burrough, Bryan. 2011. "Lessons in Communication, for Newspapers Themselves." *New York Times*, June 26, 4.

Byers, Dylan. 2011. "Occupy Wall Street Is Winning." *Politico*, November 11. http://www.politico.com//blogs/bensmith/1111/Occupy_Wall_Street_is_winning .html (accessed July 8, 2012).

Calhoun, Craig. 1992. "Introduction: Habermas and the Public Sphere." In *Habermas and the Public Sphere*, edited by Craig Calhoun, 1–48. Cambridge, MA: MIT Press.

Carnegie, Marc. 2004. "Cranks and Jokesters Take US Protest to the Streets." *Agence France-Presse*, July 27.

Carr, David. 2011a. "Comic's PAC Is More Than a Gag." *New York Times*, August 22, B1.

———. 2011b. "Ugly Details in Selling Newspapers." *New York Times*, June 20, B1.

Carter, Bill, and Brian Stelter. 2010. "In 'Daily Show' Role on 9/11 Bill, Echoes of Murrow." *New York Times*, December 27, B1.

Cave, Damien. 2004. "Interests and Ideals Meet, and Usually Get Along." *New York Times*, July 19, B3.

CBS. 2000. *CBS Evening News*. Factiva transcript, July 30, 6:00 P.M., Federal Document Clearing House.

Chastain, Emma. 2004. "Right Attitude." *New Republic Online*, August 30. http://tnr.com/docprint.mhtml?i=express&s=chastain083004 (accessed September 3, 2004).

Clarke, Richard A. 2004. *Against All Enemies: Inside America's War on Terror*. New York: Free Press.

Clifford, James. 2001. "The Last Discussant." In *Irony in Action: Anthropology, Practice, and the Moral Imagination*, edited by James W. Fernandez and Mary Taylor Huber, 253–59. Chicago: University of Chicago Press.

Clines, Francis X. 1984. "Convention in Dallas: The Republicans." *New York Times*, August 24. http://www.nytimes.com/1984/08/24/us/convention-in-dallas-the-republicans-convention-journal.html?scp=3&sq=Convention%20in%20Dallas:%20The%20Republicans%20August%2024,%201984&st=cse (accessed March 19, 2012).

CNN. 2004. "Live Today," Carol Lin and Bob Franken, February 19. Copyright eMediaMillWorks, Federal Document Clearing House.

Coffey, Brendan. 2011. "Protest Movement Starts 'Rebranding' Billionaire Koch Brothers." *Forbes*. http://www.forbes.com/sites/brendancoffey/2011/05/12/protest-movement-starts-rebranding-billionaire-koch-brothers (accessed February 25, 2012).

Colebrook, Claire. 2004. *Irony*. London: Routledge.

Collins, Chuck, Mike Lapham, and Scott Klinger. 2004. *I Didn't Do It Alone: Society's Contribution to Individual Wealth and Success*. Boston: United for a Fair Economy.

Collins, Chuck, and Felice Yeskel. 2000. *Economic Apartheid in America: A Primer on Economic Inequality and Insecurity*. New York: New Press.

Collins, Jane. 2012. "Theorizing Wisconsin's 2011 Protests." *American Ethnologist* 39(1):6–20.

Collins, Jane L., Micaela di Leonardo, and Brett Williams, eds. 2008. *New Landscapes of Inequality: Neoliberalism and the Erosion of Democracy in America*. Santa Fe, NM: School of American Research.

Collins, Jane L., and Victoria Mayer. 2010. *Both Hands Tied: Welfare Reform and the Race to the Bottom of the Low-Wage Labor Market*. Chicago and London: University of Chicago Press.

Comaroff, Jean, and John Comaroff, eds. 1991. *Of Revelation and Revolution: Christianity, Colonialism, and Consciousness in South Africa*, Volume One. Chicago and London: University of Chicago Press.

———. 2001. *Millennial Capitalism and the Culture of Neoliberalism*. Durham, NC: Duke University Press.

Conniff, Richard. 2002. *The Natural History of the Rich: A Field Guide*. New York: Norton.

Couldry, Nick. 2000. *The Place of Media Power: Pilgrims and Witnesses of the Media Age*. London: Routledge.

Cox, Christopher. 2008. "Swapping Secrecy for Transparency." *New York Times*, October 19, 12.

Crapanzano, Vincent. 2003. "Reflections on Hope as a Category of Social and Psychological Analysis." *Cultural Anthropology* 18(1):3–32.

Crew, Robert. 1985. "Top Cats Leaving Show but Producers Project Running into Summer." *Toronto* (Ontario) *Star*, October 23, B1.

Critchley, Simon. 2002. *On Humor*. London and New York: Routledge.

Croll, Andy. 2012. "Follow the Dark Money." *Mother Jones*, July/August. http://www.motherjones.com/print/178416 (accessed June 22, 2012).

Darnton, Robert. 1984. *The Great Cat Massacre and Other Episodes in French Cultural History*. New York: Perseus Books.

Davidson, Adam. 2012. "Are the Rich Worth a Damn?" *New York Times Magazine*, May 6, 34–40.

Davis, Natalie Zemon. 1975. *Society and Culture in Early Modern France: Eight Essays*. Stanford, CA: Stanford University Press.

Day, Amber. 2011. *Satire and Dissent*. Bloomington: Indiana University Press

De Martino, George. 2000. *Global Economy, Global Justice: Theoretical Objections and Policy Alternatives to Neoliberalism*. London: Routledge.

Debord, Guy. 1988. *Comments on the Society of Spectacle*. London: Verso.

Della Porta, Donatella. 2011. "Social Movements." *Oxford Bibliographies Online*. http:www.oxfordbibliographiesonline.com (accessed December 28, 2012).

Democracy Now. 2012. "Occupy the SEC: Former Wall Street Workers Defend Volcker Rule Against Banks' Anti-Regulatory Push," February 24. http://www.democracynow.org/2012/2/24/occupy_the_sec_former_wall_street (accessed February 24, 2012).

Dentith, Simon. 2000. *Parody*. London: Routledge.

DeParle, Jason. 2011. "Top Earners Not So Lofty in the Days of Recession." *New York Times*, December 13.

Desjarlais, Robert, and C. Jason Throop. 2011. "Phenomenological Approaches in Anthropology." *Annual Review of Anthropology* 40:87–102.

di Leonardo, Micaela. 1998. *Exotics at Home: Anthropologies, Others, American Modernity*. Chicago: University of Chicago Press.

———. 2008. "The Neoliberalization of Minds, Space, and Bodies: Rising Global Inequality and the Shifting American Public Sphere." In Collins, di Leonardo, and Williams 2008, 190–208.

Dickey, Sara. 1997. "Anthropology and Its Contributions to Studies of Mass Media." *International Social Science Journal* 153(September): 413–28.

Didion, Joan. 2008. "Obama: In the Irony-Free Zone." *New York Review of Books*, December 18.

DiFilippo, Dana. 2000. "A Funny Way to Run a Protest." *Philadelphia* (PA) *Daily News*, July 29, 7.

DiStaso, John. 1999. "Candidate Forbes Takes Tax 'Pledge.'" *New Hampshire Union Leader* (Manchester), March 17, A10.

Donaldson-Evans, Catherine. 2007. "Environmental Group Delivers Lumps of Coal to Merrill Lynch to Protest Texas Power Plant Project." *FOXNews.com*, January 30. http://www.foxnews.com/printer_friendly_story/0,3566,248782,00.html (accessed December 28, 2012).

Donham, Donald. 1990. *History, Power, Ideology: Central Issues in Marxism and Anthropology*. Cambridge (MA) and New York: Cambridge University Press.

Douglas, Mary. 1968. "The Social Control of Cognition: Some Factors in Joke Perception." *Man* 3(3):361–76.

Downey, Greg, and Melissa S. Fisher. 2006. "Introduction: The Anthropology of Capital and the Frontiers of Ethnography." In *Frontiers of Capital: Ethnographic Reflections on the New Economy*, edited by Melissa S. Fisher and Greg Downey, 1–30. Durham, NC: Duke University Press.

Dudley, Kathryn Marie. 2000. *Debt and Dispossession: Farm Loss in America's Heartland*. Chicago: University of Chicago Press.

Duncan, Ian. 2011. "'Earthalujah!' Shouts Reverend Billy." *New York Times*, March 16. http://eastvillage.thelocal.nytimes.com/2011/03/16/earthalujah-shouts-reverend-billy/ (accessed December 28, 2012).

Duncombe, Stephen. 2007a. *Dream: Re-imagining Progressive Politics in an Age of Fantasy*. New York: New Press.

Duncombe, Stephen, with Andrew Boyd. 2007b. "Learn from Las Vegas: Spectacular Vernacular." In Duncombe 2007a, 28–50.

Dunn, John, ed. 1992. *Democracy: The Unfinished Journey, 508 BC to AD 1993*. Oxford: Oxford University Press.

Duranti, Alessandro, and Donald Brenneis, eds. 1986. "The Audience as Co-author." Special issue of *Text* 6(3).

Dworkin, Ronald. 2010 "The Decision That Threatens Democracy." *New York Review of Books*, May 23. http://www.nybooks.com/articles/archives/2010/may/13/decision-threatens-democracy/ (accessed January 20, 2011).

Dwyer, Jim. 2008. "Is Satire in a Slump? 'Yes' and 'No.'" *New York Times*, February 16. http://www.nytimes.com/2008/02/16/nyregion/16about.html (accessed December 28, 2012).

Economist. 2006a. *Pocket World in Figures*. London: The Economist and Profile Books.

Economist. 2006b. "The Rich, The Poor and The Growing Gap Between Them." June 17, 28–30.

Edelman, Marc. 1999. *Peasants Against Globalization: Rural Social Movements in Costa Rica*. Stanford, CA: Stanford University Press.

———. 2001. "Social Movements: Changing Paradigms and Forms of Politics." *Annual Review of Anthropology* 30:285–317.

———. 2005. "When Networks Don't Work: The Rise and Fall and Rise of Civil Society Initiatives in Central America." In Nash 2005, 29–45.

———. 2009. "Synergies and Tensions Between Rural Social Movements and Professional Researchers." *Journal of Peasant Studies* 36(1):245–65.

Edelman, Marc, and Angelique Haugerud, eds. 2005. *The Anthropology of Develop-*

ment and Globalization: From Classical Political Economy to Contemporary Neoliberalism. Oxford: Blackwell.

Edelman, Murray. 2001. *The Politics of Misinformation.* New York: Cambridge University Press.

Eggen, Dan. 2010. "Poll: Large Majority Opposes Supreme Court's Decision on Campaign Financing." *Washington Post*, February 17. http://www.washingtonpost.com/ wp-dyn/content/article/2010/02/17/AR2010021701151.html (accessed December 28, 2012).

Escobar, Arturo. 2008. *Territories of Difference: Place, Movements, Life, Redes.* Durham, NC: Duke University Press.

Fallows, James. 1997. *Breaking the News: How the Media Undermine American Democracy.* New York: Vintage.

Farnell, Brenda, and Laura Graham. 1998. "Discourse-Centered Methods." In *Handbook of Methods in Cultural Anthropology*, edited by H. Russell Bernard, 411–57. New York: AltaMira Press.

Farrar, Margaret E., and Jamie L. Warner. 2008. "Spectacular Resistance: The Billionaires for Bush and the Art of Political Culture Jamming." *Polity* 40(3):273–96.

Feder, Barnaby J. 2001. "The Long and Winding Cyberhoax: Political Theater on the Web." *New York Times*, January 7. http://www.nytimes.com/2001/01/07/weekin review/word-for-word-tweaking-wto-long-winding-cyberhoax-political-theater -web.html (accessed December 28, 2012).

Fernandez, James W., and Mary Taylor Huber. 2001a. "Coda: Irony, Practice, and the Moral Imagination." In *Irony in Action: Anthropology, Practice, and the Moral Imagination*, edited by James W. Fernandez and Mary Taylor Huber, 261–64. Chicago: University of Chicago Press.

———. 2001b. "Introduction: The Anthropology of Irony." In *Irony in Action: Anthropology, Practice, and the Moral Imagination*, edited by James W. Fernandez and Mary Taylor Huber, 1–37. Chicago: University of Chicago Press.

Feyerick, Deborah. 2004. "Sunday Morning." CNN, transcript, August 29. http:// transcripts.cnn.com/TRANSCRIPTS/0408/29/sm.01.html (accessed December 28, 2012).

Financial Crisis Inquiry Commission. 2011. *The Financial Crisis Inquiry Report.* New York: Public Affairs.

Financial Times (London). 2004. "Convention Games." August 11, 10.

Foley, Elizabeth. 2004. "Who's Who in Protest?" *Newsday* (New York), August 24, A34.

Foucault, Michel. 1979. *Discipline and Punish.* New York: Vintage.

Fox, Jonathan A. 2009. "Coalitions and Networks." In *International Encyclopedia of Civil Society*, edited by Helmut Anheier and Stefan Toepler. New York: Springer. http://escholarship.org/uc/item/1x05031j (accessed December 28, 2012).

Fox News Special Report. 1999. With Brit Hume. Federal Document Clearing House, March 16, 6:00 P.M.

Frank, Raphie, and Mindy Bond. 2004. "Interview with Andrew Boyd." *Gothamist*,

October 29. http://gothamist.com/2004/10/29/andrew_boyd_cultural_activist
_and_founder_billionaires_for_bush.php (accessed December 28, 2012).

Frank, Robert. 2007a. "The Billionaire Political Smackdown." *Wall Street Journal Online*, October 1. http://blogs.wsj.com/wealth/2007/10/01/the-billionaire-political-smackdown/ (accessed January 1, 2013).

———. 2007b. *Richistan: A Journey Through the American Wealth Boom and the Lives of the New Rich*. New York: Crown.

Frank, Robert H. 2007. "Reshaping the Debate on Raising Taxes." *New York Times*, December 9. www.nytimes.com/2007/12/09/business/09view.html (accessed December 28, 2012).

———. 2010. "A Gift the Wealthy Don't Need." *New York Times*, August 8, BU7.

Frank, Thomas. 2012. *Pity the Billionaire*. New York: Metropolitan Books.

Frank, Thomas, and Matt Weiland, eds. 1997. *Commodify Your Dissent*. New York: Norton.

Fraser, Steve, and Gary Gerstle, eds. 2005. *Ruling America: A History of Wealth and Power in a Democracy*. Cambridge, MA: Harvard University Press.

Freud, Sigmund. 1960. *Jokes and Their Relation to the Unconscious*. New York: Norton.

Fry, William F. 1963. *Sweet Madness: A Study of Humor*. Palo Alto, CA: Pacific.

Frye, Northrop. 1957. *Anatomy of Criticism*. Princeton, NJ: Princeton University Press.

Fussell, Paul. 1975. *The Great War and Modern Memory*. New York: Oxford University Press.

———. 1983. *Class: A Guide Through the American Status System*. New York: Simon & Schuster.

Gamerman, Ellen. 2008. "The New Pranksters." *Wall Street Journal*, September 12. http://www.online.wsj.com/article/SB122119092302626987.html (accessed December 28, 2012).

Gamson, William A. 2007. "Bystanders, Public Opinion, and the Media." In *The Blackwell Companion to Social Movements*, edited by David A. Snow, Sarah A. Soule, and Hanspeter Kriesi, 242–61. Oxford: Blackwell.

Ganz, Marshall. 2003. "Another Look at Farmworker Mobilization." In Goodwin and Jasper 2003, 283–300.

Gardner, Matthew. 2007. "Progressive Taxes Are a Good Deal: The Fundamentals of Our Federal Tax System." In *10 Excellent Reasons Not to Hate Taxes*, edited by Stephanie Greenwood, 10–21. New York: New Press.

Garnham, Nicholas. 1992. "The Media and the Public Sphere." In *Habermas and the Public Sphere*, edited by Craig Calhoun, 359–76. Cambridge, MA: MIT Press.

Gates, William H., Sr., and Chuck Collins. 2003. *Wealth and Our Commonwealth: Why America Should Tax Accumulated Fortunes*. Boston: Beacon Press.

Gilmore, David. 1975. "Carnaval in Fuenmayor: Class Conflict and Social Cohesion in an Andalusian Town." *Journal of Anthropological Research* 31:331–49.

Gilson, Dave, and Carolyn Perot. 2011. "It's the Inequality, Stupid." *Mother Jones*, March/April. http://motherjones.com/print/99036 (accessed December 28, 2012).

Ginsburg, Faye D. 1991. "Indigenous Media: Faustian Contract or Global Village?" *Cultural Anthropology* 6(1):92–112.

Ginsburg, Faye D., Lila Abu-Lughod, and Brian Larkin. 2002. "Introduction." In *Media Worlds*, edited by Faye D. Ginsburg, Lila Abu-Lughod, and Brian Larkin, 1–36. Berkeley: University of California Press.

Gitlin, Todd. 1993. *The Sixties: Years of Hope, Days of Rage*. New York: Bantam Books.

———. 2003. "The Media in the Unmaking of the New Left." In Goodwin and Jasper 2003, 301–11.

———. 2012. "Occupy's Expressive Impulse." Possible Futures: A Project of the Social Science Research Council, May 21. http://www.possible-futures.org/2012/05/21/occupys-expressive-impulse/ (accessed June 29, 2012).

Giugni, Marco, Doug McAdam, and Charles Tilly, eds. 1999. *How Social Movements Matter*. Minneapolis: University of Minnesota Press.

Gledhill, John. 2000. *Power and Its Disguises: Anthropological Perspectives on Politics*. London: Pluto.

———. 2004. "Neoliberalism." In *A Companion to the Anthropology of Politics*, edited by David Nugent and Joan Vincent, 332–48. Oxford: Blackwell.

Gluckman, Max. 1965. *Politics, Law and Ritual in Tribal Society*. Chicago: Aldine.

Goffman, Erving. 1974. *Frame Analysis*. New York: Harper Colophon.

Gold, Daniel M. 1999. "Pressing the Issue of Pay Inequality." *New York Times*, February 7, 11.

Goldstein, Daniel M. 2004. *The Spectacular City*. Durham (NC) and London: Duke University Press.

Goldstein, Donna. 2003. *Laughter Out of Place: Race, Class, Violence, and Sexuality in a Rio Shantytown*. Berkeley and London: University of California Press.

Goode, Judith, and Jeff Maskovsky, eds. 2002. *The New Poverty Studies: The Ethnography of Power, Politics and Impoverished People in the United States*. New York: New York University Press.

Goodman, Peter S. 2008. "Taking a Hard Look at a Greenspan Legacy." *New York Times*, October 9, A1.

Goodwin, Jeff, and James M. Jasper, eds. 2003. *The Social Movements Reader: Cases and Concepts*. Oxford: Blackwell.

———. 2004. "Caught in a Winding, Snarling Vine: The Structural Bias of Political Process Theory." In *Rethinking Social Movements: Structure, Meaning, and Emotion*, edited by Jeff Goodwin and James M. Jasper, 3–30. New York: Rowman and Littlefield.

Goodwin, Jeff, James M. Jasper, and Francesca Polletta, eds. 2001. *Passionate Politics*. Chicago: University of Chicago Press.

Goodwin, Liz. 2012. "Multimillionaires for Mitt: Occupy Protesters Stake Out Romney NYC Fundraising Event." Yahoo! News, March 14. http://news.yahoo.com/blogs/ticket/multimillionaires-mitt-occupy-protesters-stake-romney-nyc-fundraising-18623833.html (accessed March 20, 2012).

Graeber, David. 2007. *Possibilities: Essays on Hierarchy, Rebellion, and Desire*. Oakland, CA: AK Press.

——. 2009. *Direct Action: An Ethnography*. Oakland, CA: AK Press.

——. 2011. "Occupy and Anarchism's Gift of Democracy." *Guardian*, November 15. http://www.guardian.co.uk/commentisfree/cifamerica/2011/nov/15/occupy-anarchism-gift-democracy (accessed February 18, 2012).

Graetz, Michael J., and Ian Shapiro. 2005. *Death by a Thousand Cuts: The Fight over Taxing Inherited Wealth*. Princeton, NJ: Princeton University Press.

Gramsci, Antonio. 1971. *Selections from the Prison Notebooks*, translated by Quentin Hoare and Geoffrey Nowell Smith. New York: International.

Gray, Jonathan, Jeffrey P. Jones, and Ethan Thompson, eds. 2009. *Satire TV: Politics and Comedy in the Post-Network Era*. New York and London: New York University Press.

Gray, Kathleen. 2004. "Actors Use Humor to Make Point About Bush—Troupe Mocks Him for Aiding Rich, But It Ignores Some Facts." *Detroit Free Press*, August 10, 3.

Greenhouse, Carol. 2010. "Introduction." In *Ethnographies of Neoliberalism*, edited by Carol J. Greenhouse, 1–10. Philadelphia: University of Pennsylvania Press.

Grote, Jason. 2002. "'The God That People Who Do Not Believe in God Believe In': Taking a Bust with Reverend Billy." In *Cultural Resistance Reader*, edited by Stephen Duncombe, 358–68. New York and London: Verso.

Gusterson, Hugh, and Catherine Besteman, eds. 2010. *The Insecure American: How We Got Here and What We Should Do About It*. Berkeley: University of California Press.

Haberman, Clyde. 2004. "In Defense of Privilege, With a Wink." *New York Times*, November 9, B1.

——. 2011. "Noblesse Oblige Among the Protesting Masses." *New York Times*, October 17. http://cityroom.blogs.nytimes.com/2011/10/17/noblesse-oblige-among-the-protesting-masses/?pagemode=print (accessed December 11, 2011).

Habermas, Jürgen. 1989 [1962]. *The Structural Transformation of the Public Sphere: An Inquiry into a Category of Bourgeois Society*, translated by Thomas Burger. Cambridge, UK: Polity Press.

Hacker, Jacob S. 2006. *The Great Risk Shift: The Assault on American Jobs, Families, Health Care, and Retirement*. Oxford: Oxford University Press.

Hacker, Jacob S., and Paul Pierson. 2010. *Winner-Take-All Politics: How Washington Made the Rich Richer and Turned Its Back on the Middle Class*. New York: Simon & Schuster.

Haidt, Jonathan. 2012. *The Righteous Mind: Why Good People Are Divided by Politics and Religion*. New York: Pantheon.

Hall, Stuart. 2002 [1981]. "Notes on Deconstructing 'The Popular.'" In *Cultural Resistance Reader*, edited by Stephen Duncombe, 185–92. London and New York: Verso.

Hall, Stuart, Dorothy Hobson, Andrew Lowe, and Paul Willis, eds. 1980. *Culture, Media, Language*. London: Hutchinson.

Hann, Chris, and Keith Hart. 2011. *Economic Anthropology: History, Ethnography, Critique*. Malden, MA: Polity Press.

Hanser, Richard. 1952. "Wit as a Weapon." *Saturday Review*, November 8, 13–14, 51.

Hari, Johann. 2004. "Why Would a Wal-Mart Shelf-Stacker Vote Republican?" *Independent* (London), September 3, 39.

Harper, Jennifer. 2005. "Anti-Bush Inaugural Bashes to Abound." *Washington Times*, January 15, A1.

Harris, Lyle V., and John Mintz. 1986. "40,000 Activists March Against Abortion Ruling." *Washington Post*, January 23, C1.

Hart, Keith, Jean-Louis Laville, and Antonio David Cattani, eds. 2010. *The Human Economy: A Citizen's Guide*. Malden, MA: Polity Press.

Harvey, David. 1989. *The Condition of Postmodernity*. Oxford: Blackwell.

———. 2000. *Spaces of Hope*. Berkeley: University of California Press.

———. 2003. *The New Imperialism*. Oxford: Oxford University Press.

Hastings, Reed. 2009. "Please Raise My Taxes." *New York Times*, February 6, A27.

Haugerud, Angelique. 2010. "Neoliberalism, Satirical Protest, and the 2004 U.S. Presidential Campaign." In *Ethnographies of Neoliberalism*, edited by Carol J. Greenhouse, 112–27. Philadelphia: University of Pennsylvania Press.

———. 2012. "Satire and Dissent in the Age of Billionaires." *Social Research: An International Quarterly* 79(1):145–68. www.socres.org.

Hayek, Friedrich A. 1994 [1944]. *The Road to Serfdom*. Chicago: University of Chicago Press.

Heaney, Joe. 1998. "Congressmen Throw a Little Tea Party in the Hub." *Boston Herald*, April 16, 4.

Hedges, Chris. 2012. "Occupy Will Be Back." *Nation of Change*, June 19. http://www.nationofchange.org/occupy-will-be-back-1340111087 (accessed July 1, 2012).

Heider, Karl G. 1988. "The Rashomon Effect: When Ethnographers Disagree." *American Anthropologist* 90(1):73–81.

Helm, Mark. 2004. "New York Bracing for Massive GOP Convention Protests." *Salt Lake* (UT) *Tribune*, August 22, A5.

Henry, Neil. 2007. *American Carnival: Journalism Under Siege in an Age of New Media*. Berkeley: University of California Press.

Herman, Ken. 2004. "Big-Bucks Donors Backing Both Sides." *Austin* (TX) *American Statesman*, August 14.

Hermann, Andrew. 1999. "Shouting 'Fire' on a Crowded Street." *American Theater*, December 1, 6–7.

Hitt, Jack. 2004. "The Birth of the Meta-Protest Rally." *New York Times Magazine*, March 28, 20.

Holland, Dorothy, Donald M. Nonini, Catherine Lutz, and Lesley Bartlett. 2007. *Local Democracy Under Siege: Activism, Public Interests, and Private Politics*. New York and London: New York University Press.

Hollar, Julie 2012. "NATO Protesters Free to Shout Down a Hole." *Extra! The Magazine of Fairness and Accuracy in Reporting (FAIR)—The Media Watch Group* 25(7):7–8.

Holmes, Douglas R., and George E. Marcus. 2005. "Cultures of Expertise and the Management of Globalization: Toward the Re-Functioning of Ethnography." In *Global Assemblages: Technology, Politics, and Ethics as Anthropological Problems*, edited by Aihwa Ong and Stephen J. Collier, 235–52. Oxford: Blackwell.

Holston, James, and Arjun Appadurai. 1999. "Introduction: Cities and Citizenship." In *Cities and Citizenship*, edited by J. Holston, 1–18. Durham, NC: Duke University Press.

Huizinga, Johan. 1955. *Homo Ludens: A Study of the Play-Element in Culture*. Boston: Beacon Press.

Hungerford, Thomas L. 2012. *Taxes and the Economy: An Economic Analysis of the Top Rates Since 1945*. Washington, DC: Congressional Research Service, September 14.

Hutcheon, Linda. 2000. *A Theory of Parody: The Teachings of Twentieth-Century Art Forms*. Urbana: University of Illinois Press.

International Herald Tribune. 2007. "The Truth About Coal." February 25. http://www.nytimes.com/2007/02/25/opinion/25iht-edcoal.4712371.html (accessed January 1, 2013).

Jacobs, Lawrence R., and Theda Skocpol, eds. 2005. *Inequality and American Democracy: What We Know and What We Need to Learn*. New York: Russell Sage Foundation.

Jacoby, Susan. 2008. *The Age of American Unreason*. New York: Pantheon.

Jamieson, Kathleen Hall, and Paul Waldman. 2003. *The Press Effect: Politicians, Journalist, and the Stories That Shape the Political World*. New York: Oxford University Press.

Jasper, James M. 2003. "The Emotions of Protest." In Goodwin and Jasper 2003, 153–62.

Johnson, Alan. 2000. "It's Come to This: Billionaires for Bush, Texas Truth Squad." *Columbus* (OH) *Dispatch*, October 11, 5A.

Johnston, David Cay. 2001. "Dozens of Rich Americans Join in Fight to Retain the Estate Tax." *New York Times*, February 14, A1.

———. 2003. *Perfectly Legal: The Covert Campaign to Rig Our Tax System to Benefit the Super-Rich—and Cheat Everybody Else*. New York: Portfolio.

———. 2006. "The Ultra-Rich Give Differently from You and Me." *New York Times*, July 2, Section 4, p. 3.

Johnston, Hank. 2011. *States and Social Movements*. Cambridge (UK) and Malden (MA): Polity Press.

Jones, Jeffrey P., Geoffrey Baym, and Amber Day. 2012. "Mr. Stewart and Mr. Colbert Go to Washington: Television Satirists Outside the Box." *Social Research* 79(1):33–60.

Jurgensen, John. 2004. "Party Crashers." *Hartford* (CT) *Courant*, June 27, A1.

Juris, Jeffrey S. 2008. *Networking Futures: The Movements Against Corporate Globalization*. Durham, NC: Duke University Press.

———. 2012. "Reflections on #Occupy Everywhere: Social Media, Public Space, and Emerging Logics of Aggregation." *American Ethnologist* 39(2):259–79.

Kahn, Richard, and Douglas M. Kellner. 2006. "Oppositional Politics and the Internet: A Critical/Reconstructive Approach." In *Media and Cultural Studies: Key-Works*, edited by Meenakshi Gigi Durham and Douglas M. Kellner, 703–25. Oxford: Blackwell.

Kaiser, Robert. 2004. "Convention Diary: New York City, August 30–September 2." *Washington Post Online*. http://www.washingtonpost.com/wp-srv/politics/inter actives/diary/republican/conventionDiary.html (accessed September 6, 2004).

Kakutani, M. 2008. "Is This the Most Trusted Man in America?" *New York Times*, August 17, Arts and Leisure Section, 1, 18–19.

Keister, Lisa A., and Stephanie Moller. 2000. "Wealth Inequality in the United States." *Annual Review of Sociology* 26:63–81.

Keller, Bill. 2005. "Introduction." In *Class Matters*, by correspondents of the *New York Times*, ix–xviii. New York: New York Times Books and Henry Holt.

Kertzer, David I. 1988. *Ritual, Politics, and Power*. New Haven, CT: Yale University Press.

Kiernan, Laura A. 1999. "Peterson Hopes to Get Lawmakers to Think '1%.'" *Boston Globe*, March 21, 8.

Kirkpatrick, David D. 2001. "A Nation Challenged: The Commentators; Pronouncements on Irony Draw Line in the Sand." *New York Times*, September 24. http://www .nytimes.com/2001/09/24/business-nation-challenged-commentators-pronounce ments-irony-draw-line-sand.html (accessed January 1, 2013).

Klein, Amy. 2004. "Tuxedos, Pearls and Satire Fill the Streets: 'Billionaires' Stage Anti-Bush Stroll." *Record* (Bergen County, NJ), September 1, A12.

Klein, Naomi. 2002. *No Logo*. New York: Picador.

Koopmans, Ruud. 2007. "Protest in Time and Space: The Evolution of Waves of Contention." In *The Blackwell Companion to Social Movements*, edited by David A. Snow, Sarah A. Soule, and Hanspeter Kriesi, 19–46. Oxford: Blackwell.

Kroll, Andy. 2012. "Follow the Dark Money." *Mother Jones*, July/August. http://www .motherjones.com/print/178416 (accessed June 22, 2012).

Krueger, Alan B. 2003. "Connecting the Dots from Tax Cuts for the Wealthy to Loss of Benefits." *New York Times*, October 16, 2.

Krugman, Paul. 2002. "The End of Middle-Class America (and the Triumph of the Plutocrats): For Richer: How the Permissive Capitalism of the Boom Destroyed American Equality." *New York Times Magazine*, October 20, 62–68, 76, 78, 141–42.

———. 2004a. "Reading the Script." *New York Times*, August 3, A19.

———. 2004b. "Triumph of the Trivial." *New York Times*, July 30. http://www.nytimes .com/2004/07/30/opinion/30krugman.html (accessed December 28, 2012).

———. 2006. "Wages, Wealth and Politics." *New York Times*, August 18, A17.

———. 2007. *The Conscience of a Liberal*. New York: Norton.

———. 2011. "The Centrist Cop-Out." *New York Times*, July 29, A27.

Krupat, Arnold. 2001. "An Apollonian Response." In *Irony in Action: Anthropology, Practice, and the Moral Imagination*, edited by James W. Fernandez and Mary Taylor Huber, 133–42. Chicago: University of Chicago Press.

Lakoff, George. 2004. *Don't Think of an Elephant: Know Your Values and Frame the Debate*. White River Junction, VT: Chelsea Green.

Larson, Gary. 1984. Cartoon. http://anthropology.net/2007/09/14/watch-out-the -anthropologists-are-coming/anthropologists-anthropologists/ (accessed June 12, 2011).

Leondar-Wright, Betsy. 2005. "Who Is the Elite?" In *Inequality Matters: The Growing Divide in American and Its Poisonous Consequences*, edited by James Lardner and David A. Smith, 215–27. New York: New Press.

Leonhardt, David. 2008. "The Return of Larry Summers." *New York Times*, November 26, B1, B4.

———. 2011. "Why Taxes Will Rise in the End." *New York Times*, July 13, B1, B5.

Leonnig, Carol D. 2010. "Activists Protest to Demand Congress to Stop Fundraising from Corporate Lobbyists." *Washington Post*, July 1. http://www.washingtonpost .com/wp-dyn/content/article/2010/06/30/AR2010063005316.html (accessed December 28, 2012).

Lessig, Lawrence. 2011. *Republic, Lost: How Money Corrupts Congress—and a Plan to Stop It*. New York and Boston: Twelve, Hatchette Book Group.

Lessner, Richard. 1999. "Presidential Follies: Short Take." *New Hampshire Union Leader* (Manchester), March 19, record number OF544EDA2820B48B, Access World News, NewsBank.

Lewis, Diane E. 1998. "The 'Radical Rich' Turn Giving into a Mission." *Boston Globe*, May 3, J1.

Lewis, Michael, and David Einhorn. 2009. "The End of the Financial World As We Know It." *New York Times*, January 4, WK9–10.

Lewis, Paul. 1997. "The Killing Jokes of the American Eighties." *Humor* 10(3):251–83.

Lichtblau, Eric. 2010. "The Proud Lobbyist: Tony Podesta Says It's About Information, Not Influence." *New York Times*, July 2, B1, B6.

LiPuma, Edward, and Benjamin Lee. 2004. *Financial Derivatives and the Globalization of Risk*. Durham, NC: Duke University Press.

Lukes, Steven, ed. 1986. *Power*. New York: New York University Press.

MacPherson, Myra. 1984. "GOP Women in the Age of Ferraro; Money, Motherhood and Fighting Off the ERA." *Washington Post*, August 22, B1.

Madrick, Jeff. 2007. "They Can Strengthen the Economy." In *10 Excellent Reasons Not to Hate Taxes*, edited by Stephanie Greenwood, 31–44. New York: New Press.

Mahon, Maureen. 2000. "The Visible Evidence of Cultural Producers." *Annual Review of Anthropology* 29:467–92.

Manza, Jeff. 2011. "Class." *Oxford Bibliographies Online*. http://www.oxfordbibliogra phiesonline.com (accessed December 28, 2012).

Marcus, George E. 2001. "The Predicament of Irony and the Paranoid Style in Fin-de-Siècle Rationality." In *Irony in Action: Anthropology, Practice, and the Moral Imagination*, edited by James W. Fernandez and Mary Taylor Huber, 209–23. Chicago: University of Chicago Press.

Marcus, George, and Michael Fisher. 1999 [1986]. *Anthropology as Cultural Critique:*

An Experimental Moment in the Human Sciences. 2nd ed. Chicago: University of Chicago Press.

Marcus, George E., with Peter Dobkin Hall. 1992. *Lives in Trust: The Fortunes of Dynastic Families in Late Twentieth-Century America.* Boulder (CO) and San Francisco: Westview Press.

Maurer, Bill. 1995. "Complex Subjects: Offshore Finance, Complexity Theory, and the Dispersion of the Modern." *Socialist Review* 25(3–4):113–45.

Mayer, Jane. 2010. "Covert Operations: The Billionaire Brothers Who Are Waging a War Against Obama." *New Yorker,* August 30, 44–55.

Mbembe, Achille. 1992. "Provisional Notes on the Postcolony." *Africa* 62(1):3–37.

McChesney, Robert. 1999. *Rich Media, Poor Democracy: Communication Politics in Dubious Times.* New York: New Press.

———. 2006. "A Cornerstone of the Media Reform Movement." *Extra!* January–February, 6–9.

McGrath, Charles. 2012. "How Many Stephen Colberts Are There?" *New York Times Magazine,* January 8.

McIntire, Mike. 2000. "Protesters' Messages Miss Mark." *Hartford* (CT) *Courant,* August 4, A13.

McIntire, Mike, and Michael Luo. 2012. "Fine Line Between 'Super PACs' and Campaigns." *New York Times,* February 26, A1, A14.

McKelvey, Tara. 2004. "Class Will Out." *American Prospect,* August, 8.

McLeod, Douglas M., and James K. Hertog. 1999. "Social Control, Social Change and the Mass Media's Role in the Regulation of Protest Groups." In *Mass Media, Social Control, and Social Change: A Macrosocial Perspective,* edited by David Demers and K. Viswanath, 305–30. Ames: Iowa State University Press.

McLuhan, Marshall. 1994. *Understanding Media: The Extensions of Man.* Cambridge, MA: MIT Press.

Media Matters for America. 2006. "Media Touted Bush's Routine at Correspondents' Dinner, Ignored Colbert's Skewering," May 1. http://www.mediamatters.org/print/research/200605010005 (accessed April 8, 2012).

Melucci, Alberto. 1996. *Challenging Codes: Collective Action in the Information Age.* Cambridge, UK: Cambridge University Press.

Mitchell, Timothy. 1990. "Everyday Metaphors of Power." *Theory and Society* 19:545–77.

———. 2002. *Rule of Experts: Egypt, Techno-Politics, Modernity.* Berkeley: University of California Press.

Miyazaki, Hirokazu. 2004. *The Method of Hope: Anthropology, Philosophy, and Fijian Knowledge.* Stanford, CA: Stanford University Press.

Mogil, Christopher, and Anne Slepian, with Peter Woodrow. 1992. *We Gave Away a Fortune: Stories of People Who Have Devoted Themselves and Their Wealth to Peace, Justice and the Environment.* Philadelphia: New Society.

Moore, Henrietta L., and Todd Sanders. 2006. "Anthropology and Epistemology." In

Anthropology in Theory: Issues in Epistemology, edited by Henrietta L. Moore and Todd Sanders, 1–21. Malden (MA) and Oxford: Blackwell.

Morgen, Sandra, Jennifer Erickson, and Patrick Hayden. 2012. "Taxing Subjects: Towards an Anthropology of DeKeynesinization." Paper presented at New York Academy of Sciences Anthropology Section and Wenner-Gren Foundation, New York, September 24.

Moyers, Bill. 2008. *Moyers on Democracy*. New York: Doubleday.

Myers, Gustavus. 1910. *History of the Great American Fortunes*, Volume One. General Books. www.General-Books.net.

Nash, June, ed. 2005. *Social Movements: An Anthropological Reader*. Oxford: Blackwell.

Naughton, Keith, and Rich Thomas. 2001. "Billionaire Backlash." *Newsweek*, February 26, 48.

New York Times. 1989. "Northeast Journal: Only Men Need Apply." January 22, 30.

———. 2005. "The Bush Economy: New Hope for the Fabulously Wealthy." June 7, A22.

———. 2006. "Editorial: Downward Mobility." August 30, A22.

———. 2007. "The Richest of the Rich, Proud of a New Gilded Age." July 15, A1, A20–21.

———. 2008a. "Editorial: The Corporate Free Ride." August 18, A18.

———. 2008b. "When the Watchdogs Don't Bark." December 31, A26.

———. 2010. "Governments Go to Extremes as the Downturn Wears On." August 6, A1.

———. 2011. "The Truth About Taxes." August 7, A10.

Newman, Andy. 2004. "Park Grass Survives, Unsmoked, Mildly Trodden." *New York Times*, August 30, P14.

———. 2008. "Irony Is Dead. Again. Yeah, Right." *New York Times*, November 23, ST1, ST12.

Newman, Katherine S., and Victor Tan Chen. 2007. *The Missing Class: Portraits of the Near Poor in America*. Boston: Beacon Press.

O'Brien, Keith. 2004. "RNC Coverage: Where the Billionaires Are." *PR Week*, September 2. http://www/prweek.com/news/printer.cfm?ID=220925 (accessed October 14, 2004).

Offer, Avner. 2006. *The Challenge of Affluence: Self-Control and Well-Being in the United States and Britain Since 1950*. Oxford: Oxford University Press.

Ortner, Sherry. 2003. *New Jersey Dreaming: Capital, Culture, and the Class of '58*. Durham, NC: Duke University Press.

Ortner, Sherry B. 1995. "Resistance and the Problem of Ethnographic Refusal." *Comparative Studies in Society and History* 37(1):173–93.

Orwell, George. 1968. "Funny, but Not Vulgar." In *The Collected Essays, Journalism and Letters of George Orwell*, edited by Sonia Orwell and Ian Angus. New York: Harcourt Brace.

Ottawa Citizen. 2004. "Billionaires' March." July 29, A4.

Panitch, Leo. 2000. "The New Imperial State." *New Left Review* 2(March–April):5–20.

Patomaki, Heikki. 2001. *Democratising Globalisation: The Leverage of the Tobin Tax.* London: Zed Books.

Patriot Ledger (Quincy, MA). 1998. "Tea Party Re-enactment Draws Counterprotest." April 16, 8.

Pear, Robert. 2011. "Top Earners Doubled Share of Nation's Income, Study Finds." *New York Times*, October 25. http://www.nytimes.com/2011/10/26/us/politics/top-earners-doubled-share-of-nations-income-cbo-says.html (accessed March 1, 2012).

Pedelty, Mark. 1995. *War Stories: The Culture of Foreign Correspondents.* New York: Routledge.

Peters, Jeremy W., and Brian Stelter. 2011. "A Federal Study Finds That Local Reporting Has Waned." *New York Times*, June 9, B3.

Phillips, Kevin. 2002a. "Dynasties! How Their Wealth and Power Threaten Democracy." *Nation*, July 8, 11–14.

———. 2002b. *Wealth and Democracy: A Political History of the American Rich.* New York: Broadway Books.

Polanyi, Karl. 1957 [1944]. *The Great Transformation: The Political and Economic Origins of Our Time.* Boston: Beacon Press.

Pomorska, Krystyna. 1984. "Foreword." In Bakhtin 1984 [1968], vii–xii.

Portelli, Alessandro. 1991. *The Death of Luigi Trastulli and Other Stories: Form and Meaning in Oral History.* Albany: State University of New York Press.

Posner, Richard A. 2005. "Bad News." *New York Times Book Review*, July 31, 1, 8–11.

Postill, John. 2009. "What Is the Point of Media Anthropology?" *Social Anthropology* 17(3):334–44.

Prokosch, Mike, and Laura Raymond, eds. 2002. *The Global Activist's Manual.* New York: Thunder's Mouth Press/Nation Books.

Public Citizen, Congress Watch, and United for a Fair Economy. 2006. "Spending Millions to Save Billions: The Campaign of the Super Wealthy to Kill the Estate Tax." April. http://www.citizen.org/documents/EstateTaxFinal.pdf (accessed December 28, 2012).

Purdy, Jedediah. 2000. *For Common Things.* New York: Vintage.

———. 2012. "Rediscovering Politics." Possible Futures: A Project of the Social Science Research Council, June 11. http://www.possible-futures.org/2012/06/11/rediscovering-politics (accessed June 29, 2012).

Quiggin, John. 2010. "Five Zombie Economic Ideas That Refuse to Die." *Foreign Policy*, October 15. http://www.foreignpolicy.com/articles/2010/10/15/five_zombie_economic_ideas_that_refuse_to_die?hidecomments=yes (accessed March 10, 2012).

Radin, Charles A. 2000. "Causes Vie to Be Heard on Street." *Boston Globe*, January 27, A19.

Razsa, Maple John, and Andrej Kurnik. 2012. "The Occupy Movement in Žižek's Hometown: Direct Democracy and a Politics of Becoming." *American Ethnologist* 39(2):238–58.

Reed, Matt. 1999. "Forbes Re-Enacts Tax Protest in Portsmouth Campaign Stop." *New Hampshire Union Leader* (Manchester), April 16, A15.

Reich, Robert. 2006. "A Few Hundred Supernovas." *American Prospect Online*, October 2. http://www.prospect.org/article/few-hundred-supernovas (accessed January 1, 2013).

———. 2007. *Supercapitalism: The Transformation of Business, Democracy, and Everyday Life.* New York: Knopf.

———. 2010a. *After-Shock: The Next Economy and America's Future.* New York: Knopf.

———. 2010b. "Foreword." In *The Spirit Level: Why Greater Equality Makes Societies Stronger*, by Richard Wilkinson and Kate Pickett, v–viii. New York: Bloomsbury Press.

———. 2010c. "How to End the Great Recession." *New York Times*, September 3, A21.

———. 2011. "Getting Away with It: An Account of the Financial Crisis Highlights Individuals Who Played Crucial Roles of Responsibility." *New York Times Book Review*, May 29, 9.

Reyner, E. 1657. *Rules Govt. Tongue* 227, quoted in *Oxford English Dictionary Online*, Oxford University Press, 2004. http://dictionary.oed.com/cgi/entry/00121255?query _type=word&qu . . . (accessed July 7, 2004).

Rheingold, Howard. 2002. *Smart Mobs: The Next Social Revolution.* Cambridge, MA: Perseus Books.

Rich, Frank. 2004. "Happy Talk News Covers a War." *New York Times*, July 18, AR1.

———. 2006. *The Greatest Story Ever Sold: The Decline and Fall of Truth from 9/11 to Katrina.* New York: Penguin.

———. 2010a. "The Billionaires Bankrolling the Tea Party." *New York Times*, August 29, WK8.

———. 2010b. How to Lose an Election Without Really Trying. *New York Times*, August 8, WK8.

———. 2010c. "Time for This Big Dog to Bite Back." *New York Times*, September 12, WK11.

Riegert, Kristina. 2007. "Introduction." In *Politicotainment: Television's Take on the Real*, edited by Kristina Riegert, 1–19. New York: Peter Lang.

Riles, Annelise. 2001. *The Network Inside Out.* Ann Arbor: University of Michigan Press.

Ronfeldt, David, John Arquilla, Graham E. Fuller, and Melissa Fuller. 1998. *The Zapatista Social Netwar in Mexico.* Santa Monica, CA: Rand.

Rose, Nikolas. 1999. *Powers of Freedom: Reframing Political Thought.* Cambridge, UK: Cambridge University Press.

Rosen, Ralph M. 2012. "Efficacy and Meaning in Ancient and Modern Political Satire: Aristophanes, Lenny Bruce, and Jon Stewart." *Social Research: An International Quarterly* 79 (1):1–32.

Rosenthal, Elisabeth. 2004. "Election Is Turning Novices into Political Advocates." *New York Times*, April 3, A11.

Rosin, Hanna. 2004. "Suddenly Politics Is Hot Again. Sometimes Really Hot." *Washington Post*, October 17, D1.

Ross, Carne. 2011. *The Leaderless Revolution: How Ordinary People Will Take Power and Change Politics in the 21st Century*. New York: Penguin.

Roubini, Nouriel, and Stephen Mihm. 2010. *Crisis Economics: A Crash Course in the Future of Finance*. New York: Penguin.

Sawyer, Suzana. 2004. *Crude Chronicles: Indigenous Politics, Multinational Oil, and Neoliberalism in Ecuador*. Durham (NC) and London: Duke University Press.

Schudson, Michael. 1992. "Was There Ever a Public Sphere? If So, When? Reflections on the American Case." In *Habermas and the Public Sphere*, edited by Craig Calhoun, 143–63. Cambridge, MA: MIT Press.

Schutz, Charles E. 1977. *Political Humor: From Aristophanes to Sam Ervin*. Cranbury, NJ: Associated University Presses.

Scott, James C. 1976. *The Moral Economy of the Peasant*. New Haven, CT: Yale University Press.

———. 1985. *Weapons of the Weak: Everyday Forms of Peasant Resistance*. New Haven, CT: Yale University Press.

———. 1990. *Domination and the Arts of Resistance: Hidden Transcripts*. New Haven, CT: Yale University Press.

Scott, Janny, and David Leonhardt. 2005. "Shadowy Lines That Still Divide." In *Class Matters*, by correspondents of the *New York Times*, 1–26. New York: New York Times Books and Henry Holt.

Segal, David. 2008. "'Zero Dollar' for Zero Sense: Artist's Print Derides Wall Street Bailout." *Washington Post*, October 8, C01.

Seigworth, Gregory J., and Melissa Gregg. 2010. "An Inventory of Shimmers." In *The Affect Theory Reader*, edited by Melissa Gregg and Gregory J. Seigworth, 1–25. Durham, NC: Duke University Press.

Sennett, Richard, and Jonathan Cobb. 1993. *The Hidden Injuries of Class*. New York: Norton.

Shapiro, Ian. 2003. *The State of Democratic Theory*. Princeton, NJ: Princeton University Press.

Shepard, Benjamin, and Ronald Hayduk, eds. 2002. *From ACT UP to the WTO: Urban Protest and Community Building in the Era of Globalization*. London: Verso.

Sherzer, Joel. 2002. *Speech Play and Verbal Art*. Austin: University of Texas Press.

Slack, Donovan. 2004. "Billionaires for Bush? Well, Yes and No." *Boston Globe*, March 26, A16.

Slackman, Michael, and Colin Moynihan. 2004. "Now in Previews, Political Theater in the Street." *New York Times*, February 19, A18.

Slinger. 1988. "Domed Stadium, Anonymous Malls Unite 'Trawna' with 'Noo Orlins.'" *Toronto Star*, August 19, A4.

Smart, Tim. 1999. "Pay Gap Widens Between Worker, Boss." *Washington Post*, August 30, A06.

Smith, Gavin. 2004. "Hegemony." In *A Companion to the Anthropology of Politics*, edited by David Nugent and Joan Vincent, 216–30. Oxford: Blackwell.

Smith, Matthew Noah. 2012. "Reflections on Occupy's May Day: All Play Doesn't Work." Possible Futures: A Project of the Social Science Research Council, May 7. http://www.possible-futures.org/2012/05/07/reflections-occupys-day-play-work/ (accessed June 29, 2012).

Smith, Mike. 2009. Cartoon. *Las Vegas Sun*, King Features Syndicate, republished in *New York Times*, March 22, WK2.

Smith, Neil. 2005. *The Endgame of Globalization*. New York: Routledge.

Sneed, Michael. 2004. "Free Spa Pampers Media Messengers with Massages." *Chicago Sun-Times*, September 1, 32.

Snow, David A., Sarah A. Soule, and Hanspeter Kriesi. 2007. "Mapping the Terrain." In *The Blackwell Companion to Social Movements*, edited by David A. Snow, Sarah A. Soule, and Hanspeter Kriesi, 3–16. Oxford: Blackwell.

Speier, Hans. 1998. "Wit and Politics: An Essay on Laughter and Power." *American Journal of Sociology* 103(5):1352–401.

Sperber, Dan, and Deirdre Wilson. 1981. "Irony and the Use-Mention Distinction." In *Radical Pragmatics*, edited by Peter Cole, 295–317. New York: Academic Press.

Spiegelman, Art. 2004. *In the Shadow of No Towers*. New York: Pantheon.

Spitulnik, Debra. 1993. "Anthropology and Mass Media." *Annual Review of Anthropology* 22:293–315.

———. 1997. "The Social Circulation of Media Discourse and the Mediation of Communities." *Journal of Linguistic Anthropology* 6(2):161–87.

Stallybrass, Peter, and Allon White. 1986. *The Politics and Poetics of Transgression*. Ithaca, NY: Cornell University Press.

Stein, Ben. 2006. "In Class Warfare, Guess Which Class Is Winning." *New York Times*, November 26, B3.

Stelter, Brian. 2012. "Colbert for President: A Run or a Comedy Riff?" *New York Times*, January 12.

Stewart, Kathleen. 2007. *Ordinary Affects*. Durham, NC: Duke University Press.

Sturr, Chris. 2011. "AP and USA Today Fall for GE Tax Repayment Hoax." *Dollars and Sense: Real World Economics*, April 13. http://dollarsandsense.org/blog/2011/04/ap-and-usa-today-fall-for-ge-tax-repayment-hoax.html (accessed December 28, 2012).

Suskind, Ron. 2004. *The Price of Loyalty: George W. Bush, the White House, and the Education of Paul O'Neill*. New York: Simon & Schuster.

Taibbi, Matt. 2010. *Griftopia: Bubble Machines, Vampire Squids, and the Long Con That Is Breaking America*. New York: Spiegel and Grau.

Tarrow, Sidney. 1998. *Power in Movement: Social Movements and Contentious Politics*. Cambridge, UK: Cambridge University Press.

Taylor, Astra, Keith Cessen, and editors from *n+1, Dissent, Triple Canopy and The New Inquiry*. 2011. *Occupy! Scenes from Occupied America*. London: Verso.

Thomas, Landon. 2006. "A Gift Between Friends." *New York Times*, June 27, C1.

Thompson, E. P. 1993. *Customs in Common: Studies in Traditional Popular Culture.* New York: New Press.

Thompson, John B. 1995. *The Media and Modernity: A Social Theory of the Media.* Cambridge, UK: Polity Press.

Tilly, Charles. 2004. *Social Movements, 1768–2004.* Boulder, CO: Paradigm.

———. 2007. *Democracy.* Cambridge, UK: Cambridge University Press.

Trigaux, Robert. 2004. "Satire in the Streets." *St. Petersburg* (FL) *Times Online,* August 31. http://www.sptimes.com/2004/08/31/Columns/Satire_in_the_streets.shtml (accessed December 28, 2012).

Turner, Robert L. 1995. "Presidential Timber." *Boston Globe Magazine,* January 8, 18.

Turner, Victor. 1974. *Dramas, Fields and Metaphors: Symbolic Action in Human Society.* Ithaca, NY: Cornell University Press.

———. 1995 [1969]. *The Ritual Process: Structure and Anti-Structure.* New York: Aldine De Gruyter.

Twain, Mark. 1897. "Pudd'nhead Wilson's New Calendar." In *Following the Equator.* Hartford, CT: American Publishing Company.

United for a Fair Economy. 1997. "Born on Third Base: The Sources of Wealth of the 1997 Forbes 400." http://www.faireconomy.org/press_room/1997/born_on_third _base_sources_of_wealth_of_1997_forbes_400 (accessed December 28, 2012).

United Nations. Human Development Indicators. 2006. http://hdr.undp.org/en/media/ Human_development_indicators.pdf (accessed February 1, 2012).

Varon, Jeremy. 2004. *Bringing the War Home: The Weather Underground, the Red Army Faction, and Revolutionary Violence in the Sixties and Seventies.* Berkeley: University of California Press.

———. 2005. "Killing the Field of Dreams: George W. Bush, Empire, and the Politics of Misrecognition." *Fast Capitalism* 1(2). http://www.fastcapitalism.com (accessed December 28, 2012).

Veblen, Thorstein. 1899. *The Theory of the Leisure Class.* New York: Macmillan.

Warner, Jamie. 2007. "Political Culture Jamming: The Dissident Humor of *The Daily Show with Jon Stewart.*" *Popular Communication* 5(1):17–36.

Warner, Michael. 1992. "The Mass Public and the Mass Subject." In *Habermas and the Public Sphere,* edited by Craig Calhoun, 377–401. Cambridge, MA: MIT Press.

Waxman, Sharon. 2006. "Paradise Bought." *New York Times,* July 2, H1.

WBUR Here and Now. 2004. "Billionaires for Bush," transcript, July 28. http://www .here-now.org/shows/2004/07/20040728_13.asp (accessed October 4, 2004).

Weber, Max. 1973 [1946]. *From Max Weber: Essays in Sociology,* edited and translated by H. H. Gerth and C. Wright Mills. New York: Oxford University Press.

Wedel, Janine R. 2009. *Shadow Elite: How the World's New Power Brokers Undermine Democracy, Government, and the Free Market.* New York: Basic Books.

White, Hayden V. 1973. *Metahistory: The Historical Imagination in Nineteenth-Century Europe.* Baltimore: Johns Hopkins University Press.

Wilkinson, Richard, and Kate Pickett. 2009. *The Spirit Level: Why Greater Equality Makes Societies Stronger.* New York: Bloomsbury Press.

Williams, Brett. 2004. *Debt for Sale: A Social History of the Credit Trap*. Philadelphia: University of Pennsylvania Press.

Williams, Raymond. 1977. *Marxism and Literature*. Oxford: Blackwell.

Willis, Ellen. 2006. "Escape from Freedom: What's the Matter with Tom Frank (and the Lefties Who Love Him)?" *Situations* 1(2):5–20.

Willis, Paul. 1977. *Learning to Labor: How Working Class Kids Get Working Class Jobs*. New York: Columbia University Press.

Wootton, David, ed. 2003. *The Essential Federalist and Anti-Federalist Papers*. Indianapolis (IN) and Cambridge (MA): Hackett.

Worcester (MA) *Telegram and Gazette*. 1998. "Protesters Use Tax Day for Batting Practice: Few Believe They'll Really Score a Major Overhaul." April 16, A1.

Wright, Erik Olin, ed. 2005. *Approaches to Class Analysis*. New York: Cambridge University Press.

Writers for the 99%. 2011. *Occupying Wall Street: The Inside Story of an Action That Changed America*. New York and London: O/R Books.

Yarwood, Dean L. 2004. *When Congress Makes a Joke: Congressional Humor Then and Now*. New York: Rowman and Littlefield.

Yes Men. 2004. *The Yes Men: The True Story of the End of the World Trade Organization*. New York: Disinformation Company.

Zald, Mayer N. 1992. "Looking Backward to Look Forward: Reflections on the Past and Future of the Resource Mobilization Research Program." In *Frontiers in Social Movement Theory*, edited by Aldon D. Moris and Carol McClurg Mueller, 326–48. New Haven, CT: Yale University Press.

Zerubavel, Eviatar. 2006. *The Elephant in the Room: Silence and Denial in Everyday Life*. Oxford and New York: Oxford University Press.

Zijderveld, Anton C. 1983. "The Sociology of Laughter and Humor." *Current Sociology* 31(Winter):1–103.

Zimmer, Ben. 2010. "Truthiness: The Fifth Anniversary of Stephen Colbert's Introduction of a Zeitgeisty Word." *New York Times Magazine*, October 17, 22.

Zinn, Howard. 2003. *A People's History of the United States*. New York: Harper Perennial.

Zitner, Aaron. 1998. "Tax Code Foes Find Nation Indifferent." *Boston Globe*, April 16, A1.

Index

Page numbers in italic type indicate photographs.

Abbeys of Misrule, 84
ABC, 25
Absurdity, 29, 35–36, 46
Abu Dhabi Investment Authority, 66
Accountability, 18, 31, 77
Acting, 139–40
Activism. *See* Political activism; Satirical/ironic activism
ACT UP, 45
Adams, Samuel, 96
Adorno, Theodor, 44, 168, 236*n*21
Advertising, 111
Affinity groups, 230*n*58
AFL-CIO, 88
Agence France-Presse, 179
Agency, 15, 39, 198, 218*n*96, 240*n*135
Agit-Pop Communications, 26, 45, 51, 192
Air America radio, 127
Alinsky, Saul, 82
Altman, Robert, 74
America Coming Together, 127
American Action Network, 26
American Revolution, 96
Anderson, Benedict, 189
Anthropology. *See* Ethnography
Antiausterity protests, 14, 193

Antiritual, 82–83, 106
April Fool's Day press conferences, 83, 86–87
Arab Spring, 193
Ariely, Dan, 60
Aristocracy, original American opposition to, 73
Aristophanes, 6
Aristotle, 31
Armey, Dick, 96–102, 104, 106
Art and Revolution Collective, 226*n*47
Associated Press, 100
Attardo, Salvatore, 32
Atton, Chris, 167
Austerity programs, 14, 193
Avedon, Richard, 15, 16, 49, 112, 163

Bagdikian, Ben, 170
Bailouts. *See* Financial bailouts
Bakhtin, Mikhail, 30
Bank for International Settlements, 78
Barotse, 81, 106
Barrali, Kristin, 97–98, 100, 106–7
Bartels, Larry, 4, 60
Bates, Melody (pseudonym: Ivy League Legacy), 58, 139, 164, 197, 198
Beautiful Trouble (book), 38, 192

Beeman, William O., 142, 144
Beers, David, 33
Ben & Jerry's, 88
Beverly Park, California, 9–10
Bichlbaum, Andy, 46–47
Big Money United, 90, 106, 113, 118
Billionaire Croquet Party, 1, 2, 15–17, 197, 211n2
Billionaire Follies, 25, 109, 125, 131, 132, 136, 139
Billionaires: media coverage of, 8–10;
    politically progressive, 23–24, 27–28, 59,
    68, 71–72; prevalence of, 1, 59, 73. See also
    Billionaires (activists)
Billionaires (activists): accomplishments of,
    191; actions of, 1, 2, 3, 3, 6, 15–16, 25–26, 37,
    113–21, 125, 129–32, 145–53; aims of, 7, 8;
    audience for, 53, 57–58; branding,
    marketing, and public presentation of,
    24–25, 44–45, 109–12, 119, 120, 123, 133, 139,
    151, 152, 157–58, 176, 215n7; bystander
    responses to, 17, 41, 132–33, 143–53;
    candidates and causes supported by, 5,
    24–27, 71, 72, 79; characteristics of, 8,
    73–74; convergences of, 37, 126; costumes
    of, 1, 2, 3, 16–17, 41, 109, 117, 133–34, 158;
    criticisms of, 125, 146–47, 149, 151;
    distinguished from traditional protestors,
    110, 112, 114, 134, 152–53, 164, 168, 177–78,
    185–86, 187; between elections, 124–29, 182;
    ethnography of, 36–42; funding of, 25,
    125–26; growth of, 24, 118–21, 122, 131, 156,
    182; interpretations of, 13, 142–53; and
    irony, 34–36, 154; Last Huzzah celebration,
    118, 198, 242m; media coverage of, 1, 15–16,
    25–27, 40, 116, 120–21, 134, 156, 163–68, 175–
    86, 191; media strategy of, 164–67;
    meetings of, 36, 40, 135–37, 184–85, 201–2;
    membership of, 123–24, 131, 136, 138, 158–
    59; messages and themes of, 57–58, 116, 118,
    121–23, 129, 133–34, 157, 159–61, 181, 183–85,
    189–90, 229n51, 235n71; names
    (pseudonyms) of, 36, 122, 144; ordinary
    lives of, 14, 192, 199–200; organizational
    structure and operation of, 110–11, 117, 118,
    121–23, 125–26, 128, 153–57, 194, 230n78;
    origins of, 84, 90, 112, 123; paid staff of,
    125–26, 231n88; performance challenges
    for, 138–42; personal experiences of (see

Personal experiences of satirical activism);
    personas of, 23, 140; pledge of allegiance
    of, 49, 220n49; political leanings of,
    235n70; precursors of, 81–107; reputation
    of, 7–8; Reverend Billy compared to,
    50–51; Reverend Billy's canonization of,
    48–50, 55, 198; slogans of, 13, 35, 56, 63, 67,
    73, 74, 113, 144, 157, 166, 191; social
    interaction and relationships of, 197–98;
    studies of, 215n77; targets of, 7, 14, 58, 77,
    118–19, 125–28, 198; Yes Men compared to,
    47, 195
The Billionaires Are in the House (CD), 125,
    215n7
Billionaires for Bailouts, 5, 25–26, 175, 182
Billionaires for Bush, 1, 2, 3, 3, 5, 6, 15–17, 24–25,
    36–38, 47, 74, 109–10, 112, 120, 125–33, 145–
    52, 158–60, 177–80, 182, 191
Billionaires for Bush (book), 132
Billionaires for Bush (or Gore), 5, 24, 93, 110,
    117–24
Billionaires for Bush or Bloomberg, 125
Billionaires for Bush's War, 125
Billionaires for Closed Debates, 230n67
Billionaires for Coal, 181, 182
Billionaires for Forbes, 5, 24, 79, 110, 112–18
Billionaires for More Media Mergers, 125, 168,
    191, 230n67
Billionaires for Plutocracy, 5, 194
Billionaires for Social Insecurity, 26
Billionaires for Tar Sands, 27, 182
Billionaires for the One Percent, 194
Billionaires for Wealthcare, 5, 26, 182
Billionaires for [X] concept, 90, 95, 115, 117
Bloomberg, Michael, 48
Bogad, Larry, 49, 215n77
Bonanno, Mike, 46, 195
Booth, Wayne, 31–32
Born, Brooksly, 75
Boston Globe (newspaper), 25, 85, 94, 100, 102,
    116, 176–78
Boston Herald (newspaper), 102
Boston Marathon, 89
Boston Tea Party Ship prank, 95–104, 101, 116
Bourdieu, Pierre, 237n21
Boyd, Andrew (pseudonym: Phil T. Rich), 1, 2,
    13, 17–18, 26, 27, 35–38, 40–42, 43, 45, 49, 50,

85, 88–92, 95, 97–100, 104, 106, 113–15, 118–
    21, 123–24, 126–27, 129, 131, 133, 136, 137, 142,
    157, 159, 161, 166–68, 177, 183, 187, 192, 196,
    198, 201–2, 215*n*77, 226*n*47, 231*n*88; *The
    Activist's Cookbook*, 85, 89, 90
Boyer, Dominic, 19, 46, 172, 190
BP (British Petroleum), 45–46
Bradley, Bill, 4
Branding, 109–12. *See also* Billionaires
    (activists): branding, marketing, and
    public presentation of
Brave New Foundation, 51, 216*n*23
Bread and Puppet Theater, 8
Bridges, Steve, 188
Brill, Carol, 226*n*22
Buffett, Warren, 7, 23–24, 56, 59, 67–68, 69, 74,
    160, 211*n*1, 224*n*115
Burdick, John, 161
Burning Man festivals, 120, 128
Burns, Ginny, 226*n*22
Bush, George W., 24, 25, 34, 37, 43, 60, 73, 83,
    94, 118–19, 125–29, 136, 143, 147, 151, 160,
    172–73, 178, 180, 187, 188, 199, 201, 235*n*53
Bush, Jeb, 136

Calhoun, Craig, 241*n*3, 241*n*6
Cameron, Carl, 116
Campaign contributions: Colbert's satirical
    attacks on, 51–52; public financing and, 79,
    92–93; regulation of, 7, 52, 212*n*22; from
    wealthy donors, 7, 62
Camus, Albert, 35
Canright, Lois (pseudonym: Ivana Reitoff),
    28–29, 120, 137–38, 141, 200
Capital gains, 67
Carnegie, Andrew, 68, 73, 224*n*115
Carnival, 8, 82, 84, 183, 225*n*4
Carter, Graydon, 32
Case, Dave (pseudonym: Fillmore Barrels),
    40–41, 183
CBS Evening News (television show), 180
Ceglie, Marco (pseudonym: Monet Oliver de
    Place), 132, 157
Character, adoption and performance of, 139–41
Charisma, 137
Charivaris, 84, 183, 225*n*4
Chastain, Emma, 134

Cheap Labor Day, 132
Cheney, Dick, 25, 173
Chicago Sun-Times (newspaper), 177
Christmas caroling, 145–47
Church of Earthalujah, 48, 50, 51
Citizens for a Sound Economy, 96
Citizens Trade Campaign, 138
Citizens United decision (2010), 7
Citizens United vs. *Federal Election
    Commission* (2010), 26, 51–52, 190, 199,
    212*n*22
Clark, Wesley, 120
Clarke, Richard, 127
Class, American attitudes about, 60–61. *See
    also* Middle class
Class Acts, 85, 88
Class warfare, 7
Cleveland Plain Dealer (newspaper), 94
Clifford, James, 33
Clinton, Bill, 93, 170
Clown Brigade, 196
CNN, 25, 100, 177, 185, 232*n*33
Coaching, in performance, 139–40
Code Pink, 8, 192
Cohen, Ben, 69
Colbert, Stephen, 8, 20, 24, 26, 31, 33, 42, 51–52,
    172, 188–89, 237*n*25
The Colbert Report (television show), 34, 52,
    111, 164
Colebrook, Claire, 32
Coleman, Norm, 72
Collective action, 5
Collins, Chuck, 58, 69–70, 85–90, 95–101, 105,
    106, 113–17, 120, 133, 223*n*98, 225*n*20
Collins, Jane, 225*n*20
Collins, Steve, 85–87, 90, 225*n*20
Comedy: economy represented as, 13;
    neoclassical economics as, 11; reassuring
    and conciliatory nature of, 10, 18, 35;
    satire's relationship to, 10, 18, 35, 202;
    wealth as subject of, 10–11. *See also*
    Humor; Irony; Satire
Commodity Futures Modernization Act, 75
Common Cause, 120, 192
Commonwealth Coalition, 93
Communications Workers of America (CWA),
    148, 151

Communitas, 16–17, 94, 193, 197–98, 202, 214n67

Conservatives: brand image of, 112, 134, 158; deceptive campaign contribution practices of, 68; economic narratives of, 57–58, 63; market emphasis of, 65; media bias favoring, 171–73; systemic capacity of, 72; and taxes, 70–71. *See also* Neoconservatism

Contentious politics, 5

Corporations: as persons, 1, 7, 13, 16, 27, 52, 212n22; political power of, 18, 26, 128; public opinion on, 29; tax liability of, 27, 64, 222n62

Costumes: Billionaires, 1, 2, 3, 16–17, 41, 109, 117, 133–34, 158; Fat Cats, 93–94; IMF Loan Sharks, 119–20; Rallies for the Really Rich, 87

Court jesters. *See* Jesters

Cox, Christopher, 75

Credit-default swaps, 75

Credit-rating agencies, 225in47

Critchley, Simon, 28

Critical Mass, 45, 51, 128

Culture jamming, 8, 46, 56, 95, 100–101, 190–91

Currency transaction tax, 78, 225n44

Cycling, 45

Dadaism, 8, 35

The Daily Show (television show), 4–6, 32, 34, 111, 127, 164, 172

David and Goliath metaphor, 102, 104, 165, 198

Day, Amber, 215n77

Death tax, 70–71. *See also* Estate tax

Debord, Guy, 43–44

Deception: by politicians and officials, 33–34; on taxes, 67–68, 223n98

Deep poverty, 60

DeMartino, George, 11

Democracy: citizens' voice in, 17–18; direct, 194; financial corruption of, 76, 79, 106, 113; media in relation to, 169; political humor in, 31; wealth's place in, 3

Democracy 21, 52, 192

Democratic National Committee (DNC), 128–29

Democratic Party, 75, 125

Democratic Party conventions, 25, 93, 120–21, 165, 172–73

Derivatives, 74–75, 77–78

Dickens, Charles, *Our Mutual Friend*, 1

Didion, Joan, 34

di Leonardo, Micaela, 238n69

Direct action, 123, 174, 194

Direct Action Network, 85, 123, 153

Direct democracy, 194

Discrepancies. *See* Incongruities and discrepancies

Disney Store, 50, 51

DIY. *See* Do-it-yourself (DIY) techniques

Do-it-yourself (DIY) movement, 111, 121, 226n47

Donham, Donald, 11, 213nn42,46, 214n51

Douglas, Mary, 28, 30, 82

Dow Chemical, 46

Dramas of citizenship, 105

Duncombe, Stephen, 9, 43–44, 48, 49, 111, 119, 215n77, 219n29

Dworkin, Ronald, 7

Dynasty tax, 71

Easterly, William, 61

Economic inequality. *See* Wealth inequality

Economic justice/fairness, 18, 55, 59, 79, 118, 192–94

Economic mobility, 56, 58, 69, 73

Economic risk, 58

Economy: human economy, 193; morality and, 195; popular narratives about, 56, 63; public opinion on, 56; role of statistics in, 56. *See also* 2008 economic crisis

Edelman, Marc, 42, 161

Edelman, Murray, 57, 214n72

Edwards, John, 173

Elephants in the room, 7, 189–90, 212n20

Embarrassment, 82, 106

Empathy, 28

Enron, 124–25

Equal economic opportunity, 60

Estate tax, 27, 59, 66–71, 106, 222n75

Ethical spectacles, 43–44

Ethnography: Billionaires as subject of, 36–42; humor as subject for, 19; intellectual obstacles in, 42; ironies in, 36–40; narrative plot models in, 11; observer-observed relationship in, 39–42

Expert subjects, 41, 42

FAIR (media watch group), 174
Fairness Doctrine, in journalism, 170
Family farms, 70
Farrar, Margaret, 215n77
Fat Cats, 84, 90, 91–95, 113
Federal Communications Commission (FCC), 125, 168, 170
Federal Deposit Insurance Corporation, 12
Federal Election Commission, 51–52
Federal Emergency Management Agency (FEMA), 65
Federal Reserve Board, 12
Ferguson, Charles H., *Inside Job*, 29
Fernandez, James, 33–34
Ferrell, Will, 235n53
Fey, Tina, 8, 31, 188
Financial bailouts, 63, 64, 75
Financial Crisis Inquiry Report, 29
Financial industry, 74–79
Financial speculation, 75–76
First Amendment, 50
Flag-draped coffins, 43
Flashmobs, 25, 26, 51
Flat tax, 96–101, 104, 113, 116–17
Follies. *See* Billionaire Follies
Fools. *See* Wise fools
Forbes, Steve, 24, 96, 101, 113–17, 229n26
Forbes Magazine, 59, 140
Ford, Gerald, 60
Foucault, Michel, 44
Founding Fathers, 26, 45, 73, 213n37
Fox, Jonathan, 190
Fox, Vicente, 9
Fox News, 116, 173, 181
Fracking, 48–49
Framing and reframing: of Billionaires, by media, 178–80; of estate tax, 68–69; in European vs. U.S. news, 179; of flat tax, 96, 100–101; in humor, 144–45; of liberalism, 58; in news coverage, 165, 172–73; of political issues, 8; of protest, 173–75, 180
Frank, Robert, 235n70
Frank, Robert H., 66
Frank, Thomas, 213n38, 236n15
Franken, Al, 127

Fraser, Steve, 61, 71
Freedom, 64–65, 72, 224n112
Free Trade Agreement protests (Quebec, 2001), 42
Freud, Sigmund, 30, 217n50
Frick, Henry C., 73
Friedman, Milton, 47
Frye, Northrop, 213n36, 213n42
Fussell, Paul, 32

Gamson, William, 82, 111, 166, 182, 185
Ganz, Marshall, 123
Gates, William (Bill), Jr., 59, 211n1, 216n30, 224n115
Gates, William, Sr., 20, 27, 56, 58, 59, 69–72, 216n30, 223n98
General Agreement on Tariffs and Trade (GATT), 46
General Electric, 27
Gerstle, Gary, 61, 71
Gilded Age, 23, 61, 73, 76. *See also* New Gilded Age
Gilligan's Island (television show), 140, 144
Gingrich, Newt, 101
Gitlin, Todd, 165–66, 173–74, 195–96
Glass-Steagall Act, 12
Golden Fleece Award, 226n26
Goldin, Claudia, 61
Goldstein, Donna, 19
Gore, Al, 24, 118–19, 125, 127
Government intervention, 79
Government regulation, 12, 65, 75, 170
Government services, 63, 66–67
Government spending, 63–66
Graeber, David, 215n77, 237n29, 242nn36,38
Great Compression, 61
Great Depression, 23
Greene Dragon, 128, 232n19
Green Party, 48
Greenspan, Alan, 144
Greenwald, Robert, 51
Grote, Jason, 50
Group solidarity. *See* Communitas
Guerrilla Girls, 8, 45
Guerrilla theater, 8
Gund, Agnes, 68
Guthrie, Woody, "This Land Is Your Land," 197

Haberman, Clyde, 178

Habermas, Jürgen, 189, 241*m*3, 241*m*6

Hacker, Jacob, 58, 62

Half-baked Sales to Save Human Services, 84, 87–88

Hall, Stuart, 13

Halliburton, 46

Hancock, John, 96

Hands Off Washington, 138

Harper, Jennifer, 180

Hartman, Chris (pseudonym: Arby Trajj), 16–17, 95, 97–98, 100, 104, 105

Hastings, Reed, 23

Health care, 26

Hegemony, 13, 186, 214*n*57

Heinz-Kerry, Teresa, 180

Hermann, Andy, 117, 229*n*41

Hertog, James, 174

Hilton, Paris, 70

Hitt, Jack, 177, 181

Hoffman, Abbie, 43

Holmes, Douglas, 42

Home Coalition, 85

Hope, 13, 15

Horkheimer, Max, 44, 168, 236*n*21

House Un-American Activities Committee, 143, 166

Huber, Mary Taylor, 33–34

Huizinga, Johan, 196, 199

Human economy, 193, 241*n*30

Humor: ambiguous nature of, 31, 190–91; effects of, 30–31, 191, 196, 203; ethnographic study of, 19; and framing, 144–45; missing vs. getting, 142–44; performance of, 138; political leaders' fear of, 30–31; as political tool, 189–91, 200; serious concerns addressed through, 4–6, 8, 150–51, 190–93; social stability reinforced by, 30–31; value of, 5; vulnerability humor, 14. *See also* Comedy; Irony; Jokes; Satire

Hungry March Band, 119

Hurricane Katrina, 64

Hurricane Sandy, 194

Hussein, Saddam, 172

Hutcheon, Linda, 35

Identity correctors, 46

IMF. *See* International Monetary Fund

IMF Loan Sharks, 119

Impersonation of officials, 46–47, 83

Income: declining value of, 58, 59, 62; of top one percent, 59. *See also* Wealth inequality

Incongruities and discrepancies: comedy based on, 10; humor based on, 28, 31; irony based on, 32, 33; satire based on, 28–29

The Independent (newspaper), 179

Indymedia, 167

Inequality. *See* Wealth inequality

Inheritance, 66–71, 74, 106, 222*n*75

Institute for Policy Studies, 192

Insult, 12

International Herald Tribune (newspaper), 181

International Monetary Fund (IMF), 78, 118, 119

Internet, political activism's use of, 122, 126, 167–68, 232*m*09

Intertextuality, 144

Investment banking, 75

Iraq War (2003–2011), 32, 43, 124, 125, 128, 172

Irony: activists' use of, 5; Billionaire activists and, 34–36; as check on certainty, 33–34; in contemporary culture, 32–34; defining, 31–32, 149–50; ethnography and, 36–40; function of, 33, 35, 203; goal of, 11, 13; morality and, 33; as narrative paradigm, 11; and power, 33; and truth, 33–34; types of, 32–33, 38; use-mention distinction concerning, 212*n*33. *See also* Comedy; Humor; Satire

Jacobs, Lawrence, 64

Jamieson, Kathleen Hall, 101, 166, 171, 178, 239*m*03

Jesters, 5, 30, 82

Jokes: as anti-rites, 82; performance of, 138; political leaders' fear of, 30–31; social structure for, 28, 82–83, 142–44. *See also* Humor

Journalism: "balanced" reporting in, 67, 68, 171–72, 179; Billionaires' appeal for, 165; conventional wisdom and accepted truths in, 14, 101, 166, 172–74; corporate news, 169–73; goals and functions of, 189; "he said, she said" style of, 67, 179; nonjudgmental nature of, 9; "objective" reporting in, 171, 174, 181, 239*n*103; professional norms in, 172; working conditions in, 171–72. *See also* Media

Juris, Jeffrey, 215*n*77, 242*n*38

Kahn, Richard, 167
Kaiser, Robert, 2, 25, 175
Kehler, Randy, 92
Keller, Bill, 171
Kellner, Douglas, 167
Kerry, John, 127, 160, 173, 180
Kertzer, David, 105
Keynes, John Maynard, 225*n*44
Keystone XL, 27
Kiefer, Megan, *Get on the Limo*, 132
Kieschnick, Michael, 126
Kirkpatrick, David D., 32
Klein, Naomi, 38, 110, 111, 112, 118
Klinger, Scott, 69–70
Koch, David H., 26, 49, 51, 220*n*49
Koch Brothers, 51
Krueger, Alan, 67
Krugman, Paul, 169, 172

Ladies Against Women, 8, 90–91, 227*n*51
Lapham, Mike, 69–70, 89, 97–99, 104, 115–16
Larson, Gary, 39
Last Huzzah celebration, 118, 198, 242*n*
Latinos, 159
Lee, Benjamin, 75
Leno, Jay, 30
Leondar-Wright, Betsy, 85–87, 89
Letterman, David, 30
Liberalism: critical of corporate excess, 75; framing of, 58; public opinion in line with, 63–64
Lies. *See* Deception
Limbaugh, Rush, 12, 100
Limo Tours, 132, 157
Lincoln Center, New York, 26, 51, 216*n*23
LiPuma, Edward, 75
Lobbyists and lobbying: and campaign funding, 26, 45; financial industry and, 12; political influence of, 7, 46
Lobbyists for McCain, 5, 175, 182
Loopholes, 27, 86

Los Angeles Times (newspaper), 25
Lower East Side Collective, 120, 125, 155–56, 218*n*88
Luntz, Frank, 70

Marcus, George, 39, 42
Mardi Gras, 84
Margo, Robert, 61
Market: freedom linked to, 65; morality in, 11–12; as natural, 10, 11, 12; political construction of, 13; romanticization of, 64; rules and regulations governing, 79; society of spectacle as governed by, 43–44
Massachusetts, satirical actions in, 84–90, 92–102
Massachusetts Human Services Coalition (MHSC), 85–86
Maurer, Bill, 77
Mayer, Ken (pseudonym: Ivan Tital), 41, 73, *74*, 137, 167, 180, 189, 199
McCain, John, 4
McCarthy, Eugene, 129
McDowell, Pete, 94
McLeod, Douglas, 174
McLuhan, Marshall, 189
Mda, Zakes, *Cion*, 182
Meaker, Alice (pseudonym: Iona Bigga Yacht), 1, 126, *155*, 155–56
Media: activists' use of, 82, 93–94, 112, 117; Billionaires as subject of, 1, 15–16, 25–27, 40, 116, 120–21, 134, 156, 163–68, 175–86, 191; Boston Tea Party Ship prank coverage by, 98–103; challenges to, 168, 169; conservative, 12; conservative bias in, 171–73; consolidation of, 169–72, 237*n*42; and cultural others, 168; democracy in relation to, 169; humor used to attract, 85; income inequality as topic of, 194–95; issues and stories ignored by, 14, 15, 76, 100, 116, 172–75, 178–79, 239*n*103; new, 167–68; political information available through, 34, 44, 76, 170–71, 187; protest and, 173–75; proto-Billionaires covered by, 88, 100, 102–3; public opinion on, 170; representations of wealth in, 8–10, 13; social movements as subject of, 163; on tax issues, 68, 70; technological changes in, 237*n*43. *See also* Journalism

Media hoaxes, 27, 46, 83
Media mergers, 118, 124, 125
Memes, 91, 115
Meredith, Judy, 226n22
Merrill Lynch, 181
Methods of research, 36–42, 209–10
Middle class, 58, 61, 62, 73
Million Billionaire March, 3, 15–17, 25, 41, 120, 131, 134, 152, 197
Mitchell, Dave Oswald, 38
Mitchell, Tim, 56
Moby (Richard Melville Hall), 24
Molé, Noelle, 37–38
Mondschein, Ken, 183–84
Moody's, 78
Moore, Michael, *Fahrenheit 9/11*, 127
Morality: of economic life, 195; of elites, 71; irony and, 33; of satirical activism, 104–5; spectacle and, 44; wealth inequality and, 60
Morgen, Sandra, 72
Movement for a New Society, 226n47
MoveOn, 25, 26, 127–29, 167
Moyers, Bill, 63, 76, 166, 169, 171, 173
MSNBC, 25
Multi-Millionaires for Mitt, 5, 27
Murdoch, Rupert, 127

Nader, Ralph, 4, 119, 125
Narrative plot models, 10–11, 213n41
The Nation (magazine), 121
National Journal (newspaper), 94
Neoclassical economics, 11
Neoconservatism, 65
Never Mind the Rabble (CD), 125, 215n7
New Deal, 61, 63, 64, 72
New Democratic Majority, 37
New Gilded Age, 59, 61, 72, 73, 76
New Hampshire Citizen Action, 94
New Hampshire Union Leader (newspaper), 116, 117
Newman, Paul, 69
New media, 167–68
Newsweek (magazine), 25
New Yorker (magazine), 16, 25, 112, 163
New York Post (newspaper), 94
New York Times (newspaper), 9–10, 16, 25,

47–48, 52, 70, 91, 116, 129–31, 134, 170, 177, 178, 179, 181, 182
9/11 First Responders legislation, 14, 19
Norquist, Grover, 64, 72
North Carolina Alliance for Democracy, 94
Northeastern Citizen's Action Resource Center, 93
Norton, Michael I., 60
"No You Can't" video spoof, 25, 182

Obama, Barack, 25, 34, 76, 197
Occupy movements, 4
Occupy Sandy, 194
Occupy the SEC, 12, 194
Occupy Wall Street, 7, 14, 18, 27, 29, 60, 76, 77, 78, 124, 153, 193–96
Offshore finance, 77–78
Oligarchy, 75, 77
Olson, Victoria (pseudonym: Fonda Sterling), 117, 131
O'Neill, Paul, 127
The Onion (satirical newspaper), 111, 164
Opportunity. *See* Equal economic opportunity
Opprecht, Kurt (pseudonym: Thurston Howell IV), 49, 111–12, 131–32, 133, 140, 175, 185, 190, 198, 200–201
Oral history, 83, 103, 107
O'Reilly, Bill, 12
Orwell, George, 30
The Other 98%, 26, 51, 192, 216n23
Others, media's treatment of, 168
Outfoxed (documentary), 127

Palin, Sarah, 31, 188
Pareto optimality, 11
Paris Hilton Tax Cut, 70
Parody, 35, 143–45, 190–93. *See also* Satire
Partisanship, 127
Patomaki, Heikki, 78
Patriot Ledger (newspaper), 102
Pedelty, Mark, 179
Pentagon Building, 43
Performance, 137–45; challenges of, 138–42; coaching in, 139–40; effects of, 141–42, 145–52; uncertainties in, 142–44
Personal experiences of satirical activism: ambivalence and discomfort, 99, 115;

empathy for targets, 104, 115; enjoyment, 136, 200–201; exhilaration, 99, 103, 104, 106, 115, 130, 200–201; media attention, 185; moral justification, 104–5, 115–16; motivations, 199; performance challenges, 138, 140–42; pride, 115; solidarity, 197–98; triumph, 115; various, 15–16

Personal responsibility, 64

Philadelphia Daily News (newspaper), 103

Phillips, Kevin, 3, 63

Pickett, Kate, 62

Pierson, Paul, 62

Pioneer Valley Pro-Democracy Campaign, 92–93

Plame, Valerie, 188

Plato, 196

Play: effects of, 195–96; political value of, 196; protest as, 84; seriousness in relation to, 8; as subversion, 5

Plutocracy, 4, 5, 7, 14, 18, 187

Plutonium Players, 90, 227n51

Polanyi, Karl, 56, 65

Political activism, advertising as model for, 111. *See also* Satirical/ironic activism

Political center, silence of, 5–6

Political imagination. *See* Public political imagination

Political satire: public reception of, 188; study of, 19. *See also* Satirical/ironic activism

Politics: humor as threat to, 30–31; money's influence on, 7; in twenty-first century, 189

Pomorska, Krystyna, 30

Poor People's Economic Human Rights campaign, 126, 192

Portelli, Alessandro, 83, 103

Potter, Trevor, 52

Poverty, 60, 72

Powell, Michael, 170

Power: challenges to, 183; disruptions of, 81–82, 191; humor as challenge to, 14, 30–31; irony and, 33

Powerless, tools of. *See* Weapons of the weak

Precision Cell Phone Drill Teams, 84, 88–89, 118

Press conferences, fake, 83, 86–87

Protest: journalistic trivialization/marginalization of, 91, 116, 163, 165, 168, 173, 175, 176, 179–81; media framing and

coverage of, 173–75, 180–81. *See also* Satirical/ironic activism; Spectacular dissent

Proxmire, William, 226n26

Public Campaign, 120

Public Citizen, 106, 192

Public financing, of campaigns, 79, 92–93

Public opinion: campaign contributions, 7; construction of public opinion by, 57; corporations, 29; economy, 56; erroneous, 76–77; on estate tax, 66; government spending, 14–15, 63–64; on liberal-conservative spectrum, 64; on media consolidation, 170; poll construction's effect on, 220n7; taxes, 15, 29, 66–67, 102, 214n64; wealth inequality, 60

Public political imagination, 12, 13, 19, 189, 191

Purdy, Jedediah, 13, 33, 195

Qatar Investment Authority, 66

Rachel Maddow Show (television show), 26

Radical Clown Front, 121

Rainforest Action Network, 181

Rallies for the Really Rich, 83, 86–87

Rally to Restore Sanity and/or Fear (2010), 26, 42–43

Rat Race skit, 89

Reagan, Ronald, 65

Reagan for Shah, 90

Reclaim the Streets, 8, 20, 45, 85, 119, 120, 123, 125, 219n29, 226n47

Reform, elite sponsorship of, 71–72. *See also* Billionaires: politically progressive

Reframing. *See* Framing and reframing

Regulations. *See* Government regulation

Reich, Robert, 17–18, 79

Religion, as off-limit topic, 122, 160

Republican Party: corporations and, 26; and financial industry legislation, 75; satirical attacks on, 1–3, 25–27, 52, 91, 129–31; and taxes, 72, 96, 102

Republican Party conventions, 2, 3, 16, 25, 91, 93, 120–21, 159–60, 177, 180

Resource mobilization theory, 197

Responsible Wealth, 27

Reuters, 100, 152

Reverend Billy (Bill Talen), 20, 24, 41, 47–51, 55, 198, 220*n*53

Reversal, rituals of, 81–82, 84, 106

Revolutionary Anarchist Clown Bloc, 42, 121

Rich, Frank, 34, 172

Rich People's Liberation Front (RPLF), 84, 85–86, 90, 99

Rituals: jokes as interruption of, 82; of reversal, 81–82, 84, 106

Roaring Twenties, 23

Robber barons, 23, 112

Rockefeller, John D., 73, 224*n*15

Rockefeller family, 23, 35, 69

Romney, Mitt, 27, 51–52, 173

Roosevelt, Franklin D., 23–24, 61, 72, 224*n*12

Roosevelt, Theodore, 23

Roosevelt family, 69

Rosen, Ralph M., 6, 53

Rosin, Hanna, 111, 168

Ross, Carne, 78

Roubini, Nouriel, 5–6

Rove, Karl, 25, 129–31

Rove action, 25, 129–31, 133, 232*n*33

RTE (television network), 172

Rubin, Jerry, 143, 166

Ruckus Society, 192

Rude Mechanical Orchestra, 51

Satire: activists' use of, 5; audience for, 53; comedy's relationship to, 10, 18, 35, 202; goal of, 8, 10, 203; missing vs. getting, 142–44; as narrative paradigm, 11; premise of, 6; in relation to media, 14; techniques of, 10, 213*n*50; truth in relation to, 179. *See also* Comedy; Humor; Irony; Parody; Political satire; Satirical/ironic activism

Satirical/ironic activism: effects of, 14, 19, 71, 89, 95, 104–6, 136, 141–42, 145–52, 150–53, 178, 191, 195–96, 199–200, 202; goal of, 13, 52–53, 79; historical conditions for, 11, 19, 28–30, 188–89; power challenged by, 14; serious approaches in tandem with, 192; targets of, 77; techniques of, 94; tips for, 89, 100, 102–3, 115. *See also* Personal experiences of satirical activism; Political satire

Saturday Night Live (television show), 31

Save Our Loopholes Day, 86

Schlafly, Phyllis, 91

Schutz, Charles E., 10, 30

Scott, James C., 186, 225*nn*3,4,5, 240*n*36

Securities and Exchange Commission, 12, 194

Seidenberg, Ivan, 148

Self-made wealth, 69

Sellers, John, 192

Seneca, 1

September 11, 2001 attacks, 32–33, 124, 172. *See also* 9/11 First Responders legislation

Share the Wealth, 85

Shepherd, Ben, 49

Sherrill, Ken, 126

Shiller, Robert, 4

Shriver, Eunice Kennedy, 9

Shultz, Howard, 111

Sierra Club, 37, 130, 133, 177

Silver Spoon Awards, 86

Situationists, 8, 35, 43, 45, 90, 130, 219*n*29, 232*n*32

Skocpol, Theda, 64

Skomarovsky, Matthew (pseudonym: Seymour Benjamins), 125–26

Smith, Adam, 65

Smith, Gavin, 186, 214*n*57, 240*n*37

Smith, Matthew Noah, 195–96

Social justice, 117–18

Social movements: Billionaires in relation to, 124; defined, 5; effects of, 190; media coverage of, 163; motivations of participants in, 196–97; participants in, 111; strategic capacity of, 123; tactics of, 196

Social safety net, 63, 73, 84, 86–87

Social Security, 26, 67, 73

Society of spectacle, 43–44, 219*n*29

Socrates, 13, 33

Sojourners, 120

Solidarity. *See* Communitas

Soros, George, 23, 35, 59, 68, 69, 160, 180

Spectacle, society of, 43–44, 219*n*29

Spectacular dissent, 42–52, 84, 166

Speculation, financial, 75–76

Spencer, Susan, 180

Sperber, Dan, 212*n*33

Der Spiegel (newspaper), 25

Spiegelman, Art (pseudonym: Milty National), 16, 126–27, 132, 163
Spirit possession, 141–42
Spunkmeyer, Bob, 46
Starbucks, 111
Status reversal, 81–82, 84
Stay the Course (CD), 125
Stewart, Jon, 4–6, 8, 12, 14, 19, 31, 32, 34, 42, 52, 127, 172, 187, 188, 189
Stewart, Kathleen, 15, 198, 199
Stiob (parodic overidentification), 19, 190
Stop Shopping Gospel Choir, 48
Street theater, 8, 89. *See also* Satirical/ironic activism
Summers, Larry, 62
Sundance Channel, 152
Super PACs, 51–52
Surrealism, 8
Suskind, Ron, 34
Swedlund, M. A., 90, 92–95

Talen, Bill. *See* Reverend Billy
Tarrow, Sidney, 192–93
Tar sands, 27
Tasner, Clifford J. (pseudonym: Felonius Ax), 109, 125, 174, 215*n*7, 233*n*2, 234*n*37
Tauzin, Billy, 96–102, 104, 106
Tax day actions, 6, 25, 37–38, 86, 96–102, 116
Tax Equity Alliance for Massachusetts (TEAM), 85–86
Taxes: capital gains, 67; corporations and, 27, 64; on currency transactions, 78, 225*n*44; in earlier periods, 61; economic growth in relation to, 61; on inherited wealth, 27, 59, 66–71, 106, 222*n*75; public opinion on, 15, 29, 66–67, 102, 214*n*64; Republican Party and, 72, 96, 102; Social Security, 67. *See also* Flat tax
Tax reform, 96
Tea Party, 12, 51, 75
Telecommunications Act, 170
Ten Chairs skit, 88–89
Think tanks, 72
Tilly, Charles, 5
Tobin, John, 225*n*44
Tobin tax, 78, 225*n*44
Tocqueville, Alexis de, 61

The Today Show (television show), 88
Torn, Rip, 130
Torn, Tony, 130, 232*n*31
Toronto Star (newspaper), 90–91
Training, for performance, 139–40
Trickle-down economics, 76
Tricksters, 14
Trudeau, Garry, 4
Trump, Donald, 148
Trump Tower, New York, 145–46
Truth, 33–34, 179. *See also* Deception
Truthiness, 33–34
Turner, Ted, 69
Turner, Victor, 16, 106, 193, 214*n*67
Twain, Mark, 4, 23
2008 economic crisis, 5, 12, 29, 75, 77, 171, 195

UFE. *See* United for a Fair Economy
UK Uncut, 216*n*25
Union organizing, 148–52
United for a Fair Economy (UFE), 85–86, 88, 90, 92, 95–106, 113–14, 118–23, 125, 138, 165, 192, 227*n*71, 230*n*78
United for Peace and Justice, 17, 125
United Nations Charter of Human Rights, 47
United States: Boston Tea Party, 96; class in, 60–61; political shift in, 62; poverty in, 60; relationship of wealth and democracy in, 3; socioeconomic crises in, 5, 12, 29, 55–79; tax rates in, 67; wealth inequality in, 60
Upward mobility, 4, 59–63, 72–77
USA Today (newspaper), 25, 94
U.S. Congress, 14, 72, 93
U.S. Constitution, 50
U.S. Justice Department, 52
U.S. Supreme Court, 7, 125
U.S. Supreme Court Building, 26
U.S. tax code, 96–102, 116
US Uncut, 27, 192, 216*n*25
Usury, 75

Varon, Jeremy (pseudonym: Merchant F. Arms), 12, 21, 23, 44, 127, 129, 130, 133, 135, 140, 154, 159, 163, 176, 182, 198, 200
Verizon Wireless, 148–52
Volcker Rule, 12
Vulnerability humor, 14

Waldman, Paul, 101, 166, 171, 178, 239*n*03
Wallace, Chris, 6
Wall Street Journal (newspaper), 25
Wall Street regulations, 12, 29
Walton, Sam, 211*m*
War, ironies of, 32
Warner, Jamie, 215*n*77
Washington Post (newspaper), 25, 45, 91
Washington Times (newspaper), 179–80
Wasserman, Dan, 90
Waxman, Sharon, 9–10
Wealth: attitudes toward, 1, 3, 9–10, 18; comic
    treatments of, 10–11; democracy's
    compatibility with, 3; factors in
    accumulation of, 69–70, 75–76; freedom
    linked to, 65, 72; historical periods of, 23;
    historical sketch of, 73; inherited, 27, 59,
    66–71, 74, 106; perils of, 4; political
    favortism toward, 63; political influence
    of, 7; self-made, 69; as social-political
    construction, 10
Wealth inequality: downplaying of, 9–10, 18,
    65; elite attitudes toward, 71–72; emotional
    and physical health effects of, 62; empathy
    gap and, 28; "envy" as frame for discussion
    of, 173; extent of, 4, 7, 58–63; factors in, 62;
    financial speculation and, 75–76;
    justifications of, 60; media coverage of,
    194–95; neoclassical economics on, 11;
    perils of, 27, 59, 68; as political issue, 4, 7;
    public opinion on, 60, 72; questioning of,
    18; reduction of, 62, 73
Weapons of the weak, 84, 104
Weber, Max, 137

WEF Billionaires: Wasn't Enron Fun, 125
Weinstein, Deborah, 85, 87–88, 90
Weld, William, 86, 94
Wertheimer, Fred, 52
White, Hayden, 10, 11, 35, 213*n*36, 213*n*41,
    213*n*42, 213*n*44
Wikipedia, 167
Wilkinson, Richard, 62
Will.i.am, 25
Wilson, Deirdre, 212*n*33
Winfrey, Oprah, 85
Wisconsin, 14, 193
Wise fools, 5, 82, 189
Witter, Lisa, 112
Worcester Telegram and Gazette (newspaper),
    102
Working Group on Electoral Democracy, 92
World Bank, 78, 118, 119, 224*m*41
World Economic Forum, 118, 124–25
World Trade Organization (WTO), 46–47, 119
World Trade Organization protests (Seattle,
    1999), 13, 18, 42, 88, 117–18

Yarwood, Dean, 14
Yeskel, Felice, 85
Yes Lab, 51
Yes Men, 8, 13, 20, 24, 27, 46–47, 189, 192, 195–
    96
Yippies, 8, 44, 84, 120, 129, 143
Yurchak, Alexei, 19, 46, 190

Zell, Sam, 171
Zijderveld, Anton, 217*n*50, 203
Zimmer, Ben, 33